THE RETURN OF A
1918-

The Return of Alsace to France, 1918–1939

ALISON CARROL

OXFORD
UNIVERSITY PRESS

OXFORD
UNIVERSITY PRESS

Great Clarendon Street, Oxford, OX2 6DP,
United Kingdom

Oxford University Press is a department of the University of Oxford.
It furthers the University's objective of excellence in research, scholarship,
and education by publishing worldwide. Oxford is a registered trade mark of
Oxford University Press in the UK and in certain other countries

© Alison Carrol 2018

The moral rights of the author have been asserted

First Edition published in 2018

Impression: 1

Published in the United States of America by Oxford University Press
198 Madison Avenue, New York, NY 10016, United States of America

British Library Cataloguing in Publication Data
Data available

Library of Congress Control Number: 2017962347

ISBN 978–0–19–880391–1

Printed and bound by
CPI Group (UK) Ltd, Croydon, CR0 4YY

Preface

This is the story of a borderland in transition. Today Strasbourg has become a synonym for European integration. As the site of the European Parliament, the European Court of Human Rights, and the Council of Europe, the Alsatian capital represents an emblem of cross-border connection. In many ways this reflects the history of the city and the region that surrounds it, which, as this book suggests, has been shaped by cross-border flows, interactions, and tensions. It also reflects Strasbourg's long history as a symbol, whether of the defensive might of the French monarchy through the Vauban fortifications built during the reign of Louis XIV, or of interaction, as in the 1923 choice of the city for the home of the oldest of the European institutions, the Central Commission for the Navigation of the Rhine. These two themes—first of Alsace as France's territorial limits and frontier of Frenchness, and second of Alsace as a bridge between France and Germany and the heart of a cross-border community—shaped the region's reintegration into French institutions and systems after 1918, and they run through the following chapters. Crucially, even when the border divided national populations, the region was always a site of contact between the two nations. Contact took many forms, from shopping and visiting family to smuggling, sharing political ideas, or outright conflict. This book aims to understand the dynamics of these processes and their implications for Alsace's return to France.

This book is the product of a long time thinking about Alsace, and during this time I have amassed a great many debts. I hope that these acknowledgements go some way to showing just how grateful I am for all of the help and support that I have received. I first arrived at Alsace through a PhD on the Alsatian Socialist Party's transfer from the SPD to SFIO at the University of Exeter. At Exeter, my biggest 'thank you' is to my PhD supervisor, Martin Thomas, for his insights and efficiency, and above all for always encouraging me to think about the bigger picture, both during my PhD and in the years since. I'd also like to thank others at Exeter who commented on my work or offered encouragement and advice, particularly Tim Rees, Andrew Thorpe, and Jeremy Noakes, and I owe special thanks to Timothy Baycroft of the University of Sheffield for his constructive comments on my PhD and for his support since acting as my external examiner. As I moved on from Exeter, first to Murray Edwards College at the University of Cambridge and then to Birkbeck at the University of London, the insights of colleagues and friends formed the backdrop to the development of my thinking on the topic. And most of the writing was completed at Brunel after I joined the Department of Politics and History in 2011. At Brunel, I have benefited greatly from discussions with many colleagues, but would like to extend particular thanks to Martin Folly and Tom Linehan for their insights and advice, and to Tamson Pietsch and Astrid Swenson for opening my eyes to new ways of thinking about history (and much more). Finally, my thoughts on borders were shaped by my teaching at Brunel, so special thanks go to all the students in my third-year course on borders and borderlands for helping me to refine my thinking, while constantly surprising me with their own interpretations and insights.

In addition to institutional support, this work would not have been possible without the support of a number of funding bodies. The AHRC, British Academy, Society for the Study of French History, German History Society, and Scoloudi Foundation (as well as the University of Exeter, Murray Edwards College, Birkbeck, and Brunel University London) have all offered financial and institutional support at various stages. I am also extremely grateful to Jean Boutier and the Association des Amis du Musée du Cloître, who awarded my doctoral research the Prix Etienne Baluze d'histoire locale européenne, which opened up tremendous opportunities, and to the Association Alsace Mémoire du Mouvement Sociale for the ever instructive discussions. I have also benefited from the advice of numerous extremely knowledgeable and generous archivists and librarians who offered advice on sources at the Archives Départementales du Bas-Rhin, Archives Municipales de la Ville et de l'Eurométropole de Strasbourg, Archives Nationales de France, Archives Municipales de Mulhouse, Archives Municipales de Colmar, Bibliothèque Universitaire de Strasbourg, and the National Archives at Kew.

The map on page xiii was drawn by Louisa Zanoun and originally published in the *European Review of History/Revue d'Histoire Européenne*, and is reprinted here with permission and thanks. Sections of Chapters 6 and 7 were originally published in the article 'Out of the Border's Shadow. Reimagining Urban Spaces in Strasbourg, 1918–1939' in the *Journal of Contemporary History*, and I am grateful for permission to include this material in the book. At Oxford University Press, Christopher Wheeler offered invaluable advice on the shape of the book at the very beginning, and since his retirement Robert Faber and Cathryn Steele have been hugely supportive, insightful, and efficient. I would also like to thank the anonymous readers for their extremely helpful comments.

I have presented much of this work at conferences and seminars, and my work has been improved by the questions and discussions at these events, and particularly by the always lively debates at the annual conference of the Society for the Study of French History. And, as one of the convenors of the IHR's Modern French History seminar, I have learned a tremendous amount from both presenters and my fellow convenors over the last five years, and I am very grateful to them for the eye-opening conversations. Amongst the wider community of French historians, I owe a great debt to many generous colleagues and friends who offered comments on my work, shared their insights in discussion, or informed my work in other ways, and I'd like to offer particular thanks to Karen Adler, Laird Boswell, Claire Eldridge, Charlotte Faucher, Laure Humbert, François Igersheim, Peter Jackson, Colin Jones, Simon Kitson, Chris Millington, Kevin Passmore, Andrew Smith, Léon Strauss, Karine Varley, and Louisa Zanoun. I have also been lucky to work closely with Ludivine Broch on a number of projects, and have learned a huge amount from doing so.

Finally, huge thanks are due to my friends and family and particularly to Jen, Richard, Peter, Fiona, and James for making sure that there was always a life outside Alsace. I owe immeasurable thanks to my parents for the tremendous love, support, and encouragement that they have offered over the years, and for sparking my interest in the history of France and its regions on many happy family holidays. The final thanks go to Mark, who has listened to my thoughts on Alsace, diverted holidays to visit border sites, read (and improved) many drafts, and brought laughter and wine to the writing process, and to our son Jack, who arrived almost exactly forty-eight hours after I sent off the manuscript, and who has made the world a sunnier place ever since. Thank you.

Contents

List of Figures and Tables

FIGURES

TABLES

Map

Map. Alsace-Lorraine 1871–1914.

Adapted from Dan P. Silverman, *Reluctant Union: Alsace-Lorraine and Imperial Germany, 1871–1918* (Pennsylvania, 1972). Originally published in Alison Carrol and Louisa Zanoun, 'The View from the Border. A Comparative Study of Autonomism in Alsace and the Moselle, 1918–1929', *European Review of History*, 18:4 (2011), pp. 465–86.

Note on Place Names

The transfers of sovereignty over Alsace in 1871, 1918, 1940, and 1945 resulted in different French and German names for Alsatian cities, towns, and villages. For the sake of clarity, this book uses French place names. These were the names used following the region's return to France in 1918, and are those in use today.

Introduction

When two dynasts, encamped on lands that they exploit, share the costs of putting down boundary markers adorned with their coats of arms along the edge of a field, or mark an ideal line of demarcation down the middle of a river, that is not a border. It is a border when, having crossed that line, you find yourself in a different world, among a set of ideas, feelings and enthusiasms surprising and disconcerting to the foreigner. In other words, what engraves a border powerfully in the earth is not policemen or customs men or cannons drawn up behind ramparts. It is feelings, and exalted passions—and hatreds.

Lucien Febvre, 1935[1]

Alsace lies between the Vosges mountains and the River Rhine on the border between France and Germany. Today, its capital city is the site of the European Parliament, and the south forms part of the TriRhena Euroregion, one of Europe's first cross-border Euroregions. This symbolism as a site of Franco–German integration reflects its long history of connection. Yet such connection has been closely linked to conflict, and in the late nineteenth century Alsace found itself at the heart of a major European confrontation when France's defeat in the Franco–Prussian War led to the region's transfer from French to German rule in 1871. Its annexation triggered a debate that saw French and German ideas about nationhood develop in opposition to each other, as the notion that France was a 'civic' nation, where citizenship was based upon popular will, crystallized in interaction with understandings of Germany as a 'cultural' nation that based belonging upon ethnicity. In the following years, both France and Germany embarked upon policies of nation-building and through the creation of a national symbolism, introduction of new education systems, construction of railways, establishment of compulsory military service, and the fixing of their boundaries, they attempted to disseminate a sense of national attachment amongst their populations. The new state borders formed part of the constitutive myth of the nation state, as ideas of national unity drew upon notions of a shared language, a common history and culture, and a bounded, delimited territory.[2]

After the outbreak of the First World War in 1914, the return of Alsace-Lorraine became France's most talked-about war aim. Allied victory in 1918 triggered the

[1] Albert Demangeon and Lucien Febvre, *Le Rhin. Problèmes d'Histoire et d'Economie* (Paris, 1935), p. 129.
[2] Peter Sahlins, 'Natural Frontiers Revisited: France's Boundaries since the Seventeenth Century', *The American Historical Review* 95 (1990), pp. 1423–51, p. 1424.

region's return to French rule, and on their entry into Alsace French troops were welcomed by cheering crowds waving tricolour flags, leading French President Raymond Poincaré to confirm that the 'plebiscite is complete'. But reintegration proved far more difficult than these first scenes and encounters suggested. The return of Alsace to France was a process negotiated over the following two decades, and it remained incomplete in 1940 when Alsace was de facto annexed into the Third Reich. This book charts the region's experiences over these years.

This history of Alsace after its return to France in 1918 is the story of a region in the throes of fundamental change. It traces return and follows the difficult process of Alsace's reintegration into French society, culture, political and economic systems, and legislative and administrative institutions. It connects the microhistory of the region with the 'macro' levels of national policy, international relations, and transnational networks, and with the cross-border flows of ideas, goods, people, and cultural products that shaped daily life in Alsace as its population grappled with the meaning of return to France. These crossings may have generated 'feelings, and exalted passions—and hatreds', to return to Lucien Febvre's 1935 words.[3] But they also led to interactions and connections that transcended the boundary. This dual sense of difference and connection that developed from living 'on the border' shaped daily life in Alsace, and marked the return to France after 1918. This book traces these processes. It considers how return was imagined, discussed, and understood in the region, and the interaction of Alsatian ideas of return with the broader national and European context. This book, then, is a study of what it meant for Alsace to become French again after 1918.

THE RETURN OF ALSACE TO FRANCE AFTER 1918

The problems of reintegrating Alsace into France emerged almost immediately after the French troops marched triumphantly into the region in November 1918. They affected society, culture, politics, and the economy, and persisted throughout the interwar years, as the French state's nation-building initiatives interacted with local expressions of belonging. Parisian administrators had anticipated neither the strength of regional attachment nor the particular ideas of Alsace that developed amongst the region's population before and after 1918, while many in the region itself had not expected such sharp differences to emerge between distinct plans for their future. The result was 'a clash of understandings' that persisted throughout the following two decades.

This clash lent Alsatian reintegration a particular urgency, but pressure increased in light of the region's strategically important location on the eastern French border, across the Rhine from Germany. In the atmosphere of Franco–German tension that followed the First World War, French authorities were not keen to

---

[3] Much of *Le Rhin* was focused on the river's connecting role, yet Febvre still described the moment of crossing the border in terms of passions and hatreds, and in so doing summed up an important way of thinking about borders in interwar Europe.

[handwritten top margin: strategic forgetfulness of the region's past to buttress national ambition at the centre]

recognize that Alsace had long been an economic, linguistic, cultural, and religious meeting point for the two nations: Alsatian industrialists had built and developed trade networks that stretched across France, Germany, the Low Countries, and Central Europe; Alsatian intellectuals had been prominent translators in the eighteenth-century republic of letters; the University of Strasbourg boasted both the author Goethe and the chemist Louis Pasteur amongst its alumni; and Mozart and Parisian theatre troupes had performed in the region. Thus, Alsace's connections to Germany had been consolidated during the years of German rule between 1871 and 1918, but they reflected long-standing traditions and relationships. What is more, cross-border encounters continued and persisted after 1918, through the crossing of people travelling to visit family, shop, or seek work, through cross-border networks and associations, and through the movement of goods and ideas across the Rhine. Such interactions defined the parameters of Alsace's reintegration into France throughout the interwar years. *[handwritten: ← KEY POINT]*

As a result, Alsace's return was shaped by conflicting understandings of borderland life. French government attempts to remove German influence while classifying the population according to descent, introducing the French language, institutions, and systems, realigning politics and the economy, and constructing a French landscape met with wide-ranging responses in Alsace. Individuals in the region resisted, appropriated, and offered alternative ideas about the nature and meaning of return. In part, the resulting clash reflected the lack of a unified voice in either Paris or Alsace. In Paris, governments and ministers collapsed rapidly, sometimes lasting for just a few months, while in Alsace, political, economic, cultural, and religious elites competed to voice the concerns of the groups that they represented. In this environment, reintegration adopted the form of a multicentred struggle that revealed divergent understandings of Alsace's place within France. For many politicians, theorists, and writers in Paris and in Alsace, Alsace represented France's limits and its last line of defence against Germany. But this was a view that was challenged by an alternative vision of Alsace as a 'bridge' between France and Germany that connected the two nations. Both ideas reflected daily life, as Alsatians lived with the checkpoints and customs guards that marked the limits of the national territory, while maintaining familial, religious, cultural, political, and economic connections with populations living across the border. *[handwritten: ← different conceptions of what the border meant / symbolised]*

These ideas of Alsace as 'limit' or 'bridge' coexisted throughout the interwar years, responding to national and international events. But they were rarely articulated simultaneously, and the border rhetoric of Alsace as a meeting point frequently evaporated at moments of political, economic, or cultural crisis, to be replaced by an emphasis on its dividing or limiting role. What is more, these ideas were shaped at the grass roots through social and cultural practices. Indeed, Alsace's return to France was defined by the interaction between local problems and national and international questions. Thus, the notorious *malaise alsacien* that emerged in the region in the early 1920s had distinct local causes connected to the return to France. But it was also part of the broader sense of crisis that gripped Europe as the continent grappled with the impact of war, which had wiped out a generation of young men, devastated large sections of the landscape, and wrought

[handwritten marginal notes, right side: dialogue (even if one end of conversation silenced); key quote "multi-centred"]

[handwritten marginal notes, left side: key point 'Alsace as 'limit' or a 'bridge'; borders as political metaphor]

[handwritten marginal notes, right: key point (malaise alsacien) local causes]

[handwritten bottom notes: its why they play on 1789 so much. a particular context at that - within a post-war. transnational / war-national / having the same memory is so key; they dates commemoration → local causes]

economic havoc.[4] The aftermath of the conflict equally posed new questions about changing gender roles, international relations, and political allegiance as hopes for a better world appeared to be dashed.[5]

In this altered political, social, and economic landscape, France's first elections in 1919 returned a chamber dominated by the nationalist and conservative *Bloc national* which worked to bring Germany to account and concentrated on ensuring the delivery of the reparations payments agreed at Versailles.[6] A political swing came in 1924 with the election of the centre-left *Cartel des gauches*, which embarked upon the task of dismantling the *Bloc*'s work and Aristide Briand, foreign minister from 1925, who began working towards Franco–German reconciliation, a programme which led to the 1925 Locarno Treaty.[7] From 1929, economic crisis hit Europe. In France, the depression caused a steep rise in levels of unemployment and wiped out the savings of many of the nation's middle classes.[8] The 1930s also saw developments across Europe's colonial empires, and the backdrop to France's showcasing of its empire at the Vincennes Exhibition of 1931 was the increasingly vocal demands for indigenous rights voiced by nationalist movements in the colonies.[9]

Meanwhile, across the continent politics appeared to give way to the extremes; the Third Reich replaced Weimar democracy in Germany, Fascist Italy flexed its muscles through the invasion of Abyssinia in 1935, civil war broke out in Spain, and the Soviet Union launched purges of the Bolshevik party and the army.[10] In France, leagues of the extreme right grew in strength, and riots on 6 February 1934 in Paris precipitated the overthrow of the government of Radical Edouard Daladier.[11] The parties of the left responded with the formation of the anti-Fascist Popular Front of Radicals, Socialists, and Communists, which triumphed in the

---

[4] Stéphane Audoin-Rouzeau and Annette Becker, *14–18: Understanding the Great War* (London, 2002); Jean-Jacques Becker and Serge Berstein, *Victoire et frustrations 1914–1929* (Paris, 1990).

[5] E. H. Carr, *Twenty Years Crisis. An Introduction to the Study of International Relations* (Basingstoke, 2001); R. J. Overy, *The Interwar Crisis* (Harlow, 2007); on questions of gender and politics, see Sian Reynolds, *France between the Wars. Gender and Politics* (London, 1996); on international relations, see Zara Steiner, *The Lights that Failed. European International History, 1919–1933* (Oxford, 2005) and Zara Steiner, *The Triumph of the Dark. European International History, 1933–1939* (Oxford, 2011); Peter Jackson, *Beyond the Balance of Power. France and the Politics of National Security in the Era of the First World War* (Cambridge, 2013).

[6] J. F. V. Keiger, *France and the World since 1870* (London, 2001).

[7] Jean-Noël Jeanneney, *Leçon d'histoire pour une gauche au pouvoir. La faillite du Cartel 1924–1926* (Paris, 1977).

[8] Matt Perry, *Prisoners of Want. The Experience and Protest of the Unemployed in France, 1921–1945* (Aldershot, 2007); Kenneth Mouré, *Gold Standard Illusions: France, the Bank of France and the International gold standard* (Oxford, 2002).

[9] Martin Thomas, *The French Empire between the Wars* (Manchester, 2005).

[10] See Richard Evans, *The Coming of the Third Reich* (London, 2003); Jane Caplan (ed.), *Nazi Germany* (Oxford, 2008); Philip Morgan, *Italian Fascism, 1919–1945* (Basingstoke, 2001); Helen Graham, *The Spanish Civil War. A Very Short Introduction* (Oxford, 2005); Sheila Fitzpatrick (ed.), *Stalinism. New Directions* (London and New York, 2000).

[11] Brian Jenkins and Chris Millington, *France and Fascism. February 1934 and the Dynamics of Political Crisis* (Oxford, 2015); Samuel Kalman, *The Extreme Right in Interwar France: The Faisceau and the Croix de Feu* (Aldershot, 2008); Sean Kennedy, *Reconciling France against Democracy: The Croix de Feu and the Parti Social Français, 1929–1935* (Montreal, 2007); Robert Soucy, *French Fascism: The Second Wave* (New Haven, 1995). For a broader perspective on the right, see Kevin Passmore, *The Right in France. From the Third Republic to Vichy* (Oxford, 2012).

1936 elections with the slogan of 'Peace, Bread and Work'.[12] In Alsace, these political, social, and economic changes jostled for attention with problems presented by the region's return to France. Police surveillance reports demonstrate the continued priority given to local issues, even as just across the border Hitler's troops marched into the Rhineland in March 1936.[13] Indeed, many of the administrative, legislative, political, cultural, and linguistic issues that faced the government in 1918 remained unresolved as international tensions intensified at the end of the 1930s and much of the Alsatian population was evacuated in anticipation of the outbreak of war. The national and the regional interacted, and international events were filtered through local understandings. As a result, the return of Alsace to France was shaped by the region's cross-border connections and the rapidly changing national and European situation, and it was understood according to this context.

NATIONS, NATIONALISMS, AND HISTORIANS: ALSACE IN EUROPE

From the late nineteenth to the early twentieth century Alsace achieved a unique symbolic importance in French nationalism, as both border and borderland. After 1871 republicans attempted to consolidate the newly founded Third Republic, and in the nascent national symbolism the statue of Strasbourg in Paris's Place de la Concorde became a site of pilgrimage, maps of France depicted the lost provinces Alsace-Lorraine in black or purple (the colours of mourning), and nationalists treated the region as a key repository of French national identity.[14] The shock of the loss dulled in the later years of the nineteenth century, yet a group of Alsatian émigrés in Paris ensured that the region remained within the national consciousness, where it was treated as the epitome of all things French. Consequently the lost territories occupied an important place in the new republican curriculum in French primary schools and in the broader programme of institutionalizing and commemorating the Revolution. Cultural representations of Alsace-Lorraine, from the caricatures of the artist Hansi to the paintings of Gustave Doré and Jean-Jacques Henner, formed part of this new national symbolism alongside the Marseillaise, 14 July celebrations, the tricolour flag, the naming of streets, and the erection of statues of Marianne.[15] In this way they stressed the devotion of the 'lost

---

[12] Julian Jackson, *The Popular Front in France: Defending Democracy 1934–1938* (Cambridge, 1998); Jessica Wardhaugh, *In Pursuit of the People. Political Culture in France, 1934–1939* (Basingstoke, 2009).

[13] Archives Départementales du Bas-Rhin (hereafter ADBR) 286D 345 Commissaire Spécial to Commissaire Division de Police Spéciale, Report on a political meeting in Rhinau, 31 March 1936; ADBR 285D 345 Commissaire Spécial to Commissaire Division de Police Spéciale, Report on a political meeting in Marckolsheim, 31 March 1936.

[14] Karine Varley, *Under the Shadow of Defeat. The War of 1870–71 in French Memory* (Basingstoke, 2008), especially pp. 175–202.

[15] On the consolidation of the Republic, see Timothy Baycroft, *France. Inventing the Nation* (London, 2008); James McMillan, *Modern France, 1880–2002* (Oxford, 2003), p. 4. On the place of

provinces' to France, while the idea of the Rhine as France's natural and historic frontier and essential to the harmony of the French *Hexagone* ensured that the border was also part of this symbolism.[16] During the First World War the cult of Alsace-Lorraine meant that the region's return became a prominent war aim, with the result that notions of French 'sacrifice' to 'liberate' the so-called lost provinces formed the backdrop to the region's return.

Late nineteenth-century French policies of nation-building were underpinned by the republican conception of nationhood, according to which the nation was not the product of race or ethnicity, but a 'daily plebiscite'.[17] Developing an understanding of the nation first articulated at the French Revolution, republican elites in France came to express a notion of nationhood that was predicated on linguistic, cultural, and political unity.[18] The annexation of Alsace-Lorraine in 1871 was crucial in the evolution of French ideas of nationhood, but critically these ideas developed in opposition to (and interaction with) definitions of the German nation. When the German historian Theodor Mommsen argued in 1870 that the annexation of Alsace was justified on the basis of the Alsatians' Germanic ethnicity, language, and culture, the French medievalist Numa Fustel de Coulanges countered that Alsace should remain within France as a result of the population's will to be French.[19] Fustel de Coulanges' ideas were taken further in Ernest Renan's stress on the importance of voluntary adhesion to the nation, upon which the republican conception of nationality was based.[20] It was through these exchanges that French perceptions of Germany as an 'ethnic nation' hardened, while on the east bank of

Alsace in this symbolism, see Michael E. Nolan, 'The Elusive Alsatian', in *The Inverted Mirror. Mythologizing the Enemy in France and Germany, 1898–1914* (Oxford, 2005). On the place of Alsace in the history curriculum, see Mona Ozouf, 'L'Alsace-Lorraine, mode d'emploi. "La question d'Alsace-Lorraine dans le Manuel général, 1871–1914"', in *L'école de la France: essais sur la Révolution, l'utopie, et l'enseignement* (Paris, 1984), pp. 214–30.

[16] Laurence Turetti, *Quand la France pleurait l'Alsace-Lorraine. Les 'provinces perdues' aux sources du patriotisme républicain, 1870–1914* (Strasbourg, 2008).

[17] Ernest Renan, *Qu'est-ce que c'est une nation? Conférence faite en Sorbonne le 11 mars 1882*, 2nd edn (Paris, 1892).

[18] On expressions of the nation at the Revolution, see David A. Bell, *The Cult of the Nation in France. Inventing Nationalism, 1680–1800* (Cambridge, MA, 2001). Thus, while some theorists of nationalism have stressed the ancient character of sentiments of collective identification, it was after the French Revolution that nationalism became a dominant political ideology across Europe and that French republican thinkers honed their understanding of the nation. For an analysis that stresses the deep roots of nationalism, see Adrian Hastings, *The Construction of Nationhood: Ethnicity, Religion and Nationalism* (Cambridge, 1997) and Anthony D. Smith, *The Ethnic Origins of Nations* (Oxford, 1986). On nationalism as a modern phenomenon, connected with industrialization and the development of the modern nation state, see Ernest Gellner, *Nations and Nationalism* (Oxford, 1983); John Breuilly, *Nationalism and the State* (Manchester, 1982); Eric Hobsbawm, *Nations and Nationalism since 1780. Programme, myth, reality* (Cambridge, 1990); Timothy Baycroft, *Nationalism in Europe, 1789–1945* (Cambridge, 1998). On nationalism in France, see in particular Michel Winock, *Nationalisme, anti-sémitisme et fascisme en France* (Paris, 1990) and Robert Tombs (ed.), *Nationhood and Nationalism in France from Boulangism to the Great War, 1889–1919* (London, 1991). The emergence of nationalism as a political ideology contributed to a widely held belief that the political and national units should be congruent and that the nation represented the supreme value.

[19] For an account of the discussion between Mommsen and Fustel de Coulanges, see Paul Smith, 'A la recherche d'une identité alsacienne', *Vingtième Siècle* 50 (1996), pp. 23–35.

[20] Renan, *Qu'est-ce que c'est une nation?*

the Rhine thinkers contrasted France's civic stance with their own, apparently more natural, ethnic conception of nationhood.[21]

The annexation of Alsace and the debate that followed thus had an important role in the development of French and German views of each other. However, this civic–ethnic dichotomy has since been challenged by a number of important historical studies that have shown that the French could be just as xenophobic as their neighbours, and that German citizenship legislation is more complicated than the stress on ethnicity would suggest.[22] And, as in the early stages of the debate over rival conceptions of citizenship and nationhood, Alsace has played an important part in revising the dichotomy. First, the *option* clause of the Treaty of Frankfurt which ratified the annexation of Alsace and a section of Lorraine in 1871 gave Alsatians the option of choosing French nationality, showing that the German state was prepared to consider choice as a criterion for citizenship (albeit choice for those who had the financial means to leave). Second, after the First World War the French government adopted an ethnic version of belonging to prevent Alsatians who had been born in the region to German parents from becoming French citizens. This was put into practice through the identity cards issued to Alsatian citizens and the purge trials that sought to remove undesirable 'German' elements from the province's population.[23]

The crystallization of attitudes towards nationhood in France and Germany after 1871 was accompanied by conscious programmes of nation-building in each nation state, with the intention of creating a shared sense of connection to the nation. Scholars have argued that during these years the establishment of a system of compulsory education, the invention of a national culture, the construction of railways, and the introduction of compulsory military service combined to sweep away old commitments and transform 'peasants into Frenchmen', to borrow Eugen Weber's phrase.[24] A number of influential works have studied the role of institutions, symbols, commemorations, and '*lieux de mémoire*' in creating a common sense of national attachment. These studies have revealed the symbolic character of nationalism, and are generally united in identifying a homogeneous

---

[21] See Patrick Weil, *How to be French: Nationality in the Making since 1789* (Durham, NC, 2008), p. 184. On Franco-German opposition, see Nolan, *The Inverted Mirror*.

[22] On France, see Patrick Weil, *La France et ses étrangers: L'aventure d'une politique d'immigration, 1938–1991* (Paris, 1991) and Peter Sahlins, *Unnaturally French: Foreign Citizens in the Old Regime and After* (Ithaca, NY, 2004). On Germany, see Andreas Fahrmeir, *Citizens and Aliens: Foreigners and the Law in Britain and the German States, 1789–1870* (New York, 2000); Eli Nathans, *The Politics of Citizenship in Germany: Ethnicity, Utility and Nationalism* (New York, 2004), and Joyce Mushaben, *The Changing Face of Citizenship: Integration and Mobilization among Ethnic Minorities in Germany* (New York, 2008). For an elegant analysis of the dichotomy, see Rogers Brubaker, *Citizenship and Nationhood in France and Germany* (Cambridge, MA, 1992).

[23] Tara Zahra, 'The "Minority Problem" and National Classification in the French and Czechoslovak Borderlands', *Contemporary European History*, 17:2 (2008), pp. 137–65; Laird Boswell, 'From Liberation to Purge Trials in the "Mythic Provinces". Recasting French Identities in Alsace and Lorraine, 1918–1920', *French Historical Studies*, 23:1 (2000), pp. 129–62; David Allen Harvey, 'Lost Children or Enemy Aliens? Classifying the Population of Alsace after the First World War', *Journal of Contemporary History*, 71:3 (1999), pp. 552–84.

[24] Eugen Weber, *Peasants into Frenchmen. The Modernization of Rural France 1870–1914* (Stanford, 1976).

sense of national sentiment that was firmly rooted in France and Germany by the late nineteenth century.[25]

This work has broken important ground in revealing the constructed nature of nationalism and its connection to modernity. But the danger in treating the nation state as the obvious culmination of a long process of modernization is that regions, or a sense of local belonging, are relegated to little more than a stage of development in a preordained path, or, as Blackbourn and Retallack put it, 'either something that is overcome or a piece of grit in the machine'.[26] In this way, it echoes the ideas of nineteenth-century liberal nationalists who contrasted the modern and dynamic nation state with the backward-looking regions. In recent decades, important new scholarship has suggested that nation-building initiatives did not come solely from governments and administrators in Europe's capital cities, and has revealed the role of local actors and institutions in forging local attachment to the nation. Thus, studies of education in the French Third Republic have argued that, far from seeking to stamp out regional language, schoolteachers, who were often born and trained in the regions in which they worked, tolerated local idioms and forged fresh links between region and nation for their students.[27] And across the Rhine local historical societies intended to complement, rather than replace, the German National Museum with their activities.[28] This work has stressed that the process of national integration is interactive, and that rather than the imposition of a fixed set of beliefs, the creation of national identity is a process 'continually in the making'.[29]

Similarly, case studies of France and Germany's regions reveal that nation-building did not involve the imposition of national identity by the centre onto the periphery, and they suggest that both state and local society adopted the role of 'motive force' in the formation and consolidation of the nation.[30] Thus, while elite groups in Paris and Berlin engaged in the creation of a national culture, this did not result in the replacement of provincial values with national ones. And surveys of local and urban politics and memory in France and Germany have stressed that regional or state-based loyalties and identities existed alongside national attachment, and thus contributed to the development of attachment to the nation.[31]

---

[25] Eric Hobsbawm and Terence Ranger (eds), *The Invention of Tradition* (Cambridge, 1983). On France, see in particular the monumental series edited by Pierre Nora: *Les Lieux de mémoire*, 7 vols (Paris, 1984–6).

[26] David Blackbourn and James Retallack (eds), *Localism, landscape and the ambiguities of place: German-speaking central Europe, 1860–1930* (Toronto, Buffalo, and London, 2007), pp. 15–16.

[27] Jean-François Chanet, *L'Ecole Républicaine et les petites patries, 1879–1940* (Paris, 1990); Deborah Reed-Danahay, *Education and Identity in Rural France: The Politics of Schooling* (Cambridge, 1996); Anne-Marie Thiesse, *Ils apprenaient la France* (Paris, 1997) and Thiesse, *La création des identités nationales* (Paris, 1999).

[28] Abigail Green, *Fatherlands: State-Building and Nationhood in Nineteenth Century Germany* (Cambridge, 2001).

[29] Caroline Ford, *Creating the Nation in Provincial France: Religion and Political Identity in Brittany* (Princeton, NJ, 1993), p. 5. See also David Laven and Timothy Baycroft, 'Border Regions and Identity', *European Review of History—Revue Européenne d'histoire*, 15:3 (2008), pp. 255–75.

[30] Peter Sahlins, *Boundaries: The Making of France and Spain in the Pyrenees* (Berkeley, CA, 1989), p. 8.

[31] Celia Applegate, *A Nation of Provincials: The German Idea of Heimat* (Oxford, 1990); Tony Judt, *Socialism in Provence, 1871–1914. A Study in the Origins of the Modern French Left* (Cambridge,

A similar picture emerges from scholarship on nations across Europe: studies of Spain and Russia have underlined the interactive character of nation-building; and, in Italian historiography, where questions of nation-building speak to the debate over the integration of the south into the nation state, work over the past three decades has also engaged with the problem of how we should think about the dissemination of national values and the construction of a national community.[32] This work has shown that each region understood the nation in ways that were filtered through local values and experiences, and were adapted according to the local context. What is more, this did not mean that individuals gave up their previous identity as they took on a national one; rather, they developed a 'complex network of identities, sometimes conflicting, and sometimes in parallel'.[33]

In recent years, this debate has taken a new turn through a focus upon Europe's border regions as scholars pay increased attention to processes of exchange and transfer. This new movement in historical studies is, in part, a response to the changes in the political map of Europe that resulted from the fall of the Iron Curtain, the enlargement of the European Union, and globalization.[34] These global political events encouraged the emergence of borderlands research, and important work has turned to borders in order to challenge the acceptance of the nation as the dominant category of analysis that underpins many histories of modern Europe. James Bjork, Pieter Judson, Tara Zahra, and others working on east and central Europe have analysed borderlands to explore the limits of nationalism and revealed populations that appeared resistant, or 'indifferent', to processes of nationalization (absorption or inclusion into the nation).[35]

As Zahra has argued, this 'national indifference' could and did change over time, and was no more consistent in its form or meaning than nationalism itself. Thus while the modernist paradigm established by Ernest Gellner, Eugen Weber, and Eric Hobsbawm and Terence Ranger has treated nationalization as a step towards the homogeneous nation state, this research has suggested that national indifference could and did flourish in moments of high nationalist agitation. These studies speak to a broader movement to shift the focus of historical analysis from the

---

1979); Alain Corbin, *Archaïsme et modernité en Limousin au XIX siècle*, 2 vols (Paris, 1975); Martin Simpson, 'Republicanizing the City: Radical Republicans in Toulouse, 1880–90', *European History Quarterly*, 34 (2004), pp. 157–90.

[32] Miguel Cabo and Fernando Molina, 'The Long and Winding Road of Nationalization: Eugen Weber's Peasants into Frenchmen in Modern European History', *European History Quarterly*, 39 (2009), pp. 264–86.

[33] Timothy Baycroft, 'Changing Identities in the Franco–Belgian Borderland in the Nineteenth and Twentieth Centuries', *French History*, 13:4 (1999), pp. 417–38, p. 417.

[34] Bernhard Struck, 'Border Regions', *European History Online* (2013). Struck identifies the turn towards cultural history, microhistory, local history, and *Alltagsgeschichte* (the history of everyday life) as playing an important part in the turn towards borders and borderlands as objects of historical research.

[35] Pieter M. Judson, *Guardians of the Nation. Activists on the Language Frontier of Imperial Austria* (Cambridge, MA, 2006); James E. Bjork, *Neither German nor Pole. Catholicism and National Indifference in a Central European Borderland* (Michigan, 2008); Tara Zahra, *Kidnapped Souls: National Indifference and the Battle for Children in the Bohemian Lands, 1900–1948* (Ithaca, NY, 2008). See also Jeremy King, *Budweisers into Czechs and Germans: A Local History of Bohemian Politics, 1848–1948* (Princeton, NJ, 2005).

nation state through new approaches to the past, whether through comparative, entangled, global, international, regional, local, or transnational history.[36] Shaped by cross-border flows and interactions, many European borderlands were defined by transnationality, and as a result they have rich potential for a history that seeks to understand 'past lives and events shaped by processes and relationships that transcended the borders of the nation-state'.[37] Yet this literature also has implications for our understanding of nationalism, as indifference should be understood as a response to modern politics and a constitutive part of the evolution of the nation.[38] It is therefore also a vital element of the story of how nations have been constructed.

Alternatively, scholars (and particularly those working on western Europe) have focused on border regions in order to complicate and better understand the formation of nations, treating borderlands as laboratories where, through a complex process of negotiation, national identities are honed and contested. Indeed, borderlands are being revisited, as Laird Boswell has suggested, by historians seeking to analyse the interaction between 'local popular representations and strategies, state policies, and multiple national myths' through which nationhood was forged at these meeting points between nations.[39] This work has suggested that identities are fluid, contested, and frequently oppositional.[40]

In his path-breaking study of the Franco–Spanish borderland, Peter Sahlins showed that peasants living on the French side of the Cerdanya valley in the Pyrenean mountain range experienced a sense of difference from the population on the Spanish side and began to describe them as 'Spanish' before talking about themselves as French. In this way the nation 'emerged at the periphery' before taking shape at the centre.[41] Crucially, such oppositional identity, or 'othering' (with one nation opposed to another), did not exist in isolation. In Sahlins' case, it existed alongside overlapping identities that he describes as a series of concentric circles from the local through the regional to the national, so an individual identified with a village within a region within a nation. This model has been nuanced by Timothy Baycroft, who used the case of Flanders to point to the existence of non-concentric overlapping identities; in this case the region of Flanders crosses both the French and Belgian nations, so the region (Flanders) contains a group of

---

[36] Tara Zahra, 'Imagined Noncommunities: National Indifference as a Category of Analysis', *Slavic Review*, 69 (2010), pp. 93–119, p. 94.

[37] Ann Curthoys and Marilyn Lake, 'Introduction', in *Connected Worlds: History in Transnational Perspective* (Canberra, 2005). See Paul Readman, Cynthia Radding, and Chad Bryant (eds), *Borderlands in World History, 1700–1914* (Basingstoke, 2014).

[38] Zahra, 'Imagined Noncommunities', p. 98.

[39] Laird Boswell, 'Rethinking the Nation at the Periphery', *French Politics, Culture & Society*, 27:2 (2009), pp. 111–26, p. 120. See also Henrice Altink and Sharif Gemie (eds), *At The Border: Margins and Peripheries in Modern France* (Cardiff, 2008); Michel Baud and Willem van Schendel, 'Toward a Comparative History of Borderlands', *Journal of World History*, 8:2 (1997), pp. 211–42; Peter Schöttler, 'The Rhine as an Object of Historical Controversy in the Inter-war Years. Towards a History of Frontier Mentalities', *History Workshop Journal*, 39 (1995), pp. 1–22.

[40] Hastings Donnan and Thomas Wilson, *Border Identities. Nation and State at International Frontiers* (Cambridge, 1998).

[41] Sahlins, *Boundaries*.

people (the Belgian Flemish) who do not belong within the nation (France).[42] Meanwhile, Alon Confino has shown that the concept of *Heimat* in Germany actually helped to consolidate German national unity in the Wilhelmine Empire by allowing citizens to reconcile local and national attachments.[43] These identities were not necessarily fixed or permanent; Peter Thaler has pointed to 'fluidity' in borderland identities in central Europe, while Caroline Ford's work on Brittany has presented national identity as a process 'continually in the making'.[44]

The literature on western European borderlands has thus offered new insights into identity construction, notably demonstrating that discrete aspects of identity overlapped, and suggesting that individual understandings were inseparable from broader, collective identity. As Dror Wahrman has noted (on a very different topic):

> Identity…encompasses within it…a productive tension between two contradictory impulses: identity as the unique individuality of a person (as in 'identity card') or identity as a common denominator that places an individual within a group (as in 'identity politics'). In the former sense, sometimes akin to self, identity is the essence of difference: it is what guarantees my quintessential specificity in relation to others. In the latter sense, identity is the obverse, or erasure of difference. It is what allows me to ignore particular differences as I recognise myself in a collective grouping.[45]

In interwar Alsace these 'productive tensions' brought into conversation individual identity and identity as part of one of a number of collective groupings, whether Alsatian, French, German, Catholic, Protestant, Jewish, Socialist, Communist, departmental, village, or any of the multiple layers of identity that Alsatians experienced and articulated. Thus, while the French government often saw identity and nationalization in binary terms as pro- or anti-French, identities in Alsace might be better understood as falling on a spectrum. Alsatians had a range of different languages that they could and did draw upon to describe themselves and their situation, and they were not always consistent in doing so. In this sense, identities in Alsace were multiple, contested, and in a state of becoming.

Alsace occupies an important place in this lively field on both national integration and borders. The symbolism invested in the 'lost provinces' of Alsace-Lorraine at a high point of nation-building means that the region enjoys a unique space in the French national consciousness, while its experience of alternate French and German rule at this pinnacle of European nation-building and subsequent contests over the region have resulted in a unique position in European history.[46] And Alsace's historiography reflects its status as a borderland; scholars from

---

[42] Timothy Baycroft, *Culture, Identity and Nationalism. French Flanders in the Nineteenth and Twentieth Centuries* (Woodbridge, 2004).

[43] Alon Confino, *The Nation as a Local Metaphor: Württemberg, Imperial Germany and National Memory, 1871–1918* (London, 1997).

[44] Peter Thaler, 'Fluid Identities in Central European Borderlands', *European History Quarterly*, 31: 4 (2001), pp. 519–48; Peter Thaler, *Of Mind and Matter: The Duality of National Identity in the German–Danish Borderlands* (Purdue, IN, 2009); Ford, *Creating the Nation*, p. 5.

[45] Dror Wahrman, *The Making of the Modern Self. Identity and Culture in Eighteenth Century England* (New Haven and London, 2006), p. xi.

[46] Jean-Marie Mayeur, 'Une memoire frontière: L'Alsace', in Pierre Nora (ed.), *Les lieux de memoire, Vol. II: La Nation* (Paris, 1966), pp. 14–20.

distinct national traditions have used the region to illuminate local, national, and comparative history.[47] The local history of Alsace has received more attention than almost any other French region, and Léon Strauss, Jean-Claude Richez, François Igersheim, Alfred Wahl, Bernard Vogler, and others have uncovered the practices and sensibilities of the region's social classes and groups over the modern period to reveal a great deal about the rich fabric of daily life in the region.[48]

What is more, over the past three decades a series of important works have adopted a comparative focus to contrast French and German policies of nation-building and to analyse how they were experienced in terms of primary schooling, universities, and politics, or their impact upon the population according to class or gender.[49] Through this work, Steven Harp, John A. Craig, David A. Harvey, Elizabeth Vlossak, Christopher Fischer, and Christian Baechler have contributed much to our understanding of nation-building and, crucially, have underlined just how similar French and German projects frequently were. Yet, comparative history has its pitfalls, not least in the sense that it brings with it the danger of affirming distinct national historiographies or of assuming that national cultures are distinct and closed.[50] Work on borderlands in central and eastern Europe offers a reminder of the influences that neighbouring societies and cultures brought to bear upon one another, and it is important to recognize that French and German programmes of nation-building were not only similar in important ways; they were also formed by imitating one another and through rivalries that drove their distinct national projects.[51] And in the case of the Franco–German borderland, Catherine T. Dunlop's work on map-making offers an instructive example of just how far rival projects

[47] Alison Carrol, 'Les anglophones et l'Alsace: une fascination durable', *Revue d'Alsace*, 138 (2012), pp. 265–83.

[48] Jean-Claude Richez, 'Malaises et crises après le retour à la France', *Langue et culture régionales*, 15 (1990), pp. 65–92; Jean-Claude Richez, Léon Strauss, François Igersheim, and Stéphane Jonas, *Jacques Peirotes, 1869–1935 et le socialisme en Alsace* (Strasbourg, 1989); Jean-Claude Richez and Léon Strauss, 'Tradition et renouvellement des pratiques de loisirs en milieu ouvrier dans l'Alsace des années trente', *Revue d'Alsace*, 113 (1987), pp. 217–37; François Igersheim, *Politique et Administration dans le Bas-Rhin, 1848–1870* (Strasbourg, 1993); Bernard Vogler (ed.), *Chroniques d'Alsace 1918–1939* (Barcelona, 2004); Bernard Vogler, *Histoire Politique de l'Alsace* (Strasbourg, 1995).

[49] Stephen Harp, *Learning to be Loyal. Primary Schooling as Nation Building in Alsace and Lorraine, 1850–1940* (DeKalb, 1998); John E. Craig, *Scholarship and Nation Building. The Universities of Strasbourg and Alsatian Society, 1870–1939* (Chicago, 1984); Christopher J. Fischer, in *Alsace to the Alsatians? Visions and Divisions of Alsatian Regionalism, 1870–1939* (New York and Oxford, 2010); Christian Baechler, *Le Parti Catholique Alsacien 1890–1939: Du Reichsland à la République Jacobine* (Strasbourg, 1982); David Allen Harvey, *Constructing Class and Nationality in Alsace, 1830–1945* (DeKalb, 2001); Elizabeth Vlossak, *Marianne or Germania? Nationalizing Women in Alsace, 1870–1946* (Oxford, 2010).

[50] Michel Espagne, 'Sur les limites du comparatisme en histoire culturelle', *Genèse*, 17 (1994), pp. 112–21; Micol Seigel, 'Beyond Compare: Comparative Method after the Transnational Turn', *Radical History Review*, 91 (2005), pp. 62–90. On the value of comparative history, see Marc Bloch, 'Pour une histoire comparée des sociétés européenes', in Bloch, *Mélanges historiques*, 2 vols (Paris, 1963).

[51] On the transnational in central and eastern European history see Tara Zahra, 'Looking East: East Central European "Borderlands" in German History and Historiography', *History Compass*, 3: 1 (2005), pp. 1–23. For an excellent study that addresses the question of how France and Germany (and England) imitated and rivalled each other's nation-building projects, see Astrid Swenson, *The Rise of Heritage. Preserving the Past in France, Germany and England, 1789–1914* (Cambridge, 2013).

were driven by exchange as well as competition with regard to this area of life.[52] Thus, while this comparative literature has underlined the role of border regions in the formation of national attachment, and of the similarities between distinct national projects, we do not know as much about the role of cross-border flows, connections, and encounters in shaping experiences.

Scholars have also focused on the dynamics of rule by either France or Germany in order to illuminate relations between the national centre and its periphery and questions of national integration. In his study of Alsace's annexation into Germany, Dan P. Silverman addressed the implications of German rule, while Anthony Steinhoff and Detmar Klein have considered the role of religion and folklore in shaping experiences of the annexation.[53] Work focused on the return to France has similarly told us much about distinct aspects of daily life; François Dreyfus has analysed politics, while Samuel Goodfellow has described the strength of the regional Fascist movement, and Laird Boswell has demonstrated Alsace's role in refashioning notions of Frenchness after 1918.[54] This work has underlined the role of the Alsatian population in forging their own sense of identity, but it begs larger questions about how return was experienced across the region's population, and over how distinct aspects of daily life (such as culture, the economy, and the landscape) influenced and informed each other.

What is more, the literature tends to treat the borderland as the geographical location of the study, but neglects the role that the border itself played both in shaping daily life in the region, and in forging Alsace's relationship with France. This book seeks to build upon this literature, but it adopts a different focus by treating the border as a driver of change: it considers how return was affected by the border, and by the cross-border contact that it generated. In so doing, this book seeks to shift the emphasis of the debate by situating Alsace's regional history within a national and transnational framework that has implications for each of these scales of existence and analysis. It considers the dynamics of return and analyses how reintegration into France was shaped by cross-border contact with Germany.

Of course, the fundamental point here is that Alsace's European history is inseparable from its French history. The return of Alsace, imbued as it was with

[52] Catherine Tatiana Dunlop, *Cartophilia. Maps and the Search for Identity in the French–German Borderland* (Chicago, 2015).

[53] Dan P. Silverman, *Reluctant Union: Alsace-Lorraine and Imperial Germany, 1871–1918* (University Park, 1972); Anthony J. Steinhoff, *The Gods of the City. Protestantism and Religious Culture in Strasbourg 1870–1914* (Boston, 2008); Detmar Klein 'The Virgin with the Sword. Marian Apparitions, Religion and National Identity in Alsace in the 1870s', *French History*, 21: 4 (2007), pp. 411–30; Detmar Klein, 'Folklore as a Weapon: National Identity in German Annexed Alsace, 1890–1914', in Timothy Baycroft and David Hopkin (eds), *Folklore and Nationalism in Europe during the Long Nineteenth Century* (Leiden, 2012), pp. 161–91.

[54] François G. Dreyfus, *La vie politique en Alsace, 1919–1936* (Paris, 1969); Samuel Huston Goodfellow, *Between the Swastika and the Cross of Lorraine: Fascisms in Interwar Alsace* (DeKalb, 1999); Laird Boswell, 'Franco–Alsatian Conflict and the Crisis of National Sentiment during the Phoney War', *Journal of Modern History*, 71: 3 (1999), pp. 552–84; Laird Boswell, 'From Liberation to Purge Trials in the "Mythic Provinces": Recasting French Identities in Alsace and Lorraine, 1918–1920', *French Historical Studies*, 23:1 (2000), pp. 129–62.

political, economic, social, and cultural connections to Germany, had significant implications for the making of the French nation, and Alsatian responses to French nationalism played an important role in reframing the boundaries of the French national community in the twentieth century. The following chapters chart the late Third Republic's problems in coming to terms with regional particularity as it encountered it in Alsace, and suggest that the successive problems of reintegration were not a result of the failures of left or right, but rather of a cultural predisposition on the part of administrators and governments to regard paths to Frenchness as inherently progressive, and undeniably beneficial.

This book offers a contribution to debates over how France has dealt with cultural difference, both in its colonial empire and within its own national boundaries.[55] It exposes just how uncomfortable the resulting assumptions could be for the Alsatian population, many of whom were deeply attached to their regional versions of belonging. And it suggests that for many in Alsace nationalization did not represent a pathway to the homogeneous nation state, yet the perceived menace of national ambiguity in the recovered departments led successive governments to define ever more closely the boundaries of the national community as Alsace triggered critical questions about what was French. Alsatian responses to government attempts to make the region French are thus a vital element of the story of the construction of the French nation. Furthermore, in their reading of the Alsatians' multiple and varied responses to return, administrators and politicians in Paris reveal the growing cultural and political insecurities of the Third Republic in ways that are suggestive of both stability and instability in twentieth-century France. Yet this book is 'a national history written outward from Alsace,' rather than from Paris, and, throughout, the transnational flows, exchanges, and conflicts that it charts worked to shape the French nation, rather than to supplant the national framework.

This book thus suggests that a focus on Alsace's return to France allows consideration of 'how regional and national history is bound up with the transnational past,' and encourages the linking-up of local experience to developments on the macro level of international relations and cross-border flows. This raises questions of how we should understand Alsace: was it part of France or a transnational space? And what did it mean to be Alsatian? The answers to these questions were not straightforward. In many ways, Alsace was defined by transnationality as people, goods, and ideas crossed the border. But while these flows transcended the border, they also helped to *make* it, as they stimulated anxieties that led to new efforts to control and monitor the region's cross-border associations and crystallized a sense of difference. After 1918 Alsace was restored to its position within France's boundaries, yet its cultural differences proved unsettling to mainstream republican

[55] Alice Conklin, *A Mission to Civilize: The Republican Idea of Empire in France and West Africa, 1895–1930* (Stanford, CA, 1997); Clifford D. Rosenberg, *Policing Paris: The Origins of Modern Immigration Control between the Wars* (Ithaca and London, 2006); Mary Dewhurst Lewis, *The Boundaries of the Republic: Migrant Rights and the Limits of Universalism in France, 1918–1940* (Stanford, CA, 2007); Gerard Noiriel, *Le Creuset français: Histoire de l'immigration XIXe–XXe siècle* (Paris, 2006).

thought. How different levels of government, administrators, local politicians, and civil society attempted to negotiate this dilemma tells us much about political France: notably, how it coped with difference and the meaning of both integration and inclusion.

Central to this history is consideration of the role that the border itself played in shaping experiences of return. It is this book's contention that the contribution of a focus on borderlands to understandings of national integration is that it encourages us to think beyond interactions between centre and periphery in the making of nations. Indeed, the very notion of 'peripheries' creates a sense of geographical marginality, and it is important not to fall into the trap of treating peripheral communities as passive partners in a two-way relationship with the centre. Instead, a focus on the border suggests that nations are formed (in part, at least) through cross-border interactions. State-based actors such as diplomats, politicians, and cultural intermediaries negotiated the limits of state power, competed with each other, and imitated and reflected developments in rival nations. At the same time national populations interacted, and borders and borderlands allowed encounters between agents of the state, such as crossing guards and border police, and local populations. It is at these crux points, or fault lines, that nations are formed, through both limiting and defining the nation, and through interaction with neighbours. Edith Sheffer's work on the border between East and West Germany after 1945 has shown that it is not only the case that borders shape identities, but also that people shape borders and invest them with meaning.[56] In this spirit, this book treats the border not simply as the geographical focus; it also seeks to write the history of the border into the history of the borderland.

THE BORDER AS A CATEGORY OF ANALYSIS

border, n. A side, edge, brink, or margin; a limit, or boundary; the part of anything lying along its boundary or outline.

Oxford English Dictionary

Questions of borders, nations, and identities raise issues of definition. After all, as Joan Wallach Scott has pointed out, 'Words, like the ideas and things they are meant to signify, have a history.'[57] When it comes to borders between two nations, distinct national historical contexts shape the ways in which words and concepts are understood. In French, the linguistic distinction between boundaries (*limites*) and frontiers (*frontières*) dates to the thirteenth century, when the French monarchy began to distinguish between a frontier, a zone which faced an enemy (and thus implied bellicose expansion), and a boundary, a linear line which established the

---

[56] Edith Sheffer, *Burned Bridge: How East and West Germans Made the Iron Curtain* (Oxford, 2011).

[57] Joan Wallach Scott, 'Gender as a Useful Category of Analysis', *American Historical Review*, 91: 5, (1986), pp. 1053–75, p. 1053.

limits of two jurisdictions.[58] The German word *Grenze*, meanwhile, corresponds to both *frontière* and *limite*, but German has developed distinct compounds to distinguish between different types of borders: the cultural boundary (*Kulturgrenze*), the border of cultural soil (*Grenze des Kulturbodens*), the border of the folk or people's soil (*Grenze des Volksbodens*), and the border of the empire (*Reichsgrenze*).[59]

In many ways, these different etymologies reflect France's and Germany's distinct national histories. The French state unified much earlier, although it was only in the nineteenth century that Nice and Savoy were incorporated into France, and of course Alsace and the Moselle returned most recently in 1945. What is more, a unified nation state does not signify a homogeneous nation state, as work on the persistence of regional identities in France reminds us.[60] Nevertheless, an earlier connection between territory, nation, and state shaped the development of understandings of these words, and Peter Sahlins has shown how ideas of 'natural' and 'historical' frontiers shaped French foreign policy during the seventeenth and eighteenth centuries.[61] For Germany, on the other hand, the fluidity in notions of borders reflected both its later unification and the fact that Germans had lived for generations beyond the borders of the German lands; as Karl Schlögel points out, German discourse on borders was 'always ambiguous'.[62] All the same, in both France and Germany ideas about borders were central to understandings of the nation, and part of what Benedict Anderson has termed 'imagined communities'.[63] These imagined communities united individuals who did not enjoy face-to-face contact, but who nevertheless imagined themselves to be connected to each other as a result of their shared identification with their common nation state. The crucial point is that the very idea of the 'border', or the 'borderland', is a construct invented by nationalists.

The vocabulary in anglophone scholarship also varies. Many histories of borders draw a distinction between the 'border' or 'boundary' as a linear and politically constructed line, and the 'frontier' which, following Frederick Jackson Turner's influential notion, is treated as a zone of expansion. In Turner's example of the American West, the pioneers' engagement with the wilderness and the special character of frontier life shaped American values.[64] Others have viewed the frontier simply as the area stretching away from the borderland. Bernhard Struck has also distinguished between, first, Europe's 'old' natural, geographical, and 'immobile' borders such as the Rhine, the Alps, the Danube, and the Pyrenees; second, the economic, confessional, and social borders 'which wax and wane'; and third, the

---

[58] Sahlins, 'Natural Frontiers Revisited', p. 1426.

[59] Karl Schlögel, 'Europe and the Culture of Borders: Rethinking Borders after 1989', in Manfred Hidermeier (ed.), *Historical Concepts between Eastern and Western Europe* (New York and Oxford, 2007).

[60] See in particular Sharif Gemie, *Brittany 1750–1950: The Invisible Nation* (Cardiff, 2007).

[61] Sahlins, 'Natural Frontiers Revisited'.

[62] Schlögel, 'Europe and the Culture of Borders', in Hidermeier (ed.), *Historical Concepts*, p. 79.

[63] Benedict Anderson, *Imagined Communities. Reflections on the Origins and Spread of Nationalism* (London, 1991).

[64] Frederick Jackson Turner, *The Significance of the Frontier in American History* (New York, 1920). The original paper was delivered at a meeting of the American Historical Association in July 1893.

territorial boundaries which are redrawn by means of war and diplomacy.[65] It is important to pin down meanings in order to establish continuities and discontinuities across different border regions and, in so doing, to reflect upon what is distinctive in the Alsatian case.' The language used by interwar actors to describe the border also offers an insight into their worldviews, and it is notable that in the redrawing of the border after 1918 French administrators, politicians, and military officers universally used the term *frontière* rather than *limite*.[66] Language has also had an effect upon the historiography of Alsace; after all, to speak of 'annexation' in 1871 and 'return' in 1918 implies legitimacy in 1918, but not in 1871.

A focus upon the border offers a reminder that nation states are not formed in isolation, but rather through cross-border, transnational, and sub-national interactions, encounters, and frictions. It points to Europe's multiple and connected histories and reminds us of the grassroots agency that persisted in the face of rapid change, such as that which occurred in Alsace in the years after 1918. The case of Alsace thus underscores that borders can be both a 'privileged site for the articulation of national distinctions', to quote Peter Sahlins, and a transitional zone where identity can be particularly fluid.[67] Alsace's symbolic and strategic importance encouraged a stress upon the nation in everyday life, and the region's relationship to France and Germany dominated political debate, which, in turn, was frequently expressed in national language. Nevertheless, the literature on national indifference offers a reminder that we should not take the nation for granted, and nor should we assume that nationalization reached all sections of the population. While the context of return may have made 'indifference' to the nation impossible (or at the very least extremely difficult) in interwar Alsace, it is important to recognize that Alsatians responded to the nation in different ways, and nationalization might thus be better understood as a spectrum of loyalties, rather than a binary 'for or against' dualism. In Alsace, national instability contributed to a reinforcement of other structures and points of attachment such as the village, religion, and the family, and Alsatian expressions of regional attachment similarly reflected responses to the region's experience.

What is more, work on peripheral agency reminds us that while the Alsatian population may have stood on the margins of alternate national communities throughout the nineteenth and twentieth centuries, their daily life was also given shape by a series of cross-border exchanges, networks, transfers, and relationships.

[65] Bernhard Struck, 'Border Regions', *European History Online* (2013). Daniel Nordman notes the term 'frontier' evokes the aggression of one state against an enemy and suggests the threat of war. See Daniel Nordman, 'Des limites de l'Etat aux frontières naturelles', in Pierre Nora (ed.), *Les Lieux de memoire*, vol. 1 (Paris, 1997), pp. 1125–46, p.1137. Timothy Baycroft takes this distinction further, arguing that the politically constructed nature of the border gives it flexibility, and allows it to be shifted as a result of war or diplomatic dealings, while frontiers (as natural geographic divisions or characteristics of the human landscape) are much more difficult to displace, remove, or create. In this view a border does not necessarily imply a frontier, if no important distinction can be made between the two sides, and the border is not a limit to some significant physical or human characteristic; Baycroft, 'Changing Identities', p. 418.

[66] See the documents and correspondence in the collection on the redrawing of France's eastern borders after 1918: ADBR 121AL 518–25.

[67] Sahlins, *Boundaries*, p. 271.

And the region's spatial and relational context was constructed not only by regional and national actors, but also by international and transnational ones, such as the Catholic Church, the Socialist party, and cross-border trade networks and cultural associations. As a result, Alsace was a place of exchange and a meeting point of cultures, as well as a national boundary. This invites consideration of how the border shaped daily life in Alsace, that is to say, of how the Alsatian population lived with it, understood it, transgressed it, and made it meaningful.

OUT OF THE BORDER'S SHADOW

This book is a study of the return of Alsace to France after 1918. Its central concern is with transition in the borderland, as it traces how return was discussed, imagined, and understood across daily life: citizenship, laws, and administrative institutions; politics; the economy; social and cultural identities, and the landscape. It considers both how the border shaped return to France and daily life in the borderland, and how it was given form and meaning by the population living alongside it, and by politicians, administrators, and others outside the region. As a result, this history of Alsace is based largely on sources produced by the French state: records of prefects, police surveillance officers, local government bodies, and municipal councils all produced significant quantities of documents as they charted the increasingly difficult process of the region's return. These documents speak directly to the challenges that France identified as it attempted to reintegrate its lost borderland into the French nation, but as with all documents produced by a state they risk reproducing the state's own anxieties and concerns, notably in terms of Alsatian regionalism and autonomism. All the same, as the return of Alsace to France cannot be understood without some consideration of the broader European and international context, this book also seeks to write this international history into what is, in many ways, a very local story.

During the two decades after Alsace's return to France, the French state's nation-building initiatives interacted with local programmes and attitudes at grass-roots level. This process was not straightforward; this book questions the assumptions of studies that present Alsace's return to France as a series of frustrated exchanges between a centralizing government and a conservative, regionalist, and often autono-mist population. Instead, it treats national integration as a complex and contested struggle that engaged a variety of national and international stakeholders. Local expressions of belonging were not consistent, and the range of attitudes displayed by the population and their political, economic, and religious representatives are suggestive of the competing sensibilities that interacted in negotiations over the region's place within the nation. Far from being uniform, the Alsatian population was fractured along lines of politics, class, confession, geography, gender, and lan-guage, and this had implications for their responses to their return to France. They also made use of existing assumptions about the border in an attempt to describe their own situation, and did so in ways which were not always consistent or clear-cut. As we will see, ideas of the border as a bridge between France and

Germany were mobilized in favour of a variety of positions, from greater integration into France to increased local autonomy. Furthermore, those very individuals who argued for "Alsace as a bridge" could also develop ideas of the border as the *limite*, and a dividing line between France and Germany when it suited their aims and objectives.

The book opens with a discussion of Alsace's long-standing connections to France and Germany in the years before 1918. Alsace came under French rule between the high point of the French monarchy and the Revolution of 1789. After spending over half of the nineteenth century within the French nation, the region was then ruled by Germany at the pinnacle of European nation-building between 1871 and the First World War, which broke out in 1914. The first chapter traces this history, and stresses both the increasing importance of the border and the connections and interactions that continued in spite (or because) of this ever more important boundary. It outlines the impact of national instability, which contributed to a reinforcement of societal structures, such as religion, the village, or the region, and considers the implications of major political events upon Alsatian identities. The following chapters treat themes in the return to French rule after 1918, and the region's increasingly problematic integration into French systems.

The second chapter discusses the renegotiation of Frenchness after 1918 through an analysis of citizenship, administration, and legislation. It places French programmes to make Alsace French again alongside regional responses, and suggests that government attempts to Frenchify the region by removing German influence brought into question the very character of Alsace and raised the issue of 'What is Alsatian?' It is thus suggestive of the ways in which the nation was reshaped from the periphery as it analyses the involvement of internal and external actors in the reintegration process. Reintegration, Chapter 2 suggests, was not a two-way interaction between centre and periphery; rather, it is better understood as a multi-centred struggle involving a range of internal and external actors. Chapter 3 pursues this consideration of national integration by considering how focus upon questions of reintegration distorted Alsatian politics. This single issue dominated political discussions within parties, between politicians, and at political meetings. Indeed, it eventually became more important than divisions between left and right, leading to some unorthodox alliances in the 1920s. By the 1930s, international issues supplanted local questions as the threat of war came to dominate Alsatian political life.

The fourth chapter turns the focus to the economy, and considers the successive crises of return and problematic reintegration that hit Alsatian economic structures, while the cross-border flows that had historically shaped economic life in the region floundered in light of difficulties in Franco–German relations. It is indicative of the implications of transition and change of national regime upon existing regional economic structures, and stresses the ultimate vulnerability of the regional economy to changes at the national and international level. Chapter 5 discusses attempts to reimagine Alsatian identities after the region's return to French rule. In a region where the vast majority of the population spoke a German dialect but little or no French, language, cultural products, and festivities were all mobilized to articulate different visions of belonging, as Alsatians attempted to articulate regional identities and ideas of Alsatianness that could encompass connections to France and Germany. These local understandings of identity came into conflict with visions of Alsace articulated at the French centre, which frequently viewed the region and its population in terms of 'for or against France', and failed to take account of the locally accepted coexisting and overlapping aspects of identity. Chapter 6 focuses on border rhetoric and analyses how the border was described and imagined in efforts to remake the Alsatian landscape. It considers how the rival understandings of the border as, on the one hand, France's limits and, on the other, the heart of a transnational cross-border community, found expression in discussions over the Alsatian landscape and built environment. These ideas coexisted, the chapter suggests, but they were not articulated simultaneously.

Running through all of the chapters are themes of interaction, transition, and tension. Alsace emerges as a place of both intense clarity and complicated ambiguity, which as Daphne Berdahl has argued, is the paradox of the borderland.[68] Throughout, the remarkable element in the story of Alsace's return to France is that, in spite of the change of national regime and the shifts in Franco–German relations, the border remained a point of contact. This contact was not always positive; it frequently took the form of misunderstandings and tensions alongside shared initiatives or friendships, and this book seeks to understand the various forms that this contact adopted. It questions how these cross-border interactions, encounters, and frictions contributed to Alsace's return, and as a result to the formation of the French nation. To return to Lucien Febvre, who epitomized many interwar ideas about borders in his 1935 work on the Rhine, the border between France and Germany was not formed either when the French and German governments fixed the boundary markers along the new borderline in 1918, or when Alsatians and Germans crossed the border to find themselves in a different world; these two dynamics interacted and fuelled the construction of a border that became a meaningful division through the encounters centred upon it.[69]

[68] Daphne Berdahl, *Where the World Ended. Reunification and Identity in the German Borderland* (Berkeley, 1999), pp. 141 and 155.
[69] Demangeon and Febvre, *Le Rhin*, p. 129.

1

A Bridge across the Rhine

Alsace has a long history as a crossroads. The region has been shaped by the interaction of different peoples, religious communities, and cultures. Lying on a plain between the Rhine and the Vosges mountains, it borders Germany to the north and east, Switzerland and the Franche-Comté to the south, and Lorraine to the west. The Rhine river, which lies to the east of the region, has left a particular mark on Alsace, moulding its surrounding landscape and shaping the civilizations that developed along its banks by providing a link to the neighbouring area; goods flowed down the river, the bishopric of Strasbourg straddled both banks, and, as Victor Hugo noted in his Rhineland tour, the river conveyed ideas as well as goods and people, connecting the communities that lay beside its banks.[1]

These interactions shaped Alsace, yet the region was also affected by political change, and particularly by the emergence of nationalism following the French Revolution. As a system of nation states came to cover the European continent, new national governments created languages of nationalism and attempted to turn the inhabitants of their provinces into national citizens through the introduction of national symbols, languages, education systems, military service, and railway networks. Feelings of belonging and shared identification with the nation led to the construction of 'imagined communities' that brought together individuals who saw themselves as connected to each other, in spite of the fact that they did not enjoy face-to-face contact.[2] And local populations played an important part in shaping these imagined communities and in giving the nation meaning as it emerged in the regions.[3] Cross-border interaction and political change thus combined to shape the lives of the Alsatian population, which was marked by diversity in terms of confessional, gendered, class, and local identities. And shared experience of the political developments of the eighteenth and nineteenth centuries acted as a unifying force for this heterogenous population.

The development of nationalism played a crucial role in Alsace's history during these years, most notably in raising questions about the relationship between nation and territory, as well as over the place of the region within the nation, and how the very term 'region' should be understood.[4] Of course, if the nation is an

[1] Victor Hugo, *Le Rhin. Lettres à un ami*, 2 vols, vol. 1 (Paris, 1912), pp. 189–90.
[2] Benedict Anderson, *Imagined Communities: Reflections on the Origin and Spread of Nationalism* (London, 1983).
[3] Oliver Zimmer, *Nationalism in Europe 1890–1940* (Basingstoke, 2003), p. 5; Timothy Baycroft and Mark Hewitson, *What is a Nation? Europe 1789–1914* (Oxford, 2006), p. 2.
[4] Catherine Tatiana Dunlop, *Cartophilia. Maps and the Search for Identity in the French–German Borderland* (Chicago, 2015), p. 5.

imagined community, the same is true of the region as a subnational space, and the 'region' and the 'local' are mental constructs just as the nation is. Yet while the 'nation', the 'region', or the 'local' may have been ideas and cultural constructs, they were also part of lived reality and generated powerful loyalties and attachments. What is more, assumptions about the relationship between territorial space and identity were shaped by distinct national and historical contexts; whereas the centralized French state treated the nation as a *grande patrie* or 'large homeland' comprising of many 'little homelands' (*petites patries*), the German nation understood home through the concept of *Heimat*, which can be translated as 'home', 'homeland', or 'country' and applied to the village, the region, and the nation.[5] The Alsatian population's Germanic dialect made them more familiar with the emotionally resonant term *Heimat,* and this had implications for their relationship with both France and Germany, as while the *petite patrie* was part of the *grande patrie,* this was not necessarily the case for the *Heimat.*

The history of Alsace prior to its return to France in 1918 was thus shaped by changing ideas about nations and regions, but also by evolving attitudes towards borders, which represented the limits of the territorial nation state and became meaningful divisions between communities and powerful symbolic divides between national cultures. Nevertheless, the most conspicuous element of this history of Alsace is that the region and the border were always sites of contact. Even closures of the border for political or military reasons created new industries in smuggling and illegal crossing which ensured that it remained a point of contact for borderland populations. This fits with the growing consensus that has emerged from the burgeoning field of borderlands literature, and which suggests that borders in modern Europe have functioned as points of contact more often than they have acted as limits.[6] Yet this experience of contact coexisted with a border rhetoric that focused on boundaries as divisions between national communities and the limits of nation states. This chapter introduces Alsace and Alsatian society, and contextualizes the region's interwar experience by tracing its longer history. It addresses the question of *how* this border represented a point of contact, and considers the interaction between cross-border flows and encounters, and the ideas and reality of the border as a dividing line. It opens with a discussion of Alsatian society.

ALSATIAN SOCIETY: UNITY AND DIVERSITY OF EXPERIENCES

Alsace is the smallest historical region in metropolitan France, but it has long been one of the most densely populated. Its population levels, along with the particularities of its social structure, reflected long-term trends, short-term political change, and geography. The Rhine valley was traditionally one of the most highly populated areas of Europe as a result of the river transport that linked the

---

[5] Celia Applegate, *A Nation of Provincials: The German Idea of Heimat* (Oxford, 1990).
[6] Bernhard Struck, 'Crossroads: Border Regions', *European History Online* (January 2013).

surrounding lands and encouraged the establishment of industries in the area. Alsatian marriage rates and levels of live births sat between French and German figures throughout much of the nineteenth and twentieth centuries, although during the interwar years the total live births per head of population in Alsace rose above the figure for both France and Germany.[7] Nevertheless, Alsace's population also fluctuated as a result of political change, increasing after annexation into Germany in 1871 before declining slightly following return to France in 1918, when wartime fatalities and the departure of approximately 200,000 Germans and Alsatians in the aftermath of war led to a drop in population levels. The arrival of incomers from France (known locally as *Français de l'Intérieur*), whether returning after opting for France in 1871 or entering the region for the first time to take up jobs or to start businesses, went some way towards replacing the departed Germans, and population levels increased gradually throughout the 1920s. But the region's population in 1931 was still around 14,000 lower than its 1910 total.[8]

Alsatian society was also characterized by diversity in terms of religion, class, gender, and the rural–urban division. Amongst the Alsatian population there was a layering of different aspects of identity; and regional, national, confessional, gendered, class-based, and political identities (amongst others) interacted to shape how the population understood the world around them, and each affected how Alsatians would respond to return to France after 1918. The majority of the population of Alsace was Catholic, but the region was also home to significant Protestant and Jewish minorities.[9] Protestants and Jews were traditionally well represented in certain professions or parts of the region, thus the majority of the Alsatian industrial class was Protestant and there were large Protestant communities around the city of Mulhouse and in the rural areas that surrounded Colmar, Riquewihr, Munster, and Sainte-Marie-aux-Mines in the Haut-Rhin, and around Saverne and Wissembourg in the Bas-Rhin.[10] With the exception of the Calvinist centres close to the Swiss border at Mulhouse and Bischwiller, the majority of Alsatian Protestants were Lutherans and, as a result, shared religious culture with Protestants in Germany.[11] Pastoral reports from all religious communities described a general habit of religious practice, and note that even the less diligent members of the flock

[7] Marcel Koch, 'Les Mouvements de la Population', in Comité alsacien d'études et d'informations, *L'Alsace depuis son retour à la France*, 3 vols, vol. 1 (Strasbourg, 1932), p. 350. In 1929 Germany registered 184 marriages per 10,000 head of population, while France recorded 162. The equivalent figures for the Bas-Rhin and the Haut-Rhin were 168 and 176. That year, 192 births were recorded in the Bas-Rhin and 191 in the Haut-Rhin, while the French and German figures were 177 and 179, respectively.

[8] Koch, 'Les Mouvements de la Population', in *L'Alsace depuis son retour à la France*, vol. 1, p. 336.

[9] According to the 1926 census, Catholics represented 61.6 per cent of the Bas-Rhin population in 1926, while Protestants represented 28.4 per cent, Jews represented 2 per cent, and the total undeclared was 7.7 per cent. The equivalent figures for the Haut-Rhin were 86 per cent Catholic, 10.5 per cent Protestant, 1.1 per cent Jewish, and 2 per cent non-declarations. See Koch, 'Les Mouvements de la Population', in *L'Alsace depuis son retour à la France*, vol. 1, pp. 344–5.

[10] Michel Hau and Nicolas Stoskopf, *Les dynasties alsaciennes du XVIème siècle à nos jours* (Paris, 2005), p. 47. In the nineteenth century, the Haut-Rhin textile barons included only one Catholic family, the Herzogs in Colmar.

[11] Anthony Steinhoff, *The Gods of the City. Protestantism and Religious Culture in Strasbourg 1870–1914* (Boston, 2008).

turned out for the celebration of religious festivals at Christmas and Easter or for pilgrimages or processions.[12] When Archbishop Ruch of Strasbourg organized a celebration to commemorate the 1200th anniversary of the foundation of the Hohenbourg convent in July 1920, 100,000 people attended.[13]

Early twentieth-century folklorists pointed to the region's distinctive religious festivals, such as the Fête-Dieu celebrated fifteen days after Pentecost, which saw Alsatian streets decorated with flowers.[14] Alfred Wahl and Jean-Claude Richez also describe Alsatian festivals which reveal the influence of cross-border connections, such as the advent *couronne de verdure*, with its four candles to represent the four weeks before Christmas and the four millennia of waiting for the Messiah, or the *Judasfeuer* or *Judasverbrenne*, in which a doll or tree representing Judas Iscariot was burned for his part in the death of Christ. Both traditions were shared with the German Rhineland, and French traditions could be slow to take root. *Père Noël*, for example, was only accepted after the Second World War, and throughout the interwar years and earlier the *Christkindel* had visited children on the night before Christmas.[15] Alongside cross-border interactions and connections, contemporary observers pointed to the interaction of different religions; churches existed alongside temples and synagogues in towns across the region and, in certain villages, the two populations were almost equal. In many of these villages, the church was shared between Protestant and Catholic communities.

Religious interaction was reflected in the number of mixed marriages, which increased steadily, particularly during the nineteenth and twentieth centuries. In Colmar the total of mixed marriages rose from 18.8 per cent in 1873 to 24.1 per cent in 1900.[16] Nevertheless, evidence suggests that the Catholic clergy applied pressure to ensure that the children of mixed marriages were not baptized as Protestants. Wahl and Richez cite a 1909 case in Kaysersberg when a Protestant mother wanted to give her child a Protestant baptism, but the local Catholic priest told her that if she did so he would be unable to bury her Catholic husband. The child was baptized in the Catholic church.[17] Such cases continued throughout the interwar years, and burials remained separate until after the Second World War, with mixed couples buried in separate graves.

Prefect of the Bas-Rhin René Paira recalls friendly confrontation between Catholic and Protestant communities, such as on the Protestant festival of Good Friday, when Catholics would be sure to be seen doing disagreeable work; *vignobles* in Riquewihr would smoke their vines and send smoke through the village in the process, while women would wash and hang up their laundry, leaving their

[12] Alfred Wahl and Jean-Claude Richez, *La Vie Quotidienne en Alsace entre France et Allemagne, 1850–1950* (Paris, 1993), pp. 123–5.

[13] Jean-François Kovar, 'Religion et Éducation: De la concorde à la discorde', in Bernard Vogler (ed.), *Chroniques d'Alsace 1918–1939* (Barcelona, 2004), pp. 46–9, p. 49.

[14] Charles Spindler, *L'âge d'or d'un artiste en Alsace. Mémoires inédits 1889–1914* (Colmar and Nancy, 2009), p. 63; Anselme Laugel, *Costumes et coutumes d'Alsace* (Colmar and Nancy, 2008; 1st edn 1902).

[15] Wahl and Richez, *La Vie Quotidienne en Alsace*, pp. 130–5.

[16] Wahl and Richez, *La Vie Quotidienne en Alsace*, p. 113.

[17] Wahl and Richez, *La Vie Quotidienne en Alsace*, p. 112.

doors open to allow everyone to see it. Then on 15 August Protestants took their revenge by threshing wheat and ensuring that they encountered Catholics on their way to Mass for the festival of the Assumption.[18] These encounters were deliberately provocative and affirmed belonging to a distinct confessional group, but they also allowed the two communities to interact and provided a point of contact between them. *This theme stressed throughout entire book*

Confession was thus an important component of many Alsatian identities, but experience in the region was also shaped by gender, class, and milieu, as well as by cross-border connections and interactions, and by the particular place that Alsace and Alsatians adopted in French and German cultures of nationalism. During the years of annexation into Germany, French nationalists transformed the Alsatian woman, or *Alsacienne*, into a symbol of resistance to Germanization. Dressed in regional costume and wearing the distinctive large black or red bow (known as the *coiffe*), Alsatian women were depicted in Hansi's anti-German *images d'Epinal*, in the art of Jean-Jacques Henner, and in the political satire of Henri Zislin as guardians of French patriotism patiently waiting for return to the lost *mère patrie*. German nationalists shared the underlying idea that women were the guardians and disseminators of national culture and, as a result, worried about Alsatian women's resistance to Germanization and their influence on their children. Of course, Alsatian women did not represent the homogeneous group that such images would suggest, and Alsatian men's experiences were equally shaped by ideas and expectations of masculinity and manliness. During the First World War, for example, the French had encouraged Alsatian men to abandon their traditional, masculine role as soldiers and defenders of the nation, and to desert rather than fight, which had significant implications for gender relations. Gendered identities also interacted with class and nation. The region's nobility and middle classes had traditionally maintained close links with France, notably in their use of the French language and in their professional and social networks, although (again) this situation was complicated by the presence of French-speaking working communities in the Bruche valley, and of noble families whose networks stretched east across the Rhine.

In the region's three large towns, workers employed by Mulhouse's textile and chemical factories, Colmar's small manufacturers, or Strasbourg's breweries rubbed shoulders with artisans and professional middle classes. Equally, the character of Strasbourg and Colmar was shaped by the former's status as the region's administrative and cultural centre and the latter's importance in the Haut-Rhin as the home of the departmental prefecture. Women represented around a third of the working population in Alsace, and the majority in certain industries, such as textile manufacturing and the confection industry, for much of the nineteenth and twentieth centuries.[19] And, as a result of the initiatives of factory owners in

---

[18] René Paira, *Affaires d'Alsace, Souvenirs d'un préfet* (Strasbourg, 1990), p. 51.

[19] Jean-Claude Richez with the collaboration of François Igersheim and Peter Armand, *Il y a cinquante ans, le Front Populaire... Sorglos sunnen? Travail et Temps libre en Alsace*, Exposition présenté par La CFDT et l'Atelier Alsacien le 23 au 28 juin en la Salle de la Mairie de Schiltigheim, p. 25.

the mid-nineteenth century and the introduction of Bismarckian social insurance after 1871, working conditions and the social insurance afforded to Alsatian workers were in advance of those in France at the time. This created an important point of distinction between Alsace and France, and contributed to differences in terms of campaigns for welfare reform and labour legislation after the region's return in 1918.

The rural population represented just over half of the total Bas-Rhin population in 1921 (51.1 per cent) and slightly under half of the Haut-Rhin population in the same year (46.8 per cent).[20] The countryside consequently played an important part in Alsatian society and politics, and was often central to representations of Alsace.[21] The majority of rural inhabitants made their living from the land, and the region contained a high concentration of small proprietors, particularly in Catholic areas, and, with an abundant labour force and small plots, Alsatian farmers were slow to mechanize. Nevertheless, the division between town and country remained fairly porous into the interwar period. Many urban workers returned home to their family smallholdings at weekends to help, while others worked their own small plots of land.[22]

It is also important to recognize geographical diversity across Alsace: numerous interwar commentators saw differences between the southern Alsatian department of the Haut-Rhin, with its more Catholic, wine-drinking, and apparently Francophile population, and the beer-drinking Bas-Rhinois in the north of the region.[23] And geography affected the cross-border connections of the two departments, with the Haut-Rhin looking south to Switzerland and southern Baden, and the Bas-Rhin facing the north of Baden, the Palatinate, and the Saar. Such cross-border personal, familial, economic, and cultural links shaped experiences for the Alsatian population, and interacted with the layering of identities created by the diversity of confession, class, gender, and milieu as they experienced gradual incorporation into France, and then annexation into Germany, between the seventeenth and nineteenth centuries. Across this period, political change contributed to a reinforcement of social structures, which interacted with the growing importance placed upon the shifting national boundary line as a symbol and component of nationhood. Each of these factors would shape the region's experience of gradual incorporation into France in the eighteenth century, German rule in the nineteenth, and return to France after 1918.

---

[20] Koch, 'Les Mouvements de la Population', in *L'Alsace depuis son retour à la France*, vol. 1, p. 341. In 1850, 62 per cent of the total regional population lived in villages of less than 2,000 inhabitants. This figure declined slowly from 49.8 per cent of the population in 1900 to 41 per cent in 1954. See Wahl and Richez, *La Vie Quotidienne en Alsace*, p. 18.

[21] At the 1937 World's Fair the French Pavilion featured a rural Alsatian interior as one of its four provincial interiors alongside Brittany, Savoy, and Arles, and women in traditional Alsatian costume marched in the French contingent at the Fair's inaugural parade. Shanny Peer, *France on Display: Peasants, Provincials and Folklore in the 1937's World Fair* (Albany, NY, 1998), p. 168.

[22] For diaries that describe this experience see, for example, Philippe Husser, *Un Instituteur Alsacien. Entre France et Allemagne. Le Journal de Philippe Husser, 1914–1951* (Paris, 1989).

[23] Marcel Nast, *Le Malaise Alsacien-Lorrain* (Paris, 1920), p. 36.

BEYOND NATIONAL FRONTIERS:
ALSACE BEFORE 1871

Alsace has long been shaped by interactions and transition. Roman rule gave way in the fourth century to rule by the Alemanni, who in turn were defeated by Clovis and the Franks in 496. The region formed part of the Holy Roman Empire for much of the medieval period, before a number of Alsatian territories were given up to the French crown under the Treaty of Westphalia in 1648. Louis XIV then turned his attention to incorporating the remaining areas of Alsace into France, and in 1681 he succeeded in annexing Strasbourg. But even after the annexation of much of Alsace into France in the seventeenth century, the region retained its distinctive linguistic, religious, and trade structures, although Louis XIV and his successors each expressed their desire to Gallicize the province, particularly in terms of language.[24] This met with some success, and during the eighteenth century the Alsatian nobility and bourgeoisie began to use French, rather than the Germanic Alsatian dialect spoken by the majority of the region's population.

Such cultural transitions were paralleled by religious interactions after much of Alsace adopted the Lutheran faith during the Reformation, while sections close to the Swiss border in Mulhouse and Bischwiller adopted Calvinism. Although the ruling Habsburgs, and later the Bourbons, attempted to eradicate heresy in Alsace, the Edict of Fontainebleau of 1685 (which revoked the substantial rights granted to Protestants by the Edict of Nantes) was never applied to the region. This led Huguenots from the north of France to settle in the region, and François-Michel le Tellier, Marquis de Louvois and Secretary of State for War under Louis XIV, introduced the requirement that if seven Catholic families moved to a village, the village needed to give up some space in the church to allow both faiths to worship. This created a situation known as *simultaneum*, which was the case for 150 Alsatian communes in 1871. The region was also home to a sizeable Jewish community; as the revolutionary National Assembly debated the question of Jewish assimilation, Alsace and Lorraine were home to around 90 per cent of the Jews in France.[25] Legislation passed in 1791 granted all French Jews complete and immediate civic equality, yet social prejudices continued to exclude Jews from certain professions. The status of all three religions was formalized under the Napoleonic Empire through the Concordat of 1801, which organized the three Christian churches, and the imperial decree of 1808, which created central and regional consistories for the Jewish faith.

Throughout the seventeenth and eighteenth centuries Alsace was a meeting point, and analysis of travel memoirs has shown that the border between the region and the Holy Roman Empire was hardly perceptible to the travellers who crossed it. Johann Friedrich Carl Grimm, a court physician from Gotha, described

[24] David A. Bell, 'Nation Building and Cultural Particularism in Eighteenth Century France: The Case of Alsace', *Eighteenth Century Studies*, 21:4 (1988), pp. 472–90, p. 472.
[25] Vicki Caron, *Between France and Germany. The Jews of Alsace-Lorraine, 1871–1918* (Stanford, 1988), p. 13.

crossing the Rhine at Kehl as akin to passing through a zone of overlapping cultures, in which outward signs such as language, architecture, or customs changed only gradually, while the novelist Sophie von La Roche did not even describe the moment of crossing the national border, as in her eyes entering what she termed 'actual France' meant that all traces of the 'former German national character' had vanished. She saw this as the case only after she had crossed into Lorraine. To these travellers, the connected borderland ensured that France and Germany did not appear as clearly divided entities, but rather as entangled through their border spaces.[26]

Such attitudes towards the border interacted with changing ideas about national boundaries, notably about the natural and historical frontiers that gave shape to the nation as an imagined space. These ideas adopted particular force in France, which as an established state had different priorities to its neighbours to the east, where the left bank of the Rhine was organized in small units under the umbrella of the Holy Roman Empire. After all, ideas about borders developed at different times, and took on distinct forms in different contexts. Cardinal Richelieu's *Political Testament* described France as bounded by 'the limits that Nature has traced': the Atlantic, the Rhine, the Alps, and the Pyrenees. This idea provided both a justification and an organizing principle of French foreign policy in the seventeenth and eighteenth centuries, as Peter Sahlins has shown, by providing a concrete goal that determined short- and long-term policy decisions.[27]

In the Alps, French policy focused upon maintaining control over towns and fortresses on the eastern flank, while in the Pyrenees, France seized strongholds on the southern side of the chain to encourage Spain to begin peace negotiations. Indeed, the Peace of the Pyrenees in 1659 made reference to the mountain range as the 'ancient' separation of 'the Gauls from the Spains'.[28] At the Rhine, Richelieu secured the fortifications at Philipsburg and Breisach in 1634 and 1639, and the Treaty of Münster in 1648 forbade the Habsburg emperor from building any fortresses on the right bank of the Rhine between Basel and Philipsburg. Louis XIV continued Richelieu's policy towards the Rhine; French armies occupied Freiburg in 1679 and the military engineer Sébastien Vauban constructed a series of fortresses at Fort-Louis, Kehl, and Huningue on the banks of the river during the 1680s. Not all of these acquisitions were permanent, however. Following France's defeat at the hands of the Augsburg League, the Peace of Ryswick in 1697 removed France's conquests on the right bank of the Rhine. Throughout, the idea of frontiers as an area for expansion (as opposed to a dividing line or limit) permeated discussions over the boundary.

[26] Bernhard Struck, 'Conquered Territories and Entangled Histories: The Perception of Franco–German and German–Polish Borderlands in German Travelogues, 1792–1820', in Karen Hagemann, Allan Forrest, and Etienne François (eds), *War Memories: The Revolutionary and Napoleonic Wars in 19th and 20th Century Europe* (Basingstoke, 2012), pp. 95–113, pp. 103–4; Sophie von La Roche, *Journal einer Reise durch Frankreich* (1787); Johann Friedrich Carl Grimm, *Bemerkungen eines Reisenden durch Deutschland, Frankreich, England und Holland in Briefen an seine Freunde*, 3 vols (1775).

[27] Peter Sahlins, 'Natural Frontiers Revisited: France's Boundaries since the Seventeenth Century', *The American Historical Review*, 95 (1990), pp. 1423–51.

[28] Sahlins, 'Natural Frontiers Revisited', p. 1430.

Peter Sahlins has argued that in eighteenth-century France discussions of borders shifted in their emphasis from natural frontiers to natural limits. This meant that greater weight was placed upon defence rather than expansion, as 'limits' were deemed to represent both a state's right, and a constraint on its expansion.[29] This coincided with the end of the era of annexation in French policies of state-building, as the *ancien régime* made its final territorial acquisitions of Lorraine in 1766 and Corsica in 1768, and switched its focus to governing the acquired territories.[30] The goal of the French state was primarily to create an enclosed, unified state in order to assure the efficient administration of the realm; clear boundaries would repress military desertion and fiscal fraud, and create a unified economic space.

Ideas of 'natural' boundaries thus had a long history in 1789 when revolution swept France. As the remaining free Alsatian city-states joined France in the following years, concepts of natural frontiers mingled with ideas of France's boundaries as marked by the principle of liberty.[31] This understanding inspired the sign hoisted up on the bridge across the Rhine at Kehl that read, 'Here Begins the Country of Liberty.' Alsatian enthusiasm for the revolution swelled, and it was in the house of Strasbourg's mayor, Friedrich de Dietrich, that the Marseillaise was reportedly composed in 1792. This period also triggered greater Alsatian integration into France as the revolutionary government redirected trade by moving the French customs barrier from the Vosges to the Rhine, abolished the provincial institutions of Alsace, divided the territory into the new departments of the Bas-Rhin in the north and the Haut-Rhin in the south, and reorganized municipal governments of the cities and towns.

Following the outbreak of war with Prussia and Austria in the spring of 1792, the revolutionary armies marched into Savoy, Nice, and the Rhineland, meaning that Alsace no longer represented France's eastern frontier. Through the peace treaties of Basel in 1795 and Campo Formio in 1797, four French-style departments were created in the Rhineland: Roer, Rhin-et-Moselle, Sarre, and Mont-Tonnerre.[32] The National Convention was deeply divided on what to do with the conquered territories; Assembly Deputy Camille Desmoulins voiced wider fears that by annexing these areas the regime would be mimicking the actions of the old monarchy that it had replaced. Others, such as Lazare Carnot and Georges Danton, countered that the populations of these territories had freely expressed their desire to be united to France, and so annexation was a response to popular will. A number of Girondin

[29] For a persuasive exposition of the idea of limits, see Jean-Jacques Rousseau, 'Extrait du projet du paix perpétuelle de l'Abbé de Saint Pierre [1756]', in C. E. Vaughn (ed.), *The Political Writings of Jean-Jacques Rousseau* (Cambridge, 1915), p. 370.

[30] Sahlins, 'Natural Frontiers Revisited', pp. 1437–8.

[31] Mulhouse, which had been a free and independent Calvinist republic associated with the Swiss Confederation, joined France following a vote by its citizens on 4 January 1798.

[32] It is important to note, however, that the region was only legally incorporated into France through the Treaty of Lunéville in 1801. By the end of Napoleonic rule in 1814, some 1.6 million German-speaking inhabitants had become French citizens. See Michael Rowe, 'France, Prussia or Germany? The Napoleonic Wars and Shifting Allegiances in the Rhineland', *Central European History*, 39:4 (2006), pp. 611–40; Michael Rowe, *From Reich to State: The Rhineland in the Revolutionary Age, 1780–1830* (Cambridge, 2003); Michael Rowe, 'Between Empire and Home Town: Napoleonic Rule on the Rhine, 1700–1814', *The Historical Journal*, 42:3 (1999), pp. 643–74.

deputies also invoked the idea of natural frontiers to describe the Rhine boundary as the Rhine 'barrier', a symbol of strategic defence against Prussian and Austrian aggression.[33] Thus ideas of territory and understandings of popular will interacted as the revolutionary emphasis upon nationality and self-determination mingled with the state's need to fix its strategic and military goals.

It was through the French Revolution that modern ideas of nationhood developed, and in debates over the nation language adopted an important role. Louis XIV and his successors encouraged the spread of French through Alsace, yet when the Englishman Arthur Young arrived in Alsace just as the revolution broke out in Paris, he noted that he found himself 'to all appearance veritably in Germany . . . here one person in a hundred has not one word of French'.[34] The region's literary societies attempted to reconcile the population's use of German with attachment to France by arguing that language did not present a barrier to commitment to the nation.[35] Their stance was not questioned by the revolutionary government, which translated laws and constitutional decrees into German for dissemination in Alsace, and it was only after 1793 that the Convention called for the replacement of Alsatian dialect with French, and issued a series of decrees to rename streets, suppress German in public affairs, and encourage Alsatian women to abandon their traditional costumes.[36] These plans met with little success, but such changing attitudes towards language are revealing of how war and political crisis affected ideas about citizenship and national cohesion. The domestic tensions faced by the Convention meant that it became more difficult to accept the idea that patriotic citizens of the Republic would speak enemy languages, and led to a stress upon the importance of speaking French.

These plans were never fully implemented before Napoleon seized power in 1799 and reportedly dismissed the importance of dialect when he recruited Alsatians to join his armies with the often-repeated phrase, 'Little matter if they speak German, as long as they fight in French.'[37] The fact that Alsatians spoke German proved an advantage when Paris recruited administrators for the new departments on the east bank of the Rhine; then the preference for bilingual Frenchmen meant that Alsatians were appointed in large numbers, and regional representatives argued that they acted as a bridge between French and German cultures.[38]

The Napoleonic Wars came to an end in 1815, and the Treaty of Vienna that established the peace reduced France to its 1792 boundaries (although the southern

---

[33] Sahlins, 'Natural Frontiers', pp. 1444–6.

[34] Arthur Young, *Arthur Young's travels in France during the years 1787, 1788, 1789* (New York, 1906).

[35] Bell, 'Nation Building and Cultural Particularism', pp. 485–6.

[36] David A. Bell, 'Lingua Populi, Lingua Dei: Language, Religion, and the Origins of French Revolutionary Nationalism', *The American Historical Review*, 100 (1995), pp. 1403–37, p. 1414. In much of France, the replacement of local with national was not acted upon, but, as David Bell has argued, the presence of German armies made Alsace a special case. The result was a series of measures against local clothing, the Gothic typeface, public signs in German lettering, and a programme for primary schools. See Bell, 'Nation Building and Cultural Particularism', p. 486.

[37] *Pneu Michelin Guide Régional Alsace de Strasbourg à Mulhouse Hautes Vosges* (Paris, 1935–6).

[38] Rowe, *From Reich to State*, p. 121.

Alsatian city of Mulhouse, which had joined France in 1798, remained within the national borders). Not only did German nationalists express great disappointment that Alsace remained in France, the crisis triggered by the wars led to new understandings of the border as a dividing line. In 1819 the merchant Johann Daniel Mutzenbecher travelled from Kehl to Strasbourg, but before entering France he stopped at the 'border of my fatherland', reflecting on the Rhine, which he had been longing to see 'for the first time in life as every German does'. He judged France and its inhabitants to be 'completely different from us in terms of customs and behaviour' and, above all, as 'morally corrupted'; he was also convinced that the French people were already longing to take revenge.[39] For Mutzenbecher, the war had encouraged the nationalization of the border, and a sense of difference between himself and those living on the other side.

Disputes over the exact location of the boundary continued into the 1820s and were only resolved following an agreement between Prussia and France in October 1829, when both states agreed upon border fortifications. Then, in 1840 a new Rhine crisis broke out, triggered by French attempts to claim territory west of the Rhine as compensation for a diplomatic defeat in the Middle East. This resulted in a renewed outpouring of nationalist sentiment in Germany, with Nikolaus Becker publishing the 'Rhine Song' (*Rheinlied*) in September 1840 and August Heinrich Hoffmann von Fallersleben writing lyrics to the 'Germany Song' (*Deutschlandlied*) the following year. Thomas Höpel has described this border crisis as the trigger of the emergence of modern German nationalism.[40]

Yet, for those living alongside the new border life continued much as before. Border residents were exempt from the passports normally needed to leave or enter national territory, and in any case inspection was only loosely enforced.[41] Fully fledged border controls were a rarity, and long stretches of the border were not visible as there were no markers or stones to delimit the national territory. Trade connections continued; indeed, they were improved as the delegates at the Treaty of Vienna chose to retain the French administrative reorganization of territories west of the Rhine, and this increased uniformity stimulated trade with Alsace and Lorraine. The de Wendel saltworks in Dieuze and the forges at Hayange and Moyeuvre in Lorraine imported coal from the Prussian mines in the Saar and Nassau, Prussian coal merchants set up warehouses in Metz and Nancy, and the Adt family from Einsheim in the Palatinate opened a factory in Forbach, in the Moselle district. The opening of a rail link between Strasbourg and Kehl in 1861 connected the Paris–Strasbourg railway with the rail network in Baden, and in 1865 a border station opened at Wissembourg. A common motif of mid-nineteenth-century Alsatian memoirs is the description of Sunday day trips from Strasbourg to Kehl,

---

[39] Struck, 'Conquered Territories', p. 104.

[40] Thomas Höpel, 'The French–German Borderlands: Borderlands and Nation-Building in the 19th and 20th Centuries', *European History Online* (August 2012).

[41] John Torpey, *The Invention of the Passport. Surveillance, Citizenship and the State* (Cambridge, 2000); François Roth, 'The making of the eastern frontier: the French–German border, 1815–70', in Sharif Gemie and Henrice Altink (eds), *At the Border. Margins and Peripheries in Modern France* (Cardiff, 2008), pp. 40–57, p. 43.

or from Mulhouse to the Black Forest.[42] As revolution swept through Europe in 1848, Alsace became a meeting place for exiled revolutionaries, while Alsatians participated in revolutionary movements on both sides of the Rhine.

The region was also home to a large number of foreign workers throughout the first half of the nineteenth century. The Haut-Rhin, which had long been a significant textile centre, recorded around 60,000 foreign workers in 1848, while there were approximately 20,000 in the Bas-Rhin.[43] According to police reports, relations between Alsatians and foreign workers were generally good, although they were prone to break down at moments of economic or political tension. The economic problems of the 1840s triggered demands for the expulsion of foreign workers from the region, yet as David A. Harvey has pointed out, 'foreign' could mean French workers, or even those from other parts of Alsace. In one case in Bischwiller local workers protested against the hiring of workers from the neighbouring commune of Gries by lying in wait along the road between the two communities and attacking the incomers.[44] Once again, crisis (although this time economic, rather than military) encouraged a sense of difference and opposition between the two communities.

By the second half of the nineteenth century, the region's industry had expanded, and foreign workers remained an important presence in the region, where many had settled into Alsatian communities.[45] The region's upper classes and bourgeoisie spoke French and mimicked Parisian trends, while the working and agricultural classes spoke Alsatian dialect and retained regional styles of dress, eating habits, and customs. The majority of the population was Catholic, especially in the Haut-Rhin, yet religious interactions with the significant Protestant and Jewish minorities continued. This was the situation in July 1870 when war broke out between France and Prussia, along with its southern German allies. German troops crossed the Rhine into Alsace on 4 August 1870. The war brought a rapid series of German victories, culminating in the capture of Napoleon III and his army at Sedan in September 1870, the defeat of Strasbourg following a six-week siege on 27 September, and the entry of Prussian troops into the outskirts of Paris by the winter.[46] Although the suppression of French resistance took several weeks, calls to annex Alsace and Lorraine were first made from the beginning of the conflict.

At the outbreak of the fighting Alsatian workers were in the midst of a strike over wage levels, but they rallied to the French cause and police reports pointed to the widespread 'outpouring of patriotic sentiment' that they witnessed.[47] This was

[42] Wahl and Richez, *La Vie Quotidienne en Alsace*, p. 219; Emile Boissiere, *Vingt ans à Mulhouse, 1855–1875* (Macon, 1876), p. 19.

[43] François G Dreyfus, 'Les socialismes en Alsace de 1912 à 1962', *Bulletin de la Faculté des Lettres de Strasbourg*, 44:1 (1965), pp. 511–34, pp. 512–13. By 1907 there were 106,000 workers in the Bas-Rhin industry and 101,000 in the Haut-Rhin industry. In total, this represented 40 per cent of the Bas-Rhin working population and 55 per cent of the Haut-Rhin working population.

[44] David Allen Harvey, *Constructing Class and Nationality in Alsace, 1830–1945* (DeKalb, 2001), p. 41.

[45] Greg Burgess, 'The Foreign Presence in the early-industrial Haut-Rhin, 1820–22: a short history from the pre-history of immigration to France', *French History*, 28 (2014), pp. 366–84.

[46] Rachel Chrastil, *The Siege of Strasbourg* (Cambridge, MA, 2014).

[47] Harvey, *Constructing Class*, p. 66.

not simply a matter of the police seeking to reassure their worried superiors about a volatile borderland population. The changes brought about by the revolution, as well as the shared experience since 1789, had all tied Alsace to France, and large sections of the population greeted the prospect of annexation into Prussia with trepidation. While this was partly concern at the unknown, the region's long history of interactions with states on the opposite bank of the Rhine meant that different sectors of Alsatian society were well aware of what they had to fear from annexation: the industrial bourgeoisie were apprehensive about the economic dislocations and loss of French markets that the changing national frontiers might bring; the Catholic community worried about annexation by Protestant Prussia; the Jewish population feared a reduction of their political rights in Germany; and labour leaders celebrated the proclamation of the Third Republic in Paris and opposed annexation by the Prussian state.[48] Upon their temporary relocation to Bordeaux, Alsace's elected representatives took to the floor of the National Assembly to argue that the region should not be allowed to fall into German hands.[49]

In spite of such protest, Bismarck annexed the whole of Alsace, with the exception of Belfort, which had withstood the German siege, and the eastern part of the neighbouring region of Lorraine, leaving the majority of Lorraine under French rule. Prussia recognized that direct annexation would be likely to provoke opposition amongst the other German states, but was concerned that attaching Alsace and Lorraine to one of the southern states could create a Catholic rival to Prussia. As a result, the annexed area formed a new zone, the Reichsland Elsass-Lothringen (Imperial Territory of Alsace-Lorraine), to be governed from Berlin. The decision on the limits of the annexed territory was based in part upon strategic concerns, as the new border needed to be defendable, but it was equally rooted in the economy, and the eventual line chosen also placed the vast steel mines in Lorraine under German rule. Victory in the war of 1870–1 provided a catalyst for German unification, and annexation of Alsace-Lorraine was also intended to incite nationalist fervour in the rest of the newly unified German nation. The region now lay on the German side of the border between the two nations, and the Alsatian population was divided from the French communities east of the Vosges by the new national boundary line.

BETWEEN FRANCE AND GERMANY: ALSACE UNDER GERMAN RULE

The Treaty of Frankfurt, which ratified the annexation of Alsace-Lorraine, gave the population of the annexed territory the option to retain French citizenship, on condition that they left the region by 1 October 1872. In total, 6.5 per cent of the population of Lower Alsace (the department of the Bas-Rhin), 2.3 per cent

[48] Paula E. Hyman, 'Citizenship. Regionalism and Identity. The Case of Alsatian Jewry, 1871–1914', in Judith Frishman, David J. Wertheim, Ido de Haan, and Joël Cahen (eds), *Borders and Boundaries in and around Dutch History* (Amsterdam, 2011).
[49] François G. Dreyfus, *La vie politique en Alsace, 1919–1936* (Paris, 1969), p. 68.

of the population of Upper Alsace (the Haut-Rhin), and 6 per cent of annexed Lorraine opted for France.[50] However, some took the declaration but didn't leave, while others left without declaring their intention to do so, and others left but returned after 1872. As a result, the exact numbers of those who opted for France (known as *optants*) remain unclear. In the Haut-Rhin, where the *Ligue d'Alsace* promoted opting for France as a matter of principle, the percentage of *optants* who actually emigrated was very low, while in annexed Lorraine the total number of *optants* was lower but that of actual emigrants higher.[51] Figures that cover entire departments also mask further differences; proportionally, the most *optants* came from regions that were either francophone, such as Molsheim, or strongly Catholic, such as Altkirch, Sélestat, and Ribeauville. Urban areas also saw greater numbers leave; the Lorrainer city of Metz witnessed the departure of 20.5 per cent of its population.[52]

That higher numbers came from francophone and Catholic areas is testament to the greater concern amongst these communities about their future within the German Empire, while the higher numbers of urban *optants* reflects the fact it was much easier for French officials, professionals, or other elements of the urban bourgeoisie to emigrate than workers or agricultural workers, as their education, prosperity, and greater mobility granted them choices not always available to the rural or working classes. Those who left included 50 of 300 pastors, the majority of university and *lycée* lecturers, and a large section of the administrative bourgeoisie.[53] Some patrons transferred their factories across the Vosges, and in these circumstances their workers generally went with them, but for any worker whose employer did not emigrate the decision to leave was risky, as they had no guarantee of finding work in France. The option clause should not be viewed as a gesture to French civic notions of citizenship and belonging on the part of the *Kaiserreich*, however, as the conditions on departure and the risks that faced those who left meant that it was not a realistic option for most Alsatians.

Upon leaving, the majority headed for Paris or the departments that neighboured Alsace and annexed Lorraine.[54] Others set off for the French colonies or North America, and many boarded ships for Algeria after the National Assembly voted to grant 100,000 hectares of Algerian land to Alsatians and Lorrainers. Yet, as Fabienne Fischer has demonstrated, this didn't lead to a notable spike in migration. Patterns of emigration from Alsace to Algeria were well established before the war, and the period between 1871 and 1874 saw only around 6,000 people take advantage of the Assembly's decree.[55] Between 1871 and 1914 the figures increased slightly, with between 12,000 and 15,000 Alsatians and Lorrainers emigrating to Algeria, where they established new settler towns named as reminders of the lost provinces, such as Strasbourg and Colmar. Such connections allowed the creation

[50] Carolyn Grohmann, 'Problems of Reintegrating Annexed Lorraine into France, 1918–1925' (PhD diss., University of Stirling, 2000), p. 5; Dreyfus, *La Vie Politique*, p. 9.
[51] Alfred Wahl, *L'Option et L'Emigration des Alsaciens-Lorrains (1871–1872)* (Paris, 1974).
[52] Grohmann, 'Problems of Reintegrating Annexed Lorraine', p. 7.
[53] Dreyfus, *La Vie Politique*, pp. 9–10.   [54] Wahl, *L'Option et L'Emigration*.
[55] Fabienne Fischer, *Alsaciens et Lorrains en Algérie. Histoire d'une migration, 1830–1914* (Nice, 1998).

of an imagined, symbolic link between Alsace and Algeria, based on the notion that Algeria would act as a kind of compensation for the loss of Alsace-Lorraine.

In the region, the departing Alsatians and Lorrainers were replaced by new migrants from across the Rhine who arrived as soldiers, bureaucrats, teachers, and pastors, or in search of employment in the region's textile mills or farms. By 1895, nearly a quarter of a million Germans from other states of the Empire had arrived in the Reichsland, where the departments of the Bas-Rhin and Haut-Rhin were redesignated *Bezirke* (districts) and renamed Unterelsass and Oberelsass, respectively, while the annexed section of Lorraine became *Bezirk* Lothringen.[56] An *Oberpräsident* presided over regional affairs, and was responsible to the Kaiser but not the Reichstag. The *Landesausschuss*, a quasi-parliament for the Reichsland, was created in 1874 to give some semblance of self-rule to the annexed territories, but its decisions could be overruled by the government or the Reichstag, and its members were chosen by an indirect voting system with a limited franchise.

The Reichsland thus enjoyed far less independence than other German states, which had their own legislature, administration, and Bundesrat representatives. To make matters worse, the new authorities left the existing legal framework in place, including some laws that the Third Republic repealed. Many permitted increased surveillance or repression, such as the so-called dictatorship paragraph, which had been introduced in the reaction following Napoleon III's *coup d'état*, and allowed house searches, the expulsion of agitators, and the prohibition of publications and organizations. This law remained in force in Alsace until 1902. Meanwhile, not all German laws were introduced; for example, the labour code was not introduced until 1889 (twenty years after taking effect elsewhere in the Reich). This left the population enjoying neither the benefits of the new masters, nor those of their old ones.

Opposition to German rule dominated politics in the first two decades after 1871. Prior to the Franco–Prussian War, Alsace had developed a reputation for electing republican and leftist candidates, but after 1871 Alsatian political life was dominated by the *protestation* movement, a loose political grouping led by local notables, industrialists, and Catholic priests that united all classes of Alsatian society around rejection of German annexation.[57] In 1874 *protestataire* candidates swept all eleven seats in the first elections held in the Reichsland, and then used the Reichstag as a platform to assert their continued opposition to the annexation. Rejection of annexation meant that they did not join any party faction in the parliament and had limited impact upon policymaking.[58]

Popular anti-German attitudes began to fade over the following years. In part, this was the result of growing economic prosperity in Alsace, particularly in the local cotton and wine industries, the development of the railway network and potash mines, and increased commercial activity in the region. But it was also connected

[56] Harvey, 'Lost Children or Enemy Aliens? Classifying the Population of Alsace after the First World War', *Journal of Contemporary History*, 34 (1999), pp. 537–54, p. 538.

[57] François G. Dreyfus, *Histoire de l'Alsace* (Paris, 1979), pp. 255–8.

[58] Harvey, *Constructing Class*, pp. 72–3.

to the introduction of social and welfare legislation and the liberalization of the Reichsland's administrative structures. In 1879 the post of *Statthalter* (Governor) was created to preside over all three districts from Strasbourg; in 1902 the dictatorship paragraph was repealed; and in 1911 the Reichstag approved a constitution for Alsace-Lorraine. Nevertheless, although the Reichsland had gained significant autonomy, it was still not on an equal footing with the other states of the Empire. The Kaiser retained the choice of the *Statthalter*, and the First Chamber remained a nominated body that could only accept or reject, but not amend, legislation passed in the elected Second Chamber.[59]

During these years Alsatian society experienced both continuity and change. First, the region remained an area of inward and outward migration. Migrants came from Germany, Italy, France, and the Polish territories seeking jobs, and by 1895 foreigners represented around 20 per cent of the total regional population.[60] The German presence was particularly evident in Strasbourg, the regional capital. Diaries and memoirs describe the line that divided these 'old Germans' from the locals; Robert Redslob described the distance between Alsatians and 'foreigners' that existed from childhood. Although the Germans were 'everywhere', he wrote, the Alsatians 'didn't know any of them'.[61] Meanwhile, Saxon-born university professor Friedrich Meinecke described his experience as akin to life in a colony.[62] Outside the middle and upper classes, however, many incomers found the line between old and new Alsatians to be reasonably porous, particularly in large towns and cities where they intermarried with the local population, established businesses, and integrated themselves into local communities. In Strasbourg, marriages between German men and Alsatian women represented almost 25 per cent of all marriages registered during the years of the Reichsland.[63]

The region was also marked by continued religious interaction; churches existed alongside temples and synagogues in towns across the region, and in a number of villages the Catholic and Protestant populations were almost equal. The Catholics remained the majority across the region and in Lower Alsace 70 per cent of the population was Catholic, while the equivalent figure for Upper Alsace was 89 per cent.[64] The Jewish population declined sharply after 1871 when the region's Jews opted for France in disproportionate numbers; the total shrank by a third between 1871 and 1932, and those that remained were clustered in the urban centres of Strasbourg, Mulhouse, and Colmar.[65]

---

[59] See Jean-Marie Mayeur, *Autonomie et Politique en Alsace: La constitution de 1911* (Paris, 1970).

[60] Harvey, *Constructing Class*, p. 78.

[61] Robert Redslob, *Entre la France et l'Allemagne. Souvenirs d'un Alsacien* (Paris, 1933), pp. 1–28, p. 29.

[62] Friedrich Meinecke, *Straßburg, Freiburg, Berlin. Erinnerungen 1901–1919* (Berlin, 1949), p. 22.

[63] François Uberfill, *Mariages entre Alsaciens et Allemands à Strasbourg de 1871 à 1914. Etude de processus du formation des unions mixtes* (Strasbourg, 1993); François Uberfill, *La Société strasbourgeoise entre France et Allemagne (1871–1924)* (Strasbourg, 2001); Alfred Wahl, 'L'immigration allemande en Alsace-Lorraine (1871–1918)', *Recherches germaniques*, 3 (1973), pp. 202–17; Harvey, *Constructing Class*, p. 78.

[64] Christopher J. Fischer, *Alsace to the Alsatians? Visions and Divisions of Alsatian Regionalism, 1870–1939* (New York and Oxford, 2010), p. 14.

[65] Goodfellow, *Between the Swastika and the Cross of Lorraine*, p. 20. See also Caron, *Between France and Germany*, and Hyman, 'Citizenship. Regionalism and Identity'.

In the eyes of the government there was a clear connection between religion and national sentiment, and in 1871 administrators classified the eighteen Protestant mayors as pro-German and favourable to the new government, and divided the two Catholic mayors into one 'hostile' and one 'undecided'.[66] Of course, nothing was quite so straightforward, and the apparent link between national attachment and confessional identity belied a range of attitudes, loyalties, and attachments. While many Catholics' concern about their position within the Prussian-dominated German Empire may have encouraged feelings of greater affinity to France in 1871, this was not the case for all, and others welcomed return in spite of the French state's avowed secularity. Equally, loyalty to France amongst the region's Jewish population was shaken by the anti-Semitic rhetoric that followed the accusation that Alfred Dreyfus was a spy, and Protestantism didn't guarantee attachment to Germany, as the memoirs of the avowedly Francophile Protestant Robert Redslob suggest.[67]

The fading of overt opposition to annexation reshaped the political landscape, and the *protestation* movement was gradually replaced by political parties that participated in national politics in imperial Germany. Political life was dominated by three movements: the Catholics (Centre Party of Alsace-Lorraine), the Socialist *Sozialdemokratische Partei Deutschlands* (SPD), and the Liberals (National Liberals and *Elsässische Volkspartei*). In the last elections held in the Reichsland in 1912, votes in Lower Alsace (the Bas-Rhin) were split, with 31.4 per cent to the SPD, 31.3 per cent to the Centre, and 26.4 per cent to the Liberals, while Upper Alsace (the Haut-Rhin) saw the Socialists take 39 per cent of votes, the Centre 45.5 per cent, and the Liberals 15.4 per cent.[68] The Centre won most of its seats in Catholic rural areas, while the Liberals collected votes largely from Protestant rural areas, and the SPD had its centres of support in the region's towns and cities.

The Catholics and Socialists were both able to capitalize on anti-German sentiment. For the Alsatian Catholic Party (affiliated from 1906 to the German Centre), the leadership and stability that the Catholic clergy had provided upon the departure of many local notables after 1871 gave the clergy a significant political voice. This was combined with the *Kulturkampf*, Bismarck's attack on the Catholic Church, and allowed the Catholic party to present itself as a shield against Germanization in Alsace.[69] The Socialists similarly capitalized on the fact that the imperial government labelled them 'enemies of the Reich' and, after 1878, banned them from speaking at public meetings and suppressed trade unions through the anti-Socialist law. Across Germany this piece of legislation had the effect of creating a sense of community amongst workers, but in Alsace this 'anti-Socialist law' also helped the party to win votes from sections of the population who maintained their opposition to German rule, notably the francophone, urban middle classes in Strasbourg,

---

[66] Wahl and Richez, *La Vie Quotidienne en Alsace*, p. 242.

[67] Redslob, *Entre la France et l'Allemagne*; Michael E. Nolan, *The Inverted Mirror. Mythologizing the Enemy in France and Germany, 1898–1914* (New York and Oxford, 2005), p. 73.

[68] Dreyfus, *La vie politique*, p. 14.

[69] Christian Baechler, 'Le Clergé Catholique alsacien et la politique, 1871–1939', *Revue d'Alsace*, 111 (1985), pp. 125–48, p. 125; Dreyfus, *La vie politique*, p. 10.

Colmar, and Mulhouse.[70] In 1887 the police commissioner in Guebwiller reported that anti-German sentiment was a driver in encouraging workers to join the SPD, which recruited its members 'primarily from the anti-German elements of the proletariat'.[71] The Liberals faced a different set of challenges, as Liberal parties (notably the National Liberals) were more closely associated with the German political system and attracted much of their support from 'old German' migrants to the region. Nonetheless, Eric Kurlander has identified a distinct Alsatian branch of liberalism in the republican particularism of the *Elsässische Volkspartei* that attracted support from some middle-class Alsatians, although it never rivalled the Catholic or Socialist parties in terms of its regional support.[72]

Lingering anti-German sentiment thus contributed to the emergence of a distinctive Alsatian political environment, which equally kept a close eye on developments in France and was shaped by cross-border connections. This was a very specific type of internationalism. It was based, in important ways, upon grass-roots political interactions such as the large numbers of Alsatians who headed to Belfort and Nancy to join the festivities on 14 July. But it was also based upon networks, which stretched from the highest echelons of the region's parties to members of its local sections.[73] Alsace was a symbolic site for joint meetings such as the Sainte-Marie-aux-Mines meeting organized by German SPD leader August Bebel and French Socialist leader Jules Guesde in September 1896, but it was also a space that facilitated cross-border encounters, and Alsatian leaders, including Colmar deputy Jacques Peirotes, were frequently invited to speak at the meetings of the Nancy section of the SFIO (Parti Socialiste: Section Française de l'Internationale Ouvrière). The police regularly banned such meetings, indeed they prevented both Bebel and Guesde's 1896 meeting and the arrival of Peirotes in 1913, suggesting once again the limits placed upon the border as a site of contact by such moments of crisis.[74] Meanwhile, many Catholic politicians, such as Abbé Emile Wetterlé, maintained links with France through frequent visits, and the regional Catholic press kept the Alsatian population up to date on the situation for French Catholics.[75]

The gradual process of integration was interrupted by the Saverne Affair.[76] In October 1913 Lieutenant Günter Baron von Forstner, a young officer in the 99th Regiment of the XV Army Corps garrisoned in the Vosges town of Saverne, referred to a group of Alsatian recruits using the derogative term 'Wackes'. After the Catholic daily *Der Elsässer* reported on the incident, it spread through the local

[70] Vernon Lidtke, *The Outlawed Party: Social Democracy in Germany, 1878–1890* (Princeton, 1966).

[71] Quoted in Harvey, *Constructing Class*, p. 99.

[72] Eric Kurlander, *The Price of Exclusion. Ethnicity, National Identity and the Decline of German Liberalism, 1918–1933* (New York and Oxford, 2006), pp. 135–84.

[73] *Der Republikaner*, 9 December 1918.

[74] Archives Nationales (hereafter AN) Fonds Panthéon, F7 15990; *Echo de Paris*, 1 May 1913. 'Le député allemande à la recousse'; *L'Humanité*, 3 May 1913. 'Une réunion interdite à Nancy'.

[75] Christian Baechler, *Clergé Catholique et Politique en Alsace, 1871–1940* (Strasbourg, 2013), pp. 127–8.

[76] Agnès Bouhet. 'L'Affaire Saverne: Novembre 1913–Janvier 1914 (Un exemple de conditionnement international indirect)', *Guerres mondiales et conflits contemporains*, 173 (1994), pp. 5–17.

press, where it was treated as an insult to the entire Alsatian people. Crowds gathered to protest in Saverne, and on the evening of 28 November several dozen Alsatians, including judges from the local court, were arrested for their part in the protests. When Forstner's trial in January 1914 ended in a mild reprimand, Alsatian anger increased. The military reported continued abuse from the public; in one notorious case the Alsatian caricaturist and author Hansi ran into two German officers in the dining room of the Central Hotel in Colmar, and responded by lighting a piece of alcohol-soaked sugar on their chairs and pronouncing, in French, that their seats had been disinfected.[77]

Although the crisis provoked by the affair interrupted Alsace's integration into Germany, the response reflected years of disquiet over Alsace's place within the Empire. When this bubbled to the surface over Saverne, it was expressed in terms of national difference, both by Forstner and by the Alsatian and Lorrainer deputies who used their platform in the Landtag to question why they were treated as second-class citizens within the German Empire. Thus the Saverne Affair had a complicated legacy. On the one hand, it revealed just how fragile Alsace's integration into German institutions and systems was, yet on the other, that the case proved so shocking is suggestive of the level of integration that had taken place.

One of the barriers to integration in the eyes of German nationalists was Alsace's continued connections with France, and in response nationalist societies and publications attempted to stress the region's shared history with the German lands (and by implication, to disassociate Alsace from France). These attempts were, however, countered by rival claims launched by French and Alsatian elites, who stressed alternatively connections to France or a vision of the region as a bridge between France and Germany, with a double culture that demonstrated the legacy of interactions with the two nations.

VISIONS OF ALSACE

The imperial government introduced specific measures into Alsace in order to win over the loyalties of a population that many German nationalists argued had been corrupted by years of 'decadent' French rule. Primary-school education, modelled on the Prussian system, was made compulsory for all boys and girls in the Reichsland by mid-April 1871, and in history lessons teachers emphasized the region's long association with the German Reich, while military service became compulsory in October 1872. Towns and streets were given German names, and new national holidays, such as the Kaiser's birthday, were celebrated with parades and official ceremonies. The University of Strasbourg reopened on 1 May 1872, and became a flagship centre of German academia after its ranks were joined by prestigious professors including Friedrich Meinecke in History, Otto Mayer in Law, and the Nobel prizewinners Röntgen and Braun in Physics. Pro-German publications attempted to instil a sense of connection between Alsace and Germany, while

[77] Fischer, *Alsace to the Alsatians?* p. 94.

downplaying or omitting the region's links to France, and nationalist associations promoted pan-German ideas and military values, and celebrated the Kaiser and the Hohenzollern family.

The police in both France and Germany monitored the success of these attempts at 'Germanization', although they didn't always arrive at the same interpretation; the German police reports on the Kaiser's visit to Strasbourg in May 1904 described the enthusiastic reception he received, while reports from the French Special Commissioner just across the border in Avricourt suggested that these celebrations were 'orchestrated by the administration' with the support of Strasbourg's German population, and that the indigenous population remained 'indifferent'.[78] The French did not simply monitor activity and attitudes in Alsace, however, they also actively promoted attachment to France through associations and literature, while Alsatians found ways of signalling their French patriotism; veterans kept medals won while serving France, and *sapeurs-pompiers* held on to their old uniforms and gave commands in French, even though most understood only Alsatian.[79]

According to German journalist and politician Alexander zu Hohenlohe-Schillingsfürst, it was easy to recognize a Francophile bourgeois Alsatian by his Napoleon III-style moustache and particular cut of trousers.[80] This points to a certain expression of connections to France amongst the regional bourgeoisie and upper classes, who typically sent their sons to French universities, enrolled their daughters in French finishing schools, and maintained links with friends and family across the border. Others made more overt displays of attachment to France, such as the celebration of anniversaries of French military victories over Germany.[81] Punishments were meted out for such seditious behaviour, and singing the Marseillaise, wearing red, white, and blue, or shouting 'Vive la France!' were all subject to penalties.[82]

Alongside these Germanophile and Francophile movements, a regionalist movement emerged from the 1890s through the establishment of the Alsatian museum in Strasbourg, the launch of the regionalist publications *Images Alsaciennes*, *Cahiers alsaciens*, and the *Revue Alsacienne Illustrée* which covered landscape, history, and popular art, and the creation of the dialect theatre, which promoted regional language, costumes, and traditions. This movement stressed Alsatian specificity in relation to Germany, but also foregrounded Alsace's 'double culture', treating it as a bridge between the French and German nations. For certain proponents of this 'double culture', Alsace could educate Germany and transmit to it western European notions of democracy and civilization, while introducing German culture

[78] AN F7 12933 Commissaire Spécial de Police, Rapport, Avricourt, 13 May 1904; Commissaire Spécial de Police, Rapport, Avricourt, 11 May 1905. See also Redslob, *Entre la France et l'Allemagne*, p. 28.

[79] Wahl and Richez, *La Vie Quotidienne en Alsace*, pp. 229–30.

[80] Wahl and Richez, *La Vie Quotidienne en Alsace*, p. 231.

[81] AN F7 12933 Commissaire Spécial Avricourt, 21 December 1905.

[82] Detmar Klein, 'Battleground of Cultures: "Politics of Identities" and the National Question in Alsace under German Imperial Rule (1870–1914)' (Royal Holloway, University of London, Unpublished PhD Thesis, 2004), pp. 115–16.

to France. This allowed Francophile Alsatian regionalists to promote France within Germany, while stressing regional cultural distinctiveness.[83]

The so-called 'lost provinces' also adopted an important part in French cultures of nationalism. In classrooms across the Third Republic, maps of the nation depicted Alsace-Lorraine in shades of black or purple (the colours of mourning), while teachers referred to the loss as an 'amputation', and textbooks on France's history and geography reminded students of the loss of the 'twin sisters'.[84] The most popular text of the period, Bruno's *Tour de France par deux enfants*, told the story of André and Julien, two orphans from Phalsbourg in the Moselle, who left their home region after the Franco–Prussian War in order to acquire French citizenship. The pair travelled around France, introducing themselves and the reader to the various French regions while stressing the links between France and its 'lost provinces'.[85]

Yet this was an Alsace that was invented (or reinvented) after 1871 in the cartoons and *images d'Epinal* of Hansi, tourist guides, the literature of Alphonse Daudet, and the Alsatian brasseries which opened in Paris and revised the recipe for choucroute by cooking it in wine or goose fat.[86] In this way, the image of the 'lost province Alsace' came to occupy an important place in French nationalism, all the while becoming increasingly distant from daily life in the region. Indeed, Jean-Claude Richez describes 'Alsace' as a new idea at the end of the nineteenth century and a word that had been rarely used before the annexation.[87] Inseparable from the idea of 'Alsace' was the border, which became a recurring motif in literary depictions of the region after 1871. From André and Julien's crossing of the border into France in *Le Tour de France par deux enfants* to René Bazin's *Les Oberlé*, which describes the difficulties faced by three generations of the Oberlé family as a result of the region's annexation into Germany, and concludes with Jean (the third generation) crossing the border in a hail of gunfire from the border guards, the border was increasingly treated as a symbol used to artificially divide two communities.[88] Yet the border also served a unifying function, rallying the population of the German Empire through the unification of German-speaking populations on both sides of the Rhine, or rallying the French population around themes of loss, absence, and

[83] See Christopher Fischer's discussion in *Alsace to the Alsatians?* pp. 20–72.

[84] *Mona L. Siegel, The Moral Disarmament of France: Education, Pacifism, and Patriotism, 1914–1940* (Cambridge, 2004), p. 139; Laurence Turetti, *Quand la France pleurait Alsace-Lorraine. Les 'provinces perdues' aux sources du patriotisme républicain* (Strasbourg, 2008); and Karine Varley's chapter 'The Lost Provinces', in *Under the Shadow of Defeat. The French War of 1870–71 in French Memory* (Basingstoke, 2008).

[85] G. Bruno, *Le Tour de la France par deux enfants* (Paris, 1877). See also Jacques Ozouf and Mona Ozouf, 'Le tour de la France par deux enfants: Le petit livre rouge de la République', in Pierre Nora (ed.), *Lieux de Mémoire* (Paris, 1984); John Strachan, 'Romance, Religion and the Republic: Bruno's Le Tour de France par deux Enfants', *French History*, 18:1 (2004), pp. 96–118.

[86] Alphonse Daudet, *La dernière classe. Récit d'un petit Alsacien* (Paris, 1873).

[87] Jean-Claude Richez, 'L'Alsace revue et inventée. La Revue Alsacienne Illustrée 1895–1914', *Saisons d'Alsace*, 119 (1993), pp. 83–94. See also Georges Bischoff, 'L'invention de l'Alsace', *Saisons d'Alsace*, 119 (1993), pp. 35–70; Wahl and Richez, 'La Petite Patrie' and 'Se Souvenir' in *La Vie Quotidienne en Alsace*.

[88] René Bazin, *Les Oberlé* (Paris, 1901).

revenge as the old ideas of the Rhine as France's natural and historic frontier, and essential to the harmony of the *Hexagone*, became an argument against annexation. This unifying function was articulated by the diplomat and historian Albert Sorel, who stressed that the quest for 'natural limits' had too often been a mask for expansionist programmes, and that a consideration of history revealed that rather than being a natural frontier, rivers had often acted as a means of communication and 'a link between peoples'. To make a river a frontier was therefore 'to violate nature by separating arbitrarily that which history has united'.[89]

In many ways this reflected the experience of those who lived alongside the new border between France and Germany; while crossing retained a symbolic importance for certain Alsatians who later reported crossing 'just to feel French soil', in general after 1873 the border between France and Germany was one that could be crossed fairly easily.[90] All the same, this did not prevent illegal crossings, whether in order to visit family or to see France, and the memoirs of Francophile Alsatian Robert Redslob describe the fear of those who sneaked back into the region to visit friends or family.[91] Others crossed for adventure: regionalist painter Charles Spindler, for example, described borrowing a friend's passport and crossing by bicycle. Or they crossed for economic reasons, and the border created new industries in smuggling.[92] French police reports also tell the stories of French citizens arrested when chopping wood, hunting, foraging for mushrooms, or fishing on the German side of the border.[93] The report on M. Belard, shot when caught hunting on German territory, notes that nothing explained his presence there, 'as the boundary was clearly marked'.[94] Through such transgressions, the border acquired meaning in the eyes of the region's inhabitants. Indeed, making such crossings a transgression created a sense of difference and opposition between the French on one side, and the Alsatians and Lorrainers on the other.

---

[89] A. Sorel and T. Funck-Brentano, *Précis du Droit des gens* (Paris, 1887), pp. 18–19; this critique was taken up by the historian Gaston Zeller in 'Histoire d'une idée fausse', *Revue de Synthèse*, 56, 2 (1936), pp. 115–32.

[90] On the symbolism of crossing see Alfred Wahl and Jean-Claude Richez, *La Vie Quotidienne en Alsace*, p. 220. On exceptional closures (notably 1887–91) see Didier Francfort, 'From the Other Side of the Mirror: the French–German border in landscape and memory', in Altink and Gemie, *At the Border. Margins and Peripheries in Modern France* (Cardiff, 2008), pp. 79–95, p. 80; Wahl and Richez, *La Vie Quotidienne*, p. 219. There were, of course, exceptions to this ease of crossing: any Alsatian or Lorrainer who had opted for France in 1871 needed authorization (and between 1888 and 1892 a visa from the German ambassador in Paris), and anyone who had left for France to avoid service in the German army was not allowed back into Alsace until after they had turned 55 and were no longer eligible for military service. What is more, specific moments of crisis could overturn the existing regime. This occurred in the wake of the diplomatic crisis triggered by Boulanger in France and the success of the Alsatian *protestataire* candidates in the 1887 Reichstag elections, when for a short spell passports were required. See François Roth, 'La frontière franco–allemande 1871–1918', in Wolfgang Haubrichs and Reinhard Schneider (eds), *Grenzen und Grenzregionen* (Saarbrücken, 1994), pp. 131–45.

[91] Robert Redslob, *Entre la France et l'Allemagne*, pp. 50–5.

[92] AN F7 12933 Rapport, Commissaire Spécial de Police de Sainte Dié, 6 July 1901.

[93] AN F7 12933 Préfet des Vosges to Ministre de l'Interieur, 30 May 1912; F7 12933 Commissaire Spécial, 8 October 1903; F7 12933 Commissaire Spécial, Rapport, 20 August 1904; F7 12933 *La Patrie*, 11 October 1901; F7 12933 Commissaire Spécial d'Avricourt, 21 December 1905.

[94] AN F7 12933 Administrateur du Préfet du territoire de Belfort, 20 March 1909 to Président du Conseil.

In other cases, individuals were tricked and pulled over. M. Binder, a cafe owner from the border town of Drumont, was reportedly asked by a customs guard dressed in plain clothes to sell him some cigars. When he did so, the guard and a colleague pulled Binder over, arrested him on French territory, and fined him 50 marks.[95] In another case, the German police spotted an Alsatian named Schwartz, who was wanted in Germany but was now working at a French hotel in the border town of Schlucht. On seeing him, the German officers pulled him across the border. According to the report in the Parisian press, several French tourists were present and tried to pull him back—but without success.[96] Such stories were very rare, but they were enough to create a sense of difference between the borderland and the centre, and to present the frontier as wild and unsafe.

The border also became an important focal point for political demonstrations, so on 14 July Alsatians and Lorrainers would head to the border to celebrate. And the border became a tourist destination, especially at its more scenic points in the Vosges, and generated a postcard industry centred on the symbols of the border. Indeed, so many tourists visited Schlucht that the Vosges section of the French alpine club protested about the commercial exploitation of the site and its impact on the landscape and nature of the mountains. Meanwhile, the police reported cases of the destruction of the border's symbols; an 1886 report described a case of damage to a border post at Avricourt and the removal of a post at Audan, and a report from 1890 noted the switching of signposts at Bonhomme so that the signpost for Germany pointed to France, and vice versa.[97]

The region was a crux point between the two nations, and existing tensions were played out differently at the periphery from how they developed elsewhere in France and Germany. This was the case with the Morocco crisis of 1906. While the French border police recorded no indication of hostility on the German side, they nevertheless reported rumours spreading through the border towns of the Vosges that reservists had been arriving in garrisons in Alsace-Lorraine, that the German authorities were requisitioning horses and cars, and that the orders for horseshoes placed by Germany in February 1906 were three times higher than normal.[98] The local press added to this concern with reports that the German general staff had sent thirty-eight officers to the Lorraine border to survey the frontier.[99] As the border had divided friends and families, letters sent from friends living on the German side added to the rumour mill by reporting that young men in Strasbourg had received letters telling them what to do in case of mobilization.[100] The border population thus kept an eye on the international situation, but such issues were understood in terms of their local impact and felt particularly keenly because of the

[95] AN F7 12933 Président du Conseil to Ministre de l'Intérieur, 26 January 1913.

[96] AN F7 12933 'Un incident de Frontière', *Echo de Paris*, 22 September 1909.

[97] Laurence Turetti, *Quand la France pleurait l'Alsace-Lorraine. Les 'provinces perdues' aux sources du patriotisme républicain, 1870–1914* (Strasbourg, 2008), p. 35.

[98] AN F7 12726 Commissaire Spécial de Police, Pagny-sur-Moselle, 25 June 1903; Direction de la Sûreté General, Rapport, Avricourt, 21 February 1906.

[99] *Journal d'Alsace-Lorraine*, 28 February 1906.

[100] AN F7 12726 Direction de la Sûreté General, Rapport, Avricourt, 3 February 1906.

presence of the frontier.[101] Indeed, a frontier mentality emerged in the border towns which left them highly attuned to the possibility of war.

There were also cases of outright confrontation. In 1901 the police reported on a fight that broke out in Arnaville, when neighbouring villages on the two sides of the border came together to celebrate the patronal festival, which was held on the French side. The fight occurred when one of the young people from the French side called 'Lucien' to get the attention of one of his friends. The population from the German side thought that he had called 'Prussien' (although the Special Commissioner notes that he thought this was a pretext). A scuffle broke out, and those involved were thrown out of the celebration, but when out in the street some of the French men were cut with knives. The Germans brought the suspects to the border for identification, and assured the French that all those identified would be taken to the prison in Metz to await trial.[102] In this case, those involved in the fracas used national language to justify their actions. Even if, as the commissioner believed, this was a pretext, this does nothing to diminish its importance. Indeed, the fact that those involved believed that the presumed insult in labelling them 'Prussians' would serve as a pretext is suggestive of the perceived significance of this apparent affront. What this example suggests is that borders don't create a sense of difference by isolating populations, but also (or instead) by generating frictions through contact and encounters.

The border remained a point of contact even after it divided the Alsatians from the populations east of the Vosges, with whom they had previously shared membership of the French nation state. Yet this contact was not all positive, and it was through contact that a sense of difference developed on the two sides of the new border. The border emerged as a collective construction, formed by the populations living alongside it as much as by the nation states that agreed on where the boundary line should go in the aftermath of the Franco–Prussian War. At this stage Alsatians began to talk about '*France de l'intérieur*', a signal of their growing sense of difference and separation from France that nonetheless suggested continued connection to the national whole, and this was a term that would continue to be widely used throughout the interwar years. Alsatians equally stressed

---

[101] AN F7 12726 Commissaire Spécial de Police, Pagny sur Moselle, 25 June 1903; Direction de la Sûreté General, Rapport, Avricourt, January 1906; Direction de la Sûreté General, Rapport, Avricourt, 3 February 1906 Direction de la Sûreté General, Rapport, Avricourt, 6 February 1906; Direction de la Sûreté General, Rapport, Avricourt, 21 February 1906; *Journal d'Alsace-Lorraine*, 28 February 1906; Direction de la Sûreté General, Rapport, Avricourt, 9 September 1911; Direction de la Sûreté General, Rapport, Avricourt, 21 September 1911. See also the plans, maps, and reports held in AN F7 12641.

[102] AN F7 12933 Rapport, Comissaire Spécial de Police, Pagny sur Moselle, 24 July 1901. While there were checks on passage at the border, and military fortifications were built along the borderline, another function of this border was its show of strength at this moment of nation-building. This purpose was reflected in the French government's negotiation that France retain certain monuments, such as that to the revolutionary general Louis Desaix on the Rhine bridge at Strasbourg (which was to be looked after by a French war veteran as a reminder of the so-called 'natural frontier'). What is more, frontier architecture became a statement; a particular case is the village of Avricourt in Lorraine, which was split in two and had two railway stations—the French station was designed to signal unity, while the German structure was intended as a showcase of German architecture.

the significance of the region, and local relationships were to become increasingly important after the outbreak of war in 1914, which led to a further reinforcement of existing social structures.

WAR AND REVOLUTION

The outbreak of war in 1914 took many Alsatians by surprise, and challenged attitudes to Germany and France.[103] The diary of Mulhouse schoolteacher Philippe Husser records his belief that Germany bore no responsibility for starting the conflict, so he hoped for rapid German victories to bring an end to the fighting.[104] Right from the outbreak of the conflict, however, the authorities monitored expressions of anti-German sentiment in Alsace, and any incidents were quickly reported on by the German national press. In Metz German troops were fired upon from two houses, while on 25 August the *Kölnische Zeitung* accused the inhabitants of Saarburg of treason and of looting the houses of absent Germans.[105] The problem for the authorities attempting to deal with such cases was that it was difficult to disentangle anti-militarism from anti-Prussianism, and the two were often expressed together; for example, one steelworker tried at Thionville in annexed Lorraine on 17 August 1914 was sentenced for shouting 'Down with the war, down with Prussia...Vive la France, merde à la Prusse!'[106] Following the Battle of the Marne in September 1914, opinion began to turn against Germany as an early German outright victory became increasingly unlikely.

Over the course of the war shortages of food and economic difficulties became an important cause of grumbles about the regime.[107] Bread rations fell from 2 kilograms per day in 1916 to 160 grams per day in July 1918.[108] Such shortages were not unique to Alsace, but as they were coupled with suspicion over the population's national loyalties, their effect was sharpened. Husser noted his disquiet as the authorities Germanized French street and town names, banned the use of French in the streets or taverns, and insisted on German in business correspondence.[109] He described their impact upon spirits in Alsace:

> [I]n Alsace...understandable sympathy (and family links) with France have driven many to forget their...duty, behaviour which the war council reprimands with severity. These lamentable incidents have had a demoralizing effect, even on the Germanophile Alsatians.... They could have hoped for more understanding towards

---

[103] Christian Baechler, 'L'Alsace entre la Guerre et la Paix: Recherches sur l'opinion publique, 1917–1918' (Thèse pour le Doctorat de Troisième Cycle, Université de Strasbourg, 1969), p. 52.

[104] Philippe Husser, *Un Instituteur Alsacien. Entre France et Allemagne. Le Journal de Philippe Husser, 1914–1951* (Paris, 1989), p. 34. Husser also shared his lack of animosity towards France in an article penned for the *Elsass-Lothringische Schulzeitung* on 17 October 1914. See Husser, *Un Instituteur Alsacien*, p. 54.

[105] Alan Kramer, 'Wackes at War: Alsace-Lorraine and the Failure of German National Mobilization, 1914–1918', in John Horne (ed.), *State, Society and Mobilisation in Europe during the First World War* (Cambridge, 1997), pp. 105–21, p. 107.

[106] Kramer, 'Wackes at War', p. 108.   [107] Husser, *Un Instituteur Alsacien*, p. 102.

[108] Fischer, *Alsace to the Alsatians?* p. 108.   [109] Husser, *Un Instituteur Alsacien*, pp. 56–7.

Alsace, a more empathetic approach to treat these particular cases, and a less summary judgement on we other Alsatians. That is what we would wish.[110]

As Husser suggests, another problem for the authorities was that not all sections of the population behaved in the same way, so some mirrored the government's attempts to suppress French: 'French names are starting to disappear', Husser noted in December 1914. 'The Charles hide behind Karl, or lose their –es, just like the Georges.'[111] Some denounced friends or family for anti-German sentiment, while others used French in public as a demonstration of their hostility to the military or the Empire, and others ignored their call-up papers, or deserted.[112]

For the approximately 380,000 men from Alsace who served in the German army, suspicion over their loyalty lowered morale.[113] Military regulations banned Alsatians and Lorrainers from serving in any position with access to sensitive information, while there were also general restrictions on leave and special censorship that were not applied to the other minorities of the German Empire. The Prussian War Ministry banned the use of French, but it did not introduce equivalent measures for the Polish minority from Germany's eastern border. Instead, as Alexander Watson has pointed out, the army actually used the Polish language to strengthen discipline and morale; so Poles were read the military code detailing their duties as soldiers in their own language on enlisting, the army recruited Polish-speaking priests to hear their confessions and, whether stationed at the front or recovering from wounds in hospital, they were permitted to receive Polish-language correspondence.[114]

From March 1915 the army introduced a new deployment policy which involved singling out unreliable Alsatians, separating them from their fighting units, and sending them to the eastern front. There, disaffected Alsatians and Lorrainers found themselves gathered together, and Alsatians who were sent to the east for military (rather than national) reasons resented the suggestion of disloyalty that came with their transfer. Orders were issued to distribute Alsatians and Lorrainers across units equally, but so many were sent east that by the end of 1917 the Army High Command feared that they would predominate on this front. The French also offered special treatment to any Alsatian troops that were captured as POWs and divided them according to their attitude towards France. So-called 'sympathetic' Alsatian soldiers were dressed in French uniforms, offered generous rations of tobacco and alcohol, and asked to participate in flag-raising ceremonies as part of a wider effort to win them over to the French cause.

---

[110] Husser, *Un Instituteur Alsacien* p. 72.　　　[111] Husser, *Un Instituteur Alsacien*, p. 57.

[112] Fischer, *Alsace to the Alsatians?* p. 109. By the end of the war there had been at least 2,389 prosecutions for showing an anti-German attitude, with about 80 per cent of them successful. In terms of desertion at the start of the war, at least 7,000 court-martial cases for desertion were pending, while 17,650 Alsatian and Lorrainer men served in the French army. At least 3,000 men escaped to France, while there was a continual flow into neutral Switzerland. See Kramer, 'Wackes at War', pp. 109–11.

[113] This represented around 40 per cent of the total population. Harvey, *Constructing Class*, p. 118; Kramer, 'Wackes at War', p. 106.

[114] Alexander Watson, 'Fighting for Another Fatherland: The Polish Minority in the German Army, 1914–1918', *English Historical Review*, 126 (2011), pp. 1137–66, p. 1145.

On the home front, meanwhile, the war unravelled communities where 'old Germans' and Alsatians had lived side by side for years, and friends, neighbours, and colleagues denounced each other for their 'Francophile' or 'un-German' behaviour. When Mulhouse was recovered by German forces after a brief spell under French occupation in early 1918, 'old German' SPD councillor Leopold Emmel denounced his Alsatian SPD colleagues Jean Martin and August Wicky to the returning German authorities for the enthusiastic welcome that they had offered to the French troops. Martin was imprisoned, and Wicky was incorporated into the German army and did not return to Alsace until after the armistice.

During the conflict French troops occupied the south-western corner of Upper Alsace, and at separate moments they occupied Mulhouse, Cernay, Guebwiller, the western outskirts of Colmar and the middle Vosges, and a strip of Lorraine for a few days, weeks, or months at a time. There they were able to introduce some French policies, such as the use of the French language, into primary schools, while leaving others (notably religious education) in place in an attempt to win over the local population. But these efforts to secure local loyalties needed to work alongside the military requirements to secure the area, including evacuation of suspect sections of the population, such as German migrants to the region, and Alsatian public-sector workers who had married Germans, or those who had been denounced by their neighbours. They were then sent to internment camps in the French interior. Once there, many reported being treated 'like Prussians', and their frequently problematic relations with the French citizens they encountered pointed to trouble ahead in terms of relations between France and Alsace.[115]

As the war drew to a close in November 1918, revolution swept through Alsace and Lorraine. Soldiers and sailors formed councils and soviets, and the last imperial government attempted to contain the movement in the Reichsland (and prevent the region from falling into French hands) by finally granting the long-standing demand for the creation of the state of Alsace-Lorraine.[116] The German government named Mayor of Strasbourg Rudolf Schwander as *Statthalter*, and Karl Hauss, leader of the Catholic Centre of Alsace-Lorraine, as Secretary of State, charged with forming a new government and elaborating a new constitution for the Reichsland. Rumours spread through the region that this signalled the first steps towards autonomy, while others anticipated a transfer to French rule.[117] The plan faltered, however, when leading Catholic politician Joseph Pfleger stated publicly that he was in favour of a return to France, and the influential Abbé Xavier Haegy pointed out that the status of Alsace-Lorraine needed to be a matter for the peace congress. This left Hauss isolated within the Centre Party, while the Socialists, the second largest party in the Alsatian Landtag, refused to participate. As a result, this attempted

[115] Fischer, *Alsace to the Alsatians?* pp. 111–14.

[116] For a discussion of the debate over Alsatian neutrality, see Christian Baechler, 'La question de la neutralité de l'Alsace-Lorraine à la fin de la Première Guerre Mondiale et pendant le Congrès de Paix (1917–1929)', *Revue d'Alsace*, 114 (1988), pp. 185–208.

[117] Husser, *Un Instituteur Alsacien*, p. 115.

government lasted just a few days and was unable to prevent the outbreak of revolution in early November 1918.

The Alsatian Revolution brought together soldiers, workers, politicians, and Alsatians who had spent the war on the home front. This eclectic mix was reflected in the revolutionary manifestos, whose demands ranged from parallels of those of councils across Germany, such as the protection of property, the orderly withdrawal of troops, and the liberation of prisoners, to particular local demands, notably the organization of resistance to the arrival of French troops.[118] On 7 and 8 November demonstrators marched through the streets of Strasbourg and Colmar and attacked prominent buildings including the Aubette building, the prison on the rue du Fil, and the residence of Prince Joachim von Hohenzollern in Strasbourg. By 9 November, the first groups of mutinying soldiers arrived in Haguenau, Strasbourg, and Mulhouse in Alsace and Thionville in Lorraine. French administrators wrote the movement off as an 'import from Germany', but research on the revolutionaries has suggested that the majority of those involved were Alsatian.[119] Indeed, in November 1918 it was Alsatians who formed the region's first soldiers' councils. Alsatian soldiers also refused orders to head towards the eastern front and headed instead for the west, and Alsatian sailors sang the Marseillaise in the uprising in Danzig in 1917.[120]

The first soldiers' councils were formed on the nights of 9 and 10 November following the declaration of the Republic in Germany, and workers' councils were formed in Strasbourg, Metz, Colmar, Sélestat, and Mulhouse. But the question mark hanging over the region's future created tensions, as head of the workers' council and SPD leader Bernhard Boehle argued that the revolution consolidated Alsace's place within Germany, while the group around rival Socialist Charles Hueber used the opportunity to demand Alsatian neutrality, and the majority of local Socialist leaders demanded the region's return to France. On 11 November 1918, revolutionaries marked the signature of the armistice by flying the red flag from the cathedral in Strasbourg in what Jean-Claude Richez has described as an 'internationalist' gesture to French and German troops, while the Alsatian and Lorrainer deputies proclaimed the *Conseil national d'Alsace-Lorraine* and demanded return to France.[121] Over the following weeks, French troops marched into towns and villages across Alsace, where they were greeted by crowds whose enthusiastic welcome was rooted as much in relief at the end of the conflict as in the desire to become French again. As Husser had noted at the end of October, 'Whether we are to be neutral, or autonomous, or French (!) all that we ask is peace. Calm. Something to eat! This is what we all want.'[122]

[118] Jean Claude Richez, 'Novembre 1918 en Alsace: Conseils Ouvriers et Conseils de Soldats', *Cahiers de l'Alsace Rouge*, vol. 1, 1977, pp. 1–22, p. 5; Harvey, *Constructing Class*, p. 126.
[119] Christian Baechler, 'Espoirs et désillusions: l'entre-deux-guerres et l'occupation nazie (1918–1944)', in Georges Livet and François Rapp (eds), *Histoire de Strasbourg* (Toulouse, 1987).
[120] Jean Claude Richez, 'La Révolution de Novembre 1918 en Alsace dans les petites villes et les campagnes', *Revue d'Alsace*, 107 (1981), pp. 153–68, p. 154.
[121] Richez, 'Novembre 1918 en Alsace', p. 15.   [122] Husser, *Un Instituteur Alsacien*, p. 117.

CONCLUSION

Alsace has long been a site of contact and interaction, and contact persisted throughout the changes of regime that the region experienced. This contact survived (or resulted from) the increasing importance placed upon the border as a dividing line. Of course, not all of this contact was positive, and this chapter has traced some of the forms that it took, from tourism or assembling at the border to celebrate Bastille Day to fights over who called whom '*Prussien*'. Contemporaries were well aware that cross-border contact was a defining characteristic of daily life in the region, and this was articulated through the idea of Alsace's 'double culture' based upon connections with France and Germany. For many Alsatians in the Reichsland, the notion of the double culture allowed the region to reconcile its connections to both nations, especially after their incorporation into the *Kaiserreich* in 1871. Yet there was a widespread understanding that regional culture not only bore the influence of the region's connections to France and Germany, but also offered the potential to provide a 'bridge' between the two nations based on interactions across the Rhine and the Vosges. This bridge would generate new connections and breed greater closeness, but the problem was that this idea evaporated at moments of crisis, whether political, economic, or international, and was replaced by an emphasis on the border as a limit or dividing line.

Transition shaped the interactions that made Alsace, and war brought integration into the French nation state in 1648, and then change of national regime in 1871 and again in 1918. Each transfer triggered movement in the location of the national border, and subsequent integration into the nation state introduced national language, laws, and institutions to the region. These experiences had an impact on attitudes and, notably, they crystallized the identities expressed by Alsatians and encouraged the articulation of a sense of difference and opposition between communities. As the spread of nationalism in the nineteenth century transformed national boundaries into increasingly meaningful divisions, the 1871 border divided the population of Alsace from those *Français de l'Intérieur* living west of the Vosges, and the widespread use of this term spoke to the sense of difference from France that emerged in the region. In this sense, through these shifts the population faced and contributed to the evolution of ideas about borders and their function.

Cross-border contact and interaction had multiple effects on attitudes in Alsace; most notably they led to the creation of a sense of difference across the border. Tourism, smuggling, or illegal crossings brought neighbouring populations together, and this contact bred an understanding of difference. Thus neighbouring communities articulated understandings of themselves as distinct from those living on the other side of the boundary line, as in the fight in Arnaville. Furthermore, the new border served a unifying function within the nation, bringing together the population in the German Empire through the unity of German speakers on both sides of the Rhine, and rallying the French population over the loss of the Alsatian departments and part of Lorraine. Yet while this created a sense of difference between Alsatians and those living across the border, it also fostered feelings of otherness within the nation, whether France or Germany. This was articulated in the protests over 'foreign' (French) workers in the nineteenth century, or through the Saverne affair, which tested the region's place within imperial Germany in 1913. Such contact and interactions took place against a backdrop of evolving ideas about borders, which during the nineteenth century were increasingly described as dividing lines between states. This is a crucial element of the story of Alsace, as the region's strategically important position between the Rhine and the Vosges led to it becoming an object of contestation between two of the most powerful nation states in Europe.

War, annexation, and national instability thus played an important part in shaping experiences and identities in Alsace, and exerted a unifying effect upon a regional population that was divided by class, confession, gender, political identity, and milieu. Alongside political change, encounters with France and Germany also had significant effects upon the regional population, and cross-border interactions helped to shape identities in the region. 'Contact and closeness bred a clear sense of difference,' and Alsatians were acutely aware of the distinctiveness of Alsatianness. The Alsatians thus played an important part in forging both their own sense of identity and a more widespread understanding of the border as a dividing line.

2

Remaking French Alsace
Citizenship, Administration, and Laws

When French troops entered Alsace in November 1918, they were greeted by young women dressed in traditional Alsatian costume and a sea of blue, white, and red. In Strasbourg, tricolour banners adorned the cathedral, the former imperial palace, the town hall, shops, houses, and buttonholes.[1] One hairdresser even had a window display of false hair in the colours of the national flag.[2] Wealthy Alsatians established committees to collect donations for the widows and orphans of French soldiers 'in recognition of their sacrifice', while the city's museums commissioned commemorative medals and the municipal council distributed lyric sheets for the Marseillaise, which served as a souvenir of the events as well as a prompt for anyone unfamiliar with the words.[3]

The enthusiasm that coloured these scenes was partly rooted in relief at the end of the war. Four years of conflict had seen sons, husbands, and fathers sent to the fierce fighting on the eastern front, while Alsatians on the home front had been subject to the requisition of goods, the imposition of martial law, and the introduction of far harsher policies of Germanization than those in place prior to 1914. Nevertheless, the reception of the French troops also reflected genuine enthusiasm at the return to France amongst large sections of Alsatian society. Similarly, in France the restoration of Alsace-Lorraine had become a primary war aim after 1914, and the return of the lost provinces was greeted with widespread excitement that built upon images of Alsace disseminated before and during the war.[4] Propaganda, caricature, and the *images d'Epinal* of Hansi and others had all contributed to the development of an image of Alsace as eternally French and awaiting the arrival of its liberators. Yet in spite of the jubilant atmosphere in November 1918, the return of Alsace to France raised numerous questions over reintegration, and was marked by problems that arose across all areas of daily life. Voices inside and outside the region grappled with the question of how to undo

---

[1] *L'Excelsior*, 27 November 1918.   [2] *Le Petit Parisien*, 27 November 1918.
[3] Archives Municipales de la Ville et l'Eurométropole de Strasbourg (hereafter AMVES), 81Z 39, Fonds Hugo Haug, 'L'Offrande de la Liberation aux Veuves et Orphelins des Soldats Français, Morts pour la Patrie. Comité de Strasbourg-Ville'; Medaille Commemoratif de l'entrée des Français à Strasbourg; Souvenir des Grandes Fêtes à Strasbourg en 1918. La Marseillaise.
[4] On the return of Alsace-Lorraine as a primary war aim, see J. F. V. Keiger, *Raymond Poincaré* (Cambridge, 1997), pp. 202, 229. On Alsace-Lorraine in republican cultures, see Laurence Turetti, *Quand la France pleurait Alsace-Lorraine. Les 'provinces perdues' aux sources du patriotisme républicain* (Strasbourg, 2008) and Karine Varley's chapter 'The Lost Provinces' in *Under the Shadow of Defeat. The War of 1870–71 in French Memory* (Basingstoke, 2008).

almost fifty years of German rule, and how to make the region French again. And, given that the return of Alsace had become a key war aim, these discussions were also coloured by notions of the French sacrifice during the First World War to secure the region's return. These problems proved particularly acute in the areas of citizenship, administration, and laws.

Long-standing Alsatian connections across the Rhine had been consolidated by the years of German rule, when large numbers of Germans moved to the region. Once there, many had married Alsatians, found jobs, established businesses, and built lives. Meanwhile, France had crystallized its idea of citizenship through the debates that followed the loss of Alsace, and through the expansion of its colonial territories.[5] At Alsace's return, an immediate priority for the French government was the removal of German influence. But the intermarriage and family links that they encountered in the region meant that doing so was not as straightforward as initially assumed. Indeed, the very nature of borderland society raised the question of *who* could be considered to be French, as French ideas about Alsace interacted with local understandings forged through the experience of transfers of sovereignty, war, and cross-border contact.

If citizenship raised the question of who was French, administrative and legal reintegration posed the problem of *what* was French. German rule had left the region with administrative institutions and laws distinct from those introduced in France since 1871. New structures from the Reichsland period stood alongside systems that had been left intact from the Second French Empire, which created a situation where Alsace had regional administrative institutions, some French laws that had been repealed in France, and a series of German laws distinct from their French equivalents. Many of these laws, notably in terms of welfare, were extremely popular with the local population. Meanwhile, the Third Republic had introduced its own systems of administration and legislation, and the regime rapidly became associated with centralized government and law. The resulting situation produced some important questions: should Alsace retain its distinctiveness or should French systems be introduced? And, if French institutions were to be introduced, should this take place immediately or should a transition period be allowed? Discussions over these questions were polemicized by Alsatian attachment to regional particularities on the one hand and, on the other, by the centrality of the concept of the 'one and indivisible' French Republic. Crucially, years of contact across the Rhine had given the Alsatian population a very clear idea of what was German, and of the differences between Alsace and Germany; yet Alsatian analyses of the situation were not always understood in Paris, and administrators who arrived in the region were struck by the blurring of the lines between 'Alsatian' and 'German'.

In these circumstances, citizenship and legal and administrative reintegration became pressing problems for each of the governments that took power after 1918.

---

[5] On French ideas of citizenship, see Patrick Weill, *How to be French. Nationality in the Making since 1789* (Durham and London, 2008). On the impact of debates in the colonies, see Elisa Camiscoli, *Reproducing the French Race: Immigration, Intimacy and Embodiment in the Early Twentieth Century* (Durham and London, 2009).

It was no less of a concern for political elites in Alsace, who developed their own stance on the region's reintegration, or for the Alsatian population, who appropriated and resisted Parisian initiatives in a variety of different ways. The result was mutual misunderstandings and misperceptions. But this situation did not result from a two-way dialogue between centralizers in Paris and regionalists in Strasbourg. Rather, opinion was divided at both centre and periphery, creating frustrations and ensuring that questions of reintegration remained unanswered throughout the interwar years. In these discussions, national, regional, and political prerogatives came together, but just as important was the clash of expectations, as reintegration came to dominate Alsatian life. This chapter traces these debates, focusing first on citizenship, second on administration, and third on legislation. The opening section sets out the context to these discussions.

FROM GERMANY TO FRANCE

During the First World War French troops occupied the area around Thann in southern Alsace from 1914. Upon his entry into the town, Marshal Joffre announced, 'Our return is final, you will be French forever. France brings you, with the liberty that she has always represented, respect for your liberties,...your traditions, your convictions, your way of life. I am France, you are Alsace, I bring you the maternal embrace of France.'[6] All the same, throughout the conflict German forces spread propaganda materials warning that French recovery of Alsace-Lorraine would be followed by the immediate introduction of secular laws. This proved a particular point of concern in Alsace, where the Catholic population had observed the institution of the separation of church and state in the Third Republic in 1905 with concern. The Alsatian clergy played an important part in local life, having stepped into the gap left by the departure of the region's elites after 1871, and the experience of change of national regime in 1871 had reinforced the importance of religious faith as a stable point of loyalty for much of the population. While Joffre's speech went some way towards reassuring local concerns that return to France would mean the immediate introduction of central French institutions and systems, these rival assertions pointed to the challenges ahead in terms of integration and the potential clash between France and its 'lost provinces'.

Joffre had been clear that 'the solutions that we adopt will take on a provisional nature... questions [of the introduction of French administrative and judicial institutions] are the responsibility of the Parliament, and of the Government, alone'.[7] Nonetheless, many Alsatians took to heart the implied promise that France would not attempt to introduce the separation of church and state into the

---

[6] AMVES 113Z 48, reproduction of Joffre's speech at Thann (no date).

[7] Rapport de l'Administration militaire de l'Alsace sur l'organisation des territoires, imprimé à Thann en 1917. Quoted in Peirotes' proposal on the introduction of secular education and the separation of church and state, cited in ADBR 98AL 661 *Les Dernières Nouvelles de Strasbourg*, 31 May 1927, 'Pour l'introduction des lois scolaires et sur la séparation de l'Eglise et de l'Etat'.

region, especially after these promises to respect local traditions and customs were renewed by General Gourand, when he led the French troops into Strasbourg in November 1918, and by Raymond Poincaré on his first presidential visit to Alsace in December 1918.[8]

Shortly after Joffre entered Thann in 1914, the French government began discussing the reintegration of the region in preparation for its return following a French victory. In 1915, Premier René Viviani established the *Conférence d'Alsace et de Lorraine*, which brought together high-ranking civil servants, French politicians, and Alsatian émigrés including regionalist Anselm Laugel, former mayor of Colmar Daniel Blumenthal, and Catholic priest and politician Emile Wetterlé to discuss the implications of the anticipated return of Alsace-Lorraine to France. Much of the discussion focused upon what should be done to remove German influence, but this conference was unable to reach agreement on either the removal of German citizens or the introduction of French administrative institutions and laws. It warned that the immediate introduction of French institutions (most notably the separation of Church and state) would be likely to provoke local resistance, and instead proposed a transitional period and the gradual introduction of French systems.

As France made plans for the lost provinces, groups inside Alsace proposed neutrality for the region in the final months of the conflict.[9] The Socialist Salomon Grumbach argued that the answer was a plebiscite. This, he suggested, would remove any question mark over Alsace's desire to become French again and settle the 'Alsace-Lorraine question' once and for all.[10] But concerns were raised in Paris and London that a plebiscite might not return a clear majority in favour of return to France.[11] The government in Paris attempted to avoid the issue by pointing out that as Germany had not held a plebiscite in 1871, France was under no obligation to conduct a vote in 1918.[12] Furthermore, Senator Léon Bourgeois argued that, through their protest at Bordeaux in 1871, the Alsatian deputies had expressed their opposition to the annexation, and as they were region's elected representatives, this should be taken as evidence of popular resistance to the Treaty of Frankfurt.[13] No such protest followed the return of Alsace to France. Instead, French troops had met with an enthusiastic reception, which offered, President Raymond Poincaré pointed out, all the evidence needed of their population's will to return to France, and showed, to repeat his often quoted phrase, that 'the plebiscite is complete'.[14]

---

[8] On Gourand see AMVES 81Z 39 Fonds Hugo Haug, 'Aux Habitants de Strasbourg!' General Gourand. On Poincaré see ADBR, 121AL 207 Introduction des Lois Françaises en France. Conférence faite le 1er mai 1922 par M. Albert Chéron.

[9] ADBR 121AL 207 Commissaire Générale de la République to Garde des Sceaux, Strasbourg, January 1923. See also Christian Baechler, 'La question de la neutralité de l'Alsace-Lorraine à la fin de la Première Guerre Mondiale et pendant le Congres de Paix (1917–1829)', *Revue d'Alsace*, 114 (1988), pp. 185–208; François G. Dreyfus, *La vie politique en Alsace, 1919–1936* (Paris, 1969), p. 32.

[10] 'Berne Conferees Vote for Alsace Plebiscite', *The New York Times*, 9 February 1919.

[11] The National Archives (hereafter TNA) CAB/24/70 Note by Arthur Balfour, 18 October 1918.

[12] TNA CAB/24/70 Note by Arthur Balfour, 18 October 1918.

[13] See ADBR 121AL 204 Coupure de presse, 'L'Alsace-Lorraine', *Le Temps*, 9 October 1919.

[14] David Stevenson, 'French War Aims and the American Challenge, 1914–1918', *Historical Journal*, 22 (1979), pp. 877–94, p. 884.

France thus rejected a plebiscite, but differences of opinion at the *Conférence* and elsewhere in government meant that it recovered the lost provinces without a clear plan for reintegration. Just as wartime discussions over the region's future had taken place within and outside Alsace, so debates over reintegration after the return to France engaged forces at both the Parisian centre and the Alsatian periphery. The governments of the interwar years, working with civil servants in Paris-based ministries and in the prefectures and sub-prefectures in Alsace adopted numerous strategies to negotiate the process of reintegration. But there was rarely consensus on how to proceed, and civil servants based in the region often adopted different views from those working in Paris, while changes of government complicated matters further. Their strategies were then resisted, accepted, and countered in different ways in Alsace.

In these discussions, an important role was played by the region's political parties, and in many respects party politics in interwar Alsace followed patterns established under German rule. The two largest parties were successors to the pre-1918 Catholic and Socialist parties: the *Union Populaire Républicaine d'Alsace* (UPR), Alsace's largest party during the interwar years, succeeded the Catholic Centre Party, and the Socialist SFIO (*Parti Socialiste: Section Française de l'Internationale Ouvrière*) was successor to the German SPD.[15] After 1918, the UPR kept its focus on religious questions, and also its centres of support in the region's Catholic agricultural areas, while the SFIO maintained its support amongst the urban working classes. The Socialists' profession of their attachment to France also allowed them to capture what administrators described as 'national' support from *Français de l'Intérieur*.[16] Both retained their links to Germany through networks of personal contacts.

Legacies of German rule similarly lingered in the new parties established after 1918. The Conservatives, made up of the *parti républicain démocratique* in the Bas-Rhin and the *parti républicain indépendant*, represented conservative opinion and offered a home to leaders and voters of the German Liberal Party. Both parties were unique to Alsace, and won most of their votes from middle-class Protestants. The Radicals (*parti républicain radical et radical socialiste*) were established in Alsace in 1919 by Alsatian members of the left wing of the German Liberal Party and by *Français de l'Intérieur* who had moved to the region after 1918; they demanded the introduction of all French laws and institutions, particularly centralization and secularity. The Communists (PCF, or *Parti Communiste Français*) emerged after the left wing of the SFIO broke away at the Tours Congress in 1920 to form a new party that accepted Lenin's conditions for membership of the Third International. The PCF attracted the majority of the Alsatian SFIO's members and demanded autonomy for Alsace.[17]

[15] Malcolm Anderson, 'Regional Identity and Political Change: The Case of Alsace from the Third to the Fifth Republic', *Political Studies*, 20 (1972), pp. 17–30, p. 20.

[16] Alison Carrol, 'The Socialist Party and the Return of Alsace to France', in Brian Sudlow (ed.), *National Identities in France* (Rutgers, 2012), pp. 47–64.

[17] *L'Humanité*, 9 March 1926.

The range of different voices involved in discussion over return meant that integration in the case of Alsace did not take the form of a straightforward interaction between centre and periphery. Rather, there were contentious debates in Paris and Alsace, with no clear single opinion emerging from either. What is more, ideas for Alsace's future also came from outside France, as the Weimar Republic established a research centre for Alsatian studies at the University of Frankfurt and an *Institut für geschichtliche Landeskunde der Rheinlande* at the University of Bonn, both of which stressed Alsace's links to the German lands. The German press also kept a close eye on developments and was sure to offer comments upon them.

The early discussions over Alsace's future took place against the backdrop of discussions over the peace terms in Paris between the victorious and defeated powers, which opened in January 1919 and lasted throughout that year. For the western Allies, moral condemnation based on the accusation that Germany had started the war and committed war crimes in Belgium lay at the heart of the Treaty and was stated in the 'responsibilities clauses' (articles 227–30). This attitude was rejected by German public opinion, which resisted notions of guilt and responsibility and held that the peace should have been based on dialogue and compromise on the model of the Congress of Vienna in 1815. John Horne has suggested that these sharply divergent ways of seeing not only the terms of the peacemaking, but also its nature, prolonged enmity into the years of peace.[18] This had implications for Alsace, which both France and Germany had treated as a territory essential to the integrity of the nation.

When the delegates at Versailles discussed the redrawing of the border between France and Germany, Britain and the USA supported the return of Alsace and annexed Lorraine from the outset. But France's wartime leader and 1919 Premier Georges Clemenceau wanted to go further to protect France against any further German aggression. He argued not only for the return of Alsace and Lorraine, but also for the creation of a neutral buffer state in the German Rhineland and the restoration of an independent Belgium (in order to block another historical route of German invasion of France). Both the American President Woodrow Wilson and the British Prime Minister Lloyd George rejected French demands for the separation of the Rhineland from Germany. Instead, it was agreed that the Rhineland was to become a demilitarized zone, with Germany to dismantle all fortifications within 50 kilometres of the Rhine and forbidden from sending soldiers or maintaining any military installations in that area.

The Treaty also allowed for French occupation of the Rhineland and granted the French the Saar coalfields for fifteen years; and pending a plebiscite at the end of the period, France could occupy the territory. The remaking of borders in the west was discussed in concert with ideas about those in the east, and Clemenceau argued for Polish and Czechoslovakian independence with the aim of creating strong, independent states that would provide a buttress against German expansion. He assumed that these states would fall within the French sphere of influence. This idea

[18] John Horne, 'Demobilizing the Mind: France and the Legacy of the Great War, 1919–1939', *French history and civilization: papers from the George Rudé Seminar* (2009), pp. 101–19, p. 104.

won out over the British suggestion of a smaller, more ethnically homogeneous Poland, which Lloyd George believed would prove a more stable influence in Europe.[19] The signing of the Treaty in June 1919 fixed these new borders in both east and west. But before the discussions at Versailles had started, France turned to the work of reintegrating their recovered provinces. Much of these early efforts focused upon the removal of German influence, and this was a particular and immediate problem when it came to classifying the Alsatian population.

THE RETURN TO FRENCH RULE: RENEGOTIATING CITIZENSHIP AT THE GRASSROOTS

In the wartime *Conférence d'Alsace et de Lorraine*, Abbé Wetterlé advised that it would be both 'unjust' and 'dangerous' to allow German migrants to the region to remain.[20] However, the decision of who to remove after return was not straightforward. Around 300,000 German nationals were resident in Alsace-Lorraine at the armistice, but many had families, jobs, and businesses and did not want to 'return' to Germany. What is more, there were also many Alsatians and Lorrainers who had collaborated with the Germans during the years of imperial rule or who were deemed to have harboured sympathies for the Reich, and popular pressure was building for retribution. This raised the question of whether to remove pro-German Alsatians along with the Germans, and how exactly to go about classifying the population. With no clear solution in sight, the French government recovered the lost provinces without a definite programme to make Alsace-Lorraine French and adopted a policy that Laird Boswell has described as the first French *épuration* of the twentieth century, one that preceded the purge that followed the collapse of the Vichy regime and the liberation of France in 1944–5.[21] This met the aim of implementing a policy of francization to the recovered departments, while meeting calls within France for the removal of all enemy subjects and feeding local demands for vengeance following repressive treatment at the hands of the German regime during the war.

France's citizenship policy had three parts: the first was a system of identity cards that classified the population according to their parents and place of birth; the second was the expulsion of Germans; and the third was the weeding out of supposedly pro-German Alsatians. The identity cards classified the population into four categories. The first, the A-card, was adorned with the stripes of the tricolour and issued to those who had held French citizenship, or whose parents had held

[19] See Zara Steiner, *The Lights that Failed. European International History, 1919–1933* (Oxford, 2005), pp. 15–79; Margaret Macmillan, *Peacemakers. Six Months that Changed the World* (London, 2001).

[20] David Allen Harvey, 'Lost Children or Enemy Aliens? Classifying the Population of Alsace after the First World War', *Journal of Contemporary History*, 71:3 (1999), pp. 537–54, p. 539.

[21] Laird Boswell, 'From Liberation to Purge Trials in the "Mythic Provinces". Recasting French Identities in Alsace and Lorraine, 1918–1920', *French Historical Studies*, 23:1 (2000), pp. 129–62, p. 130.

French citizenship before 1871 but had become German through the Treaty of Frankfurt. The second, the B-card, had two red stripes and was given to those born in Alsace-Lorraine with only one French or Alsatian parent. The third, the C-card, had two blue stripes and went to foreign subjects of non-enemy states (e.g. Italy), while anyone from an enemy country (Germany, Austria, Hungary, Turkey, or Bulgaria) and their children received the fourth card, the D-card, which was plain white.

More than a million (1,082,650) Alsatians and Mosellans received an A-card, while B-cards went to 183,500, C-cards to 55,050, and D-cards to 513,800.[22] Many Alsatians and Mosellans worried that the cards would be used as the basis for establishing citizenship and, as a result, the card system served to reinforce the importance of ethnicity in the minds of the population. Not having an A-card also came with certain practical disadvantages. D-cardholders received unfavourable rates of exchange for their German marks: whereas A-, B-, and C-cardholders received 1.25 francs, D-cardholders received just 0.74 francs. What is more, B-, C-, and D-cardholders had difficulties finding jobs in the civil service, post office, or railways, and in travelling to visit family in Germany or elsewhere in France.[23] As a result, many holders of B-, C-, and D-cards petitioned to have their status changed to 'A-cardholder', and a lucrative black market emerged in the sale of false identity cards. The system also highlighted the difficulties in classifying the population after years of migration into the region and intermarriage. This caused confusion for many and practical problems for others, as, for example, if a German man had married an Alsatian woman, he would receive a D-card while she would receive an A-card, and their children would be B-cardholders. Gender also cut across the allocation of cards: Elizabeth Vlossak has pointed out that in August 1919 the French authorities specified that the child of an A-card father and a D-card mother was recognized as French, whereas the child of a D-card father and an A-card mother was not.[24]

The next stage in the process of making the region French was the expulsion of German nationals. This process started with Germans who had lost their jobs and were identified as potential troublemakers, and moved on to employed Germans who were targeted in order to create jobs for unemployed Alsatians. This wave also saw the expulsion of known or suspected troublemakers, and many prostitutes, black marketeers, and beggars received orders to leave the region.[25] The *épuration* then gave way to the final stage of the process, and from early 1919 the focus shifted to the indigenous population in a series of trials known as the *commissions de triage*. As this period fell before the ratification of the Treaty of Versailles in June 1919, Alsace and the Moselle were still being governed by a civil-military administration responsible to the War Ministry. Consequently, the commissions

---

[22] Irmgard Grünewald, *Die Elsass-Lothringer im Reich, 1918–1933* (Frankfurt, 1984), p. 29.

[23] Carolyn Grohmann, 'From Lothringen to Lorraine: Expulsion and Voluntary Repatriation', *Diplomacy and Statecraft*, 16 (2005), pp. 571–87, p. 573.

[24] Vlossak, *Marianne or Germania?* p. 214.

[25] Harvey, 'Lost Children or Enemy Aliens?'; Carolyn Grohmann, 'From Lothringen to Lorraine', p. 576.

established in each district took on a decidedly military character, not least as they were headed by an officer appointed by the commanding general. Each commission's decision was reviewed by a general, who passed it on to a *triage* review commission that could uphold or reverse the judgement, before it was passed to the commanding general for the final decision, and the accused were unable to bring legal representation.

Guidelines issued in January 1919 stated that the superior officer at the head of the commission should have some knowledge of legal procedure and at least a basic understanding of German or Alsatian. In practice, however, it was difficult to find officers who met these criteria amongst the French officer corps and to transfer them to Alsace before demobilization. As a result, few of the presiding officers spoke German and even fewer had legal training. Among the French officers who did meet the criteria of knowledge of German or Alsatian were a number of members of Alsace's industrialist families; some came from family branches that had opted for France in 1871, others had chosen to fight in the French army in 1914, but all retained links to the region. Contemporary observers from the Socialist Party drew a link between the presence of members of Alsace's leading industrial families on the commissions and the disproportionate number of labour leaders who were targeted in the first trials.[26]

Alongside labour leaders, the initial defendants included civil servants and other Alsatians who had worked for the German administration; Alsatians who had been German 'cultural mediators', whether as teachers, pastors, or priests; and large numbers who had been denounced by their neighbours. The instructions failed to specify who should be a suspect, what kind of accusation merited investigation, and what constituted acceptable evidence. So the commissions frequently worked on the basis of rumours and denunciations, many of which made vague statements concerning '*boche*' sensibilities.[27] The commissions had been established to deal with pro-German Alsatians and Mosellans, but a number of German nationals found themselves in front of the commissions charged with Germanophily. This reflected the lack of communication between Paris and the commissions, but it also reveals the blurring of boundaries in borderland society, as Germans became the object of denunciation for loyalty to Germany alongside their Alsatian neighbours.

What these denunciations reveal is the impact of the experience of war and return to France on the Alsatian social fabric. Society turned in upon itself as businessmen denounced their competitors, tenants denounced their landlords, and neighbours and families denounced each other. Schoolteacher Philippe Husser described his colleague Mme Wendling as a 'victim of war', hounded to death by the *Souvenir Français* campaign against her as a supposed 'Germanophile' when she had 'merely done her duty' as a teacher in an Alsatian primary school.[28] Many of the grudges and feuds behind these denunciations predated the outbreak of war

[26] ADBR 121AL 552 Commissaire Spécial de Police to Commissaire de la République, Colmar, report on speech by Edouard Richard at meeting of the Haut-Rhin Socialist Party, Colmar, 7 November 1919.

[27] ADBR 121 899-900-901-903.   [28] Husser, *Un Instituteur Alsacien*, p. 195.

in 1914, but they had been amplified by the experience of wartime shortages and repression and the uncertainty that followed the return to France. As rumours spread that the identity cards represented an attempt to establish who was to be expelled from the region, many Alsatians sought to assert their own patriotic French credentials by denouncing others. Thus denunciations were often signed 'un bon Français', or made reference to the author's 'A-card' status. That so many would do so is an indication that even those with the coveted A-card did not feel secure of their position within France, and suggests that denouncing others appeared to offer a means to assert the patriotism of the denouncer. As Tara Zahra has pointed out, the 'many denunciations and appeals to be reclassified that flooded state offices in Alsace in 1918 reflected both the ambiguity of national loyalties in this borderland region, and the ambiguity of the very concept of nation in Europe's most celebrated nation-state'.[29]

Not everyone who left Alsace after 1918 was forced to leave. Some of the departing Germans and Alsatians had opted for voluntary repatriation as many German civil servants, politicians, schoolteachers, local administrators, railway workers, bureaucrats, university lecturers, pastors, and priests left Alsace hoping for a better professional and personal life in the Weimar Republic. Voluntary departure was a complex process which required an individual to produce identity papers, a certificate of nationality, a receipt to confirm that all taxes were up to date, and a reference from the relevant mayor for examination by the Repatriation Bureau. Once permission had been granted, applicants were given precise details on when and where to present themselves for their departure. Of course, it is possible to question how far 'voluntary repatriation' can accurately be described as voluntary given the pressures placed upon nationally or politically suspect individuals, which included the poor rate of currency exchange, lack of employment, denunciation, arrest, police enquiries, threat of imprisonment, and fear of violence from neighbours. In such circumstances, many indigenous Alsatians and Mosellans felt that they had no choice other than to leave the region.

Moreover, the same restrictions were placed upon the voluntary repatriates as were placed on the expellees; both had limits upon the amount of luggage and money that they could carry and both faced the sequestration and liquidation of any property that they left behind. Conditions on the journey were poor for all passengers, and accounts describe some trains taking thirty-six hours to complete the four-mile journey from Strasbourg to Kehl, with children contracting illnesses and women reporting ill treatment.[30] Others described the local population lining the track to bid farewell to the trains by shouting insults, or occasionally throwing stones or horse dung.[31] The expellees and voluntary repatriates all arrived in the Weimar Republic as refugees without money or accommodation, to be greeted by the chaos and disarray caused by defeat and the collapse of the imperial system.

[29] Tara Zahra, 'The Minority Problem: National Classification in the French and Czechoslovak Borderlands', *Contemporary European History*, 17 (2008), pp. 137–65, p. 158.

[30] Grohmann, 'From Lothringen to Lorraine', p. 578.

[31] Irmgard Grünewald, *Die Elsass-Lothringer im Reich, 1918–1933* (Frankfurt, 1984), p. 23.

Around 80,000 Germans left the two Alsatian departments after 1918, with over two-thirds of this figure from the Bas-Rhin.[32] Approximately 70,000 left the Moselle.[33] This was, however, only half of the total number of Germans resident in the former Reichsland in November 1918. Of those who remained, 95,893 applied for naturalization (as allowed by Article 79 of the Treaty of Versailles), and the French government accepted 77,064 of these applications.[34] Many of these newly naturalized French citizens had married Alsatians or Mosellans, while others worked in specialized occupations such as on the railways or tramways. The government had assumed that the lengthy process involved in applying for naturalization would weed out any Germans who were staying for reasons other than attachment to France, but concern lingered over those who were allowed to remain. In communication with the Mayor of Strasbourg Jacques Peirotes in 1922, Henri Borromé, the newly appointed Prefect of the Bas-Rhin, suggested that these naturalized Frenchmen should not be considered full French citizens. Borromé reminded Peirotes that nationality should be mentioned on all *livrets de famille*, to ensure that those who married in Strasbourg were not able to go to the rest of France and 'pass themselves off as true Frenchmen'. Peirotes refused for procedural reasons, but that Borromé would ask is indicative of broader concern about the continued presence of Germans in the recovered departments and their potential impact across France.[35]

Problems also arose for Alsatians who had married Germans. The French authorities allowed an exception to French nationality laws, which stipulated that a woman must take her husband's nationality on marriage, to allow Alsatian women to receive French nationality even if their husbands had been born in Germany. But eligible Alsatian women had to apply for this dispensation before 1921, and even if they received it, with their husbands facing problems finding work, many of these newly French Alsatian women faced financial hardship, and a number left the region after 1918.

This was a fate shared by some Alsatian couples. Mulhouse schoolteacher Philippe Husser's eldest daughter Marie had married a native of the Haut-Rhin commune of Riquewihr named Fritz Bronner in August 1920. After Alsace's return to France, Bronner studied for a doctorate in history at the University of Frankfurt and became an active member of the group of Alsatians and Lorrainers in Germany who attempted to keep alive the idea of a German Alsace-Lorraine. Husser's sadness at his separation from his grandchild Anne-Marie (born in 1928) is a constant theme in his diaries until the Bronners' return to Alsace in 1940, after its annexation into Hitler's Germany.[36] Other women had planned to marry German-born men before the armistice and, on going ahead with these plans, they were

---

[32] Marcel Koch, 'Les Mouvements de la Population', in Comité alsacien d'études et d'informations, *L'Alsace depuis son retour à la France*, 3 vols, vol. 1 (Strasbourg, 1932), p. 338.

[33] David Allen Harvey, 'Lost Children or Enemy Aliens?' pp. 550–1.

[34] Grohmann, 'From Lothringen to Lorraine', p. 583.

[35] ADBR 286D 174 LIVRETS DE FAMILLE; Préfet du Bas-Rhin to M. le Maire de Strasbourg, Strasbourg, April 1922; Préfet du Bas-Rhin to M. le Maire de Strasbourg, Strasbourg, 8 June 1922.

[36] Husser, *Un Instituteur Alsacien*, pp. 287, 301.

granted German nationality (the exception was made only for those who had married before 1918). The result for these couples was financial hardship, as both husband and wife found it difficult to find work. If the marriages broke down, the women then faced a long battle to win back French nationality, and doing so was crucial if they were to find work and support themselves.[37]

Between November 1918 and their eventual abolition in October 1919, the commissions processed over 11,000 cases.[38] Laird Boswell's research on north-eastern Alsace has revealed that almost half of the cases were dismissed for lack of evidence.[39] Nevertheless, appearing before the commissions was a trauma which few found easy to forget, and for those who were found guilty and punished, whether by being placed under surveillance, sent on a spell of exile in the French interior, or expelled to Germany, the commissions ruined lives. They also caused untold damage to the reputation of the new French regime. Within four months of the return to French rule, reports on public opinion in the Bas-Rhin described their negative impact upon morale and highlighted the widespread criticism of the commissions. 'People discuss not only the [opportunism] of these expulsions, but also their legality. The Alsatians consider themselves to be French, and do not understand how such measures can be taken against their compatriots when they would not be possible against French citizens from other regions', reported the High Commissioner for Upper Alsace in March 1919.[40]

These comparisons extended not only to the rest of France, but also to the rest of Europe. As contemporary observers pointed out, French policy in the recovered departments stood in stark contrast to the policies that the Allied great powers insisted upon from the new nations in central and eastern Europe. The suggestion of the Lithuanian delegate to the League of Nations that all League members should be required to respect the same standards of minority rights imposed on eastern Europe's new nation states was brushed away by the French representative, Henry de Jouvenel, who informed him that France 'has no minorities. To find minorities in France, they would have to be created in the imagination.' When a Romanian delegate pointed to the linguistic and ethnic minorities dotted around western Europe on ethnographic maps, he was told that 'minorities only exist where there is a treaty'.[41] Of course, no such treaty was applied to the population of Alsace.

Tara Zahra has compared French policy in Alsace with the situation in Czechoslovakia, and shown that the minority rights protection granted to the German minority meant that the new Czechoslovak state attempted to label citizens from

[37] ADBR 286D 174 Réintégrations 1933–1935. Papers held in the Departmental Archives of the Bas-Rhin describe the problems faced by Mme Henize (née Hild), who was granted German nationality following her marriage to a German man. After their divorce, she moved to Dossenheim but was still counted as a foreigner and so had to pay for a foreign identity card and was unable to undertake paid work. Another woman, Mme Vogel (née Tock), had to wait three years before she was restored to French nationality following her divorce.

[38] Fischer, *Alsace to the Alsatians?* p. 132.

[39] Boswell, 'From Liberation to Purge Trials in the "Mythic Provinces"'.

[40] AN AJ30 170 Rapport Hebdomadaire du Commissaire de la République de Haute Alsace, Semaine du 9 au 16 Mars 1919.

[41] C. A. Macartney, *National States and National Minorities* (London, 1934), p. 482.

its bilingual border regions as Czech in order to demonstrate a Czech majority and create a sense of legitimacy as a nation state, while hundreds of Germans in these areas demanded recognition as members of the German minority, with the associated access to German schools and cultural associations. This stood in marked contrast to what happened in Alsace, where Alsatians labelled as members of the German minority fought to be included in the French majority by trying to swap lesser cards for A-cards, defending themselves at the commissions, or denouncing their neighbours. As Zahra has stressed, France was able to take a different stance on its minority populations from that adopted by the new nations in the east as a result of international hierarchies, which positioned France as a model of national unity and democracy, and which treated the 'minority problem' as restricted to central and eastern Europe.[42] But in east and west, the minorities themselves responded by challenging the classifications applied to them, strategically invoking culture, descent, and will as they demanded to be reclassified.

The commissions remained a source of grievance throughout the 1920s, and the association for the victims of the *commissions de triage* consistently demanded revision of the decisions reached at the trials. They met with some success and a number of the commissions' decisions were reversed, allowing certain dismissed civil servants to reclaim their jobs in the 1920s.[43] However, as economic reintegration faltered in the first decade after return to France, financial reasons meant that it was simply impossible to re-employ all the dismissed *fonctionnaires*, as the General Service for Alsace-Lorraine made plain.[44] In 1928 the *conseil général* of the Haut-Rhin demanded a review of the commissions' verdicts, but the Ministry of Justice responded that nothing could be done. Meanwhile, it was a regular topic at the parliamentary commission for Alsace-Lorraine, where the region's deputies complained not only about the triage commissions but also about the expulsion of German nationals.[45] In 1929 the Catholic deputy Marcel Stürmel proposed a bill to the Chamber that granted French citizens the right to appeal the commissions' verdicts and request compensation. The bill was referred to the Commission for Alsace-Lorraine and then shelved. Stürmel proposed the same bill in June 1936, but it met with an identical fate. By the late 1920s, Paris's priorities had shifted away from the classification of the borderland population.

Laird Boswell's work on the *commissions de triage* treats them as a means to illuminate not only the renegotiation of Frenchness that followed Alsace's return to France, but also the differences between French and German models of citizenship. Boswell builds upon work that challenges the idea that there is a neat dichotomy between France's civic, voluntarist concept of citizenship and Germany's ethnic

[42] Zahra, 'The "Minority Problem" and National Classification', p. 163.
[43] AMVES 125Z 40 Letter from Georges Bonnet (Présidence du Conseil, Service Général d'Alsace et de Lorraine) to Jacques Peirotes, Paris, 29 May 1925.
[44] AMVES 125Z 40 Letter from Georges Bonnet (Présidence du Conseil, Service Général d'Alsace et de Lorraine) to Jacques Peirotes, Paris, 29 May 1925.
[45] AN C14640 Commission d'Alsace-Lorraine, Séance, 18 March 1920. Seltz complained about the expulsion of 200 Germans from Strasbourg; C14877 Commission d'Alsace-Lorraine, Séance, 25 June 1931; C14982 Commission d'Alsace-Lorraine, Séance, 6 July 1932; Commission d'Alsace-Lorraine, Séance, December 1932.

conception, based upon ethnicity, language, and blood ties.[46] This juxtaposition is based, in part, on citizenship legislation in the two countries: in France the law of 1889 recognized the principle of *jus soli*, according to which all persons born on French territory become French citizens (regardless of ethnicity), while the 1913 German citizenship law maintained the principle of *jus sanguinis*, according to which all ethnic Germans, even those born and raised outside German territory, retained German citizenship, but the children of immigrants born in Germany did not. As we have seen, the model is also based upon the debates over Alsace that followed the region's 1871 annexation, when the analyses of Theodor Mommsen, Numa Fustel de Coulanges, Ernest Renan, and Heinrich von Treitschke played no small role in defining these divergent understandings of nationality.[47]

Moreover, just as Alsace played a role in the establishment of these positions, so it played an important part in challenging this dichotomy; through the Treaty of Frankfurt the German government offered Alsatians choice in their national attachment by allowing them to opt for France (although how far this represented a genuine option for most Alsatians is debatable), and the *commissions de triage* and identity cards introduced by France abandoned the principle of *jus soli* upon which citizenship in the Republic was supposedly based in favour of an increasingly racial one. This drew upon developments in the first fifty years of the Third Republic, when the expansion of France's overseas empire in the 1880s developed ideologies of racial inferiority that justified the exclusion from citizenship of whole categories of people.[48] The racial underpinnings of colonialism then made it easier for the extreme right to promote a more radicalized anti-Semitism, particularly during the Dreyfus Affair. This racial idea of citizenship persisted throughout the interwar years, and became increasingly important in marking the boundaries of citizenship when France's economic dependence on immigrants troubled those defenders of a racially conceived 'true France', and writers including Charles Lambert, Jean Pluyette, and Georges Mauco argued for an immigration policy based on racial selection.[49]

Racial ideas of citizenship were also increasingly employed with regard to Alsace. Camille Jullian of the Collège de France wrote that the Alsatian 'race' was Gallic rather than Germanic, while the familial metaphors of 'lost daughters' employed to describe the lost provinces after 1871 reflected an emphasis on biological links between Alsace and France.[50] The Alsatian population borrowed this rhetoric and used the language of race to describe itself; Socialist leader Jacques Peirotes stated that 'the first populations of the left bank of the Rhine were Celtic, i.e. the same race as almost all the inhabitants of Gallic soil, while those on the other side of the

---

[46] Boswell, 'From Liberation to Purge Trials in the "Mythic Provinces"'.

[47] See Rogers Brubaker, *Citizenship and Nationhood in France and Germany* (Cambridge, MA, 1992).

[48] Herrick Chapman and Laura L. Frader, 'Introduction', in *Race in France: Interdisciplinary Perspectives on the Politics of Difference*, p. 5.

[49] Charles Lambert, *La France et ses étrangers* (Paris, 1928); Jean Pluyette, *La Doctrine des races et la sélection de l'immigration en France* (Paris, 1930); Georges Mauco, *Les Etrangers en France. Leur rôle dans l'activité économique* (Paris, 1932).

[50] Camille Jullian, *Le Rhin Gaulois: le Rhin français* (Paris, 1915).

Rhine were Germanic'.[51] As Boswell has argued, this pointed to profound tensions between competing visions of nationhood in France; on the one hand, the republican concept based upon voluntary adhesion to the nation, on the other, the racialized understanding in evidence during the *épuration*.[52] Indeed, ethnic and cultural considerations merged in the process, and thus it was possible to receive an A-card but still be denounced and find oneself before the commissions.

In this sense, the commissions reveal not only the renegotiation of nationhood triggered by the return of Alsace to France, but also the fractures that tore apart the very fabric of Alsatian society. Envy of A-cardholders was rife, and some A-cardholders fanned the flames of popular discontent by suggesting that their status merited privileges beyond those allowed by the system, for example complaining that holders of lesser cards should make way for them in queues. Thus the *épuration* of 1918–19 is striking in terms of the level of grass-roots participation, but also as a case that reveals how Alsatians articulated their understanding of their place within the French nation. Both France and Germany demonstrated different understandings of borderland society from that on display in Alsace; for the Alsatian population contact with Germany bred a greater understanding of difference, and many letters of denunciation were able to give examples not just of why their author was French, but also of how they were *not* German. Nevertheless, the context of return meant that there was little room for ambiguity in the eyes of the French government, and such question marks over the loyalties of the Alsatian population led to closer attempts to define and close off the boundaries of the national community. The process of determining who was French would find parallels in the next steps of reintegration: establishing *what* was French in terms of administration and legislation.

ADMINISTRATION

The Third Republic was based upon the principle of centralized government, but since 1871 Alsace's administrative institutions had been regional within the structures of the German Empire. The resulting discussions over how to reconcile the two posed important questions about the place of centralism in the Third Republic. But any decisions were postponed between the armistice of November 1918 and the ratification of the peace treaty in June 1919, as during this period Alsace and annexed Lorraine were provisionally placed under military occupation, with overall control by the Premier and Minister of War.[53] The initial changes that France introduced were tempered by the concern that further change may be necessary

---

[51] AMVES Fonds Peirotes 125Z 44 Discours de Jacques Peirotes sur l'histoire du mouvement politique en Alsace à la Société des Alsaciens-Lorrains habitant à l'Auvergne (ND); 286D 336 *Die Freie Presse*, 5 October 1920.

[52] Boswell, 'From Liberation to Purge Trials in the "Mythic Provinces"', p. 145.

[53] ADBR, 121AL 204 Projet de loi relatif au régime transitoire de l'Alsace et de la Lorraine. Exposé des motifs, 1919.

after the conclusion of discussions at Versailles.[54] The correspondence of the temporary administration is testament to the hurried character of the initial transfer from German to French rule; in January 1919 Jules Jeanneney, the Undersecretary of State for War, requested that French officials stop using German forms, as this practice was creating confusion and embarrassment.[55]

In November 1918 Premier Georges Clemenceau appointed three commissioners to manage integration in the districts of Lower Alsace, Upper Alsace, and Lorraine, with Georges Maringer, the commissioner for Lower Alsace, charged with responsibility for matters that concerned all three districts. The activity of the commissioners was overseen by two newly created bodies—the General Service for Alsace-Lorraine and the Superior Council for Alsace and Lorraine—which took responsibility for centralizing the administration. Both the General Service and the Superior Council were under the ultimate control of Clemenceau, who delegated all power to Jules Jeanneney, Maringer's brother-in-law and a Radical politician with a reputation for strident anti-clericalism.[56] Hopes that the three commissioners would function in a similar way to the departmental prefects in the rest of France were rapidly dashed, however, and their mismanagement of regional affairs provoked widespread criticism within the recovered departments. Their reception was no better in the corridors of power; President Poincaré was concerned that they were alienating local opinion, while Premier Clemenceau expressed frustration that the commissioners were not providing sufficient information on the local situation.[57]

Upon ratification of the Versailles treaty, the French government first dismantled 'Alsace-Lorraine' (and its association with Germany which had created it) by separating the Reichsland into three departments. This was completed on 17 November 1919, when the two districts of Alsace regained their pre-1871 labels and became the departments of the Bas-Rhin and the Haut-Rhin. The annexed section of Lorraine, which did not correspond to a pre-1871 department, was named the Moselle. Nevertheless, the moniker Alsace-Lorraine remained in use in Paris and in the recovered departments. Questions over how far Alsace and the Moselle should remain connected continued in discussions over the reintegration of the three departments, particularly in the Moselle, where resentment at being treated as the 'junior partner' in Alsace-Lorraine proved a driving force in local politics.[58] Administratively,

[54] ADBR, 121AL 204 Commissaire Général de la République to Président du Conseil, Strasbourg, 7 April 1919.

[55] ADBR, 121AL 33 Sous-secrétaire d'Etat à la Présidence du Conseil to MM. le Haut Commissaire de la République, les Commissaires de la République et les Inspecteurs Généraux, Paris, 29 January 1919.

[56] AMVES 113Z 48 Proposition de loi relative à l'organisation d'une région alsacienne, annexe au procès verbal de la séance du 1 juin 1934.

[57] ADBR, 121AL 204 Georges Clemenceau to Commissaires de la République, Paris, 14 February 1919; J. V. Keiger, *Raymond Poincaré* (Cambridge, 1997), p. 251.

[58] AMVES, 113Z 29 Séance du Conseil Consultatif, 19 December 1923, speech by Abbé Muller. On the Moselle's attitudes towards Alsace, see Alison Carrol and Louisa Zanoun, 'The View from the Border. A Comparative Study of Autonomism in Alsace and the Moselle, 1918–1929', *European Review of History*, 18:4 (2011), pp. 465–86. The reintegration of the Moselle adopted a different course from that of Alsace—see Carolyn Grohmann, 'Problems of Reintegrating Annexed Lorraine into France, 1918–1925' (University of Stirling, unpublished PhD thesis, 2000).

however, with Alsace-Lorraine broken up, the new government could turn to the institutions that were to govern the recovered departments.

In March 1919 Clemenceau oversaw the creation of a General Commission of the Republic in Strasbourg. This body was headed by a General Commissioner, answerable first to the Minister of War and then to the Premier. Three prefects worked under the Commissioner, who maintained close links with Paris through daily reports.[59] The first General Commissioner was Alexandre Millerand, a politician with a ministerial career dating back to 1899 and a sufficiently high profile to reassure regional politicians that Paris was taking the question of Alsace-Lorraine seriously.[60] Significantly, Millerand repeated Joffre's promise, telling an audience in Metz in September 1920, 'The values, customs and traditions, which you treasure so much, and which France, when setting foot on Alsatian land in 1914 solemnly promised by the mouth of its representatives to respect, should not only be undisturbed, but should flourish.'[61]

The creation of the Commission allowed smoother running of Alsatian administrative affairs. Crucially, it was based in Strasbourg rather than Paris, which increased efficiency, and placed the Commissioner in closer contact with the local population. This move proved popular in Alsace.[62] Nevertheless, confusion continued in Paris, and given the number of 'General Commissioners' in other ministries, it was decided that the body would adopt the title 'General Commissioner of Alsace and Lorraine' in its correspondence with the capital.[63] Up until the elections of November 1919, Alsace and the Moselle were governed in this way, with no political representation in the French parliament.

In May 1919, the Superior Council was transferred from Paris to Strasbourg to work alongside the General Commission. Again, this move improved efficiency, while sending a powerful signal that the government was prepared to consider regional administration. This impression was compounded in October 1919, when it was confirmed that the General Commission would remain in Strasbourg, albeit provisionally. Further regional administration was granted when the government created three departmental councils and a regional council to discuss local affairs. In September 1920, the Superior Council was replaced by the Consultative Council for Alsace and Lorraine, with councillors made up of members of the departmental councils and Alsatian and Mosellan members of the National Assembly. Nevertheless, the fact that the council's members were appointed rather than elected provoked criticism.[64]

In 1920, the election of the Conservative government of the *Bloc national* triggered the resignation of Georges Clemenceau, and Millerand left Alsace to

---

[59] ADBR, 121AL 205 Questionnaire No.2 de M. le Président de la Commission d'Alsace et Lorraine du Sénat.

[60] Raoul Persil, *Alexandre Millerand 1859–1943* (Paris, 1949); Marjorie Milbank Farrar, *Principled Pragmatist. The Political Career of Alexandre Millerand* (Oxford, 1991).

[61] Cited in Genevieve Baas, *Le malaise alsacien, 1919–1924* (Strasbourg, 1972), p. 119.

[62] E. Wetterlé, 'Droit national et droit local', *Le Nouveau Rhin Français*, 7 October 1919.

[63] ADBR, 121AL 199 Chef de Bataillon, Note pour le Commissaire Général, Paris, 9 June 1919.

[64] E. Wetterlé, 'Droit national et droit local', *Le Nouveau Rhin Français*, 7 October 1919.

assume the premiership. During his period in office Millerand had not only created a framework which improved the administration of the three departments, but had also restored confidence in the French government by reassuring the local population that France did not seek to remove local privileges or replace Alsatian laws with French.[65] He was equally popular amongst Alsace's politicians and established good relations with representatives of parties across the political spectrum.[66] Millerand's replacement was Gabriel Alapetite, a high-ranking civil servant who proved unable to command the political influence or popularity that Millerand had enjoyed.[67]

Under Alapetite, a series of institutional moves signalled the gradual transfer of administrative authority away from Alsace; between 1920 and 1922 control over the railways, justice, finance, mining, postal and telegraph services, and roads were all handed to Paris.[68] Alapetite himself stressed that such transfers were more symbolic than real, arguing that they had been carried out too hastily and had left the ministries concerned reliant on the General Commission.[69] Nevertheless, Alapetite's management of Alsatian affairs came under fire from the region's politicians and damaged the institution of the General Commission, which was criticized by all sides: for the Catholic UPR, the transfer of authority to Paris had reduced the efficiency of regional administration; for the Communist PCF, it was one manifestation of broader French policy which reduced Alsace to the status of a 'colony'; and in the eyes of the Radicals and the Socialists it represented an unpleasant and expensive hangover from the years of German rule, with the position of General Commissioner akin to that of *Statthalter*.[70] More significantly, it had slowed down administrative reintegration and hampered the provinces' attachment to France.[71]

Discussions over the future of the General Commission continued throughout the early 1920s, even though it had been envisioned as a temporary solution to the initial problems of reintegration.[72] In 1923 Alapetite stressed that some form of transitional body was still necessary, and he argued that the dissolution of the General Commission would need to be accompanied by the creation of an alternative administrative institution.[73] After further discussion, Premier Raymond

[65] AN 470AP/44 Fonds Millerand. Discours prononcé à la Première Assemblée de l'Office général des assurances sociales, le 5 mai 1919; see also *Le Temps*, 7 October 1919.

[66] AN 470AP/44, Fonds Millerand, Les adieux à M. Millerand à l'Alsace et à la Lorraine, du correspondent du petit journal.

[67] ADBR 121AL 1, Discours de M. Oberkirch, Président du Conseil General du Bas-Rhin au banquet offert par le Conseil Général à M. Alapetite et M. Borromée, 31 May 1924.

[68] Répertoire numérique détaillé du fonds du Commissariat Général de la République 1918–1925 par Guy de Lavareille sous la direction de François-Jacques Himly (Strasbourg, 1980), p. 3.

[69] ADBR 121AL 207, Commissaire Général de la République to Garde des Sceaux, Strasbourg, January 1923.

[70] On the views of the UPR, see Scheer's speech to the Chambre des Députés, Journal Officiel, Séance du 25 May 1925, p. 2331.

[71] AN AJ30 173 Session of the Conseil Consultatif, 2 October 1922.

[72] AMVES 113Z 29 Jean Kuntzingen to abbé Muller, Strasbourg, 6 June 1921.

[73] ADBR 121AL 207 Commissaire Général de la République to Garde des Sceaux, Strasbourg, January 1923.

Poincaré announced that the Commission would be dissolved in July 1924, but opposition in Alsace and indecision amongst administrators in Paris thwarted the plans. With opinion divided in Strasbourg and Paris, and with no suitable alternative in sight, the Commission endured until 1925. Its dissolution finally came as a result of the 1924 election of the centre-left *Cartel des gauches* government. The new Premier, Radical Edouard Herriot, set about dismantling the internal policies of the *Bloc National* by reinstating railway workers sacked for striking in 1920, granting civil servants the right to unionize, offering an amnesty to wartime pacifists accused of relations with the enemy, and withdrawing the ambassador from the Vatican.[74] In terms of Alsace and the Moselle, he announced an end to concessions to the departments' particular status.

Herriot selected Strasbourg Socialist deputy Georges Weill to be his special advisor on Alsatian issues. Weill had served as SPD deputy for Metz in the Reichstag between 1912 and 1915, and had long-standing links to France and the SFIO, having served as editor of *Le Mouvement Socialiste* in Paris between 1900 and 1901. He had been present in the Café du Croissant when SFIO leader Jean Jaurès was assassinated in July 1914, and on the outbreak of war his decision to join the French army led to him being stripped of his German citizenship. After the return to France he was elected to the General Council of the Bas-Rhin in 1919 and became SFIO deputy for Strasbourg-Campagne in 1924. Weill's presence meant that all of the *Cartel*'s plans for the region bore the stamp of the Socialist Party, which had stressed since 1918 that maintaining regional administrative authority in Alsace and the Moselle would contravene the principles of unity which had been the basis of French policy over centuries, and argued for the introduction of French administrative institutions in the recovered departments.[75] Weill's presence compounded the worries of the region's right. For the Catholic press, Herriot's parliamentary speeches on the recovered departments had already represented a 'declaration of war against the believers of Alsace-Lorraine', and Weill's appointment signalled a worrying move towards centralization.[76] Weill's actions added to their concerns; one of his first moves was to hasten the dissolution of the General Commission. Alapetite resigned in July 1924 and his replacement, Henri Cacaud, was named 'Interim Commissioner'. Rather than taking up management of regional affairs as his predecessors had done, Cacaud oversaw the dissolution of the Commission.

Amongst the Alsatian population, fears about the extent and implications of Herriot's proposed centralization provided a focus for the dissatisfaction that had developed since the return to France. But, in spite of local resistance, the process of accelerated centralization continued. According to Weill's 1924 decree on Alsatian reintegration, any regional administrative sections that had not been transferred to their respective ministries by 1925 were to be passed to a General Directorate,

[74] Rod Kedward, *La Vie en Bleu. France and the French since 1900* (London, 2005), p. 134.
[75] AMVES 125Z 18 Rapport fait au nom de la commission chargée d'examiner le projet de loi portent réorganisation du régime administratif des départements 68, 67 et 57 par Georges Weill.
[76] ADBR 121 AL 100 Note sur la presse, *Volksbote*, 'Gabriel Alapetite' par Charles Pfleger, 31 August 1924.

based in Paris, although several important sections kept their Strasbourg bases, including churches and education. The Directorate's main function was the administration of the three departments, and throughout its existence it was headed by civil servant Paul Valot. Like the General Commission, the General Directorate was intended to be a temporary solution. This kept the issue of administrative reintegration alive; in 1926 the departmental council of the Bas-Rhin described it as the 'most pressing' of all the problems facing the Alsatian population.[77] Later that year, a group of Catholic deputies demanded regional administrative autonomy for Alsace and the Moselle as a precursor to national decentralization.[78] Despite being envisioned as an interim solution, and in spite of a brief suppression in 1935–6, the Directorate remained in place in 1939.[79]

For many in Alsace, and particularly amongst the Conservative and Catholic right, administrative decentralization would allow officials to respond more effectively to local needs by placing them in close contact with local populations.[80] This would facilitate greater efficiency and encourage more sensitive responses to local problems. These principles formed the basis of a 1921 law, proposed by parliamentary deputies from the Alsatian Conservative and Catholic right with the support of Conservatives from across France. This law proposed greater autonomy for mayors and municipal councils, and the transfer of powers enjoyed by the Prefect and departmental councils to sub-Prefects and borough councils.[81] Such principles also lay at the heart of a law proposed by Alsatian Catholic deputies thirteen years later, which similarly stressed regional, rather than departmental, administration. Unlike the earlier law, however, the 1934 proposal restricted its scope to Alsace.[82] This was a significant departure from the previous demand, which presented Alsace as a model for the rest of France.[83] Having failed to secure national reform, the proposed law would at least allow administrative reorganization in the province. Again, hopes for reform were to be frustrated. And the move from a proposal for national change to regional change is reflective of a growing focus upon the region as reintegration proved ever more problematic, and the continued existence of temporary institutions left all sides feeling that their arguments were falling upon deaf ears.

[77] ADBR 286D 348 Préfet du Bas-Rhin to Garde des Sceaux, Ministère de la Justice, 6 May 1926.
[78] AMVES 125Z 20 Proposition de résolution, 6 August 1926.
[79] When the Directorate was reconstituted in 1936, Alsatian deputies proposed that it be based in Strasbourg. This was refused by the government, and by the Mosellan senator Stuhl, who stated that the Moselle did not wish to return to the days of dependency upon Strasbourg. Gustave Mary, 'L'evolution politique depuis 1932', Comité alsacien d'études et d'informations, *L'Alsace depuis son retour à la France. Premier supplément: Vie politique administrative et sociale; Vie intellectuelle; artistique et spirituelle; Vie économique* (Strasbourg, 1937), p. 28.
[80] AMVES 113Z 29 Séance du Conseil Consultatif, 19 December 1923, speech by abbé Muller.
[81] ADBR 121AL 206 Chambre des députés, Session de 1921, annexe au procès-verbal de la 2 séance du 3 juin 1921 Proposition de résolution concernant la reforme administrative.
[82] AMVES 113Z48 Proposition de loi relative à l'organisation d'une région alsacienne, annexe au procès verbal de la séance du 1 juin 1934.
[83] AMVES 113Z 29 Séance du Conseil Consultatif, 19 December 1923, speech by abbé Muller; Wetterlé, droit national et droit local.

While there was diversity in Alsatian visions of the region's future administration, the proposals from Alsace were united in their consideration of how to best position Alsace within France, and in their use of ideas about German administration to inform their positions. As with the case of citizenship, greater contact bred a clearer understanding of difference. The range of views from Alsace, as well as in Paris, ensured that reintegration did not take the form of a straightforward interaction between centre and periphery; rather, it is better understood as a complex struggle, involving a number of actors. The stakes were high: not only were French ideas shaped by the notion of the sacrifices undertaken to secure the return of Alsace during the First World War, but Alsatian discontent appeared to threaten the centrality and, as a result, the very unity of the French nation.[84] As Minister of Justice Pierre Laval explained, 'Everyone is allowed to criticise those in power; all attacks are permitted.... But there is one terrain on which no discussion is allowed: that of national unity.'[85] This meant that when making proposals for future administration, individuals in Alsace were keen to present their ideas as Alsatian rather than German.

[margin, handwritten: "create contact bred a clearer understanding of difference"]

LEGISLATION

[handwritten above heading: terminology slip up. Alsace region would be better? As technically at this stage is in France. Or should have said 'Paris', as same done throughout]

[left margin, handwritten: national idea of history...]

In 1918 Alsace had a patchwork of laws, with national and local laws introduced before 1870, and national and local laws instituted under German rule, all legislating for different aspects of life. As the Third Republic had been built upon the principle of legal as well as administrative uniformity, this situation raised the important question of whether a French region could maintain its own distinct, legislative systems. War and the return to France complicated the situation further, as pressing day-to-day problems required emergency legislation and distorted the workings of the government. In the discussions over legal reintegration, many in Alsace and France looked to French history for the roots of Alsatian laws, and presented the region's legislative framework as a model for nationwide reform.

[right margin, handwritten: dilemma of centralised Third Republic]

During the seven-month period before the ratification of the Versailles Peace Treaty, the ushering in of legislation was not possible and the new government needed instead to rely on orders to administrate for urgent issues, such as the introduction of French currency and the establishment of the exchange rate. After June 1919, the institution of French legislation met with administrative delays as local *fonctionnaires* and municipal officials attempted to accustom themselves to the French legal system.[86] Moreover, the range of ideas about how to approach legislative reintegration meant that a consensus was difficult to reach. As a result, a piecemeal approach was adopted and the government set a limit of ten years for the introduction of all French laws into Alsace and the Moselle. But by 1934 this goal

[right margin, handwritten: piecemeal approach; delays]

---

[84] Marcel Nast, *Le Malaise Alsacien-Lorrain* (Paris, 1920).
[85] Jean-Paul Cointet, *Pierre Laval* (Paris, 1993), pp. 66–7.
[86] See ADBR 286D 44 Mayor of Schiltigheim to Préfet du Bas-Rhin, 30 March 1922.

was still far from reach and a subsequent law was passed in December 1934 prolonging the period of integration to 1945.

Part of the problem lay in the different expectations in Paris and Strasbourg. While administrators in Paris had assumed that all French legislation would be introduced into the recovered departments after 1918, this plan met with significant opposition in Alsace. Resistance to the wholesale introduction of French legislation centred on two points. First, some German laws had no equivalent in the French legal system, such as the laws on the post office or on pharmacists, where Alsatian legislation covered areas ignored by the French laws.[87] Second, certain aspects of German legislation offered greater advantages to the population than French law.[88] This was the case, local politicians argued, for social security, company law, property rights, and municipal laws.[89] In the early years of French rule, this argument found a powerful supporter in General Commissioner Alexandre Millerand, who took a particular interest in the region's social and welfare framework.[90] For Millerand, as for many of the region's politicians, legislation in Alsace was not German, but Alsatian, or in other words not foreign, but French.[91] Given the political impossibility of maintaining any attachment to Germany in the recovered departments, this relabelling was intended to allow the retention of aspects of regional legislation in Alsace after its return to French rule.[92]

In order to present Alsatian legislation as local, rather than German, regional politicians took pains to stress the deeper roots of regional laws in French history. For example, Socialist Mayor of Strasbourg Jacques Peirotes tied the municipal law to the Revolution of 1789, which granted communes greater autonomy. According to Peirotes, the law was then reversed by Napoleon, but reintroduced into Alsace-Lorraine after 1870 on the initiative of the local population.[93] Moreover, the law's inspiration lay in the same historic bases as the French municipal law, rendering it totally different from the legislation in force in the other federal German states.[94] The departmental council of the Bas-Rhin stressed that the local law was based 'on French communal administration and the law of... 1837', rather than on any

[87] ADBR 121AL 207 Directeur Régional des Postes et des Télégraphes to Commissaire Général de la République, Strasbourg, 29 November 1922; *Journal Officiel*, Séance du 25 May 1925, p. 2331.
[88] ADBR 121AL 207 Note to the Secrétaire Général, Strasbourg, 27 September 1922.
[89] AMVES 125Z 52 Discours de Jacques Peirotes; ADBR 121AL 207 Commissaire Général de la République to Garde des Sceaux, Strasbourg, January 1923.
[90] AN 470AP/44 Fonds Millerand, Discours prononcé à la Première Assemblée de l'Office général des assurances sociales, le 5 mai 1919; Alexandre Millerand, *Le retour de l'Alsace-Lorraine à la France* (Strasbourg, 1923), p. 70.
[91] AN 470AP/44 Journal officiel du 2 octobre 1919. Chambre des députés, Séance du 1 October 1919.
[92] The contrary view (that this legislation was not local but German, and that it was not superior to French laws) was taken by Marcel Nast, *Le Malaise Alsacien-Lorrain* (Paris, 1920), pp. 36, 47.
[93] AMVES 125Z 32 Discours de Jacques Peirotes, nd; AMVES 125Z 38 (nd) Exposé: 'La Loi Municipale d'Alsace-Lorraine du 6 June 1895' historique, grandes et petites communes- composition et fonctionnement des conseils municipaux, la municipalité, les employés municipaux, l'autonomie communale, le budget communal, l'activité économique des communes, conclusion.
[94] AMVES 125Z 38 (nd) Exposé: 'La Loi Municipale d'Alsace-Lorraine du 6 June. 1895'.

German initiative.[95] Such arguments were not always readily accepted in Paris, however, where many politicians, administrators, and academics were keen to ensure the introduction of the French legal system and avoid the risk of another region demanding separate legislation.[96]

Local politicians were particularly keen to retain municipal legislation, as they had an eye on its advantages over French municipal laws. The mayors of Strasbourg, Colmar, and Mulhouse stressed that, in comparison to the Alsatian legislation, the French law granted communes far less autonomy, particularly over their finances, and also allowed the Prefect more authority over the communal budget.[97] The independence conferred upon Alsatian communes, they argued, allowed them to participate in the local economy and generate extra income through municipal companies.[98] The Alsatian mayors also secured the support of mayors and municipal officials from towns across France in their efforts to retain their municipal legislation and to see it introduced across France.[99]

As with administration, the major controversy over legislation broke out after the 1924 election of the *Cartel des Gauches*. When Premier Herriot announced the government's intention to introduce 'the whole of the republican legislation into Alsace and Lorraine, while respecting the situation, and looking after the material and moral interests of the population', he made clear that this meant the separation of church and state.[100] This declaration provoked an immediate and vocal response from the region, where religious communities treated it as a betrayal of Joffre's promises at Thann. Spontaneous protests and demonstrations broke out across the three departments, and controversies over separation also spilled out beyond the borders of the region, where they intersected with widespread concerns about the maintenance of a French ambassador at the Vatican and broader perceptions of the Cartel's attack on religious life. In September 1924 the French cardinals published a letter protesting against Herriot's policy, and agitation on the issue broke out amongst Catholics and republicans across France.[101] Such protest was closely monitored and reported upon triumphantly by the Alsatian Catholic press.[102]

---

[95] ADBR 121AL 740 Conseil Général du Bas-Rhin, Session de Septembre 1921. Extrait du procès verbal des délibérations, Séance du 23 septembre 1921.

[96] ADBR 121AL 207 Introduction des Lois Françaises en France. Conférence faite le 1er mai 1922 par M. Albert Chéron; Marcel Nast, *Le Malaise Alsacien-Lorrain* (Paris, 1920), p. 49.

[97] AMVES 204MW 16 Jacques Peirotes to Mayors of Alsace and Lorraine, Strasbourg, 20 November 1922; ADBR 121AL 740 Resolution of Mayors of large communes of Alsace and Lorraine, Strasbourg, 21 July 1923.

[98] AMVES 125Z 38 (nd) Exposé: 'La Loi Municipale d'Alsace-Lorraine du 6 June 1895'.

[99] In 1920 the 11th Congress of Mayors of France adopted a resolution demanding that the departments of Alsace and the Moselle should retain their law, and that the French law should be modified to bring it closer to the Alsatian law. See AMVES, 204 MW 16 Strasbourg, 23 November 1922, speech by Jacques Peirotes to assembled mayors of Alsace-Lorraine.

[100] *Le Temps*, 22 June 1924.

[101] *Le Temps*, 28 September 1924. See AN F7 14614, which contains telegrams from all over France demanding the maintenance of the ambassador to the Vatican and AN AJ30 207, which contains letters on the issue from French Radicals and Catholics as well as resolutions passed by *conseils généraux* in the Nord.

[102] ADBR 121AL 102 coupure de presse, *L'Elsässer*, 31 January 1925.

This wasn't the only viewpoint in Alsace, however, and the protests also rallied supporters of separation, who argued that the introduction of separation to the region was essential if it was to become part of the republican state.[103] It thus got to the heart of how to define what was quintessentially Alsatian; Socialist Jacques Peirotes sought to stress the existence of non-Catholic political cultures by arguing that Alsatian tradition, customs, and beliefs were not dependent on the Concordat, and that separation would not have a negative effect on regional culture.[104] Nevertheless, the voices of Socialists, Radicals, and other supporters of separation were drowned out by the region's Catholic clergy, press, and politicians. In parliament, Mosellan deputy Robert Schumann made a declaration on behalf of twenty-one of the region's twenty-four deputies:

> In the name of 21 of the 24 Alsatian and Lorrain deputies,...we were painfully shocked by the government's declaration, in that it proposes the introduction of the whole of the religious and educational legislation into the recovered departments. The governments which have taken power since 1918 have all reaffirmed the promises made during the War in the name of the French nation. We cannot watch the government outline a programme that is in total contradiction with the programmes on which seven eighths of the deputies of the affected departments were elected. Carrying out such a programme would not only be contrary to...democratic principles...but would also create serious problems in our region, for which we would take no responsibility.[105]

Schumann's opposition was echoed by departmental and municipal councils across the recovered departments. Archbishop Ruch of Strasbourg created the Committee of Action and Defence of Religious Liberty and Traditions in Alsace and Lorraine on 23 June, and penned a series of letters to the government, the local press, and the Alsatian clergy. Pasteur Kuntz, the president of the Lutheran superior consistory, voiced his objections, and the Catholic press issued passionate rejections of the plans.[106] Spontaneous protests broke out in Alsace and the Moselle; in the summer of 1924, 50,000 people participated in a demonstration over the issue in Strasbourg.[107] In particular, Alsatian women relished the opportunity for political activism and, as Elizabeth Vlossak has pointed out, were also galvanized by separation's perceived threat to their social influence by removing their role as educators.[108] Further protest met Herriot's announcement that separation would also mean the

[103] AMVES 125Z 18 Rapport fait au nom de la commission chargée d'examiner le projet de loi portent réorganisation du régime administratif des départements 68, 67 et 57 par Georges Weill; ADBR, 121AL 856, Commissaire Spécial. Rapport, Strasbourg, 13 January 1923. Report on a meeting of La Ligue des Droits de l'Homme held at Strasbourg, 12 January 1923; AN AJ30 173, Session of the Conseil Consultatif of 2 October 1922; ADBR, 286D 328 *Die Freie Presse,* 5 July 1924.

[104] AMVES 125Z 37, A14. 20 May 1927, Proposition de loi.

[105] Cited in Pierre Zind, *Elsass-Lothringen: Alsace-Lorraine. Une Nation Interdite* (Paris, 1979) p. 224.

[106] The *Elsässer Kurier* of 19 June and the *Elsässer* of 20 June demanded a referendum on the educational question in Alsace.

[107] Christian Baechler, 'Espoirs et désillusions', in Livet and Rapp, *Histoire de Strasbourg,* p. 411. The Commissaire Générale wrote that agitation was livelier and more widespread in Alsace than in the Moselle: AN AJ30 207, Commissaire Général de la République to the Président du Conseil, Strasbourg, 11 July 24.

[108] Vlossak, *Marianne or Germania?* pp. 244–5.

introduction of secular education. UPR leaders, the clergy, and the population organized a protest petition which collected 375,000 signatures, and protest resolutions were issued by the UPR, municipal councils, and Catholic associations across Alsace.[109]

Catholic, Protestant, and Jewish communities also organized in response to the proposal; and, according to the Catholic daily *Der Elsässer*, 643 communes in the two Alsatian departments—two-thirds of the total number—protested against the introduction of secular schools.[110] When Herriot climbed down and proposed the establishment of interconfessional schools, Bishop Charles Ruch of Strasbourg called a school strike for 16 March 1925.[111] This strike was observed by between 70 and 75 per cent of students in the countryside, and around 20 to 30 per cent in towns, with 50 per cent of students in the Bas-Rhin and 57 per cent in the Haut-Rhin absent from school on the day of the strike.[112]

However, the region was not as united as the Catholic press suggested, nor indeed as Herriot's government feared. For one thing, French Protestants adopted a more conciliatory stance and, rather than issue a protest concerning the proposal to introduce separation, the Protestant Federation of France's 1924 General Assembly suggested the manner in which separation might be introduced into the three recovered departments.[113] For another, large sections of the population supported Herriot's plans, and complementary elections held in the Haut-Rhin town of Thann in September 1924 are suggestive of the complexity of the issue and the views of the Alsatian population. The catalyst for the vote was the resignation of all of the council's Socialist members in protest against their colleagues' decision to vote for a resolution against the introduction of separation. The press treated the elections as a referendum on the issue of separation, and the Socialists' belief that the population supported their stance appeared vindicated when the left triumphed in the poll.[114]

The protests spilled over into the following year, when Herriot agreed to the establishment of interconfessional schools in Alsace and the Moselle. When Socialist- and Radical-controlled councils in Strasbourg, Colmar, and Schiltigheim

[109] ADBR 98AL 661 Resolution of the Ligue Catholique de Thann, Thann le 24 Mar. 1926; 1927 Ligue des Catholiques d'Alsace pamphlet entitled 'Pour Dieu et pour la France'. According to the *Elsässer*, by September 1924 509 of 946 communes in Alsace had protested against the proposed introduction of separation. *Der Elsässer*, 27 September 1924; Jean-François Kovar, 'Religion et Éducation: De la concorde à la discorde', in Bernard Vogler (ed.), *Chroniques d'Alsace 1918–1939* (Barcelona, 2004), pp. 46–9, p. 51.

[110] *Der Elsässer*, 12 February 1925.

[111] This was in protest at the decision of municipal councils in Strasbourg, Colmar, Schiltigheim, Graffenstaden, Guebwiller, and Huningue to introduce interconfessional schools.

[112] ADBR 98AL 326 Commissariat Général de la République to Président du Conseil, 20 March 1925.

[113] ADBR 121AL 95 Commissaire Spécial to Préfet du Bas-Rhin, 27 October 1924; *Le Journal d'Alsace et de Lorraine*, 24 October 1924; AN AJ30 207 Commissaire Général de la République to Président du Conseil, Strasbourg, 11 July 1924.

[114] The *liste des blocs des gauches* was elected in its entirety, and secured between 649 and 680 votes of 1,280 voters, while the Mayor's *liste des diverses groupements et confessions réunis* secured between 558 and 602 votes. ADBR 121AL 102 Préfet du Haut-Rhin to Commissaire Général de la République, Colmar, 8 September 1924.

announced their intention to interconfessionalize their primary schools, Bishop Ruch responded by organizing a further school strike. This action lasted for three days in Colmar and one day across the rest of Alsace. The Catholic daily *Der Elsässer* proudly reported that the strike had been followed by 100 per cent of children in 324 communes, by 80 per cent in 277, and by 50 per cent in 124. In only 58 communes, it noted, had the strike been followed by less than 50 per cent of children.[115] What it failed to point out, however, was that these 58 communes included all of the region's large towns, and so included more than 50 per cent of Alsatian schoolchildren. In total, around 50 per cent of children in the Bas-Rhin and 57 per cent in the Haut-Rhin missed school on the day of the strike. The number of strikers peaked in the countryside, where between 70 and 75 per cent of children participated.[116] Such protest came in spite of efforts by the prefectures to discourage participation in the strike, but often with the tacit support of UPR mayors and municipal councils.[117]

A few weeks later, the Catholic Church organized a referendum on the issue. François Dreyfus has expressed scepticism over the claim made by the Haut-Rhin Catholic daily the *Elsässer Kurier* that 83,502 of the 135,046 voters in the Haut-Rhin, and 81,919 of the 176,464 in the Bas-Rhin, were in favour of confessional schools.[118] Certain factors are likely to have contributed to a high proportion of votes cast in favour of continued religious education, notably pressure from the local clergy, the fact that the ballot was not secret, and the presence of female voters. Yet the vote appeared to have an effect, and the worries voiced by the Catholic resistance were not realized, as Herriot announced in January 1925 that the Concordat would remain in place. He resigned in April 1925, and his successors proved reluctant to carry through his plans. The following year, the Cartel fell amidst concerns about national finances. This heralded the return of the right, which made no attempt to dismantle the Concordat. In many ways, their inaction reflected continued concern for popular opinion in Alsace and Moselle; the scale of the Catholic reaction had provoked considerable anxiety amongst politicians in Paris. The threat of popular unrest within the border population represented a significant source of concern, not least as it was exploited by sections of the German press.

Moreover, it had almost completely overshadowed the support voiced for Herriot's proposals by the SFIO and Radicals.[119] As a result, the republican left's frustration grew as successive governments appeared content to leave Alsace and the Moselle to their separate regime. In 1927 Strasbourg SFIO deputy Jacques Peirotes proposed the introduction of the 1905 law on separation and the 1882

[115] *Der Elsässer*, 18 March 1925.

[116] ADBR 98AL 326 Commissariat Général de la République to Président du Conseil, 20 March 1925.

[117] ADBR 121AL 95 Préfet du Haut-Rhin to Commissaire Général, Colmar, 31 March 1925.

[118] Dreyfus, *La Vie Politique en Alsace*, p. 86.

[119] See the resolution adopted by the Federation of the Socialist Party of Bas-Rhin in a meeting on 1 July 1924, *Die Freie Presse*, 2 July 1924; ADBR 121AL 654 Commissaire de Police de Sainte Marie-aux-Mines, Sainte Marie-aux-Mines, 29 July 1924. General rapport; *Die Freie Presse*, 23 July 1924.

law on primary education into the recovered departments.[120] According to Peirotes' proposal, the legislation would be introduced in two stages: the first would establish separation and secular education, while the second would see the creation of a series of commissions to manage the transition.[121] Peirotes' project was condemned as a '*Kulturkampf*' by the Catholic right, and was defeated in parliament. The deputies proved unprepared to risk provoking further protest from Alsace, especially as Peirotes' proposal was launched against the backdrop of a movement that demanded greater autonomy for Alsace, and which rapidly won significant support in the region.[122]

The vocal nature of the response to Herriot's plans must be understood as part of a broader shift towards what Martin Conway has identified as a new and more self-conscious Catholic identity across Europe, as Catholics became increasingly concerned to assert the public presence of their religion.[123] This coincided with the Vatican's altered attitude towards politics, which encouraged a more active role for Catholic laity and greater involvement in international issues such as Franco–German reconciliation. And the result of this altered stance was that Catholic parties were encouraged to develop a less introspective vision of national and European politics, and to engage in greater cooperation with different national Catholic parties.[124]

In 1936 the newly elected Popular Front proposed the introduction of an extra year of schooling for students across France. This was to be applied in Alsace and the Moselle, even though primary-school education there already lasted one year longer than in the rest of France. National education minister Jean Zay argued that the extra year was necessary for Alsatian children, given the time spent on religious and German education. But he offered communes the opportunity to opt out of these two subjects, allowing students to leave at age 14, as they did in the rest of the country. The population erupted in protest, particularly in agricultural areas where boys began working at 14, and their anger was mobilized by UPR politicians and the clergy. A petition collected 450,000 signatures, which represented a rise from the 375,000 who had signed in 1925.[125]

This action was accompanied by protest resolutions and widespread passive resistance; teachers failed to report absences, cantonal judges gave dispensations to work at home whether or not the criteria were met, the clergy encouraged parents to disobey the law, and several mayors failed to inform their constituents of the

[120] AMVES 125Z 37 20 May 1927, proposition de loi tendant à introduire dans les départements du Haut-Rhin, du Bas-Rhin et de la Moselle, avec des mesures spéciales d'adaptation et de transition, la loi du 9 décembre 1905 sur la séparation des églises et de l'Etat et la loi du 28 mars 1882 sur l'enseignement primaire obligatoire.

[121] AN F7 13385 *Œuvre*, 7 June 1927. 'La proposition Peirotes de séparation des Eglises et de l'Etat en Alsace et en Lorraine'; ADBR 98AL 661 *Les Dernières Nouvelles de Strasbourg*, 31 May 1927, 'Pour l'introduction des lois scolaires et sur la séparation de l'Eglise et de l'Etat'.

[122] *Lothringer Volkszeitung*, 2 June 1927.

[123] Martin Conway, *Catholic Parties in Europe, 1918–1945* (London, 1997), pp. 3–14.

[124] Wolfram Kaiser, *Christian Democracy and the Origins of European Union* (Cambridge, 2007).

[125] Kovar, 'Religion et Éducation', p. 52; Harp, *Learning to be Loyal*, p. 195.

legislation.[126] This was countered by movements in support of the policy on the left; the SFIO and local unions passed a series of resolutions congratulating Blum on the legislation, which they said would bring new opportunities to all children and particularly those in working-class families.[127] Nevertheless, once again this support for secularity was drowned out by the Catholic opposition, and when Blum fell from power, the law was reinterpreted so that boys could leave school at 14 with religious and German education intact.

As the challenge to the Popular Front suggests, the Concordat continued to raise temperatures throughout the 1930s and, despite the increasingly tense international situation, it remained a popular topic at the meetings of local parties throughout the decade.[128] Ultimately, no government was able to resolve the issue. This was, in part, a reflection of the lack of consensus within administrative circles. While separation was a priority for the Radical Premier Herriot, this was not the case for the Conservative governments that held power for the majority of the interwar years. The result was that the Concordat remained in effect in Alsace and the Moselle, and, indeed, it remains in place to this day. On this issue, popular mobilization at the periphery had brought about change, or at the very least acceptance of the status quo, at the centre. The resistance that greeted attempts to abrogate the Concordat in Alsace led successive governments to leave it in place and forced recognition that secularity was not as central to the Third Republic as had been previously assumed, at least in the context of Alsace.

In spite of their different attitudes, supporters and critics of the separation of church and state both used the language of Alsace's 'dual culture' and described the region as a 'bridge' between France and Germany. This idea evolved from its nineteenth-century use, when it had explained and allowed the continuation of Alsatian difference (with the associated French characteristics that this entailed) within the German Empire. After 1918, it was used to support Alsatian difference within France by presenting the individual particularities of Alsatian legislation as Alsatian, rather than German.[129] The Concordat was retained in Alsace and the Moselle.

CONCLUSION

The return of Alsace to France posed a series of questions over how French citizenship laws and administrative and legal structures should be introduced to a region

[126] For the protest resolutions voted by Protestant representatives, see the *Elsässer* and the *Elsässer Kurier*, 25 February 1937; for the Catholic response, see 'La Question scolaire en Alsace', *L'Echo de Paris*, 15 February 1937; on the Catholic petition, see Kovar, 'Religion et éducation', p. 52. See also Harp, *Learning to be Loyal*, p. 195.

[127] ADBR 98AL 673/2 IVe résolution du Congrès Départemental du Rassemblement Populaire.

[128] ADBR 286D 345 Commissaire Spécial to Commissaire Division de Police Spéciale, 31 March 1936; ADBR 285D 345 Commissaire Spécial to Commissaire Division de Police Spéciale, 31 March 1936. Report on Socialist meeting in Marckolsheim.

[129] Thus the UPR attempted to disassociate interconfessional schools from Germany; see ADBR 121AL 857 L'Inspecteur de Police Spéciale (Mincker) to Sous-préfet d'Erstein, Erstein, 7 July 1924.

with its own separate systems. Any suggestion that German institutions should be removed wholesale, to be replaced with French, proved impractical, given that there were not always equivalent French laws or administrative institutions to be introduced in their place, and proved impossible in the face of the mixing of the borderland population and the considerable local attachment to regional laws and administration that the Alsatian population demonstrated. Consequently, discussions over citizenship and administrative and legal reintegration proved contracted, and two decades after the region's return many of the questions that they had posed in 1918 remained unanswered. The resulting debates lie at the heart of the problems of reintegrating Alsace into France.

Alsatian ideas about citizenship, administration, and legislation had been shaped by years of interaction with France and Germany, and notably by the years of German rule after 1871. This contact had contributed to local understandings of what was French, what was German, and what was Alsatian. Debates over reintegration thus reveal Alsatians attempting to carve out a space for local distinctiveness within the French nation. Early efforts to present Alsace as a model for widespread national reform gradually gave way to efforts to retain regional particularities, yet throughout these discussions Alsatian voices were united in their distinction between what was German and what was Alsatian. Of course, any apparent endorsement of German ways of doing things was problematic in interwar France, and concerns about the threat that Germany posed guided the emphasis placed upon removing German influence in France's initial policies in the region. It also rendered problematic any expression that could be interpreted as an endorsement of German systems. Yet for the Alsatian population, years of contact had created a clear understanding of difference, and debates about reintegration were coloured by these efforts to demonstrate the differences between Alsace and Germany to administrators and politicians in Paris, who exhibited very different understandings of Frenchness.

In this sense, this chapter reveals integration to be a multicentred struggle. It was not simply a two-way interaction between centre and periphery, as neither Paris nor Alsace achieved internal unity in their ideas about the region's future. Nor was the struggle restricted to within France's borders, as attempts to reimagine the region's place did not only come from Paris and Alsace. Specialist research institutes in German universities, the German press, and German politicians also intervened, and return took place against the broader context of territorial adjustments and shifting ideas about 'national minorities' that followed the First World War. Consequently, ideas from the French interior, Alsace, and outside the French nation interacted in debates about integration and the return of Alsace to France. This point is crucial, as it serves as a reminder that nations are not formed in isolation. In Alsace, debates about what was French were shaped by attempts to differentiate between Alsace and Germany, and by interactions involving France, Germany, and Europe. Connections between Alsace and Germany raised the stakes in discussions about Alsatian reintegration. The problems were also unexpected, and many of the arriving *Français de l'Intérieur* had trouble reconciling a region that had been presented as the epitome of Frenchness in the years since 1871 with the reality of the German-speaking region and the population's attachment to regional particularities. And, of course, emotions were heightened because of the perceived French sacrifice that had taken place to 'liberate' the region during the Great War.[130] The result was a wide-ranging clash as Alsatians from all walks of life attempted to reimagine the region's place within France and to grapple with the question of how to negotiate its relations with Germany.

[130] Marcel Nast, *Le Malaise Alsacien-Lorrain* (Paris, 1920), p. 12.

3

Borderland Politics

A crucial forum for many of the debates about reintegration was politics. Indeed, political life in interwar Alsace was dominated by questions posed by return. Should French systems and institutions be introduced wholesale into the recovered departments? What (if any) Alsatian particularities should be retained? Who was best placed to speak on reintegration? Further issues rooted in the region's particularities also acquired an acute importance. What role should religion play in political life? Was there any place for continued connection to Germany in a region that lay on France's eastern border? These questions ran through political life in the region, where many of the parties that debated them were unique to Alsace. This was the case for the Catholic *Union Populaire Républicaine* (UPR), the Conservative Democrats and the autonomist movement. Meanwhile, the Alsatian sections of national parties such as the Socialists, Communists, and Radicals maintained a close focus on Alsatian questions and regional organizational structures that frequently left them a step apart from the rest of their parties. These issues were discussed at political meetings and in the regional press, where the habitual language of politics was German, and when Alsatian parliamentary deputies made interventions in the chamber, it tended to be on issues restricted to the region. The result was a sense of separation between the population of Alsace and those *Français de l'Intérieur* living across the Vosges, and an air of claustrophobia surrounded Alsatian politics. In this environment, politics became both a forum where reintegration was discussed and one cause of the very difficulties of return.

Yet in spite of the focus upon local issues, political life in Alsace was also shaped by broader, transnational connections. People, ideas, and money crossed the border into and out of the region, while cross-border networks linked Alsatian movements with individuals and groups across Europe. Crucially, such flows helped to *make* the border as well as transcend it, and they stimulated anxieties that led to new efforts to control politics and monitor the region's cross-border associations. This chapter attends to these multiple impulses, and argues that the insularity and cross-border connections that shaped Alsatian politics were far from oppositional; on the contrary, they shaped each other.

Local, national, and international questions may have interacted in Alsatian politics, but during the 1920s questions of reintegration dominated political debate. It became the primary issue discussed by politicians, between parties, and at political meetings. This focus on a single topic squeezed normal political debate and eventually became more important than differences between left and right. This led to some unorthodox alliances, such as the coalition of Communists, autonomists, and Catholics that won Strasbourg's town hall in 1929. During the 1930s, international issues supplanted this focus upon the region as the increasing belligerence of the Third Reich raised the spectre of war, triggering the break-up of the alliances of the 1920s and shifting the focus of regional politics. Nonetheless, Alsatian politics did not fall into step with those in the rest of France, as the particularities of the Alsatian Popular Front suggest.

The interaction of the distinct scales of 'local', 'national', and 'transnational' was not unique to Alsace, as recent work has argued.[1] What is more, transnational encounters did not only take the form of connection and unity.[2] Transnationality could equally be manifested through tension and conflict, and transnational relationships could change over time in response to the shifting international situation. In Alsace, connections formed through international networks existed alongside rumours about German intentions, and clashes between German refugees and the French police. In this sense, thinking transnationally about Alsace also challenges notions of the 'periphery' as a marginalized and isolated space away from the capital city. While political rhetoric often focused on Alsace as the limits of France, the region was a site of multiple encounters and contact across both the Vosges and the Rhine.[3] These encounters, and the resulting understandings and frictions, shaped the local political context.

This chapter traces local politics. It considers the parties that contested the region's elections, analyses the issues that drove political debate, and traces the evolution of opinion in Alsace, as the population grappled with the dynamics of return and their place in Europe. It focuses first on the Alsatian political landscape,

---

[1] Recent work on interwar French politics has taken account of the growing literature which urges us to think transnationally about the various forces that have fashioned national political landscapes, societies, and understandings. On the transnational perspective, see Bernhard Struck, Kate Ferris, and Jacques Revel, 'Introduction: Space and Scale in Transnational History', *International History Review*, 33:4 (2011), pp. 573–84; Nancy Green, 'French History and the Transnational Turn', *French Historical Studies*, 37:4 (2014), pp. 551–64; C. A. Bayly et al., 'AHR Conversation: on transnational history', *American Historical Review* (2006), pp. 1441–64; Ann Curthoys and Marilyn Lake, 'Introduction', in *Connected worlds: History in transnational perspective* (Canberra, 2005). On the transnational and the national, see Jan Rüger, 'OXO: Or, the Challenges of Transnational History', *European History Quarterly*, 40:4 (2010), pp. 656–68; Astrid Swenson, *The Rise of Heritage. Preserving the Past in France, Germany and England, 1789–1914* (Cambridge, 2013). On the transnational and the local, see Robert Gildea and Andrew Tompkins, 'The Transnational in the Local: The Larzac as a Site of Transnational Activism since 1970', *Journal of Contemporary History*, 50:3 (2015), pp. 581–605. See also Roland Robertson, 'Globalisation or glocalisation?' *The Journal of International Communication*, 1:1 (1994), pp. 33–52; Victor Roudmetof, 'Transnationalism, Cosmopolitanism and Glocalisation', *Current Sociology*, 53:1 (2005), pp. 113–35. For recent studies of French politics that take account of the transnational turn, see Kevin Passmore 'La droite et l'extrême droite Française et la Grande Bretagne, 1870–1940: préjugés antiméridionaux, préjugés anticeltiques', in Philippe Vervaecke (ed.), *À droite de la droite. Les droites radicales en France et en Grande Bretagne au XXe siècle* (Villeneuve d'Ascq, 2012); Thomas Beaumont, 'International Communism in Interwar France', in Ludivine Broch and Alison Carrol (eds), *France in an Era of Global War 1914–1945: Occupation, Politics, Empire and Entanglements* (Basingstoke, 2015), pp. 92–110.

[2] Maud Anne Bracke and James Mark (eds), 'Between Decolonization and the Cold War: Transnational Activism and its Limits in Europe, 1950s–90s', *Special Issue of the Journal of Contemporary History*, 50:3 (2015).

[3] For an example that makes use of the notion of 'margins' see ADBR 121AL 559 Election Poster for Laurent Meyer, May 1922.

before moving on to cover the return to French politics in 1918, the emergence of a movement seeking Alsatian autonomy in the second half of the 1920s, and then the redrawing of alliances in the 1930s. Throughout, the dual impulses of the region as France's limits and of Alsace as a point of contact between nations defined the region's position. The resulting interaction between the local and the transnational shaped politics in the borderland.

THE ALSATIAN POLITICAL LANDSCAPE

Alsatian politics must be understood against the backdrop of the borderland's cultural specificities, historical experience, and geographical location, all of which affected the campaigns for and results of elections. While local parties dominated party politics, and while national, regional, and municipal elections were centred around local concerns, the region's cross-border connections also exerted a strong influence upon the local political environment. Thus Alsatian political life was shaped by the interaction between transnational flows (of people, ideas, political tracts) and the local context of return to France and a deep-rooted attachment to the locality across all sectors of society, just as Alsace was defined by its identity as a borderland.

Years of party politics as a territory of the German Empire had left a distinct mark on Alsatian political life. The region's largest parties, the UPR and SFIO, were successors to parties established under German rule, while many political leaders from these and other parties could look to the *Kaiserreich* for their formative political experiences. As a result, numerous Alsatian politicians found themselves to be the object of suspicion for the political role they had played prior to 1918. Many of these leaders chose to leave Alsace in the weeks after the armistice, and a number were able to forge new political careers in the Weimar Republic. They included Strasbourg's wartime mayor Rudolf Schwander, who joined the liberal *Deutsche Demokratische Partei* (DDP) and became *Oberpräsident* of the state of Hesse-Nassau. Others were forced to leave by the wave of purges that followed the armistice. As we have seen, labour leaders were a particular target of these commissions, which were frequently headed by members of the region's industrial families. Thus SPD deputies Bernard Böhle and Richard Fuchs were amongst the victims of the commissions forced to leave Alsace for Germany.[4]

Long after the purges had ended, Alsatian politicians used German names or records of service in the Reichstag in an attempt to discredit their political rivals; the Communist Ernest Haas, for example, launched criticism at Socialist Jacques Peirotes for having voted for war credits in the Reichstag, and accused Peirotes' SFIO colleague Georges Weill of having previously obtained Bavarian nationality before playing 'the good Frenchman'.[5] Elsewhere, Alsatian parties found themselves

[4] David Allen Harvey, *Constructing Class and Nationality in Alsace, 1830–1945* (DeKalb, 2001), pp. 133–7.
[5] ADBR 286D 345 Report on Communist meeting by Police d'Etat de Strasbourg, 5ième arrondissement, 27 April 1928.

falling upon German terms when they appeared better served to capture the cultural sense that they sought to convey; thus the UPR described plans to introduce separatism as a '*Kulturkampf*', and the Socialists equated the Conservative policies of Prime Minister André Tardieu to those of Bismarck.[6]

Throughout the interwar years, Alsace's location and history meant that regional politics remained open to exchange across the Rhine. As the German nationalist press monitored developments in the region and triumphantly reported any indication of anti-French sentiment, French administrators worried about potential German influence.[7] Most worrying for the French authorities was the funding received from Germany by certain Alsatian parties, notably the autonomist parties and Communist Party.[8] But the government saw foreign influence across the political spectrum and did not restrict its concerns to Germany; in 1919 administrators expressed their concerns about the potential danger of connections between Socialists in Basel and those in the Haut-Rhin communes that bordered Switzerland.[9] Alsatian public figures capitalized on the government's fears in order to advance their own aims and agenda; for example, UPR deputy Joseph Pfleger described Radical Premier Edouard Herriot's plans for the introduction of French laws into the region as a contribution to German propaganda.[10] Nevertheless, for many Alsatian leaders such links were a natural reflection of the region's history and geography; thus the Socialists commemorated dates in the German revolutionary calendar alongside French anniversaries, and viewed this tradition as a reflection of their local heritage.[11] In this sense, Samuel Goodfellow's observation that Alsace acted as a meeting point for different national and regional fascist strands could be applied to political life more generally.[12] Regional politics in Alsace were both insular and outward-looking, and one did not exclude the other as political life reflected long-standing links, the specific historical experience of German rule, and return to France.

A major element of Alsatian distinctiveness lay in the fact that Alsatian dialect or German had long been the language of regional politics. But reliance on German increased after 1871 when the region's politicians stood for election to the German parliament and its parties formed elements of larger, German networks. This trend

---

[6] AN F7 13383 Direction de la Sûreté Centrale, Contrôle Général des Services de la Police administrative, 1 July 1926. 'Les Socialistes et le mouvement autonomiste'. A French translation of the manifesto on autonomism of the federations of Haut-Rhin and Bas-Rhin, published in *Die Freie Presse* and *Der Republikaner*; Archives Départementales du Haut-Rhin (hereafter ADHR) 8AL 200590. Pamphlet for Salomon Grumbach, 1932 elections (iv). 'L'Heure décisive'.

[7] ADBR 286D 345. Le Commissariat Spécial to Monsieur le Directeur des Services Généraux de Police d'Alsace et de Lorraine. Reports on extract from an article from Fribourg (Baden) of 1 May 1928.

[8] AN F7 13379 Commissaire Spécial de Colmar to Préfet du Haut-Rhin, Colmar 6 March 1923.

[9] ADHR 8AL 200578 Renseignements to the Commissariat Général de la République, Strasbourg, 1 December 1919.

[10] Samuel Huston Goodfellow, *Between the Swastika and the Cross of Lorraine, Fascisms in Interwar Alsace* (DeKalb, 1999), p. 32.

[11] AN F7 13379 Commissaire Spécial de Strasbourg to Préfet du Bas-Rhin, Strasbourg, 19 March 1924.

[12] Goodfellow, *Between the Swastika and the Cross of Lorraine*, p. 3.

persisted after 1918, as parties printed most of their electoral material in German and, when pamphlets or posters were also available in French, they tended to contain less information than the German version.[13] Certain newspapers, such as the Socialist *Freie Presse* introduced bilingual versions in the 1920s, which included a small amount of French comment or adverts alongside lengthier articles in German. Others, such as the *Dernières Nouvelles de Strasbourg*, published French and German editions, but most people continued to read the German version. The vast majority of the Alsatian population read the local press, which focused on issues affecting the recovered departments, while political meetings were generally conducted in Alsatian dialect or in German.

This habitual use of German at Alsatian political meetings posed problems when external speakers were invited, as they either needed to speak German or have their speeches translated. The correspondence between the SFIO's Bas-Rhin women's section and the National Committee of Women Socialists is revealing of the difficulties encountered by local leaders when they attempted to secure German-speaking guests for Alsatian meetings. In one letter, Alsatian secretary Paulette Penner wrote: 'We [don't mind] if we don't know the comrade [that you send], we ask only that she speaks German.'[14]

Local activists occasionally invited high-profile speakers who were unable to speak German, but these efforts met with varying success. On a 1924 visit to the region, Socialist leader Léon Blum attempted to convince his audience that he realized that many in Alsace felt that France had failed to understand the grievances and concerns of the recovered departments by making reference to his Alsatian roots, which, he said, allowed him to understand 'the Alsatian soul' and the misunderstandings between Alsace and France.[15] He told his audience that the Alsatians had experienced a nation which 'was not the true France', while Alsace had sent representatives of only a fraction of the views held in the region to the Chamber, and it was for this reason that the misunderstandings had developed. Blum's audience of Socialist militants responded well, but on other occasions political rivals used visits of high-profile speakers from Paris to protest against French policy.

In 1929, with tensions between Paris and Alsace heightened following the 1928 trial of fifteen autonomist politicians for plotting against the French state, the Radical Party of the Bas-Rhin invited leading Radical Edouard Daladier to its General Assembly.[16] Daladier accepted but arrived late, complaining that he had received a phone call with instructions to leave his train in Saverne to avoid demonstrations in Strasbourg. He did so, and was collected by two men who drove him around the Vosges forest for a few hours before dumping him by the side of the road. He had been the victim of a hoax, and the con artists had capitalized on his fear of a negative response in the region to try to prevent him from attending one

---

[13] For one publication's account of the differences in French and German electoral materials, see the *Elsässer Bote*, 24 April 1929.

[14] Office Universitaire de Recherche Socialiste (hereafter OURS) Fonds SFIO 41, Liste 1, Dossier 21 Paulette Penner to Suzanne Buisson, Strasbourg, 17 January 1938.

[15] *Les Dernières Nouvelles de Strasbourg*, 10 April 1924.

[16] This trial is covered in Chapter 4.

of the most high-profile events in the Radicals' calendar.[17] Daladier responded with a virulently anti-clerical speech.[18]

Language became so contentious, in part, because of the perceived association between language and national attachment. This led to divisions between Alsatian politicians. In a 1931 meeting of the Strasbourg city council, UPR councillor Michel Walter found himself on the losing side of an argument, and Socialist Marcel-Edmund Naegelen asked him whether he would now resign, as he had threatened to resign if the vote was not passed. Walter denied having said such a thing, and suggested that Naegelen must have misunderstood as Walter had spoken in dialect and left Naegelen unable to understand.[19] His implication was that as a Socialist in favour of assimilation, Naegelen was not in tune with the Alsatian population and could not understand dialect. Four years later, in May 1935, the Conservative Charles Frey won the Strasbourg town hall from the dissident Communist Charles Hueber, and Frey began explaining the process for election of adjuncts in French. Hueber claimed that he was unable to understand him and dissident Communist councillor Ferrenbach requested that Frey speak German instead. Frey refused, but conceded to use both French and dialect in council meetings.[20] Hueber himself had previously attracted controversy after delivering a speech in Alsatian dialect in the Chamber in 1927.

Life as a territory of the German Empire had also fostered an important role for organized religion in political life. After 1871, when large numbers of Alsatian elites left the region through the option clause, the clergy had filled the resulting gap and provided a sense of leadership for the population. Priests and bishops had first adopted a leading role in the *protestation* movement, and then became important figures in the Centre Party, while pastors had protected Protestant interests within the Lutheran Church, its lay associations and the Liberal Party.[21] The Catholic clergy assumed a less overt political role in the UPR, but contemporary observers nonetheless stressed the general obedience that the clergy were able to command. This was reflected in the broad correlation between voting patterns and confessional divisions, and the low levels of abstention recorded in Catholic constituencies, such as Obernai, Sélestat, Rosheim, and Seltz.[22] One Haut-Rhin police special commissioner went so far as to describe the clergy as 'the master in the region'.[23] Even the anti-clerical Socialists felt compelled to avoid organizing meetings that clashed with religious festivals.[24] The Catholic clergy's perceived

[17] ADBR 286D 348 Commissaire de Police to Commissaire Central, Strasbourg, 25 February 1929. Report on the General Assembly of the Radicals of Bas-Rhin, and a banquet attended by Edouard Daladier.

[18] Drefyus, *La vie politique en Alsace,* p. 145.

[19] AMVES 234MW 132 Compte rendu du conseil municipal, 52e séance, 6 July 1931.

[20] AMVES 234MW 132 Compte rendu du conseil municipal, 1ère séance, 18 May 1935.

[21] See Christian Baechler, 'Le Clergé Catholique alsacien et la politique, 1871–1939', *Revue d'Alsace,* 111 (1985), pp. 125–48; Malcolm Anderson, 'Regional Identity and Political Change: The Case of Alsace from the Third to the Fifth Republic', *Political Studies,* 20 (1972), pp. 17–30.

[22] AN F7 12755 Commissaire Spécial de Mulhouse, Rapport Mensuel, 31 May 1928; ADBR 286D 346. Sous-préfet de Wissembourg to Préfet du Bas-Rhin, 20 March 1929.

[23] AN F7 12755 Commissaire Spécial de Mulhouse, Rapport Mensuel, 31 May 1928.

[24] OURS Fonds SFIO, Liste 1, Dossier 21 Liselotte Wernher, Strasbourg, 20 February 1939.

overstepping of boundaries was reflected in a popular anti-clerical anecdote about one Alsatian priest's sermon, which told the story of the death of a local man who arrived at the gates of heaven and was invited to enter as he had never stolen or killed. But, according to the priest, just before he was able to enter, Saint Peter requested his political dossier. On seeing that the man had once voted for a Radical, and later voted for a Socialist, Peter sent him to Purgatory instead.[25]

Outside political meetings, local politics relied on sociability and an associative culture that dated back beyond German annexation to the paternalist associations established in the mid-nineteenth century by the region's industrialists. Then, patrons such as Haut-Rhin textile baron Jean Schlumberger had created these organizations in the hope that they would encourage workers to avoid bars and brasseries and instead make more 'productive' use of their leisure time. This associative culture had been transformed during the years of German rule, when political parties and trade unions had created associations offering activities from music or gymnastics to instruction in Esperanto. These associations acted as political vehicles with the Socialist groups integrating lessons in socialist theory and history into their activities and Catholic associations introducing religious education. These organizations achieved such importance that Jean-Claude Richez and Léon Strauss place the associative movement alongside the party, trade unions, and cooperatives as one of the four pillars of the workers' movement in Alsace.[26] After 1918, many associations adopted symbolic French names such as 'Egalité', 'Liberté', or 'Solidarité', or affiliated to national federations.[27] Nevertheless, they retained their own distinct vocabulary, rules, and rituals. They also maintained links with associations in neighbouring countries, in spite of a 1918 ban on contact with German societies.[28] The regional associative culture thus maintained cross-border connections and reinforced Alsatian traditions and history and, in this way, they fostered a sense of regional distinctiveness informed by international links.

Such particularities found expression in the centrality of regional issues to Alsatian political debate. At political meetings, speakers frequently dealt with the problems of reintegrating Alsace, while participants' questions reflected their preoccupation with such matters.[29] A focus on regional issues was not unique to Alsace, but it did have a particular effect in the region. In his work on the Franco–Belgian frontier, Timothy Baycroft has shown that voting allowed the French Flemish population to participate in a national activity that distinguished them from their Belgian neighbours across the border. Through their involvement in French elections, the

---

[25] Parti Socialiste: Section Française de l'Internationale Ouvrière *XXVe Congrès National, tenu à Toulouse les 26, 27, 28 et 29 Mai 1928. Compte Rendu Sténographique* (Limoges, 1928), p. 260.

[26] Jean-Claude Richez and Léon Strauss, 'Tradition et renouvellement des pratiques de loisirs en milieu ouvrier dans l'Alsace des années trente', *Revue d'Alsace*, 113 (1987), pp. 217–37, p. 234.

[27] For example, the region's sporting associations affiliated to the French Workers' Sporting Federation (FST) after its creation in September 1919.

[28] See, for example, ADBR 296D 347 Préfet du Bas-Rhin to Président du Conseil, October 1928. Report sur la journée du 10 octobre 1928.

[29] See, for example, ADBR 286D 354 Commissaire Spécial de Saint Louis to Sous-préfet de Mulhouse, 27 March 1934. Report on an SFIO meeting in Bourgfelden, on 25 March 1934. Howald spoke about the Stavisky Affair; then a member of the crowd asked to speak and stressed the need for struggle against clericalism in Alsace.

French Flemish 'projected regional issues into the nation', with the result that the political border became a division in the Flemish community.[30] In Alsace, participation in French elections similarly served as a point of distinction from the Weimar Republic. However, this did not lead to integration into France. Instead, Alsatian politics were dominated by separate regional parties, which contested separate regional issues.

Having missed out on the development of the Third Republic's political culture between 1871 and 1918, Alsatian politics retained a distinctiveness that left them out of step with political life across France and made reintegration more difficult. For Parisian visitors, the unfamiliarity of Alsatian politics also contributed to misunderstandings which served to reinforce a sense of Alsatian difference. Numerous observers commented on the particularities of Alsatian political life, while administrators struggled to find comparisons that they hoped might make the region's politics more intelligible to Paris; in 1919 the *Commissaire de la République* described them as 'closer to pre-war Belgium than contemporary France'.[31] Meanwhile, national newspapers often made mistakes in their description of party politics or the region's politicians.[32] It was these regional particularities that established the context for political life in Alsace. The result was a claustrophobia that engulfed regional politics, but that coexisted alongside the transnationality and the cross-border interactions that shaped debates and experiences.

THE RETURN TO FRENCH POLITICS

In 1919 the Alsatian population was able to vote in the first election since their return to France in 1918. In an echo of the enthusiastic welcome granted to the French troops the previous year, the reconstituted parties peppered their campaigns with declarations of patriotism, and the Catholic and Conservative parties went one step further in proposing that all parties unite to form a single electoral list. Their aim was to turn the elections into a 'patriotic demonstration [to reaffirm] . . . the joy of the . . . population at their return to the homeland', while sending a powerful message to France's 'enemies across the Rhine', particularly those involved in the campaign in favour of neutrality for Alsace-Lorraine. With all the parties making up just one list, the Republic's commissar in Colmar noted, the election would be free from party-political considerations and the vote would become the plebiscite on the return to France that French authorities had decided to avoid the previous year. [33] This 'patriotic demonstration' was scuppered by the Socialists, however, who decided that standing on a single list might allow the Catholics to hijack the regional political agenda. As a result, in the Bas-Rhin Alsatian voters chose between

[30] Timothy Baycroft, 'Changing Identities in the Franco–Belgian Borderland in the Nineteenth and Twentieth Centuries', *French History*, 13:4 (1999), pp. 417–38, pp. 430–1.

[31] AN AJ30 170 Rapport Hebdomadaire du Comissaire de la République, Semaine du 17 au 24 Février 1919.

[32] For example, *L'Ami du peuple* (soir), 24 January 1929.

[33] ADHR 8AL 200578 Commissaire de la République du Haut-Rhin, Rapport, Colmar, 13 November 1919.

the Socialists, the Radicals, and the Bloc National (UPR and Conservatives). In the Haut-Rhin, with no Radical party standing, the choice was a straightforward one between the Socialists and the Bloc National.

While the parties declared their loyalty to France, administrators faced the headache of working out how French electoral legislation should be applied to the recovered departments, and who, exactly, was eligible to vote. The papers of the General Commission for Alsace and the Moselle contain letters of instruction, notes of complaint, and telegrams from administrators confused by the new legislation. The definition of citizenship applied by the French complicated matters further, as Alsatians who had lost French nationality through the Treaty of Frankfurt could vote, as could their children, but those Alsatians who had taken another nationality after the Treaty were ineligible, as were the children of pre-1870 Alsatians if their ancestors also included any post-1870 migrants to Alsace-Lorraine.[34] So, the Commissioner for the Moselle pondered, could 'an individual born in Lorraine, before 1870, with a Saarlander father and a Lorrainer mother be registered to vote?', while the Mayor of Strasbourg questioned whether 'the descendant of a non-German foreigner, who entered the country before 1870, and who married an Alsatian or Lorrain woman was eligible?'[35]

One point was clear: Alsatian and Mosellan women would not be voting in May 1919. Women in France remained ineligible to vote throughout the interwar years, yet had Alsace and the Moselle remained part of Germany, the region's women could have voted in elections in the Weimar Republic. In her analysis of women's lives under German and French rule, Elizabeth Vlossak has found little evidence that Alsatian women voiced their displeasure at seeing German women enfranchised while they remained unable to vote. But she does underline 'a sense of uneasiness' amongst some women who worried that return to France would mean a significant loss in rights acquired under German rule. She offers the example of an anonymous letter sent to *La Française*, which pointed out that having opened her bank account herself under German rule, the letter's author was now unable to manage it without the consent of her husband. Vlossak connects this to the political atmosphere, which allowed little space for dissent, as any expression of concern with aspects of return could be misinterpreted as antipathy towards France, or even a longing for Germany.[36]

In spite of these issues, 83 per cent of Alsatian and Mosellan men turned out to vote in the 1919 elections.[37] When the results were announced, Alsace paralleled

[34] Office de Statistique d'Alsace et de Lorraine. Compte rendus statistiques. Fascicule No.4, p. 9.

[35] ADBR 121AL 547 Telegram from the Commissaire de la République in Metz to the Commissaire Général, Metz, 7 June 1919; Letter from Jacques Peirotes, Président du Conseil Municipal to Commissaire Général, Strasbourg, 12 June 1919.

[36] Vlossak, *Marianne of Germania?* p. 234.

[37] ADBR 121AL 552 Office de Statistique d'Alsace et de Lorraine. Compte rendus statistiques. Fascicule No.4, p. 9. This was towards the top end of the levels of turnout normally recorded, as the Third Republic had high voter-turnout levels of between 76 and 84 per cent. See Melvin Edelstein, 'Aux Urnes Citoyens! The Transformation of French Electoral Participation 1789–1870', in Gail M. Schwab and John R. Jeanneney (eds), *The French Revolution of 1789 and its Impact* (Westport, 1995), p. 203.

Table 3.1. Votes cast in Alsace in the elections of 1912 and 1919.

	1912		1919	
	Total votes	Percentage of total votes cast	Total votes	Percentage of total votes cast
Socialist Party	80,000	34.2	83,000	36.7
Radical Party			12,350	5.4
Bloc national (Centre and Liberal Conservatives in 1912)	153,000	65.4	130,468	57.7
Total votes cast	233,800		225,818	
Total number of voters	262,000		279,000	

Sources: ADBR 121AL 552 Office de Statistique, Compte rendus, No.4, p. 10; François G. Dreyfus, *La Vie Politique en Alsace*, p. 14.

the national trend of victory for the Conservative Bloc national, formed in Alsace of the UPR and Conservatives (Parti républicain démocratique). In Alsace, the Bloc secured 53.2 per cent of votes in the Bas-Rhin and 62.1 per cent in the Haut-Rhin, while the Socialists received 36.5 per cent in the Bas-Rhin and 36.9 per cent in the Haut-Rhin, and the Radicals, who stood only in the Bas-Rhin, collected 9.4 per cent of votes in the northern department.[38] In comparison with the last elections held in the Reichsland, this marked an increase in the total number of votes received by the Socialists and a decrease for the parties of the Conservative right (see Table 3.1).

In 1912, this had translated into four seats for the Socialist SPD, six for the Catholic centre, and one for the Liberals. In 1919, however, it resulted in nine UPR deputies, six Conservatives, and one independent. French electoral reform in 1919 had been intended to produce just such results that favoured coalitions of the centre and the right, but the Socialists were incensed that across the three departments the Bloc National had polled 172,000 votes and won 24 seats, while the Socialists had received 112,000 votes but no seats.[39] Nevertheless, all the deputies sent from Alsace joined the Bloc National in the Chamber of Deputies. Across France the election had been fought, in Premier Clemenceau's words, 'for or against Bolshevism'. Fear of revolution, combined with the voting system and nature of the alliances that competed in the election meant that the Chamber of Deputies elected in 1919 was the most Conservative French parliament since 1871. It became known as the 'sky-blue' chamber, as so many deputies were veterans dressed in their sky-blue dress uniforms. And, while the left complained about the results of the elections for Alsace, the region now had representation in parliament. This meant that the political parties could turn their full attention to the business of the reintegration of Alsace.

[38] ADBR 121AL 552 Office de Statistique, Compte rendus, No. 4, p. 10.
[39] ADHR 8AL 200578 Pamphlet of the SFIO for the 1924 elections.

THE POLITICS OF REINTEGRATION

Looking back on the 1919 elections in 1922, the Haut-Rhin Prefect Charles Valette described the poll as 'a patriotic demonstration' rather than a political contest. In Valette's eyes, this obscured the results, making it difficult to predict the outcome of future elections.[40] But, alongside the patriotism on display, the 1919 elections had seen the redrawing of political rivalries: the SFIO had refused to join the single list and condemned the right's militarism, its foreign policy, its financial misman-agement, and its neglect of social problems, and demanded the nationalization of railways and mines, and the separation of church and state; and the UPR demanded the maintenance of the Concordat, the eight-hour working day, and fiscal reform. Both called for votes for women.[41] Thus divisions established under German rule were maintained, and the issues of religion, welfare, and female suffrage in particu-lar were long-standing concerns that all the Alsatian parties retained at the heart of their programmes throughout the interwar years. Later elections would echo these demands: the UPR continued to call for female suffrage, as well as decentralization or federalism and fiscal reform; and the Socialists maintained their support for an increase in the budget for unemployment and old-age relief, and demands for a peaceful foreign policy, as well as their emphasis upon the need to introduce the separation of church and state and French national administrative institutions.[42] Issues of welfare, female suffrage, and reintegration also formed part of the pro-grammes of the Conservatives, Radicals, and Communists in the region.

While many of these concerns remained constant throughout elections in the interwar years, political priorities shifted as the domestic and international situations changed, moving from tense Franco–German relations after Versailles to the spirit of optimism around Locarno, when Germany recognized French sovereignty over Alsace-Lorraine. Then, with the global depression hitting Germany from 1929 and France from the beginning of the 1930s, economic considerations increasingly affected politics during the early thirties. After 1933 Hitler's seizure of power in Germany evoked fear of another war. This meant that politics were guided by concern about the Third Reich's intentions, particularly after it embarked upon a programme of rearmament and a belligerent foreign policy that took German troops right to France's eastern frontier in 1936 with the remilitarization of the Rhineland. Alsatian fears were not eased when this was followed by the annexation of Austria and the Sudetenland in 1938, and of the remainder of Czechoslovakia in 1939.

Alongside these fluctuating national and international concerns, local issues retained their importance, and the future of Alsace within France dominated polit-ical debate in the region. On the one hand, the UPR and Conservatives demanded

[40] ADBR 121AL 102 Préfet du Haut-Rhin to M. le Ministre de l'Interieur, April 1922.
[41] ADBR 286D 349 Directeur de Police de Strasbourg to Commissaire de la République, Strasbourg, 20 August 1919; 286D 349 Report on SFIO meeting held 19 August 1919; Dreyfus, *La Vie Politique*, p. 72.
[42] ADHR 8AL 200580 Pamphlet for Klein, 1932 elections.

the retention of particular local legislation, notably the religious laws, and regional administration. The Communist Party (Parti Communiste Français, PCF) echoed their criticisms of French policy, and criticized France for treating the region 'like a colony'. The Socialists and Radicals, on the other hand, were committed to the introduction of all republican legislation into Alsace, and both parties placed a particular stress upon the urgency of introducing the separation of church and state into the recovered departments. Without them, they believed, Alsace was left 'on the margins of the Republic', to quote a 1922 SFIO poster.[43] This slogan spoke to more widespread concerns that the region's position on the nation's geographical periphery would be mirrored by it being left on the periphery of national debate. The French failure to meet the demands of either side meant that initial concerns over French policy persisted. In 1922 Valette described local politics as dominated by the questions of religion, confessional schools, and language.[44] His comments were echoed by successive prefects and sub-prefects over the following twenty years.[45]

The years between the 1919 election and the next contest in 1924 saw Alsatian politicians and parties attempt to adjust to the new political landscape. With the Bloc National in power, the Socialists criticized government policy, but tried to do so without condemning France. The Communists described French policy in Alsace and the Moselle as 'imperialist', and created closer links with the German Communist Party (Kommunistische Partei Deutschlands, KPD); Alsatian Communist leader Charles Hueber adopted a prominent role in the PCF's opposition to the French occupation of the Ruhr valley, and the local party took the opportunity to send young Alsatian Communists to Germany for training in anticipation of a European revolution in the early 1920s.[46]

The predominance of issues of reintegration created divisions within a number of parties, and the UPR and Radicals in particular were hit by internal conflict over their future. Cracks emerged first in the UPR, and on 30 October 1921 the party passed a resolution which threatened to take the French government to the League of Nations if it endangered Alsatian religious freedoms. Joseph Pfleger, the party's president, criticized the declaration and resigned from the party, making his return conditional upon the party making a public statement of its commitment to France and changing its name to reflect this. His demand was accepted by the party by a margin of 82 votes to 69; as a result, the party changed its name to the UPRN (*Union Populaire Républicaine Nationale*), although it was still known as the UPR, rendering the change more symbolic than practically meaningful. Pfleger was replaced as president by Thomas Seltz, the deputy for Rhinau.

The Radicals' problems similarly reflected difficulties in negotiating the return to France. Many Alsatian members of the party came to feel that centralized

---

[43] ADBR 121AL 559 Election Poster for Laurent Meyer, May 1922.

[44] ADBR 121AL 559 Préfet du Haut-Rhin to M. le Ministre de l'Interieur, 3 May 1922.

[45] See, for example, AN AJ30 171 Préfet du Bas-Rhin to Sous Secretaire d'État, Strasbourg, 25 June 1925; ADBR 286D 347 Préfet du Bas-Rhin à M. le Ministre de l'Interieur (reply to letter of 23 August 1928).

[46] Christine Frantz, 'Le Parti Communiste', in Jean-Claude Richez, Léon Strauss, François Igersheim, and Stéphane Jonas, *Jacques Peirotes, 1869–1935 et le socialisme en Alsace* (Strasbourg, 1989), pp. 85–8.

administration did not reflect the needs of Alsace, and began to demand regional administration. This brought them into conflict with the party's highest authorities, whose long-standing attachment to the concept of the Republic as 'une et indivisible' had become inseparable from their commitment to the revolution.[47] Across France, leading Radicals had rejected demands for decentralization, but questions of regional autonomy were complicated in Alsace due to the continued existence of the Concordat and religious education. For many Radicals, it was difficult to countenance regional administration for the recovered departments while still pushing ahead with the introduction of the separation of church and state. As a result, in the eyes of leading Radicals, when their Alsatian members questioned centralism, they were also questioning the heritage of the revolution, and by extension, the Republic itself. By the 1924 elections, these tensions were threatening to bubble over into outright conflict.

The 1924 campaigns were dominated by issues of reintegration; the UPR's programme concentrated on the retention of the Concordat, and they shared with the Socialists, Radicals, and Conservatives a focus upon the status of the Alsatian and Mosellan railways, and on the retention of local legislation, the General Commission, and religious education in the recovered departments.[48] More parties were involved than in 1919, since new parties had been founded in the intervening years, and militants launched lively campaigns as voters in the Haut-Rhin chose between the Bloc National, Radicals, Socialists, and Communists; and in the Bas-Rhin the Conservative *Comité républicain national* also stood. When the results were announced, the Bloc National's share of the vote had fallen from 53 to 44 per cent in the Bas-Rhin, and from 62 to 52 per cent in the Haut-Rhin. This meant six UPR deputies for the Bas-Rhin, alongside two Conservatives, two Socialists, and one Communist. In the Haut-Rhin, the Bloc National again won all seven seats, with four going to the UPR and three to the Conservatives.[49]

While Alsace returned the Bloc National to the Chamber of Deputies, in the rest of France the tide had turned towards the left, and a new government was formed by the Radicals with SFIO support. As we have seen, this *Cartel des Gauches* was headed by the Radical Edouard Herriot, who used his ministerial declaration to announce that 'the government…will prepare the measures that will allow the introduction of the whole of the republican legislation into Alsace and Lorraine, while respecting the situation, and looking after the material and moral interests of the population'.[50] This declaration provoked an immediate and vocal response from the Catholic parties in both Alsace and the Moselle, for whom it appeared to represent a betrayal of Joffre's wartime guarantee of respect for Alsatian traditions and customs. Consequently, it served to provide a focus for the more general dissatisfaction that had developed in the region since 1919.

[47] Serge Berstein, 'Le Parti radical et le problème du centralisme (1870–1939)', in Christian Gras and Georges Livet (eds), *Régions et régionalisme en France du XVIIIe siècle à nos jours* (Vendôme, 1977), pp. 225–40, p. 225.

[48] ADBR 121AL 553 *Dernières Nouvelles de Strasbourg*, 12 May 1924.

[49] Dreyfus, *La Vie Politique en Alsace*, pp. 75–6. [50] *Le Temps*, 22 June 1924.

The contests triggered by Herriot's declaration (that were covered in Chapter 2) meant that the issue of religion was central to the programmes of all Alsatian parties. For the leaders of political Catholicism, the maintenance of the Concordat represented a fundamental particularity in Alsace, which did not detract from the Alsatian population's attachment to the French nation. Similarly, separation of church and state was not an integral part of France, and it was possible to feel French and to favour the maintenance of the Concordat. As a result, attacks on regional religious life represented not simply a betrayal of promises to respect Alsatian culture, but also an attack on Alsace, its population, and its fundamental values.[51] Meanwhile, for the SFIO and Radicals, abrogation of the Concordat would ensure the full integration of Alsace into the French Republic, while offering an opportunity to reduce the clergy's political influence.[52] Socialists presented their Catholic and Conservative rivals as 'conditional Frenchmen', who, having found Third Republican France to be different from the France of the Second Empire, were threatening the unity of their *mère patrie*.[53]

In 1925 there were municipal elections across Alsace. As this contest closely followed Herriot's declaration on the laws of separation and the introduction of interconfessional schools, many observers treated the elections as a plebiscite on these controversial issues. When the results came in, the SFIO-Radical council in Strasbourg reinforced its hold over the council, while the Socialists and Radicals maintained their seats in Colmar, Mulhouse, and Schiltigheim. François Dreyfus has suggested that the results demonstrate support for interconfessional schools across Alsace.[54] This was certainly the case among some sections of the towns' populations, notably Socialist and Radical voters. Nevertheless, amongst wider sections of the population it is more likely that the results indicate a lack of serious opposition to the reform in the region's main cities, as well as confidence in the existing councils' sound municipal management. The SFIO-Radical councils had made significant improvements to the towns under their control between 1919 and 1925, including improving infrastructure, building social housing, and extending cultural programmes.[55] What is more, the UPR maintained its position across rural Alsace.

During the first half of the 1920s, ideas about reintegration developed within the context of existing political rivalries, leading parties and politicians to downplay the points that united them.[56] Regional politics were thus deeply embedded within the process of reintegration. The result was that proposals for reintegration developed within the limits of party-political rivalries and were confined by political priorities. At the same time, reintegration squeezed ideology, as political life became dominated by the return to France. Consequently, Alsatian parties arrived

[51] ADBR 121AL 857 *Le Courrier de Strasbourg*, 4 October 1924; ADBR 121AL 857 *L'Elsässer*, 8 December 1924.

[52] ADBR 286D 328 *Die Freie Presse*, 5 July 1924; *Die Freie Presse*, 7 November 1924.

[53] AN F7 13384 *Der Republikaner*, 23 April 1927. [54] Dreyfus, *La Vie Politique*, p. 95.

[55] AMVES US 240 *Compte rendu de l'administration de la ville de Strasbourg, 1919–1935*, Strasbourg, 1935; *L'œuvre sociale de la Ville de Mulhouse*, Mulhouse, 1931.

[56] AMVES 113Z 29 Séance du Conseil Consultatif, 19 December 1923, speech by abbé Muller.

at significant moments of unity, for example over their treatment of Alsatian institutions as Alsatian rather than German, and of Alsace's potential to act as a model for the rest of France.[57] In spite of this unity, Alsatian politicians were unsuccessful in their attempts to secure the adoption of Alsatian laws and systems, although Paul Dutton has shown that Alsatian legislation did serve as a reference point for parliamentary consideration of a nationwide system of medical insurance.[58]

That all parties gradually moved towards a focus upon regional issues reflects an increasing frustration with the narrow and rigid definition of Frenchness that Alsace encountered after 1918, and what appeared to be a tendency to label any policy ideas or activities that did not fit existing ideas about centralization as 'anti-national' or 'pro-German'.[59] The clash that this provoked between Paris and Alsace is revealing of different understandings of the borderland's relationship to both the national centre and its neighbours. While Alsatian politicians recognized the region's connections to France and Germany but stressed Alsace's distinct culture, French politicians were highly suspicious of anything that betrayed a whiff of German influence. The resulting misunderstandings coloured Alsatian politics throughout the two decades after the return to France, and in the second half of the 1920s they spilled out into outright conflict as a movement demanding regional autonomy emerged in Alsace.

AUTONOMISM

After the school strike, Alsatian political life became increasingly focused upon regional issues. Sections of the UPR became ever more frustrated with successive governments' failure to grant their demands for the protection of regional interests, and they sought out increasingly unorthodox alliances. This found its first expression in a by-election in the Haut-Rhin town of Soultz in January 1925. There, the town's UPR mayor Paul Heinrich competed with Socialist Salomon Grumbach for the seat in the Chamber. When Heinrich won, the total number of votes he received suggested that he had won support from Communist and Radical voters in the second round as well as the UPR voters who had supported him in the first. This indicates that a proportion of Communist and Radical supporters had preferred to vote for a regionalist politician than a candidate of the left. This marked the beginning of a 'tacit alliance' that continued in the July 1925 cantonal elections, when the socialist press complained about the absence of Catholic opposition for

[57] AMVES 125Z 18 Rapport fait au nom de la commission chargée d'examiner le projet de loi portent réorganisation du régime administratif des départements 68, 67 et 57 par Georges Weill; AMVES 125Z 64 Jacques Peirotes, speech (nd); ADBR 286D 336 SFIO (Fédération of the Bas-Rhin), Programme for the elections of 11 May 1924; *Journal Officiel*, Séance 25 May 1925, p. 2331.

[58] Paul V. Dutton, 'French versus German approaches to Family Welfare in Lorraine, 1918–1940', *French History*, 13 (1999), pp. 439–63, p. 462. See also Paul V. Dutton, *Origins of the French Welfare State. The Struggle for Social Reform in France, 1914–1947* (Cambridge, 2002).

[59] ADBR 286D 345 Extract de presse. *Le Temps*, 11 May 1929.

Communist candidates (and vice versa) in constituencies across Alsace.[60] Rather than the '*main tendue*' of 1936, when the Communists reached out to other parties in the interest of national unity and anti-fascism, this alliance was based on shared prioritization of regional interests. It was cemented later that year, when both the UPR and PCF refused to condemn the burgeoning movement that demanded greater autonomy for Alsace.[61]

The elections of 1925 show an increasing urban–rural divide amongst the Alsatian population, as while the cities and towns voted in left-leaning local governments, the UPR maintained its position in the countryside. Across rural Alsace, isolated frustrations that had been building up since 1918 found expression in a new weekly newspaper, *Die Zukunft*, launched in May 1925, which demanded autonomy for Alsace. By May of the following year, the publication had reached circulation levels of 35,000.[62] Then, in June 1926, 102 Alsatian and Mosellan notables signed the *Heimatbund* ('homeland league') manifesto, an appeal to all Alsatians and Lorrainers 'faithful to the *Heimat*'. The use of the German term '*Heimat*', rather than the French '*patrie*' or '*petite patrie*', reflected the dominance of German in regional political life; but it also speaks to the connection between language and understandings of home and locality rooted in Alsatian history and culture.

The manifesto stated that its signatories had been driven to action by the 'fanatical assimilationists, who sought to attack the character, the soul and the very civilization of the people of Alsace-Lorraine' and expressed the conviction that the only means of safeguarding the rights of Alsace-Lorraine was through autonomy within France. This meant a regional parliament in Strasbourg, maintenance of the religious status quo, protection of the German language, nationalization of the railways, and maintenance and development of regional social and communal laws. The signatories stressed that they were not forming a new party, but rather they wanted to cultivate and protect regional character and heritage. What is more, they stressed a vision of Alsace-Lorraine as a meeting point between two great civilizations with a role to play in forging a common European culture.[63] Thus they built upon the nineteenth-century idea of Alsace's double culture and mobilized the idea of the region as a bridge between France and Germany in order to protect local rights and customs.

Four months later, Radical leaders George Wolff and Camille Dahlet broke away from the Radical party to found the *Elsässische Fortschrittspartei* in October 1926. This followed months of debate within the Radicals over French policy in the recovered departments, and the new party demanded regional autonomy for Alsace and the Moselle.[64] In September of the following year, editors of *Die*

[60] *Die Freie Presse*, 23 July 1925; *Die Freie Presse*, 24 July 1925.

[61] Georges Weill, 'Les menées autonomistes en Alsace. Seuls le parti clérical et le parti communiste ne les ont pas condamnées', *Le Quotidien*, 3 December 1925.

[62] Christian Baechler, 'L'autonomisme alsacien entre les deux guerres', *Historiens et Géographes*, 347 (1995), pp. 249–55, p. 251.

[63] *Manifeste du Heimatbund* (Strasbourg, 1926).

[64] See *La France de l'Est*, 28 October 1925, 'Le Congrès de Nice et la politique alsacienne', for an analysis of developments in the Radical party. See also Serge Berstein, 'Le Parti radical et le problème du centralisme (1870–1939)', in Christian Gras and Georges Livet (eds), *Régions et régionalisme en France du XVIIIe siècle à nos jours* (Vendôme, 1977), pp. 225–40.

Zukunft Paul Schall, René Hauss, and Karl Roos founded the *Unabhängige Landespartei für Elsass-Lothringen* (or *Landespartei*), with the express aim of protecting local rights and particularities. Each of these new parties placed the issue of 'autonomism' or local rights at the top of their political priorities.

These developments in Alsatian politics took place against the backdrop of a thaw in Franco–German relations that began with the signature of the Locarno Treaty in 1925. Through this agreement, the signatories guaranteed Germany's western borders and the demilitarized Rhineland, and France and Germany agreed not to attack or invade each other. The Treaty was crucial in producing a new sense of hope, the *esprit de Locarno*, across western Europe; British Foreign Secretary Austen Chamberlain later described it as 'the real dividing line between the years of war and the years of peace'.[65] Indeed, Zara Steiner has pointed out that while it did represent a continuation of the French retreat from the Versailles settlement that had begun with acceptance of the Dawes Plan, it was also something new in form and direction: it was a regional and mutual security pact that opened the way to a peaceful European settlement.[66]

Ultimately, the Locarno agreement did not secure peace and, rather, left the situation on the eastern borders of Germany more precarious than they had been previously. But it did mark the beginning of a period of closer relations between France and Germany cemented by the Kellogg–Briand Pact of 1928, by which the signatories (which included both France and Germany) renounced war as a means of settling disputes. Such will for greater cooperation was still evident in the September 1931 trade agreement, but this accord would prove to be a last attempt to forge closer relations, as the death in 1929 of German Foreign Minister Gustav Stresemann and a crisis in trading relations triggered the collapse of such efforts to forge closer economic integration.[67] Subsequently, the election of Adolf Hitler to the chancellorship of Germany in January 1933 marked the beginning of a new period of tension and suspicion in Franco–German relations.

Alsatian autonomism became the dominant political force in regional politics by the end of the 1920s, although the label 'autonomist movement' suggests a unity of action and purpose that Alsatian autonomism never realized. Rather, autonomism mobilized widely held grievances connected to reintegration and brought together a broad cross section of society under the umbrella of the defence of local rights and traditions. In the words of leading autonomist René Hauss, it represented an attempt to protect Alsace's 'most sacred possessions: its religion, language, culture and traditions'.[68] While autonomists may have disagreed amongst themselves about what should be the immediate priority for their movement, they were broadly united by their demands for regional administration, an autonomous budget, and bilingualism.

[65] N. H. Gibbs, *Grand Strategy* (London, 1976), p. 43.
[66] Zara Steiner, *The Lights that Failed, European International History, 1919–1933* (Oxford, 2007), p. 408.
[67] Conan Fischer, 'The Failed European Union: Franco–German Relations during the Great Depression of 1929–32', *International History Review*, 34:4 (2012), pp. 705–24.
[68] ADBR 286D 345 'Appel', 16 April 1928.

Outside the autonomist parties, the existing parties also made demands for regional autonomy. The SFIO and Conservatives demanded the retention of regional language and certain local laws, but the emergence of autonomism had a more marked impact upon the Radicals, the Catholic UPR, and the Communist PCF. As we have seen, demands for regional autonomy caused the Radicals to split when Bas-Rhin leaders Camille Dahlet and Georges Wolff broke away to form the *Fortschrittspartei*, while Communist leader Charles Hueber had led calls for Alsatian neutrality during the revolution of 1918, and from its foundation the Alsatian PCF condemned French imperialism and demanded regional autonomy.

Several UPR leaders were involved with the autonomist movement from its early stages; Joseph Rossé and Jean Keppi were amongst the first signatories of the *Heimatbund* manifesto, and some high-profile members of the clergy became prominent spokesmen for Catholic grievances, particularly over the proposal to introduce the laws on separation into the recovered departments. In a letter to Radical leader Edouard Daladier, Bishop Ruch of Strasbourg condemned the government's treatment of Alsatians as 'imbeciles', 'slaves', or 'backward tribes' to whom the Republic needed to bring 'the light', 'freedom', and 'civilization'. In a complaint common to local religious leaders, Ruch stressed that Paris knew 'hardly anything' of Alsace and should not presume to know better what the region needed than those in Alsace itself.[69] But, as the autonomist movement gained in force, Ruch expressed his opposition to it by criticizing the *Heimatbund* for putting Alsatian interests ahead of Catholic concerns, and called on members of the League of Catholics to avoid political questions.[70] He later condemned *Die Zukunft*. This stance was supported by sections of the UPR who saw no connection between their own views and those of the autonomists. In February 1926 Joseph Weydmann, a prominent UPR leader, published a statement in the name of the Ligue des Catholics d'Alsace, which allied the League with the National Federation of Catholics, and rejected *Die Zukunft*.[71]

The emergence of autonomism coincided with a stabilization of the German economy and increased interest at the Weimar Foreign Office in the territories that Germany had lost at Versailles. While more attention was focused on the lost territories in the east, research and finances were also directed at Alsace-Lorraine, in spite of the thaw in Franco–German relations. As a result, the Alsatian autonomist movement was supported by German propaganda, finance, and institutions such as the *Deutsches Ausland-Institut* in Stuttgart, established as a centre of research and propaganda with a budget of 80 million marks in 1925, which it used to fund theatrical societies, popular libraries, and youth movements in Germany's lost territories. By 1927 the German foreign office was giving 280,000 Reichsmarks per year to the Alsatian autonomist cause, with the majority of this funding going

[69] ADBR 286D 348 Letter from Arch-Bishop Ruch to M. Daladier (nd).
[70] Dreyfus, *La Vie Politique en Alsace*, p. 103.
[71] *Le Courrier de Strasbourg*, 19 February 1926, 'Un avertissement necessaire. La Ligue des catholiques d'Alsace proteste contre la "Zukunft". La declaration de la Ligue des Catholiques d'Alsace'.

to the regional autonomist press.[72] Nevertheless, while the movement was financially supported by Germany, it must be understood as a local movement, rooted in the desire to protect regional customs and in frustration with French policy in the recovered departments.

This was not the conclusion arrived at in Paris, however, and the autonomist crisis brought the deepening cleavage between Paris and Alsace into relief. After the *Heimatbund*'s emergence, Minister of Justice Pierre Laval took sanctions against any civil servant who had signed the manifesto; all were suspended and higher civil servants faced disciplinary action. Joseph Rossé, the UPR leader and a *Heimatbund* signatory, lost his job as a teacher in a Colmar primary school. For much of the population across France, the *Heimatbund* was the first that they had heard of any problems in reintegrating the recovered departments and, as a result, it was through autonomism that the so-called 'Alsatian problem' entered French national consciousness.[73]

On 22 August 1926, French royalist and nationalist associations disrupted an autonomist rally in Colmar, crying 'down with the boches'. In the ensuing ruckus, autonomist leader Eugène Ricklin was beaten. The events drew condemnation from all sectors of Alsatian society, and the day became known as 'Bloody Sunday'. The following year, tensions reached boiling point as the abbé Xavier Haegy launched a libel trial against the Parisian journalist Edouard Helsey, who had published a series of incendiary articles that accused the autonomist movement of working in connection with Berlin, Moscow, and the Vatican, and Haegy of being a German agent. The court found in Haegy's favour, and he emerged from the trial a hero to many Alsatians who were angered by his treatment at the hands of both the court and the Parisian press.

The autonomist movement represented a serious concern for Poincaré's government, which banned three autonomist newspapers—*Die Zukunft, Die Wahrheit,* and *Die Volksstimme*—in November 1927, using 1895 legislation that outlawed foreign-language publications. The next month, the police conducted house searches and arrested twenty-four alleged autonomists, fifteen of whom were put on trial in Colmar in 1928 charged with various offences under Articles 87, 88, and 89 of the Penal Code which dated from the 1852 repression following Napoleon III's *coup d'état*. The PCF provided lawyers for the defendants and financial support to their families in protest against the actions of the government.[74] Communist support for the defendants also signalled support for autonomism itself; as Fourier, one of the Colmar lawyers stated, French actions in the region had created a community of interests amongst the disadvantaged working and lower-middle classes in the region. As a result, he pointed out, the future struggle

[72] Dreyfus, *La Vie Politique en Alsace*, pp. 90–1; Bankwitz, *Alsatian Autonomist Leaders*, p. 22.
[73] Solange Gras, 'La presse francaise et l'autonomisme alsacien en 1926', in Christian Gras and Georges Livet (eds), *Régions et régionalisme en France du XVIIIe siècle à nos jours* Vendôme, 1977), pp. 337–61.
[74] ADBR 286D 347 Inspecteur de Police Générale, Minker to M. le Sous-Préfet d'Erstein, 22 September 1928.

of the Alsatian and Lorrainer proletariat needed to take two aims into account: one socialist, the other national, which was to win autonomy for this 'petit pays where imperialism and capitalism reign'.[75]

As François Dreyfus has argued, there were two distinct types of autonomists on trial at Colmar: those who sought to win greater autonomy for Alsace within France, and those who were working for a return to Germany.[76] This distinction was not established by the prosecution, which also failed to demonstrate proof of a conspiracy or evidence of funding from Germany. As a result, the local press portrayed the trial as a farce. Eleven of the defendants were acquitted, but Joseph Rossé, Eugène Ricklin, Paul Schall, and Abbé Joseph Fasshauer were found guilty of plotting against the French state. All were imprisoned for a year and banned from entering Alsace for five years. The announcement of the verdict provoked rioting on the streets of Colmar, and in the elections of 1928 the autonomists won seats across Alsace (with the notable exceptions of Strasbourg and Mulhouse). Candidates with autonomist sympathies claimed twelve of the fifteen seats, with the Bas-Rhin population electing three UPR deputies, one pro-autonomy Communist, and one autonomist alongside the Conservative Charles Frey and Jacques Peirotes (SFIO), and the Haut-Rhin elected six UPRists and the Socialist Salomon Grumbach.

The results of the 1928 election should be understood as a protest against French policy in the region, rather than as popular endorsement for autonomism. But they also demonstrate just how far autonomism had permeated the views of the region's mainstream parties. With frustration rife over the imposition of the French language, administrative structures, and legislation, as well as over Herriot's proposals to introduce the separation of church and state, the Colmar trial had seemed to provide further evidence of the lack of French understanding of the situation in Alsace. While the autonomists saw themselves as the protectors of regional rights, the French government treated them as anti-national activists and argued that they were working for Germany. Worse was to come when the Chamber of Deputies voted to strip Rossé and Ricklin of their parliamentary mandates by a majority of 194 to 29 votes (with 350 abstentions) in response to the guilty verdict passed upon the two men.[77] By-elections were held to replace them in 1929, and returned their fellow Colmar defendants, the acquitted Marcel Stürmel and René Hauss, in a further act of protest.

Nevertheless, sections of Alsatian opinion worried that the trial tarred the entire regional population with the brush of loyalty to Germany, and brought the patriotism of 'good Alsatians' into question. As a result, the trial caused further fractures in Alsatian society. In the midst of the recriminations and fighting that followed the verdict, leading UPRist Joseph Weydmann demanded that the party place sanctions upon those militants who had collaborated with the autonomists,

[75] ADBR 286D 347 Inspecteur de Police Générale, Minker to M. le Sous-Préfet d'Erstein. 22 September 1928.
[76] Dreyfus, *La Vie Politique*, pp. 133–4.
[77] Goodfellow, *Between the Swastika and the Cross of Lorraine*, p. 37.

exclude Colmar defendants Rossé and Michel Walter from the party, and agree to make no further alliance with the Communists or autonomists. This was refused by the party committee, leading Weydmann and a circle of anti-autonomist UPR leaders to break away and form the *Alliance Populaire Nationale d'Alsace* (APNA) in December 1928.

The new party continued to defend Catholic rights, but rejected the principle of autonomy for Alsace.[78] This left the UPR free to focus on the protection of regional privileges, and to ally with parties that shared this priority. This produced some surprising alliances. In 1928 the UPR's posters in the constituency of Strasbourg II called on Catholic workers to vote for the Communist candidate Jean-Pierre Mourer to secure the maintenance of the Concordat in the region, while UPR election circulars called on Catholic voters in Saverne to support the anti-clerical Protestant Camille Dahlet of the *Fortschrittspartei* 'in spite of his position on religion', in the hope of demonstrating the strength of regional feeling in Alsace.[79]

In 1929 this strategy was formalized when the UPR allied with the Communists and autonomists in municipal elections across Alsace. These coalitions won the majority of the seats in the high-profile councils of Strasbourg and Colmar, and the Communist Charles Hueber was voted mayor of Strasbourg and the UPR's Eugène Herzog became mayor in Colmar. On hearing the news, the Catholic party's activities were condemned by Charles Ruch, Bishop of Strasbourg, who had already banned Catholics from reading the *Zukunft* and ordered priests not to read, recommend, or collaborate on the *Zukunft* or its fellow autonomist newspapers the *Wahrheit* and the *Schliffenstaan*.[80] Ruch's condemnation, combined with a decline in popular support and splintering of the autonomist movement, eventually led the UPR to disassociate itself from its alliance in the 1930s.

The Communist Central Committee was similarly aghast at the Alsatian party's failure to follow its 'class against class' strategy and insisted that all elected PCF members resign from the council or face expulsion from the party. With the exception of one Colmar councillor, all of the Communist councillors refused to resign and were expelled from the PCF in 1929. This led to a further redrawing of the boundaries of the Alsatian political landscape in October 1929, as the expelled Communists formed a new party, the *Kommunistiche Partei Opposition* (KPO), affiliated to the German-based International Communist Opposition (IVKO). In 1934 the KPO was expelled from the IVKO, and local leaders Hueber and Jean-Pierre Mourer formed the autonomist *Elsässische Arbeiter- und Bauernpartei* in 1935. The loss of Hueber and Mourer left the PCF without leadership, and although Maurice Thorez was at pains to stress that the PCF would remain the

---

[78] For further information on the APNA, see the biography of its leader, Alfred Oberkirch: Christian Baechler (ed.), *Alfred Oberkirch 1876–1947. Un médecin alsacien dans la tourmente politique* (Strasbourg, 1990).

[79] *Parti Socialiste: Section Française de l'International Ouvrière. XXVe Congrès National, tenu à Toulouse, les 26, 27, 28 et 29 mai 1928*, Compte Rendu Sténographique (Limoges, 1928), p. 257; AN F7 12751 Commissaire Spécial, Rapport mensuel, Saverne, 3 April 1928.

[80] AN F7 12751 Commissaire Spécial to M. le Directeur de Cabinet, Directeur de la sûreté générale, Strasbourg, 2 July 1927. Report on a letter of 8 June 1927 addressed to priests of his diocese.

defender of the oppressed peoples of Alsace-Lorraine, the Communist Party was never able to recapture the earlier successes that it had enjoyed in Alsace, and its share of the votes declined from 20.1 per cent in the Bas-Rhin and 13.3 per cent in the Haut-Rhin in the 1928 elections to 13.3 per cent and 7.8 per cent, respectively, in 1932.[81] Meanwhile, Hueber's and Mourer's drift towards the right meant that they lost much of their working-class support, leading Mourer to lose the 1937 cantonal elections to the Socialist Charles Hincker. Eventually the *Bauernpartei* associated itself with the Nazi party, and after Alsace's annexation into the Third Reich Hueber was reinstated as mayor of Strasbourg and Mourer became *Kreisleiter* for Mulhouse.[82]

The issue of autonomism did not only provoke fractures between Paris and Alsace, however. While much of the Alsatian population condemned 'Bloody Sunday' and applauded Haegy's victory, police across the region also reported ambivalence or outright frustration towards the autonomist movement. According to one report, by May 1927 most readers of the *Zukunft* bought the daily out of curiosity, while another noted that the populations of Sélestat and Saverne welcomed the ban placed upon the autonomist press.[83] In November 1927 the Special Commissioner of Saverne described a fight that broke out when some autonomists requested that the band play a *Heimatbund* dance at the village festival in Drulingen. According to the commissioner, the village population protested and the resulting skirmish ended with the autonomists being thrown out of the festival.[84] These reports may well have been written with a view to reassuring superiors in Strasbourg or Paris, yet they do speak of increasing division within the region, as Alsatian was pitted against Alsatian over questions of autonomy and assimilation.

Similar fractures emerged between Alsace and the Moselle. The Mosellan autonomy movement maintained important centres of support, most notably in the German- or dialect-speaking areas close to the border, although it was almost totally dependent on Alsace for funds. Yet autonomism was never as pervasive a force in the Moselle as in the Alsatian departments. Crucially, many Mosellans resented what they perceived to be Alsatian dominance of the movement and, as a result, particularism emerged as a more potent branch of departmental politics. This also fed into perceptions in Paris that the Moselle was the least troublesome of the three recovered departments.[85]

From the end of the 1920s onward, the links that many leading autonomists enjoyed with Germany led the debate to become increasingly couched in national terms; on the Strasbourg city council Socialists, Conservatives, and Radicals called

[81] Samuel Goodfellow, 'From Communism to Nazism: The Transformation of Alsatian Communists', *Journal of Contemporary History*, 27 (1992), pp. 231–58, p. 243.

[82] For further detail on their transformation, see Goodfellow, *Between the Swastika and the Cross of Lorraine.*

[83] AN F7 12751 Commissaire Spécial, Rapport mensuel, Saverne, 3 January 1928; Commissaire Spécial, Rapport Mensuel, Sélestat, 2 May 1927; F7 12751 Commissaire Spécial Sélestat, Rapport mensuel, Sélestat, 1 December 1928.

[84] AN F7 12751 Commissaire Spécial, Rapport mensuel, Saverne, 2 November 1927.

[85] Alison Carrol and Louisa Zanoun, 'The View from the Border. A Comparative Study of Autonomism in Alsace and the Moselle, 1918–1929', *European Review of History*, 18 (2011), pp. 465–86.

their *Volksfront* colleagues 'boches' or 'amis de boches' in 1930.[86] And, as German troops marched into the Rhineland, the SFIO accused autonomist politicians of 'doing Germany's dirty work'.[87] Such accusations represented a rejection of Germany that was common in much of interwar Alsatian political life, but they also played upon French fears about the potential security implications of German influence amongst its border population, and members of the government and administration similarly worried about German involvement in the movement. The prefect of the Haut-Rhin, Charles Valette, described autonomism as the work of 'Germanophiles' or the 'anational' PCF. While the majority of the Alsatian population were good French patriots, he wrote, they had been manipulated by these anti-national elements, by the Germanophile clergy, or by the large number of Germans who had been given leave to remain in Alsace by an overly generous peace settlement.[88]

Of course, not all autonomists were in favour of return to Germany and, equally, other autonomists enjoyed international links and networks that extended beyond the German lands. In February 1929 Progressist (and former Radical) Camille Dahlet went so far as to meet with the leaders of the Minorities Congress in Geneva in the hope of securing broader support for autonomism in Alsace. His trip was closely monitored by the French government, and a French consul reported with relief that the Congress leaders had demonstrated limited interest in supporting Alsatian demands for minority status.

The problem for the government was, of course, that autonomism was a heterogeneous movement, and what it meant to be an autonomist meant different things to different people. Not only is it important to distinguish between regionalism, separatism, and autonomism, but it is also necessary to distinguish between different branches within the autonomist movement. Scholarship on the movement has reflected these difficulties of classification. Christian Baechler has argued that there were three strands: the first were the separatists who wanted autonomy for Alsace, preferably within a federally reorganized Europe, and the second saw autonomism as the best means of preserving Alsatian particularities within France, although they differed over the question of religious institutions. Within this second group some, like the Protestant Camille Dahlet, preferred to leave religious questions to one side, while others in the UPR saw them as central to the 'customs and traditions' that they sought to preserve. Third, there were the regionalists who favoured decentralization of French administrative structures, and they included the Conservatives and the right wing of the UPR that broke away to form the APNA.[89]

[86] AMVES Compte-rendu du Conseil Municipal de la Ville de Strasbourg, 18 séance, 3 February 1930, Discours de Staehling, p. 203.

[87] ADBR 286D 345 Commissariat Spécial des Ponts et de Port du Rhin Strasbourg to M. le Prefect du Bas-Rhin, 23 April 1936.

[88] ADBR 121AL 102 Préfet du Haut-Rhin (Charles Valette) to M. le Ministre de l'Intérieur, Colmar, April 1922.

[89] Christian Baechler, 'L'autonomisme alsacien entre les deux guerres', *Historiens et Géographes*, 347 (1995), pp. 249–55, p. 254.

Philip Bankwitz similarly identifies three strands, but sees the divisions as between Catholic autonomists, lay liberal autonomists, and anti-French separatists.[90] And, for David A. Harvey, the autonomist movement can be divided into four: first, Catholic autonomism; second, the dialect-speaking Lutheran population of the northern Bas-Rhin; third, the Communist Party, which increasingly made autonomist demands in the late 1920s; and fourth, a strand evident in all three branches which emerged as a distinct branch in the 1930s. This was the *völkisch* German nationalism which opposed French rule on ethnic as well as cultural terms.[91]

Part of the problem in classifying autonomism is that Alsatians themselves were not consistent in how they described the movement. The regional population had different languages that they could, and did, draw upon as they strategically invoked different labels to describe themselves and their situation, or to discredit their political rivals. What is more, while it built upon a long-standing commitment to regional autonomy that had developed while Alsace was under German rule, interwar autonomism was very different from the earlier movement. It represented a response to the perceived threat to local rights and traditions that French policy represented, and won support across diverse sections of society, acquiring resonance in varied political, social, and economic contexts. But it resonated most with those Alsatians who were particularly disillusioned by the return to French rule, notably teachers, civil servants, or workers in companies sequestered by the French government. As a result, while autonomism appeared to capture the popular mood in the region, it must be viewed as a divisive, rather than a unitary, political force in 1920s Alsace.

Just as views in Alsace were divided on autonomism, so this was the case in Paris. The Communists were the only national party to back the movement in the 1920s, and they demonstrated this support through the provision of legal aid for the defendants at the Colmar trial, and through their focus upon France's exploitation of the region in the press. The Socialists expressed concern at the Catholic party's association with the movement, while Conservatives worried about its connections with Germany. But in spite of such variation in their views, when politicians or civil servants in Paris talked about autonomism they tended to view the movement as anti-French, and by implication, pro-German. This binary way of viewing autonomism reflected a broader understanding of nationalization that had little in common with realities in Alsace, where one person could describe themself as French, speak German, wave tricolour flags on 14 July, and vote for autonomist candidates in elections. Rather than revealing pro-French or pro-German attitudes, such behaviour reflected daily experience in the borderland, where nationalization is better understood in terms of a spectrum of loyalties than in binary terms. For many Alsatians, autonomism represented the political manifestation of this spectrum.

Autonomists may have differed amongst themselves over what the priorities should be, but most Alsatians could be better classed as 'regionalists' rather than autonomists or separatists, and much of the movement represented an attempt to

[90] Philip Charles Fairwell Bankwitz, *Alsatian Autonomist Leaders. 1919–1947* (Kansas, 1978), p. 4.
[91] Harvey, *Constructing Class*, pp. 155–6.

protect regional tradition that was neither pro-French nor anti-German. Paris, however, focused on the pro-German minority within the movement and treated autonomism in its entirety as distinctly anti-French. Despite the shelving of repressive policies following the Colmar trial, the French government continued to interpret the autonomist demands of Alsatian parties through the prism of the nation state. The clash between the French government's analysis of autonomism and its place in daily life in Alsace served to increase the distance between Paris and Strasbourg, while adding to the existing fractures at the centre and at the periphery, and complicating further the already difficult process of reintegration.

REDRAWING ALLIANCES IN THE 1930s

Autonomism permeated political allegiances, and provoked major shifts in the alliances formed by Alsatian parties. The Catholics and Conservatives had come together as the Bloc National in the 1919 and 1924 elections to face the Socialists and Radicals, and the two blocs had reformed in 1925 in municipal elections which saw the SFIO–Radical list face the Bloc National and PCF in cities and towns across Alsace and win notable successes in Strasbourg, Colmar, Mulhouse, Sélestat, and Sainte-Marie-Aux-Mines. In 1924 the impetus for the SFIO–Radical alliance came from Paris and had met with opposition amongst militants in the region, particularly amongst the left of the Haut-Rhin Socialist Party.[92] Nevertheless, after it was finally formed, the SFIO–Radical alliance survived the Radicals' 1926 schism and persisted throughout the 1930s. Alsatian Radicals tended to be of the centre-left, and found common ground with the local SFIO over questions of welfare, religious laws, and Alsatian reintegration. The UPR–Conservative alliance that had secured the Bloc National's 1919 and 1924 victories did not fare so well in the second half of the 1920s, however. It was shaken by autonomism, and, as the UPR increasingly foregrounded regional questions, the party found greater common ground with the newly created autonomist parties and with the Communists. As we have seen, this led to formal alliances, including the *Volksfront* of Catholics, Communists, and autonomists in Strasbourg. In this way, regional issues permeated the 1920s political landscape to the extent that the boundaries between left and right became less important than those between regionalists and assimilationists.

The 1930s saw further redrawing of Alsatian party-political alliances. Germany's increasingly belligerent foreign policy problematized autonomism's connections to Germany. For the UPR, this combined with Bishop Ruch's condemnation of autonomism and led the party to distance itself from its Communist and autonomist partners. Meanwhile, the ejection of its local leadership left the Alsatian Communist Party adrift without a clear purpose, and the Nazi seizure of power in 1933 posed fresh questions for the autonomists, as any association with Germany could be interpreted as endorsement of the Third Reich. In this changed political context, alliances were redrawn and the political register moved back towards a

[92] AN AJ30 232 Préfet du Haut-Rhin to Ministre de l'Intérieur, Colmar, April 1924.

division between left and right and away from the divide between autonomists and assimilationists that had dominated politics during the 1920s.

First, on the left, from 1934 the threat posed by domestic and international fascism led the parties of the centre-left and left to come together in an anti-fascist front to oppose the right wing leagues in France, Mussolini's Fascist Party in Italy, and Hitler's National Socialists in Germany. In Alsace, Socialists, Communists, and Radicals announced their intention to work together against fascism, although many local fronts did not get off to a good start. In the Haut-Rhin town of Guebwiller, the Socialists abstained in the municipal by-elections held in December 1934, with the result that neither the Socialists nor the Communists were able to seize the town hall.[93] Later that month, the prefect of the Bas-Rhin expressed his reservations about the developing front, remarking that the leadership of the two parties was still in opposition over the 'question of Alsace-Lorraine'.[94] This had divided the two parties since the split at Tours, but bitterness on the part of the Socialists had only increased as the Communists had edged closer to autonomism during the 1920s. The PCF's expulsion of its autonomist leaders Hueber and Mourer had not eased SFIO worries, and, as a precautionary measure, the party went as far as reaffirming its 1919 programme on Alsatian issues at its 1935 congress.[95] In spite of their differences, the Socialists and Communists joined forces alongside the Radicals to hold meetings to protest after SFIO leader Léon Blum was attacked in Paris by members of the royalist association, the *Camelots du Roi*, in February 1936.[96] Crucially, the party leaders' reluctance was not shared by Socialist or Communist militants; cooperation was accepted 'easily' by members of local branches and federations, according to police reports.[97] In the unions, the membership led the way. CGT and CGTU members held joint May Day processions from 1 May 1934, but it was only in 1936 that the Socialist CGT and Communist CGTU fused.[98]

When it came to the election of 1936, the front faced an additional problem in its title, the '*Front Populaire*'. Adopted by the Socialists, Radicals, and Communists across France, it reflected the popular mandate of the anti-fascist coalition, the 'People's Front'.[99] In German, this title translated as the '*Volksfront*', a title which had already been used by the Communist–Catholic–Autonomist coalition in Strasbourg, and was, as a result, unavailable to Alsatian Popular Front leaders. The

---

[93] ADBR 98AL 683 Préfet du Haut-Rhin to M. le Ministre de l'Intérieur, Colmar, 29 December 1934.

[94] ADBR 98AL 683 Préfet du Bas-Rhin to M. le Ministre de l'Intérieur, Strasbourg, 31 December 1934.

[95] *Die Freie Presse*, 23, 24, 25 January 1935.

[96] ADBR 98AL 683 Préfet du Bas-Rhin to Vice Président du Conseil, 18 July 1934.

[97] ADBR 98AL 683 Commissaire Divisionnaire de Police spéciale to Préfet du Bas-Rhin, Strasbourg, 28 December 1934.

[98] ADBR 98AL 684/1 Commissaire Divisionnaire de Police Spéciale Préfet du Bas-Rhin, Strasbourg, 28 October 1935; ADBR 98AL 683 Préfet du Bas-Rhin to Ministre de l'Intérieur, Strasbourg, 31 December 1934; ADBR 98AL 683 Préfet du Haut-Rhin to Ministre de l'Intérieur, Colmar, 29 December 1934; ADBR 98AL 683 Commissaire Divisionnaire de Police spéciale to Préfet du Bas-Rhin, Strasbourg, 28 December 1934.

[99] On the Popular Front, see Julian Jackson, *The Popular Front in France: Defending Democracy 1934–1938* (Cambridge, 1998).

Alsatian coalition was therefore known as the *Front Populaire*, a French-language title that stood out in the landscape of regional politics where debate was conducted in German, and fed into a widespread (and not wholly mistaken) perception that the front was an import from the French interior.

In 1935 the Popular Front successfully contested municipal elections in Colmar and Mulhouse, but not in Strasbourg, where the Socialists allied with the Conservatives and helped secure the election of Conservative Charles Frey as mayor. This served as a taster for the following year's parliamentary elections. Discipline prevailed in the Haut-Rhin, where Radical and Communist candidates stood down for the Socialist mayor Edouard Richard in Colmar, while in Mulhouse the Communists deferred to the Socialist candidate Jean Wagner. Neither Popular Front candidate was elected, however. In the Bas-Rhin, the coalition fell apart in Strasbourg when the first round returned the Conservative Garcin in first place and the autonomist Charles Hueber second. The Popular Front's candidate, the Socialist Georges Weill, came third. With the UPR instructing its voters to support Garcin, the Front decided to withdraw all of its candidates and order support for Hueber, who was elected. In Strasbourg-Campagne, the Popular Front registered its sole Alsatian success when the SFIO candidate Adolf Sorgus stood down for the PCF's Alfred Daul to secure the defeat of the Conservative Charles Frey. Yet the Haut-Rhin Popular Front survived the national collapse of the Front in 1938. When Mulhouse's deputy, the Conservative Alfred Wallach, resigned in 1939, he provoked a by-election. This saw the Radical and Communist candidates stand down in favour of the Socialist Jean Wagner on a platform focused upon domestic reaction and international fascism. In spite of this triumph for the unity of the Alsatian front, Wagner was narrowly defeated by the Conservative candidate Joseph Fega by 500 votes.[100]

With the Radicals and Communists both weakened by their splits, the Popular Front had difficulty in getting its message across to the Alsatian population. With just one deputy elected from the two Alsatian departments, the 1936 election revealed the Alsatian Research and Information Committee's report that politics in the region were evolving towards national patterns to be a touch optimistic.[101] Rather, Alsace was once again out of step with the rest of France, where the Popular Front swept to victory and the SFIO's Léon Blum became France's first Socialist prime minister. Indeed, throughout the election campaign political meetings continued to return to Alsace's status within France; police reports reveal that audience members questioned speakers on religious education and the introduction of secular legislation into Alsace and the Moselle, in spite of the orators' attempts to discuss the fascist threat, the international political situation, or the financial crisis.[102]

---

[100] ADBR, 98AL 333; *La République*, 20 February 1937.

[101] 'L'evolution politique depuis 1932' par Gustave Mary, Secrétaire de redaction de l'Office regional d'information, Comité alsacien d'études et d'informations, *L'Alsace depuis son retour à la France. Premier supplement: Vie politique administrative et sociale; Vie intellectuelle; artisistique et spirituelle; Vie economique* (Strasbourg, 1937), p. 15.

[102] ADBR 286D 345 Commissaire Spécial to Commissaire Division de Police Spéciale, 31 March 1936. Report on Socialist meeting in Rhinau; Commissaire Spécial to Commissaire Division de Police Spéciale, 31 March 1936. Report on Socialist meeting in Marckolsheim.

On the other side of the political spectrum, the Catholic parties—the UPR and APNA—entered a rapprochement during the 1930s which helped the UPR to increase its total number of votes in 1936, although sections of the UPR (and notably that around Colmar deputy Joseph Rossé) maintained their commitment to regionalism and links with both Germany and the autonomist parties. Amongst the autonomist parties, alliances shifted as the unity enjoyed during the 1920s splintered. The parties increasingly found themselves at odds with each other, and the alliances forged during the 1920s had collapsed by the 1934 cantonal elections. By the middle of the decade, many of the autonomist parties of the 1920s had lost much of their support, or had adopted a pro-German and pro-Hitler stance. Dahlet and the *Fortschrittspartei* broke away from the autonomist *Elsass-Lothringer Zeitung* in September 1933 in protest against the newspaper's increasingly positive treatment of Hitler. Their departure left the *Landespartei* isolated, and encouraged its leadership to agree to a fusion with Hueber's and Mourer's *Arbeiter- und Bauernpartei* to form the *Elsass-Lothringische Arbeiter- und Bauernpartei* in July 1939. This was banned on 31 October 1939 following the outbreak of war.

Demands for greater links or return to Germany dominated autonomism during the second decade after the return to France, as new, pro-German autonomist parties emerged.[103] This second wave was led by three organizations: the *Bauernbund*, the *Comices Agricoles (Kreisverein)*, and the *Jungmannschaft*. The *Bauernbund*, led by Joseph Bilger, had centres of strength in the Bas-Rhin and close links with the Third Reich. In 1938 a package addressed to Bilger was intercepted at customs and found to contain translated speeches by Joseph Goebbels and Nazi propaganda material. The *Comices Agricoles* had greater strength in the Haut-Rhin, and enjoyed particular support in the countryside. The *Jungmannschaft* was a proto-Nazi youth organization established by Hermann Bickler, a collaborator on the *Elsass-Lothringer Zeitung* dubbed the 'Konrad Henlein of Alsace' by the French press.[104] *Jungmannschaft* members wore brown uniforms, sang marching songs, and adopted the Nazis' leadership principle, the *Führerprinzip*. After Bickler refounded the organization as the *Elsass-Lothringische Partei* in 1931, it increased its appeal further. By 1934 it boasted 130 sections and 2,000 members, and was classified as the most dangerous pro-German party in Alsace by the French police.[105] It was banned by the French government on 21 April 1939.

Autonomism did not maintain its importance in Alsatian politics during the 1930s. François Dreyfus suggests that the autonomist parties' increasingly positive attitude towards the Third Reich in this decade explains the lack of appeal that they held for the Alsatian population.[106] But the idea that Nazism killed autonomism must be coupled with shifting relations between France and its borderland, signalled by the 1931 amnesty for those convicted at Colmar. This robbed the movement of some of its *raison d'être* as a protest movement, while

---

[103] ADBR 98AL 634 Report by V. Dauny, Inspecteur d'Academie à Bourges, Cher, 12 May 1938.
[104] Tara Zahra, 'The "Minority Problem" and National Classification in the French and Czechoslovak Borderlands', *Contemporary European History*, 17 (2008), pp. 137–65, p. 145.
[105] Bankwitz, *Alsatian Autonomist Leaders*, p. 54.
[106] Dreyfus, *La Vie Politique*, p. 211. See also Harvey, *Constructing Class*, pp. 167–8.

reductions in German funding after the depression hit the Weimar Republic in 1929 affected the propaganda possibilities of much of the autonomist press. Nevertheless, as Samuel Goodfellow has pointed out, autonomism engendered a political discourse that legitimized fascist activity, and fascist leagues established themselves in the region from the middle of the 1930s. Fascism became increasingly important in Alsace, and Goodfellow's research suggests that by 1938 the movement consisted of around 40,000 activists, split between the Alsatian Nazis and *Croix de Feu/Parti Social Français*,[107] This represented around 4 per cent of the population.

These fascist leagues and parties capitalized on increased anti-Semitism in the 1930s. Anti-Semitism had been present in Alsace throughout the interwar years; in the 1925 Soultz election, Catholic voters were reportedly ordered 'not to vote for a Jew', and in the early 1930s, Colmar deputy Joseph Rossé went so far as to demand the imposition of a *numerus clausus*.[108] This earlier anti-Semitism was connected to the widespread belief that Jews were behind the Radical party and its anti-clerical agenda, and this assumption appeared validated by the Jewish Socialist Georges Weill's close association with Edouard Herriot and the *Cartel des gauches*. Throughout the 1920s the prefects described regional anti-Semitism as connected to Jewish support of 'all that is national'.[109] But in the 1930s local anti-Semitism grew as increasing numbers of German Jewish refugees arrived in Alsace.[110] The British Foreign Office reported that after 1933 the Nazi government successfully exploited growing anti-Semitism in Alsace as a subject for German propaganda in the region.[111] The result was increased anti-Semitic activity, ranging from attacks to incidents of the type recorded by Jean Libmann, a Jewish SFIO adjunct on the Colmar municipal council, who recalled that in the 1935 municipal elections his name was crossed out on a poster listing the candidates, along with the names of Jewish candidates Dreyfus and Lehmann. The name of a fourth candidate named Weill, who was not Jewish, was mistakenly crossed out on the assumption that he was also a Jew.[112] But anti-Semitic rhetoric in the region's extreme right-wing press also took a more violent turn. In part, this reflected German influence and the movements' connections with Germany, but for certain elements such anti-Semitism represented a means of stressing their place within the French nation.

[107] Goodfellow, *Between the Swastika and the Cross of Lorraine*, pp. 5, 27.
[108] ADBR 121AL 102 Préfet du Haut-Rhin to Commissaire Général, 22 January 1925; Léon Strauss, 'L'anti-sémitisme en Alsace dans les années trente', *XVIIIe Conférence de la Société d'Histoire des Israelites d'Alsace et de Lorraine, Strasbourg, 10–11 Février 1996* (Strasbourg), pp. 77–89.
[109] ADBR 296D 347 Préfet du Bas-Rhin to Président du Conseil, October 1928. Report sur la journée du 10 octobre 1928.
[110] Vicki Caron, 'The anti-Semitic revival in France in the 1930s: the socio-economic dimension reconsidered', *Journal of Modern History*, 70 (1998), pp. 24–73, p. 57; see also Strauss, 'L'anti-sémitisme en Alsace', pp. 77–89.
[111] TNA FO 371/21621 C12861 German-speaking population of Alsace-Lorraine. Sir E. Phipps, Paris, 24 October 1938.
[112] Jean Libmann, *Mes Mémoires, Chronique d'une famille en marge de l'histoire* (Strasbourg, 1989).

While the fascists established their hold on sections of Alsatian society, elsewhere the population watched with concern as Germany reasserted its claims on Alsace-Lorraine. As we have seen, this dated from before Hitler's seizure of power; Weimar had funded pro-German activity in Alsace and, in 1932, Chancellor Brüning and President Hindenburg sent telegrams to the annual congress of the *Verein fur das Deutschtum im Ausland* (Association of Germans Living Abroad), which called on them not to regard any German territory as lost. This activity stepped up a gear after the establishment of the Third Reich; in April 1933, a demonstration on the Rhenish border led to injuries for a number of French customs officials, and the sixtieth anniversary of the establishment of the Kaiser Wilhelm University in Strasbourg triggered a series of radio programmes and demonstrations in Germany which stressed the cultural and intellectual importance of the German institution.

This propaganda attracted some Alsatians, but the majority of the population watched in horror as the Nazi government stepped up its brutality towards the German population, and as the Wehrmacht marched first into the Rhineland, then Vienna, then the Sudetenland, and then Prague. After the Anschluss in March 1938, the *Humanité d'Alsace-Lorraine*'s editorial warned that 'after Vienna, Strasbourg must be Hitler's next conquest!'[113] First-hand accounts about the regime came from the large numbers of refugees who flocked to the region (and particularly Strasbourg) from 1933 onward. These refugees were a diverse group, united by their opposition to Nazism. Many contributed to anti-Nazi activity in the region, although such activity was closely monitored by the French authorities, who worried that their propaganda would lead to tensions with the Third Reich.[114]

The second decade after Alsace's return to France saw the redrawing of political alliances and the emergence of new parties and movements, notably proto-fascist parties. Alsace was not alone in experiencing political polarization; across France, the leagues of the extreme right jostled with the PCF as they attempted to provide the answers to the questions facing the French nation.[115] And across Europe, parties of the extreme left and right battled as democracies gave way to dictatorships. This polarization of politics was inseparable from an increasingly tense international situation that led Zara Steiner to label the 1930s as a period of 'pre-war' tension distinct from the 'post-war' years that followed the end of the First World War in 1918.[116] In Alsace, questions over the region's status lingered, and interacted with concerns over its future in a Europe which had its eyes fixed on an ever more aggressive Germany.

[113] Dreyfus, *La Vie Politique en Alsace*, p. 190.

[114] ADBR 286D 345 Ministre de l'Intérieur to Préfet du Bas-Rhin, 18 November 1937.

[115] Brian Jenkins and Chris Millington, *France and Fascism. February 1934 and the Dynamics of Political Crisis* (Oxford, 2015); Samuel Kalman, *The Extreme Right in Interwar France: The Faisceau and the Croix de Feu* (Aldershot, 2008); Sean Kennedy, *Reconciling France against Democracy: The Croix de Feu and the Parti Social Français, 1929–1935* (Montreal, 2007); Robert Soucy, *French Fascism: The Second Wave* (New Haven, 1995).

[116] Zara Steiner, *The Lights that Failed. European International History, 1919–1933* (Oxford, 2005).

CONCLUSION

Political life in interwar Alsace was dominated by questions of integration. Issues such as the status of the regional railways or introduction of secular legislation dominated party programmes and political debate. The controversies provoked by these issues triggered splits in the regional political landscape, as divisions between autonomists and assimilationists became more significant than the divide between left and right in the 1920s. By the 1930s, a thaw in relations between Paris and its borderland, and changes in the political regime in Germany, led to a new relationship with Alsace that provoked further changes in local politics. The parties returned to the previous divisions between left and right as autonomism lost some of its appeal, but they retained their local distinctiveness and remained out of step with politics in the French interior. Throughout, the region's distinct history, the particular importance of religion, use of the German language, and the sense that the Alsatian population faced a particular set of concerns shaped local politics, and made reintegration more difficult.

All the same, in spite of the resulting claustrophobia that surrounded local politics, political life in Alsace was also defined by the interaction between local concerns and the cross-border flow of people, money, and ideas. These flows went in both directions, although not at the same time. In the years after the purge trials, Alsatian political leaders headed eastwards across the Rhine to restart their political careers in the Weimar Republic; then in the 1920s money flowed in the opposite direction to help fund the autonomist movement. During the late 1920s young Alsatian Communists attended training camps in Germany, and in the 1930s refugees from Hitler's Germany arrived in the region and started anti-Nazi propaganda campaigns. That these flows went in particular directions at particular moments is a reminder that neither the causes nor the outcomes of transnational movements remained static, and both changed over time. And, of course, they offer a reminder of the border's dual function as both limit and point of contact between neighbouring populations, and of how this too evolved over time.

What is remarkable is how many of these cross-border flows and encounters had both local roots and local implications. In the case of the purge trials, the commissions led to the departure of a number of politicians. Upon their arrival in Germany, some began campaigning for Alsace's return to Germany and were involved in organizing funding for the autonomist movement. Or, to take the example of autonomism, the movement emerged in order to protect local rights and sensibilities, but was fuelled by German money and the French authorities' concerns that it was a German import. Both finances and perceptions affected how the autonomists described themselves, and how other Alsatians responded to their ideas about integration. In this way the local and transnational became enmeshed and affected the development of each other. This is reflective of the broader entanglement of the two in Alsatian politics. As political life was dominated by the issue of reintegration, these cross-border interventions shaped its process and helped to determine the form of the return of Alsace to France.

Alsatian politicians were aware of these cross-border connections. They made reference to the region's double culture, called upon their networks, and made use of German words—such as '*Kulturkampf*' or '*Heimat*'—when the French word failed to capture the historical and cultural sense that they sought to convey. In this way, these links informed Alsatian understandings of their own situation. While individuals in Alsace saw such connections as a natural state in a borderland, once again the French authorities' fears about German influence in the recovered departments led them to see Germanophily, rather than the distinctively Alsatian political system that the region's population attempted to defend. Thus while contact with Germany bred a more clearly defined sense of difference for the Alsatian population, the French authorities found it difficult to distinguish between what was German and what was Alsatian.

4

Economic Reintegration

A study of the economic development of Alsace over the past one hundred and fifty years reveals that the region has been able to sustain its prosperity in spite of all of the political, economic and technical change that these years have produced.

Werner Wittich (1932)[1]

The economic section of the 1932 study conducted by the *Comité alsacien d'études et d'informations* on Alsace's return to France opens with a stress on the prosperity and adaptability of the regional economy. Alongside its celebrated textile industry, Alsace boasted chemical plants, potash mines, and metallurgical and engineering production, as well as small and medium-sized artisanal firms that produced beer and wine, leather goods, foie gras, and other luxury products. Its agricultural sector was similarly varied, and the region was a major producer of tobacco, hops, and grapes. The reason for this prosperity, according to Werner Wittich of the University of Strasbourg, was Alsace's position on the Rhine. This connected it with Germany and central Europe to the east, Switzerland to the south, and Belgium and the Low Countries to the north. And, of course, after 1918 economic success was in the interests of the French government, which treated it as a statement about Alsace's rightful place within France. However, shortly after the volume's publication, Alsace's position on the Rhine began to appear to be a liability rather than a strength. As war looked increasingly likely in the second half of the 1930s, the French government banned investment or the construction of infrastructure in the eastern-border departments, and certain companies relocated to the French interior. With a lack of investment and the requisition of farming equipment and livestock, an economic malaise set in across Alsace. This lasted until the outbreak of war in 1939.

The history of the Alsatian interwar economy is a story of the impact of national and international change upon long-standing regional economic links and ties. The region's distinct economic identity, built through centuries of trade across and along the Rhine, was subject to national and global forces. The years of German rule after 1871 encouraged the economy to turn further eastward, then 1918 represented a significant break as policies to remove German influence and to realign

[1] Werner Wittich, 'L'Alsace Economique de 1913 à 1933. Introduction', in Comité alsacien d'études et d'informations, *L'Alsace depuis son retour à la France*, 3 vols, vol. 2 (Strasbourg, 1933), p. 21.

economic structures meant that the interwar years saw a struggle to negotiate the return to French systems. In this sense, this chapter continues the theme of the interaction between the local, the national, and the transnational developed in the previous chapter, and economics were inseparable from political change. Just as the issue of reparations dominated Franco–German relations for far longer than anyone had anticipated, so political developments such as Hitler's seizure of power affected economics as the region struggled under the ban upon investment close to the border. In spite of its distinct economic identity, Alsace was always subject to shifts in government policy and affected by developments in the global economy. Indeed, in many ways it was more subject to wider forces than to local conditions, although of course it is difficult to disentangle the two. Above all, its economic reintegration was never able to escape the impact of the border.

This history is also, therefore, one of the effects of economic crisis upon social relations. Crisis in Alsace took the form of the problematic reintegration of the regional economy in the 1920s, and in the 1930s the global financial crisis had deep and lasting effects on local economic structures. Both crises affected border-land society, where the experience of war and change of national regime had crystallized identities and understandings of the regional community. The result was a clash between Paris and Alsace, as the French government attempted to remove what they perceived to be German influence and Alsatians battled to retain structures that they saw as distinctly Alsatian. In this atmosphere, the perception that the region faced a unique set of problems contributed to a sense of difference between Alsatian workers and those across the Vosges. But these crises also resulted in a clash at the centre and within the region, as differences arose in discussions over the solutions to Alsace's economic problems. What is more, problems of economic reintegration fostered a sense of difference between Alsace and the neighbouring German population, who alternately boycotted Alsatian goods and shopped in Alsace, pushing prices up. In this way, economic reintegration helped to make the border between France and Germany a meaningful division, though all the while it remained a site of contact between two communities.

This chapter traces this history. It opens with an introduction to the Alsatian economy and then considers, first, the problems of reintegration; second, the region's experience of depression in the 1930s; third, the dynamics of the border economy; and then, finally, the region's labour movement, which drew upon Alsace's connections to France and Germany. Throughout, it traces how change of national regime and fluctuations in the global economic and political situation affected the economy in Alsace after the return to France, and considers how the border shaped regional economic life.

THE ALSATIAN ECONOMY

Alsace has long benefited from its position on an economic crossroads between west and central Europe, and throughout its history the Rhine was a major trade route linking the River Rhône with Alsace, Germany, Switzerland, and the

Netherlands. In the nineteenth century, diplomatic and technological change transformed Rhine traffic. The foundation of the Rhine Commission at the Congress of Vienna in 1815 created an institution which established the laws of the river's navigation, while the development of steam power allowed goods to pass quickly up and down, connecting the countries that lay along the river's banks. This facilitated the development of the port in Strasbourg, which received goods from across Europe and beyond.

The nineteenth-century Alsatian economy combined a large agricultural sector with growing industry. Smallholdings dominated regional agriculture, and produced barley, oats, other cereals, potatoes, grapes, hops, and tobacco.[2] Agriculture retained its importance over the following years, as industrialization changed the face of the Alsatian economy. Across the region, textile manufacturers, chemical plants, engineering factories, and metallurgical enterprises sprung up alongside artisanal industries producing beer, leather, and foie gras. In the Haut-Rhin, the Mulhouse textile manufacturers dominated and shaped industrial development.[3] These family firms, many of which could trace their roots to the eighteenth century, expanded and earned global reputations for their products. Intermarriage amongst the Mulhouse textile families created what Michel Hau has dubbed 'a Mulhousian industrial dynasty', while auxiliary industries such as machine construction and chemical dyes emerged across the department to meet the needs of the textile firms.[4] Smaller firms dominated industry in the Bas-Rhin, and even in 1875 firms with five or fewer workers made up 98.4 per cent of the department's business and employed 67.9 per cent of its workforce.[5] Nonetheless, the northern Alsatian department also experienced considerable growth in the nineteenth century. The completion of the Rhône–Rhine Canal in 1834 increased Strasbourg's importance as a port, while railway construction under the Second Empire brought the city within half a day of Paris and boosted the department's De Dietrich forges and arms manufacture. On the eve of the Franco–Prussian War, Alsace was amongst the most industrialized regions in France.

The years of annexation into Germany saw farming retain its economic importance; two-thirds of countryside inhabitants worked in agriculture at the end of the nineteenth century.[6] By the early twentieth century Alsatian farmers and smallholders had created networks of support, education, and sociability. They were supported by insurance schemes that protected them against the death of livestock, agricultural savings banks which also offered loans, and well-attended winter

---

[2] During the interwar years, Alsatian agriculture remained dominated by polyculture and 90 percent of farms had less than 10 hectares. Richard Keller, 'L'Alsace Rurale: Un monde inchangé', in Bernard Vogler (ed.), *Chroniques d'Alsace 1918–1939* (Barcelona, 2004), p. 77. By 1942, 67,000 farms (61.4 per cent of the total) covered less than five hectares. Alfred Wahl and Jean-Claude Richez, *La Vie Quotidienne en Alsace entre France et Allemagne, 1850–1950* (Paris, 1993), p. 17.

[3] Marcel Moeder, *Notes sur l'industrie de Mulhouse et de ses environs* (Mulhouse, 1923).

[4] Michel Hau and Nicolas Stoskopf, *Les dynasties alsaciennes du XVIème siècle à nos jours* (Paris, 2005).

[5] David Allen Harvey, *Constructing Class and Nationality in Alsace, 1830–1945* (DeKalb, 2001), p. 17.

[6] Jean-Pierre Kintz, 'Vers une autre économie et une autre société', in Philippe Dollinger (ed.), *L'histoire de l'Alsace de 1900 à nos jours* (Toulouse, 1979), p. 140.

schools which advised on new farming techniques.[7] In industry, mergers encouraged by the establishment of Alsatian banks created a regional credit system that was able to respond to local circumstances, and the fusion of factories in the Bas-Rhin and the Haut-Rhin created the Alsatian Society of Mechanical Construction (SACM) in 1872. Meanwhile, in the textile and brewing industries the number of cotton mills dropped from forty-one to twenty between 1869 and 1914, and the number of breweries halved between 1872 and 1907 through mergers that created larger and more influential concerns.[8] Existing industries underwent expansion: the rail network grew from 862 kilometres of track to 1,958 kilometres between 1871 and 1914, while new industries also emerged.[9] One of the major success stories of the years of German rule was potash mining, which boomed after the 1904 discovery of this potassic salt, which was commonly used as a fertilizer. German investment in potash mining fostered a steady increase in production and, by 1914, the Alsatian mines produced 320,000 tonnes of potash per year.[10]

The outbreak of war hit agriculture immediately, and farmers and smallholders saw their workers called up into the army and land and crops destroyed when parts of Alsace became a zone of military operations in autumn 1914. The line hardly moved before the end of the war, preventing the resumption of agricultural activity and discouraging any further investment in the region. The Haut-Rhin's economy faltered as a lack of raw cotton, the collapse in demand, the transfer of capital into military production, and the incorporation of skilled workers into the army all forced the textile industry into crisis. When the war ended, the region was left with agricultural land devastated by conflict and industries struggling to deal with the movement towards war production.

Alsace emerged from the Great War in the throes of an economic slump. Workers returned from military service unable to find work, industries were unable to access the raw materials necessary for the resumption of normal activity, and inflation contributed to a sharp increase in the cost of living. In 1920 the Postal, Telegraph and Telephone Union estimated that living costs had risen by 544 per cent from their 1914 level, while workers' wages lagged behind with a mere 100–120 per cent increase.[11] While the union figures are higher than official estimates, they reflect a common complaint that the wage increases on offer failed to live up to the employers' wartime promises.[12] The result was a wave of isolated strikes which reached their peak in July and August 1919, when work stopped in the Haut-Rhin potash mines, the Mulhouse textile factories, and the Strasbourg tramways. This was followed by a general strike in April 1920.[13] Alongside protests about the rising cost of living, strikers demanded *Heimatrechte*,

[7] ADBR 121AL 156 *Le Petit Journal*, 26 May 1920, 'En Alsace-Lorraine' par H. Gomot.
[8] Dreyfus, *La Vie Politique en* Alsace, p. 265.   [9] Harvey, *Constructing Class*, p. 139.
[10] *L'Evénement*, 'Les richesses minières de l'Alsace-Lorraine', 25 May 1920.
[11] ADBR 121AL 878 Direction de Police, Strasbourg, 15 November 1920. Report on meeting of *cheminots* and PTT held Strasbourg, 14 November 1920.
[12] ADBR 121AL 880 Préfet du Haut-Rhin to Commissaire Général, Colmar, 22 June 1921.
[13] 'General Strike in Alsace-Lorriane', *The Daily News*, 24 April 1920.

or 'homeland rights', and condemned 'French imperialism'. It was not only the demands of the Alsatian strikers that were 'local', however. The calendar of strikes was also out of step with the rest of France, where the strikes took place in February and May, whereas in Alsace the strikes occurred in March and April.[14] Within less than two years, economic discontent became inextricably linked to wider dissatisfaction about the return to France, and pamphlets circulated by the strike committee described the 'ruin' of local industry and the struggle for the 'defence of the soil of our homeland'.[15]

As regional unemployment hit 33,000 in Upper Alsace alone by February 1919, town and city councils struggled to respond to the crisis with a combination of unemployment relief and public-works schemes.[16] By 1921, the city of Strasbourg had created 20 building sites employing 800 previously unemployed men on public-works schemes, while the town of Colmar spent 193,747 francs on unemployment relief and a further 296,930 francs on public works in 1921 alone.[17] A proportion of these costs was reimbursed by the state, but the local councils bore the brunt and found their finances squeezed.[18] In many parts of the region, these works contributed to the reconstruction of war-damaged towns, the dismantling of German constructions, or improvements to infrastructure, such as the enlargement of the port of Strasbourg or the works on the Rhône–Rhine Canal.[19] After the immediate crisis passed, the councils continued to use public-works schemes to provide employment for workers affected by seasonal work patterns, most notably construction workers, or to employ jobless workers on developments within the towns.[20] The Haut-Rhin industrialists, whose paternalist initiatives had dominated the mid-nineteenth century, attempted to challenge the decrease in their influence which accompanied municipal initiatives with the creation of new schemes, such as a family allowance in Mulhouse in 1920, but the interwar years saw their influence continue to decline as a result of increased state intervention. While local administrators preoccupied themselves with meeting the post-war crises in unemployment, infrastructure, and housing, the French government turned to the pressing problem of reintegrating the Alsatian economy.

[14] Fernand L'Huillier, 'Remarques sur les grèves de 1920 et de 1936 en Alsace', *Bulletin de la Societe d'Histoire Moderne,* 3 (1972), pp. 9–17.

[15] Harvey, *Constructing Class,* p. 147.

[16] 'La direction générale du travail, de la législation ouvrière et des assurances sociales au commissariat général d'Alsace-Lorraine: laboratoire du droit social (1919–1925)', *Les Cahiers du Comité d'Histoire,* Colloque organisé sous la responsabilité scientifique de Jeanne-Marie Tuffery-Andrieu le 11 décembre 2009, p. 21.

[17] AMVES 151MW 68 Rapport. Direction des travaux publics municipaux, envoyé à la Division III, Strasbourg, 12 February 1921; Archives Municipales de Colmar (hereafter AMC) Conseil Municipal de Colmar 36th séance, 29 December 1921, p. 1088.

[18] AMVES 151MW 68 Rapport sur les travaux organisés par les soins de la Ville immediatement après l'armistice et pendant la période de transition. (This proportion varied between towns and projects.)

[19] AMVES 151MW 68 Mayor of Strasbourg to Préfet du Bas-Rhin, Strasbourg, 14 February 1921; 151MW 68 Ministre des Travaux Publics to Jacques Peirotes, 12 September 1925.

[20] AMVES 151MW 68 Rapport au Conseil Municipal, concerne: travaux de chomage, signed Le Maire, Strasbourg, 3 October 1921.

PROBLEMS OF REINTEGRATING
THE ALSATIAN ECONOMY

The primary challenge facing both French policymakers and Alsatian economic elites after 1918 was the reintegration of the Alsatian economy into French markets and systems. During the years of German rule the Alsatian economy had turned east, and many industries created to meet the demands of the French market stagnated or relocated to sites west of the new border, while new forms of economic activity emerged. German migrants established new mining, metallurgy, and leatherwork enterprises, particularly in the Bas-Rhin. Coal, grain, and petrol arrived in Strasbourg's expanding port from centres across Germany and drove late nineteenth-century Alsatian industrialization. Potash mining became an important and valuable sector of the Alsatian economy, feeding the intensification of agricultural production in Germany and Alsace. The expansion of the railway network linked the region more closely to the rest of the German Empire. By the outbreak of war in 1914, Alsatian economic life was densely connected to Germany.

When the war reached its end, France had been severely affected by the fighting that had taken place on French soil. As Europe's leaders considered the peace, it was hoped that French heavy industry would be strengthened by the delivery of coal and iron ore from the Moselle, which would in turn aid France's economic reconstruction.[21] Yet at the Versailles Conference the Allies left the issue of reparations to the very end of the discussions and, as Robert Boyce has pointed out, they left three crucial questions unanswered: Germany's total reparations bill, how Germany would (or could) pay such a sum, and how the Allies would divide the payments up amongst themselves. As a result they postponed the crisis that emerged when it became fully apparent that covering the huge costs of the war through reparations could not be squared with the goal of rapid post-war economic recovery.[22] Thus, while recent work on French security policy has suggested that economic considerations were not as dominant as often assumed, the question of reparations and post-war economic recovery nonetheless played a role in Franco–German relations throughout the 1920s.[23] What is more, it had implications for both political and territorial security, and for the reintegration of Alsace.

When the French turned their attention to the economic reintegration of the recovered departments, their economic priorities mirrored their attitudes towards society, administration, and politics. As a result, the first step towards economic reintegration was deemed to be the separation of the Alsatian economy from Germany: the French franc replaced the German mark; companies owned by German corporations or individuals were sequestered and liquidated; and a customs border was established to separate Alsace from Germany. These early French initiatives provoked discontent and resistance in the recovered departments. In

[21] Adam Tooze, *The Deluge. The Great War and the Remaking of the Global Order, 1916–1931* (London, 2014).
[22] Robert Boyce, *The Great Interwar Crisis and the Collapse of Globalisation* (Basingstoke, 2009).
[23] Peter Jackson, *Beyond the Balance of Power. France and the Politics of National Security in the Era of the First World War* (Cambridge, 2013).

NB: note on this book: based on what France is doing - a gap in the lit is what Germany was doing - her borders as a site of contact nevertheless, remains rather one-sided

November 1918, the franc was introduced at a level determined by political rather than economic consideration; the rate created problems for businesses and was the source of much resentment.[24]

[rate of franc a prob]

[what about what claxed to Germany, they heard, not mentioned here?]

Greater problems still were caused by the sequestering of German-owned companies. German corporations which had invested in the Reichsland found themselves excluded, often without compensation. These firms were then placed under the temporary management of agents nominated by the French government, and later sold to French investors. As most of the large Haut-Rhin textile firms and the heavy industrial companies had remained untouched by outside investment, sequestration was a process that affected the new industries of Alsace and Lorraine, notably mining and railways, which had been driven by German investment. While this limited the impact of sequestering to some extent, the local significance of the industries affected served to ensure that the 'squandering' of national treasures, as Socialist deputy and Mayor of Strasbourg Jacques Peirotes described the scandal in 1927, became one of the major crises that followed the return to France in 1918.[25]

[corporations]

At the end of the war, the French government placed the German-owned potash-mining companies under government trusteeship and opened discussions about their future. The regional press launched a campaign in favour of the creation of one company to direct the mining of Alsatian potash, arguing that a single potash-mining corporation would be able to compete more effectively with potash producers elsewhere, and stressed that the 12,000 workers employed in mining were not too many for one company to manage.[26] These arguments stressed practicality and viability, but they were rooted in common criticism of the corruption that surrounded the influx of French capital into the recovered departments, and fed upon a widespread belief that the region's potash belonged to the Alsatian people. The Socialists mobilized this attitude to argue for state ownership of the mines, but the idea that the mines should be nationalized extended far beyond the organized labour movement. Indeed, it united voices from all shades of the political spectrum in opposition to French policy.[27] In spite of this opposition, the mines were placed under the ownership of the *Société Commerciale de Potasse d'Alsace* (SCPA) in 1920. But the issue remained a thorn in the side of the French government; in 1937 the sub-prefect of Mulhouse reported continued complaints about the SCPA's planned relocation from Mulhouse to Paris.[28]

[potash mining]

Similar issues of local interest were mobilized with regard to the railways. The Alsatian railway network had been significantly expanded under German rule and then administered by the imperial government, before being sequestered in 1918.

[railway]

[24] Fischer, *Alsace to the Alsatians?* p. 133. [25] Quoted in Harvey, *Constructing Class*, p. 139.
[26] *L'Express de Mulhouse*, 'L'Exploitation des mines de potasse d'Alsace. Sectionnement ou regime unitaire?' 19 March 1920; *Le Nouveau Rhin Français*, 19 March 1920; *Le Journal d'Alsace et de Lorraine*, 'L'exploitation des potasses d'Alsace', 27 May 1920.
[27] Resolution of Commission d'Alsace Lorraine AMC14640, Commission d'Alsace Lorraine, séance du 26 March 1920; *Journal de Mulhouse*, 6 May 1920 'Les mines de potasse d'Alsace et leur avenir'.
[28] ADBR 98AL 1071/1 Sous-Préfet de Mulhouse to Préfet du Haut-Rhin, Mulhouse, 18 October 1937.

While the French government tried to decide what to do with the railways, Alsatian railway workers argued in favour of the nationalization of the network, stressing that a state-owned company would put the safety of passengers over profit. Radical politician Camille Dahlet echoed their concerns, and urged the French government not to reject what had proved to be an effective system simply because they had labelled it as 'German'.[29] The Socialist Georges Weill went further and, in 1922, argued that nationalization of the railways of Alsace and the Moselle would present a model for nationalization across the French rail network. Far from being a 'local' question, Weill added, the future of the Alsatian railways was a question of 'general interest'.[30] Both arguments were considered by the government, which gave serious consideration to the idea of attaching the Alsatian railways to the Ministry of Public Works, and the ministry established a committee to study this very question.[31] Ultimately the committee rejected nationalization and instead announced on 13 December 1921 that the most economically viable option was the Alsatian railways' incorporation into the private *Compagnie de l'Est*.[32]

While the government stressed practicality, their concerns went beyond economics and they were keen to avoid nationalization of the Alsatian network lest it become a precedent for railways elsewhere. Again, Alsatian demands for widespread national reform and the presentation of Alsace as a model for broader change fell upon deaf ears. But whereas in the case of the separation of church and state local particularities were allowed to remain in place in the region, this was not the case when it came to economics, which proved more powerful than secularity. The French government refused to countenance any maintenance of the local status quo. Local opposition continued, and the Alsatian and Lorrainer Railway Workers' Union, numerous local councils, and politicians from across the spectrum expressed their opposition, but on 6 July 1922 the incorporation of the railway network of Alsace-Lorraine into the *Compagnie de l'Est* was agreed, though the network was administered by the *Compagnie d'Alsace-Lorraine* until the nationalization of all French railways into the SNCF in 1937–8.[33] The whiff of corruption that

---

[29] ADBR 121AL 156 *République*, 5 November 1922, 'Déraillements' by Camille Dahlet.

[30] AN AJ30 173 Session of the Conseil Consultatif of 21 July 1922.

[31] ADBR121AL 1105 Le Commissaire Général de la République to M. le Ministre des Travaux Publics, Strasbourg (nd), 1920; Project de Décret 1920; Rapport fait au nom de la Commission d'Alsace-Lorraine chargé d'examiner le projet de loi portant ratification du décret du 30 novembre 1920 relatif au rattachement des chemins de fer d'Alsace et de Lorraine au Ministère des Travaux Publics par M. René Baradé. Session de 1921; Note pour la Direction des Voies Ferrées et des Routes, 4 April 1923.

[32] ADBR 121AL 1105 Chambre des Députés No. 4770, Douzième Législature. Session de 1922. Annexe au procès verbal de la 2e séance du 8 juillet 1922. Projet de Loi portant approbation d'une convention passée entre le Ministre des Travaux Publics et la Compagnie des chemins de fer de l'Est pour l'exploitation des lignes du reseau d'Alsace et de Lorraine. Presenté au nom de M. Alexandre Millerand, Président de la République Française par M. Yves le Trocquer, Ministre des Travaux Publics et par M. Charles de Lasteyrie, Ministre des Finances.

[33] ADBR 121AL 1105 Le Secrétaire général du syndicat indépendent des cheminots d'Alsace et de Lorraine to M. Alapetite, Commissaire Général de la République, Président du Conseil Consultatif, 17 October 1923; Le Président de la Fédération des Syndicats Professionnels des Cheminots d'Alsace et de Lorraine to M. Alapetite, 1 October 1923; Résolution du Conseil Municipal de Reguisheim, 29 September 1923; Extrait du registre des deliberations du Conseil Municipal de la Commune

accompanied the entry of French capital encouraged condemnation of French imperialism in Alsace, while lingering questions over the future of the sequestered railways and potash mines kept the issue burning in the early 1920s.

The next means by which the French government attempted to separate the Alsatian economy from Germany was with the erection of a customs barrier between the recovered departments and the Weimar Republic. As a result, industrialists and manufacturers needed to locate new markets for Alsatian goods, which had increasingly been targeted at German markets between 1871 and 1918. Immediate separation proved impossible as Alsatian companies remained reliant on trade with Germany and many French firms hesitated before dealing with Alsatian businesses. For some firms, this reluctance was rooted in their uncertainty over whether companies based in the recovered departments were indeed 'Alsatian'. Establishments were unsure whether all German companies had been expunged from Alsace and the Moselle and feared that, in dealing with businesses based in Strasbourg, Colmar, or Mulhouse, they might end up negotiating with Germans. Correspondence with the Foreign Ministry and regional administration expressed regret that there was no 'black list' for Alsatian companies as there was for foreign establishments.[34] Elsewhere, Alsatian products did not meet the tastes or habits of French consumers, and this was a problem which proved particularly pressing in viticulture.

In 1920 Alsatian winemakers cultivated 26,000 hectares of grape vines and produced wines which they had altered to cater for the tastes of German drinkers and marketed as 'Rhineland wines'.[35] Under German rule, many producers bought new plants that allowed them to make larger quantities of wine, albeit wine of a lower quality, and the industry as a whole had been transformed by German legislation, which allowed the addition of sugared water to wine at a proportion of 4:1 and permitted wines to be improved by the supplement of grapes from another region, as long as the added grapes did not make up more than 49 per cent of the finished product.[36] The return to French rule and alignment of the Alsatian wine industry towards French markets provoked debate about both practices, as neither was permitted under French wine laws, and winemakers adopted a different position on each question. *Coupage*, or the addition of grapes from other regions, was a technique used primarily to produce red wine and was particularly widespread in

---

d'Alagrange, 16 September 1923; *Le Nouvelliste d'Alsace* 'Resolution concernant le reseau de chemins de fer d'Alsace et de Lorraine', 18 October 1923; Société pour l'expansion du port de Strasbourg et de son hinterland s.a.r.l. deliberation concernannt le projet de rattachement du reseau d'Alsace et de Lorraine à la compagnie des Chemins de fer de l'Est. See also the correspondence held in ADBR 121AL 1105. On the eventual decision, see 121AL 1105 Convention pour l'Exploitation des Lignes d'Alsace et de Lorraine par la Compagnie de l'Est, 6 July 1922.

[34] AN AJ30 215 J.M. Paillard (S.A. des Anciens Emballissements), to Ministre des Affaires Etrangères, Paris, 17 March 1919; Commissaire Générale to Maison Fournier & Fils (Seine) Strasbourg (nd); Haut Commissaire de la République to Sous- Secrétaire d'état à la Président du Conseil, Strasbourg, 28 February 1919.

[35] *L'Evenement*, 'Les richesses minières de l'Alsace-Lorraine', 25 May 1920.

[36] ADBR 121AL 1260 Conseil Consultatif d'Alsace et Lorraine, Session d'avril 1921. Procès Verbal.

the Moselle, where winemakers used it to improve the taste, acidity, and strength of their wine.[37] The technique was used in Alsace, but it was not popular amongst producers, who argued that they did not profit from the sale of wine produced in this way. Alsatian winemakers thus argued for the application of French law and a ban on *coupage* to concentrate on improving the taste and quality of red wines.[38]

Winemakers adopted a different position on the question of adding sugared water. This technique was widely used in Alsatian vineyards, where producers stressed that sugaring was necessary to allow Alsatian wines to compete globally with Rhineland wines, which contained added sugar. Even if this was a temporary measure, these winemakers argued, it would give them time to replace their existing plants with vines capable of producing quality wines to meet the tastes of French consumers.[39] Wholesalers countered that the addition of sugared water gave Alsatian wines a bad reputation. As a result, they stressed, the French law banning the technique should be introduced immediately.[40] The problem was complicated, as Alsatian wines produced in this way were not eligible for sale in France, while German Rhineland wines treated with sugared water were. When combined with the weakness of the German mark, this gave German wines a competitive edge over Alsatian products, and this anomaly was only partially resolved by the enforcement of labelling to show how the wine was produced.[41] The eventual August 1921 law applied French legislation to the recovered departments, but with the important concession that wine could be treated with sugar according to the local law, provided it was clearly labelled as such and was sold only in the recovered departments or abroad.[42] This disposition was allowed until 31 December 1925.[43] *Coupage* was also permitted on a temporary basis until 1925.[44]

In these early years, Alsatian wine producers benefited from articles 68 and 268 of the Treaty of Versailles, which allowed Alsatian and Lorrainer producers to send their goods to Germany without import duty for five years after the ratification of the treaty, on condition that the goods imported could not surpass the annual average of exports recorded between 1911 and 1913. Alsatian industry and commerce had until 10 January 1925 to continue exporting to Germany, and it was envisaged that this transition period would allow the region's industrialists, manufacturers, and businesses to realign themselves towards France. But, in the event, the transition

---

[37] ADBR121AL 198 Commissaire Général de la République to Comte de Bertier, Senateur de la Moselle, Paris, 25 July 1922.

[38] ADBR 121AL 1261 Le Commissaire Général de la République to Président du Conseil, Strasbourg, 27 June 1921.

[39] ADBR 121AL 1260 Conseil Consultatif d'Alsace et Lorraine, Session d'Avril 1921. Procès Verbal.

[40] ADBR 121AL 1260 Le Syndicat du Commerce en Gros des Vins du départment du Haut-Rhin, 6 July 1920.

[41] ADBR 121AL 1261 Président de la Chambre de Commerce de Colmar to Directeur des Services du Commerce et de l'Industrie, Colmar, 26 December 1921.

[42] ADBR 121AL 1260 Journal Officiel, 26 August 1921 (Law of 25 August 1921, signed Président de la République, Alexandre Millerand).

[43] ADBR 121AL 1260 Ministre des Finances to Président du Conseil, Paris, 28 April 1925.

[44] ADBR 121AL 198 Commissaire Générale de la République to Comte de Bertier, Senateur de la Moselle, Paris, 25 July 1922.

period coincided with a rapid depreciation of the German mark and a boycott of French goods in protest at the occupation of the Ruhr by the French army. As a result, Alsatian goods struggled to reach German consumers in the levels envisaged at Versailles, and Alsatian wine producers found themselves in an impossible situation. They were still unable to sell their wines in France, as French consumers found Alsatian wines to be 'too green, too acidic and too expensive'.[45] But Alsatian wines failed to sell in Germany either as a result of the boycott. Between January 1920 and January 1921, German consumers purchased just 180,000 hectolitres of Alsatian and Mosellan wine, and Alsatian wine exports dropped from 62.2 per cent to 9.2 per cent of their total product between 1920 and 1922.[46] But this decline did not reflect realignment to French markets; rather, it was because the majority of Alsatian wine was now consumed in the region itself.

In an attempt to adapt to the French market, Alsatian wine producers removed their hybrid plants and replaced them with quality vines. As a result, land cultivated by vineyards dropped from 19,019 hectares in 1922 to 11,344 hectares in 1938. Alsatian wine producers also came together to discuss how their wines should be presented under the auspices of the *Syndicat des negociants en vins et viticulteurs du vignoble alsacien* and the association of *viticulteurs d'Alsace* founded in 1911. The first decision was on labelling, as all wines needed to be labelled with their geographic origin. Producers and merchants debated this issue at length, arguing over whether the wine should be called 'vin d'Alsace', 'vin du Rhin d'Alsace', or 'vin du Rhin français'. In the end, the first appelation won, and the producers hoped that it would disassociate them from other Rhineland wines and create a distinctive identity for Alsatian wine.

Connected to the construction of this regional image was the wine's distinctive bottles and labels, and the shape of the Alsatian bottle was enshrined in law by a decree of 15 February 1930. Labels similarly drew on images of Alsace reminiscent of the late nineteenth-century *images d'Epinal* that featured so prominently in the cult of the 'lost provinces'. Some of the most important Alsatian artists of the interwar years designed wine labels, including Hansi, Charles Spindler, and Charles Bastian, and their labels frequently depicted a timeless, eternally French Alsace featuring women dressed in traditional costume, half-timbered villages, and storks. Alsatian wines were also promoted at a series of local fairs: Ribeauvillé in 1921, Ammerschwihr in 1922, Colmar in 1927, and Molsheim in 1934.

Sarah Howard's work on the imagery created by the French alcohol industry has underlined that, in interwar France, wine drinking was presented as a 'patriotic' activity.[47] This patriotism could also be deeply rooted in regional attachment, and Shanny Peer has pointed to the importance of the connection between consumer

[45] ADBR 121AL 1261 Président de la Chambre de Commerce de Strasbourg to Directeur des Services du Commerce et de l'Industrie, 20 April 1920.

[46] ADBR 121AL 1261 Le Commissaire Général de la République to Président du Conseil, Strasbourg, 27 June 1921; 121 AL 1261 Commissaire Général de la République to Monsieur le Garde des Sceaux, Ministère de la Justice, Paris, 30 April 1923.

[47] Sarah Howard, *Les images de l'alcool en France entre 1915 et 1945* (Paris, 2006).

goods and regional identity in the interwar years.[48] Both trends came together in an attempt to encourage the consumption of Alsatian wine. But, while progress was made in terms of creating a distinctive identity, producers were not able to make the leaps in quality that they had hoped for by 1935, when the *Institut National des Appellations d'Origine* (INAO) was created to manage the process of *appellation d'origine contrôlée* (AOC) for wines. This certification would guarantee the geographical origin of the wine, and became an important marker of quality. Alsatian wines had to wait until 1962 before they received the AOC marker, which gives some indication of just how long and difficult the process of economic reintegration was for the wine industry.

These problems of reintegration were shared by other industries; in 1913 textile producers were sending 95 per cent of their goods to Germany, and, although the Versailles Treaty allowed them to send 40,000 tonnes of cotton to Germany until 1925, the average yearly export during the transition period was just 11,400 tonnes.[49] Like the winemakers, textile producers had difficulty in replacing their lost German customers in France, especially after the textile factories in the devastated regions of the north resumed production. Textile manufacturers adopted a different strategy from the wine producers and, rather than focus on realigning their products towards French markets, they instead attempted to retain their foothold in their traditional markets in Germany. In the Franco–German commercial treaty of 17 August 1927, negotiators concentrated on maintaining a presence for Alsatian textiles in Germany. This effort met with some success, as the following year recorded a slight increase in orders from Germany.[50] But the improvement faltered with the depression that followed the Wall Street Crash, when French exports to Germany dropped from 6,000 million to 4,500 million tonnes.[51] The protectionist quotas applied in 1931–2 had further negative effects, and by 1938 Alsatian industrialists were lamenting the closure of the German markets to their products.[52]

The end of the Versailles transition period in 1925 coincided with the dissolution of the regional administrative institution of the General Commission, and the introduction of French commercial and civil legislation into the recovered departments, as well as the protests on interconfessional schooling. As a result, 1925 represented a year of turbulent change for the recovered departments. Nevertheless, the 1920s also witnessed increased integration. Successive governments gradually introduced French legislation, and a number of Alsatian banks merged with larger Parisian establishments, which incorporated the region into national financial networks. A ministerial order of May 1926 grouped the Chambers of Commerce of Colmar and Mulhouse with Belfort, Gray, Lure, and Besançon in a new economic region, which encouraged economic cooperation outside the borders of Alsace.

[48] Shanny Peer, *France on Display: Peasants, Provincials and Folklore in the 1937's World Fair* (Albany, NY, 1998).
[49] Dreyfus, *Histoire de l'Alsace*, p. 301.
[50] AN F7 12751 Commissaire Spécial de Mulhouse Rapport, 1 February 1928.
[51] ADBR 98AL 1083 2 *France de l'Est*, 1 September 1931.
[52] ADBR 98AL 1083 2 *France de l'Est*, 30 December 1938.

Such changes produced some economic success stories. The construction industry received a boost from the building of new transport links between Alsace and France, while the production of Alsatian tobacco (which had long been better suited to French pipes than German cigars) was centralized by the state in 1919. This granted producers a guaranteed income and facilitated an increase in production from 3.6 million kilograms in 1913 to 10 million kilograms in 1930.[53] The port of Strasbourg saw a major increase in traffic: coal imports increased from 934,000 tonnes in 1913 to 1,737,000 tonnes in 1929, and potash increased from 71,000 tonnes to 573,000 tonnes in the same period.[54] Meanwhile, new industries emerged, notably in car manufacture and artificial silk.

Alsatian industry and commerce also attempted to establish links with France's colonial empire. Haut-Rhin textile manufacturers established factories in Niger and Syria to cultivate cotton, and the Syrian Cotton Company, established by a collective of Haut-Rhin mills, expanded its plantation from 10 hectares in 1924 to 10,120 hectares in 1930. Similarly, Alsatian industry and commerce attempted to find new markets in France's colonial possessions: tanneries established important bases in north Africa, textiles and *petit outillage* manufacturers stepped up their exports, and metallurgical production, including railway construction and household appliances, attracted colonial orders amounting to several million francs before 1930.[55] Expanding these links was the primary motivation behind the colonial exhibition, held in Strasbourg in the summer of 1924 just as the transition period permitted by Versailles came to an end.[56] Its organizers described the exhibition as a means to 'introduce Alsace to France', and in an early planning meeting organizer Louis Proust attempted to convince a group of local businessmen of the potential of the exhibition by suggesting that it would 'give *Français de l'Intérieur* a reason to come to Strasbourg', while Mayor Peirotes wrote of the benefits that he hoped the region would reap from the exhibition, which would be of considerable 'economic and national importance' for the city, as well as for the three recovered departments and the surrounding area.[57] Two-thirds of the

[53] The value of this harvest also rose, from 2.3 million francs-or in 1913 to 56 million francs in 1930. Werner Wittich, 'L'Alsace Economique de 1913 à 1933. Introduction', Comité alsacien d'études et d'informations, *L'Alsace depuis son retour à la France,* 3 vols, vol. 2 (Strasbourg, 1933), p. 34.

[54] Wittich, 'L'Alsace Economique de 1913 à 1933', *L'Alsace depuis son retour à la France,* pp. 26–7.

[55] Marc Lucius, 'Les Relations Economiques entre l'Alsace et les Colonies Françaises', in Comité alsacien d'études et d'informations, *L'Alsace depuis son retour à la France. Premier supplement: Vie politique administrative et sociale; Vie intellectuelle; artisistique et spirituelle; Vie economique* (Strasbourg, 1937), p. 215.

[56] AMVES 234MW 296 M. Peirotes to M. le Directeur de l'Enregistrement à Strasbourg, Strasbourg, 5 April 1924; Strasbourg 28 December 1923 à Ministre des Colonies, Ministre de l'Agriculture, Ministre du Commerce; Jacques Peirotes, Maire de Strasbourg, to Edouard Daladier, Ministre des Colonies, Strasbourg, 15 January 1924; Louis Proust, 'L'Exposition Coloniale de Strasbourg', *Dernières Nouvelles de Strasbourg,* 22 February 1924; 234 MW 295 Brochure de l'Exposition Coloniale, Industrielle et Agricole de 1924; 234MW 295. Rapport sur la séance du 3 novembre 1923 à la Banque d'Alsace et de Lorraine.

[57] AMVES 234MW 295. Jacques Peirotes to Préfet du Bas-Rhin, Strasbourg, December 1923; 234MW 296 M. Peirotes to M. le Directeur de l'Enregistrement à Strasbourg, Strasbourg, 5 April 1924; Strasbourg 28 décembre 1923 to Ministre des Colonies, Ministre de l'Agriculture, Ministre du Commerce; Jacques Peirotes, Maire de Strasbourg, to Edouard Daladier, Ministre des Colonies,

total exhibition space of 15 hectares featured displays on Alsace and the French interior, while the exhibition's publicity materials featured adverts for Alsatian products and articles to encourage tourism to the region.[58] Above all, the committee envisaged economic interaction between the regional and colonial industries represented at the exhibition, and hoped to establish opportunities for economic exchange and cooperation.[59]

Integration also came with its downsides, however. Some sectors struggled to realign themselves to the French economy, and the port of Strasbourg had difficulty in establishing itself as a centre for colonial imports, as ships travelling to the port needed to pass through Antwerp, which meant that the goods that they carried became subject to tariffs, regardless of their origins in the French Empire and destination in metropolitan France. This deprived the port of an important market, and meant that industries reliant on raw materials from the colonies did not establish factories in Strasbourg.[60] In the banking system, a number of the independent Alsatian banks, particularly in the Mulhouse area, were incorporated into Parisian banks. This removed their local centre of decision-making and left them less able to respond to the regional problems that affected Alsatian industry.[61]

As Alsatian manufacturers and producers struggled to find new markets for their goods, the region's economic life also followed the ebbs and flows of the French economy. The drop in the value of the French franc from 1922 was felt particularly deeply in Alsace, where the population had experienced a drop in the value of the German mark just four years earlier at the end of war. Concern at seeing an echo of events in Germany, where hyperinflation had taken hold in the summer of 1921, led many wealthy Alsatians to convert large sums of money into dollars. It also encouraged numerous savers and property owners to withdraw significant amounts from their savings accounts.[62] In Colmar's banks, the two weeks between 14 and 31 January 1924 saw withdrawals outstrip deposits by almost one million francs (557,022 francs were deposited, while 1,566,499 francs were withdrawn) as city residents opted to invest in furniture, fabric, and other luxury goods as a means of protecting their assets.[63] This pattern was repeated across the region, and reports from Strasbourg in the same week described queues forming hours before the banks opened, as Strasbourgers rushed to withdraw their savings.[64] These fears

Strasbourg, 15 January 1924; Louis Proust, 'L'Exposition Coloniale de Strasbourg', *Dernières Nouvelles de Strasbourg*, 22 February 1924; 234MW 343, Exposition Coloniale: Rapport sur la séance du 3 novembre 1923 à la Banque d'Alsace-Lorraine, Strasbourg, 3 November 1923.

[58] See, for example, AMVES 234 MS 295 Brochure de l'Exposition Coloniale, Industrielle et Agricole de 1924, 2 August 1924; Brochure de l' Exposition Coloniale, Industrielle et Agricole de 1924, 4 October 1924. See also Alison Carrol, 'Imagining Greater France in the Provinces: The Strasbourg Colonial Exhibition of 1924', in Philip Whalen and Patrick Young (eds), *Place and Locality in Modern France* (New York, 2014).

[59] AMVES 234 MW 295 Brochure de l'Exposition Coloniale, Industrielle et Agricole de 1924.

[60] Lucius, 'Les Relations Economiques entre l'Alsace et les Colonies Françaises', *L'Alsace depuis son retour à la France. Premier supplement*, pp. 220–1.

[61] Livet, *Histoire de Mulhouse*, p. 302.

[62] ADBR 121AL 93 Préfet du Haut-Rhin to Commissaire Général, Colmar, 24 November 1923; Commissaire Spécial (Fuger) Rapport, Mulhouse, 14 December 1923.

[63] ADBR 121AL 93 Préfet du Haut-Rhin to Commissaire Générale, Colmar, 1 February 1924.

[64] ADBR 121AL 93 Commissaire Général de la République, Strasbourg, 21 January 1924.

persisted after the economic situation stabilized in 1924, and in February 1927 the *caisse d'épargne* in Saverne registered 80,000 francs of withdrawals, as opposed to just 20,000 francs deposited.[65]

Uncertainty about the future of the franc also contributed to a widespread regional reluctance to buy treasury bonds, which had the knock-on effect of leading the departmental prefects to question the patriotism of the Alsatian population.[66] Meanwhile, the weak franc encouraged shoppers from neighbouring Swiss and German towns to travel to Alsace in search of bargains. Their purchases forced local prices up and contributed to the rising cost of living in the early 1920s.[67] This meant that inflation was felt particularly keenly in Alsace, and by 1927 Mulhouse had gained the reputation of the 'most expensive town in France'.[68] The following year, reports suggested that the cost of living in the recovered departments had risen by 45 per cent since 1914.[69] Moreover, Alsatians continued to struggle under higher taxes than inhabitants of departments in the French interior, as local rates meant that a higher proportion was taken from Alsatian wage packets.[70] Such differential treatment had an impact on Alsatian attitudes and added to the bubbling sense of 'otherness' with regard to *Français de l'Intérieur*.

The first decade of French rule thus saw economic successes and failures, as well as continued interactions and adjustments to the new situation in Europe. But it was the sense of crisis and difficulty that had the larger impact on attitudes in the region; surveillance reports on the population signalled widespread discontent which increasingly manifested itself in labour conflict.[71] These issues, coupled with the problems of reintegrating the recovered departments into the French economy, ensured that in the first years after the return of Alsace to France popular discontent with economic reintegration compounded dissatisfaction with administrative and political reintegration. Nevertheless, as François Dreyfus has pointed out, there was no preferable alternative: 'revolutionary crises, economic difficulties, governmental instability and the rapid drop in the value of the Mark' ensured that economic discontent did not feed into agitation in favour of return to Germany.[72]

Throughout the 1920s the French economy did well. Post-war reconstruction was helped by the fact that much of French industry had modernized during the war, and new principles of 'scientific management' such as Taylorism had

[65] AN F7 12751 Commissaire Spécial, Rapport mensuel, Saverne, 3 February 1926.

[66] ADBR 121AL 93 Préfet du Bas-Rhin (Borromée) to Ministre de l'Interieur (Paris), 6 December 1924; Préfet du Haut-Rhin to Ministre de l'Intérieur, 20 November 1924; Préfet du Bas-Rhin to Ministre de l'Intérieur, Report, November 1924.

[67] AN F7 13380 Directeur des Services Généraux de Police d'Alsace et de Lorraine to Directeur de la Sûreté Générale, 28 February 1924. Rapport sur les activités des services généraux de police d'Alsace et de Lorraine pendant le mois de Janvier 1924.

[68] AN F7 12751 Commissaire Spécial de Mulhouse, Rapport, 1 July 1927.

[69] AN F7 12751 Commissaire Spécial de Mulhouse, Rapport, 1 March 1928.

[70] ADBR 98AL 1083 2 Dépêche de Strasbourg, 14 June 1931; AMVES 125Z A16. 9 June 1927. Rapport au nom de la Commission d'Alsace-Lorraine chargée d'examiner la proposition de resolution de MM. Peirotes et Georges Weill tendant à modifier dans les départements du Bas-Rhin, Haut-Rhin et de la Moselle les impôts locaux sur les traitements salaires et sur les professions. Présentée par Jacques Peirotes.

[71] AN F7 13014 Commissaire Spécial de Belfort to Ministre of the Interior. 28 October 1924; Commissaire Central de Belfort to Directeur de la Sûreté Général, 25 April 1924.

[72] Dreyfus, *Histoire de l'Alsace*, p. 64.

transformed certain sectors, notably the aircraft and iron-and-steel industries. In Alsace, things were a little different. Problems of reintegrating the region's economic institutions and systems, altering products for French tastes, or competing with new national competitors meant that the Alsatian economy faltered for much of the 1920s. For Alsace, economic reintegration followed the ebbs and flows of the problems of political and administrative reintegration, and, as in those areas, there was no unity in either Paris or Alsace in the ideas about how to solve the problems that emerged. After a decade of French rule, Alsace still suffered from the impact of return. During the following decade things became worse, as the local, the national, and the global intertwined as the region faced the onset of world depression.

ECONOMIC CRISIS IN THE 1930s

When the global economic crisis hit Alsace from 1930, the effects were severe, especially in the Haut-Rhin. Industrial production decreased in response to reduced demand; the amount of potash leaving the mines fell by 27 per cent between 1931 and 1932, beer produced by the breweries dropped by 20 per cent between 1930 and 1935, and agricultural production outside tobacco and potatoes entered a decline as prices dropped.[73] Tentative links with the colonies were shattered as the crisis forced the Haut-Rhin-owned Syrian Cotton Company into liquidation, and export levels to the Empire slowed down after 1930.[74] The closely integrated regional economy, which had helped to facilitate reintegration in the 1920s, became a weakness in the 1930s as crisis in the textile industry had knock-on effects in the metallurgical, chemical, and building industries which relied upon it.[75] Workers saw a further drop in their wages. In the Engel factory in Mulhouse, wages were reduced three times in the space of three months in 1933.[76]

Across France, unemployment increased in the early 1930s. Nevertheless, French unemployment levels were kept down by the forced expulsion of many of the migrant workers who had moved to the metropole from the French colonies and elsewhere in Europe.[77] Moreover, these official figures do not include the invisible unemployed, notably those female and migrant workers who did not register as unemployed as they were either ineligible for benefits, or because they did not want to expose themselves to possible expulsion.[78] For these reasons, in

---

[73] Dreyfus, *La vie politique en Alsace*, p. 324; Jean-Claude Richez, 'Malaises et crises après le retour à la France', *Cahiers Langue et culture regionales*, 15 (1990), pp. 65–92, p. 85.

[74] Lucius, 'Les Relations Economiques entre l' Alsace et les Colonies Françaises', in *L'Alsace depuis son retour à la France. Premier supplement*, p. 222.

[75] AN F7 13028 Préfet du Haut-Rhin to Ministre de l'Intérieur, Colmar, 4 June 1934.

[76] Archives Municipales de Mulhouse (hereafter AMM) D1 a1 1933 5 séance, 9 June 1933, p. 376.

[77] Matt Perry, *Prisoners of Want. The Experience and Protest of the Unemployed in France, 1921–1945* (Aldershot, 2007).

[78] Philip H. Slaby, 'Violating the "Rules of Hospitality": The Protests of Jobless Immigrants in Depression-Era France', in Matthias Reiss and Matt Perry (eds), *Unemployment and Protest. New Perspectives on Two Centuries of Contention* (Oxford, 2011).

1932 the Bas-Rhin Socialist Marcel-Edmund Naegelen estimated that less than one-third of unemployed workers in France received benefit.[79] Nevertheless, a combination of a large population of migrant workers, a significant agricultural sector, and less reliance on manufacturing than Britain or Germany helped France to weather the storm better than its neighbours to the east and west. While unemployment hit around 25 per cent in both Britain and Germany in 1933, official figures suggest that French unemployment peaked at just 4.3 per cent in February 1935.[80] However, Alsace was amongst the French regions to feel the effects of the depression most keenly. David A. Harvey points out that the number of textile workers in Mulhouse and its surrounding areas dropped from 12,008 in 1930 to 7,314 in 1935, meaning that almost 5,000 workers, or around 40 per cent of the total workforce, were without work.[81] The effects were felt particularly keenly in the Haut-Rhin, where industrial employment in 1935 was around 30 per cent lower than its 1931 level, and which became one of the worst affected departments in France.[82]

Hardest hit by the rising unemployment levels were women, unskilled workers, and foreign workers. Women represented around a third of the working population of Alsace, and made up a large proportion of the workforce in the textile industry. As this industry was particularly badly affected by the crisis, it left many female workers without work.[83] Many companies tried to keep local workers employed at the expense of foreign workers; in February 1932 the potash mines offered to pay for the return journey of the 250 Polish and Czechoslovakian workers who had been laid off.[84] Meanwhile, their presence proved a source of concern to administrators, who ensured that the police subjected these foreigners to close surveillance.[85] What is more, prefectural correspondence suggests that high levels of regional unemployment meant that foreigners became increasingly unpopular with the regional population as the economic crisis led to a crystallization of ideas about difference, and about community.[86]

Alsatian workers were also badly hit by reductions in the working week. By June 1931, the potash mines and textile manufacturers had reduced the working week significantly, and their workers counted amongst the 'partial unemployed'.[87] These

[79] AN F7 13261 Commissariat du 7ième arrondissement, Rapport Strasbourg, 16 April 1932. Report on Socialist meeting held in Strasbourg on 15 April attended by 700.

[80] Charles Sowerwine, *France since 1870: Culture, Politics and Society* (Basingstoke, 2001), p. 139.

[81] Harvey, *Constructing Class and Nationality in Alsace*, p. 164.

[82] Richard Keller, 'À l'atelier, à l'usine, au bureau', in Bernard Vogler (ed.), *Chroniques d'Alsace 1918–1939* (Barcelona, 2004), p. 113.

[83] See Jean-Claude Richez, avec la collaboration d François Igersheim et Peter Armand, *Il y a cinquante ans, le Front Populaire … Sorglos sunnen? Travail et Temps libre en Alsace*, Exposition presenté par La CFDT et l'Atelier Alsacien le 23 au 28 juin en la Salle de la Mairie de Schiltigheim, p. 25.

[84] AN F7 13040 Commissaire Spécial de Mulhouse to Préfet du Haut-Rhin, Mulhouse, 29 February 1932.

[85] AN F7 13028 Préfet du Haut-Rhin to Ministre de l'Intérieur, Colmar, 12 November 1934.

[86] AN F7 13028 Préfet du Haut-Rhin to Ministre de l'Intérieur, Colmar, 12 November 1934.

[87] AN F7 12751 Préfet du Haut-Rhin to Président du Conseil, Colmar, 16 June 1931; Préfet du Haut-Rhin to Président du Conseil, Colmar, 2 July 1931; Préfet du Haut-Rhin to Président du Conseil, Colmar, 19 August 1931; Préfet du Haut-Rhin to Président du Conseil, Colmar, 4 November 1931; AN F7 13040 Commissaire Spécial de Mulhouse, Rapport, 31 March 1931.

workers, not included in official figures, found themselves struggling to feed their families as their wages dropped in parallel with their working hours. Other groups of workers who had traditionally experienced seasonal unemployment, such as construction workers, joined the ranks of the unemployed when winter arrived and brought a stop to building work.[88]

Local councils again stepped in to provide relief for jobless workers. Prior to 1918, the Bismarckian insurance system and trade-union network had provided insurance for workers against unemployment. The movement to French systems and the separation of the Alsatian unions from the German network created a shortfall, and in many parts of the region municipal councils stepped in to fill the gap after 1918 by offering relief to unemployed workers and establishing public-works schemes. However, after the onset of the depression, these schemes became quantitively and qualitatively different. Expansion in the scale and range of works undertaken was coupled with a significant increase in spending. By 1938 Colmar's aid to the unemployed had reached 3 million francs per year, and the council had resorted to loans in an attempt to get through the crisis.[89]

The Socialist and Volksfront coalition-controlled city councils that had won power in Mulhouse, Colmar, and Strasbourg in 1929 stepped up both their existing public-works programmes and their relief systems, supplementing monetary relief with soup kitchens and free coal deliveries.[90] Timothy B. Smith has suggested that across France councils increasingly stressed the need for national responses to social issues, yet in Alsace the autonomy that councils enjoyed as a result of local municipal legislation meant that towns in the recovered departments were able to offer higher relief payments than those elsewhere.[91] The resulting gap between towns east and west of the Vosges encouraged jobless workers to move to the region in the hope of benefiting from the relief provided in Alsace. This had the effect of increasing levels of regional unemployment further. To curb this tide, the Mulhouse council placed limits on relief in 1934 and offered it only to unemployed workers who had lived in Mulhouse for at least a year.[92]

Workers responded to the situation with increased protest, and the first strike to hit the region broke out in the potash mines in 1930. But protest against unemployment was not limited to strikes by workers who still held on to their jobs, as Matthias Reiss and Matt Perry have stressed, using examples from cases across Europe.[93] In Alsace, unemployed workers across the region mobilized in protest against their situation. In the south, Communist militants Joseph Walliser and Marcel Rosenblatt attempted to organize a hunger march from Mulhouse to

[88] AN F7 13561 Préfet du Haut-Rhin to Ministre de l'Intérieur, Colmar, 5 January 1934.

[89] AMC Compte rendu des séances du Conseil Municipal de la Ville de Colmar, 37 séance, 29 December 1938, p. 136.

[90] AMM D1 a1 1936 2 séance, 21 February 1936, pp. 52–3.

[91] Timothy B. Smith, *Creating the Welfare State in France, 1880–1940* (Quebec, 2003).

[92] AMM D1 a1 1934 8 séance, 17 September 1934, p. 486.

[93] Matthias Reiss and Matt Perry, *Unemployment and Protest. Two Centuries of Contention* (Oxford, 2011).

[handwritten: part of a transnational trend — same thing was happening in France and Germany (egan Germany, new oregon book)]

Colmar in protest against the lack of action for the unemployed.[94] But when they failed to secure the support of the SFIO, the CGT, or the Mulhouse section of the *Invalides de Travail* association, the march did not take place.[95]

Workers who remained in employment also turned to protest in response to their working conditions. In 1933 a general strike hit Strasbourg after workers in the public services, CGT, and CGTU came out in support of construction workers, who had been striking throughout the summer and whose delegates were unable to secure a meeting with their employers. With the public-service workers on strike, Strasbourg's homes went without gas and electricity, the trams did not run, and rubbish filled the streets. Official sources claimed that there were 7,600 strikers in Strasbourg, but the CGTU claimed 20,000.[96] This movement ran out of steam as the trade unions were unable to agree on the priority in terms of the strike's aims. The workers returned to their posts in August 1933. *[handwritten: desperate conditions everywhere...]*

In 1936, after the election victory of the Popular Front, a strike movement spread throughout France. With 12,142 strikes and 1,830,930 strikers in June alone, they were the largest strikes in French history (and to date, only the strikes of 1968 have been on a larger scale).[97] The reasons behind the strikes varied in different industries and different parts of France, with strikers making a combination of demands ranging from social questions to shop-floor issues. The strikes were slow to break out in Alsace, in part due to the existing privileges that Alsatian workers enjoyed but largely due to a widespread sense that workers in Alsace had concerns and problems distinct from workers elsewhere in France. The government brought an end to this strike wave with the Matignon Accords signed on 7–8 June, which granted a 10 per cent increase in salaries, two weeks of paid holiday, a 40-hour working week, the election of workplace delegates, and the conclusion of collective contracts. Following the accords, the movement gained a new lease of life in Alsace. *[handwritten: running point: popular front came to power]* *[handwritten: Gov compromise to end the strikes. But Alsace not ready yet...]*

On 9 June strikes broke out in two of Mulhouse's chemical firms, and the following day the workers at the Société Alsacienne de Constructions Mécaniques (SACM) and the Charles Mieg textile factory were on strike. On 11 June PCF leader Maurice Thorez called on workers to remember that it was necessary to know to end a strike when the most important demands had been achieved. The same day, the workers at the Lingolsheim tannery occupied the factory and demanded a 15 per cent wage increase, the introduction of the 40-hour week and the reinstatement of workers sacked following the 1933 strike. The workers secured a 30-centime per hour rise on 13 June. Across Alsace workers in the chemical industry, gas factories, public transport, textile industry, potash mines, and department stores secured wage increases. In July 1936 agricultural labourers

---

[94] AN F7 13561 Commissaire Spécial de Mulhouse to Préfet du Haut-Rhin, Mulhouse, 22 May 1934.

[95] AN F7 13561 Préfet du Haut-Rhin to Ministre de l'Intérieur, 26 June 1934; Préfet du Haut-Rhin to Ministre de l'Intérieur, 19 December 1934.

[96] Léon Strauss, 'Les Grèves', in Jean-Claude Richez, Léon Strauss, François Igersheim, and Stéphane Jonas, *Jacques Peirotes, 1869–1935 et le socialisme en Alsace* (Strasbourg, 1989), p. 81.

[97] Jackson, *Defending Democracy*, p. 86.

occupied the Schlumberger farm in Guebwiller and barricaded its entrance; they won a 14 per cent increase in their salaries.[98]

Each victory was celebrated with a procession, and Eugène Zwingelstein described the strike in the Kiener textile workshop in Colmar; during the day the strikers sang and danced as the red flag flew above the factory beside a banner proclaiming 'Pain, Paix, Bonheur et Liberté'. Women brought meals to their striking husbands, the CGT provided the morning coffee, the *aubergiste* of the nearby *Taverne des Sports* sent four casks of beer, and the socialist municipality delivered packed lunches. The Kiener strikers won just 1 extra per cent on top of the 14 per cent granted to all textile workers in the Haut-Rhin, yet the lasting impression went much deeper, and the strikers remembered fondly the sense of camaraderie that resulted from their participation in the movement.[99]

The Popular Front triggered a brief upturn in the region's economic fortunes. The new government brought the end of deflation, a step-up in armament production, and increases in salary. In 1936 the Mulhouse cotton factories ended the year without a deficit for the first time since 1930.[100] But this recovery proved short-lived, as the increasingly bellicose position adopted by Nazi Germany discouraged investment in the region and destabilized Alsace's fragile economic recovery.[101] Work on the Rhône–Rhine canal had stopped almost immediately after Hitler's seizure of power in 1933. In December 1934 the Senate agreed to make the opening of any industrial establishments within 30 kilometres of the border subject to special government authorization, to be countersigned by the Minister of War. The proposal's author, Senator General Bourgeois, was mindful of a possible flow of industrialists and workers from the Saar following the plebiscite. He hoped that the measure would put a stop to the establishment of 'foreign companies' and employment of 'foreign workers' in France's borderlands, stressing that these regions represented a potential 'weak spot'.[102] But the region's Chambers of Commerce, the council of the Strasbourg port, and the city council of Strasbourg protested that the measure would have damaging effects on the region's economy.[103]

As councillors voiced fears that the measure could lead to the creation of monopolies, increased unemployment, and economic stagnation, Mayor Charles Hueber noted that the city of Bordeaux had already written to certain Strasbourg companies to offer them favourable conditions should they choose to relocate to the south-west.[104] In spite of the protests of Hueber and others, many patrons looked west and south, and important industrialists such as the De Dietrichs moved production away from the border. These fears were reflected in regional

[98] Claude Keiflin, *L'été 36 en Alsace* (Strasbourg, 1996). 　　[99] Keiflin, *L'été 36 en Alsace*, p. 60.

[100] Georges Livet, *Histoire de Mulhouse. Des origines à nos jours* (Strasbourg, 1977), p. 307.

[101] *Dernières Nouvelles de Strasbourg*, 4 June 1939.

[102] AMVES Comptes rendus des séances du Conseil Municipale de la Ville de Strasbourg, 130e séance, 10 December 1934, p. 870.

[103] AMVES Comptes rendus des séances du Conseil Municipale de la Ville de Strasbourg, 130e séance, 10 December 1934, pp. 870–86.

[104] AMVES Comptes rendus des séances du Conseil Municipale de la Ville de Strasbourg, 130e séance, 10 December 1934, pp. 870–86.

commerce and industry, as savers emptied their accounts in the *caisses d'épargne*, shoppers proved increasingly unwilling to spend money, businesses made plans to relocate, and unemployment rose, particularly in the building industry.[105] Furthermore, projects planned for Alsace were moved to the interior; in 1937 a petrol refinery proposed for Strasbourg was relocated to Donges in the Loire-Atlantique. In many ways, the economic problems summed up the paradox of the border; while the construction of fortifications offered a reminder that the region was the nation's first line of defence against Germany, the perception that the region was under threat and the actions that this triggered led to the border appearing as a potential 'weak point' for France, to quote General Bourgeois.[106]

Again, such economic problems fed into existing discontent and, as part of an enquiry into the situation in rural areas of east and north-east France, Lot-et-Garonne Communist deputy Renaud Jean reported on the widespread malaise that he encountered in the Rhine departments. For Jean, the primary cause was the possibility of war: the Alsatian population lived alongside land requisitioned for fortification, closed roads and bridges, and fields and orchards damaged by the installation of artillery batteries. This malaise had transnational roots connected to a wider sense of crisis that gripped interwar Europe, but it also had specific local causes. As Jean spoke to villagers across the Alsatian departments, they complained about the military's failure to pay indemnities for horses, vehicles, and farm equipment requisitioned, and compared French disorganization unfavourably with the organized German mobilization of 1913. Jean recommended immediate payment for requisitioned animals and allowances for farmers to let them continue their work, but admitted that the border malaise would be difficult to shift.[107] In many ways, Alsace's experience of the depression of the 1930s reflects its experience of political developments in that decade. Regional, national, and transnational developments and flows interacted and shaped local experience. And, as was the case with politics, so with economics: far from being in opposition, these processes served to shape one another. In this sense, the region's economic history was defined by the border.

THE ALSATIAN BORDER ECONOMY

In the years after 1918, the new border between France and Germany was strengthened with new customs points, while the gradual introduction of French legislation and tariff duties reinforced the barrier between the Alsatian population and

[105] TNA C13987 Joseph Pyke to Sir Eric Phipps Strasbourg, 9 November 1938; ADBR 98AL 1083 2 *Dernières Nouvelles de Strasbourg*, 4 June 1939; 98AL 634 Paul Valot to Vice-Président du Conseil, Paris, 29 October 1938.
[106] Comptes rendus des séances du Conseil Municipale de la Ville de Strasbourg, 130e séance, 10 December 1934, p. 870.
[107] AMVES 106Z 1 Rapport fait au nom de la delegation chargée par la Commission de l'Agriculture d'effectuer une enquête sur la situation des populations rurales des régions de l'Est et du Nord- Est, par M. Renaud Jean, député (February 1939).

their neighbours in Germany and Switzerland. Nevertheless, people and goods continued to cross the border. Some did so illegally as illegal migrant workers or smuggled goods, while other travellers arrived armed with visas or travel passes, and other goods entered with the necessary customs duties having been paid. Some passed through the region on their way to a final destination in the French interior or elsewhere; others remained in Alsace over the long or the short term. Alsace's border economy was an important feature of regional economic life; German states had long been significant trading partners for Alsatian industries, and while relations shifted after 1918, their importance remained constant.

For sections of the Alsatian population, transgression of the border had become commonplace under German rule. Reports on the smuggling of tobacco and other contraband goods flooded in from border guards before the Great War, and, after 1918, networks were realigned so that contraband drugs, tobacco, weapons, and other goods found their way into Alsace. In this respect, the Alsatian border had much in common with borders across Europe; Henrice Altink and Sharif Gemie have suggested that as smuggling was created and maintained by borders, it proved a near universal problem for border guards.[108] Equally, Timothy Baycroft has argued that at the Franco–Belgian frontier the border's role as a barrier to the passage of goods actually served to bring people together through the practice of illegal smuggling: 'For a long time, contraband has been an activity that has created a number of cross-border contacts. It leads to a mentality of solidarity, and cohesion amongst borderland populations.'[109] Nevertheless, all the while that smuggling increased contact and cooperation, it also reinforced the place of the border as a dividing line in the local consciousness.

In Alsace, the border was not an impermeable line, and drugs (notably cocaine) passed through the region on their way from Germany and Switzerland to France.[110] Routine searches of cars frequently turned up 'large quantities of tobacco', which the police surmised were sold to shopkeepers in the countryside.[111] Arms also passed through Alsace to destinations in France, or as far afield as Melbourne, Australia.[112] Connections with Germany and Switzerland created problems for the

---

[108] Henrice Altink and Sharif Gemie, 'Introduction: Borders: ancient, modern and postmodern: definitions and debates', in Altink and Gemie (eds), *At the Border. Margins and Peripheries in Modern France* (Cardiff, 2008), p. 15.

[109] Timothy Baycroft, 'Changing Identities in the Franco–Belgian Borderland in the Nineteenth and Twentieth Centuries', *French History*, 13:4 (1999), pp. 417–38, p. 428.

[110] AN F7 14841 Commissaire Spécial de Mulhouse to M. le Controleur Général de la Sûreté Nationale à Strasbourg, 7 March 1938; Inspecteur de Police Mobile Arnet Pierre to M. le Commissaire Divisionnaire Chef de la 16e Brigade régionale à Strasbourg, 21 August 1936; Commissaire Spécial to M. le Directeur des Services Généraux de Police d'Alsace et de Lorraine, 20 December 1924; Directeur des Services Généraux de Police d'Alsace et de Lorraine to M. le Directeur de la Sûreté Général, Strasbourg, 24 December 1924; Président du Conseil to Ministre de l'Intérieur, Paris, 7 September 1923; Commissaire Divisionnaire chef de la 14ème brigade de police mobile to M. le contrôleur général des services de recherché judiciaries, Montpellier, 20 November 1922; Commissaire Spécial de Mulhouse to M. le Controleur Général de la Sûreté Nationale à Strasbourg, 7 March 1938.

[111] AN F7 12751 Commissaire Spécial, Rapport mensuel, Saverne, 2 November 1927; Commissaire Spécial, Rapport mensuel, Saverne, 2 August 1925.

[112] AN F7 13028 Préfet du Bas-Rhin to M. le Ministre de l'Intérieur, Strasbourg, 7 May 1934; Préfet du Bas-Rhin to Ministre de l'Intérieur, Strasbourg, 15 October 1934.

police as they attempted to suppress this trade. In 1924 the Special Commissioner of the southern Alsatian town of Saint-Louis described some of the problems that his forces encountered in policing the border; thousands of people and at least a hundred cars took the road that linked the Alsatian towns of Mulhouse and Saint-Louis with the Swiss town of Basel each day, while trams crossed the border every ten minutes. In the station, the guards were unable to stop and search the compartments of the numerous night trains that crossed through on their way between Paris and Vienna or Paris and Milan without provoking complaints from passengers. And the denunciations upon which guards relied were rarely forthcoming. As a result, the Commissioner proposed either random searches or acting on precise information. But he warned that random searches were unlikely to prove productive and would reduce popular goodwill, while acting on denunciations relied on information which the service rarely received. In this situation, he advised his superiors, he found himself unable to prevent cross-border smuggling.[113]

The borderland economy was also affected by the large numbers of German shoppers who crossed the border to purchase everyday essentials and luxury goods. This practice was brought to a rapid halt when Germany launched a boycott of French products in response to French troops' occupation of the Ruhr valley in January 1923, following the Weimar Republic's failure to meet the reparations payments set down by the Treaty of Versailles. This passive resistance ended in September 1923, leading German shoppers to visit Alsatian towns in greater numbers and prompting a collective sigh of relief from Alsatian shopkeepers, who welcomed the boost to the local economy.[114] As a result, customs officials frequently turned a blind eye to the small quantities which these visitors bought.[115] But in 1924, as the collapse of the mark led to a dramatic increase in prices in the Weimar Republic, Germans entered Alsace in ever greater numbers to buy the cheaper goods on sale in Alsatian shops. Their purchase of bread, sugar, coffee, meat, vegetables, clothes, and shoes forced local prices up. In January 1924, the prefect of the Haut-Rhin estimated that Germans had spent 80,000 francs in Mulhouse in the previous week, which, when combined with Swiss purchases, had led to a 'doubling, or even a tripling' in the normal rate of purchasing.[116] Similar reports from across the region prompted the prefects of both Alsatian departments to call on the government to restrict movement between Alsace and the neighbouring occupied German territories.[117] In response, the General Commission limited border crossings by German citizens, stepped up the surveillance of those Germans who did enter, and, when necessary, turned away travellers even if they held a pass.[118]

[113] AN F7 14841 Commissaire Spécial to Directeur de la Sûreté Général, Saint-Louis, 22 December 1924.
[114] ADBR 121AL 93 Rapport, Strasbourg, 20 January 1924.
[115] ADBR 121AL 93 Commissaire Spécial, Wissembourg, Rapport, Wissembourg, 14 January 1924.
[116] ADBR 121AL 93 Préfet du Haut-Rhin to Commissaire Général, Colmar, 22 January 1924.
[117] ADBR 121AL 93 Préfet du Haut-Rhin to Commissaire Général, Colmar, 22 January 1924; Préfet du Bas-Rhin to Commissaire Général, Strasbourg, 18 January 1924.
[118] ADBR 121AL 93 Commissaire Général to Président du Conseil, 29 January 1924.

The Alsatian economy suffered from these measures, and this encouraged the local press to lobby in favour of the opening of the borders. Led by the conservative *Journal d'Alsace-Lorraine*, this press campaign argued that allowing Germans to shop in Alsace would boost the faltering regional economy.[119] But their appeals did not meet with a favourable response at the General Commission, where Gabriel Alapetite had watched the border crossings with alarm, worried that each German was 'an agent of the Reich, capable of... conducting pro-German and anti-French propaganda'.[120] Moreover, the Commission's fears appeared to be validated as surveillance officers reported that German 'tradesmen' coming to Alsace for work were to blame for the circulation of pessimistic rumours about the future of the franc, which had encouraged Alsatians to withdraw their savings from banks and to refuse to invest in treasury bonds.[121]

Many border-crossers came to the region for work, where they added to the large number of Germans who had migrated to the Reichsland in search of employment prior to 1918 and remained in the region after its return to French rule. Their presence worried local administrators; in 1918 the Strasbourg police commissioner recommended that all German workers employed at the arsenal be expelled from the region.[122] When the 1920 strike wave broke out, the Commission ascribed much of the agitation to German workers. This concern about German influence posed a particular problem for any worker born in Germany who decided to participate in the organized labour movement. In his memoirs, Prefect of the Bas-Rhin René Paira (who had been an intern at the *Direction Général* in the 1920s) recalled that inscription on the CGT's books always led to inclusion on a black list, a fate which could spell expatriation for German workers.[123]

Attitudes towards border-crossers reflect the diversity of the Alsatian population, and the resulting divisions that we have seen running through this book. While shopkeepers welcomed German crossers who spent money in Alsace and boosted the regional economy, they were unpopular with much of the regional population, who complained that they pushed prices up and created local inflation. These differences fed into divergent attitudes towards the border and how it should be controlled, but also into the distinct views on return that divided opinion in both Paris and Alsace and ensured that the reintegration of Alsace became a multicentred struggle.

The history of the region's border economy is thus suggestive of some of the ways in which borders are made. The introduction of the French franc and new customs points created a sense of the border as a division, while the notion that the boundary mattered was compounded by transgressing the border through smuggling (on a small or large scale) or through the different currencies and price scales on the two sides of the border. Interactions similarly created a sense of difference,

[119] AN F7 12751 Commissaire Spécial, Rapport Mensuel, Sélestat, 1 December 1925.
[120] ADBR 121AL 93 Commissaire Général to Président du Conseil, 29 January 1924.
[121] ADBR 121AL 93 Commissaire Général de la République to Préfet du Haut-Rhin, Colmar, Strasbourg, 19 January 1924.
[122] Harvey, *Constructing Class and Nationality*, p. 136.
[123] René Paira, *Affaires d'Alsace, Souvenirs d'un préfet* (Strasbourg, 1990), p. 114.

as the flow of shoppers from Germany and Switzerland to Alsace pushed up prices and created a sense of resentment that was reinforced by the special treatment reserved for those Germans resident in Alsace. What is more, this influx encouraged the appreciation of difference as the reforms charted in previous chapters took hold. By these means, the border was constructed from the grassroots through economic as well as political, social, and cultural interactions.

THE LABOUR MOVEMENT

It was not only regional economic systems and institutions that needed to realign themselves after the return of Alsace to France in 1918. The Alsatian labour movement (notably the trade unions) also turned west towards France. In a process that mirrored the political integration of the Socialist Party into the national SFIO, the Alsatian socialist unions (Free Trade Unions) pledged their allegiance to the coordinating French union, the CGT, in January 1919. Leaders held posts in both party and movement: Eugene Imbs, for example, was general secretary of the Bas-Rhin CGT and a municipal councillor and adjunct to the mayor in Strasbourg. This fusion proved a tricky process. Like the Socialist movement, the Alsatian unions had undergone significant expansion under German rule, as industrialization had swelled the number of workers in the region and facilitated the growth of the trade-union network. The socialist trade unions were closely connected to the SPD, which paid for secretaries and administrators for the Alsatian and Lorrainer unions.

The end of the war saw a surge in membership of the Alsatian and Mosellan socialist unions, which jumped from 25,000 in 1914 to 125,000 in 1919.[124] This increase occurred just as the Alsatian syndicates separated themselves from the German labour movement, a schism that removed an important source of funds and organizational support for the regional movement. Nevertheless, their distinct structures and continued use of German meant that the Alsatian unions also remained a step apart from their French counterparts. Furthermore, they boasted higher numbers of members, and Imbs was representative of a broader trend of labour leaders holding posts in both party and union. As a result, they had more in common with the German than the French labour movement. Such differences were highlighted by visiting speakers from the French interior. Chevalme, a Belfort unionist, praised the 'strong syndicalist' spirit and better-organized workers involved in the Alsatian labour movement, while CGT leader Léon Jouhaux expressed his admiration for the 'solid organization' of the Alsatian syndicates.[125] Such praise was a source of immense pride for the Alsatian unions, where it afforded leaders justification for their distinctiveness within the French movement.

[124] ADBR 121AL 162 *Die Freie Presse*, 24–5 June 1919.
[125] ADBR 121AL 881 Commissaire Spécial, Erstein, 14 August 1921; 121AL 882 Commissaire Spécial de Mulhouse, Mulhouse, 13 August 1922.

Before 1918, the socialist unions in Alsace had been rivalled by the Christian unions, which were connected to the Alsatian Centre Party, but failed to parallel the party's support; in 1914 the Christian unions had only 10,000 adherents for the entire Reichsland, while the socialist unions boasted over twice as many members.[126] The Christian trade unions similarly found themselves cast adrift by the return to France. In February 1919 Christian union leaders formed the *Unabhängiger Gewerkschaftsbund von Elsass und Lothringen* (UGB) and nine months later they helped to found the *Confédération Française des Travailleurs Chrétiens* (CFTC), a national Christian union. In its links with the UPR, the UGB mirrored the relations between the Alsatian SFIO and CGT, and personnel crossovers were also frequent; for example, Camille Bilger, one of its founding members, was UPR deputy for Guebwiller from 1919, and Henri Meck, general secretary of the UGB, was UPR deputy for Molsheim between 1928 and 1940. But, like the Christian unions of the years of German rule, the UGB was never able to translate the electoral pull of political Catholicism, or the religiosity of the Alsatian population, into near-dominance of the labour movement akin to that enjoyed by the Catholic political party. In a report on the situation in Mulhouse in 1921, Charles Valette, prefect of the Haut-Rhin, wrote that only around 20 per cent of the 22,000 organized workers in the town adhered to the Christian unions, whereas the remaining 80 per cent belonged to the socialist unions. The union did build on this position, however, and its membership total increased from 53,331 in 1924 to 93,678 in 1936. This was an increase from 34 to 52 per cent of the total movement, and was paralleled in an equivalent decline in the Socialist Union.[127]

A second rival for the Socialist CGT was the Communist CGTU, formed after the SFIO's split into socialist and communist wings at the Tours Congress. The two unions shared the positions on Alsace-Lorraine that separated their respective parties, as well as their bitter rivalry. For the CGT, Alsace and the Moselle needed to be subject to the same legislation as all other departments of France. As a result the Socialist Union rejected the CGTU's calls for a plebiscite over the future of the recovered departments, and Bas-Rhin CGT leader Eugene Imbs condemned such calls as 'autonomist manoeuvres' which played into the hands of German nationalists.[128] Various sections of the CGT passed manifestos echoing Poincaré's statement that the plebiscite had been achieved through the 'unanimous will' of the Alsatian people, demonstrated in the spontaneous welcome to the French troops, and rejecting CGTU calls for a plebiscite.[129]

The bitterness with which such questions were debated by both CGT and CGTU served to make the two unions fierce rivals. A 1922 police report written

---

[126] ADBR 121AL 162 *Die Freie Presse*, 24–25 June 1919. For more information see also Léon Strauss, 'Le Syndicalisme', in Richez et al., *Jacques Peirotes*, p. 73.

[127] Dreyfus, *La vie politique*, p. 210.

[128] AN F7 13381 Commissaire Spécial de la Gare de Strasbourg to Préfet du Bas-Rhin, Strasbourg, 25 September 1925.

[129] AN F7 13381 *Le Petit Journal*, Paris, 29 September 1925. The article reports on the congrès de l'union départemental de syndicats ouvriers du Bas-Rhin; *Le Journal d'Alsace et de Lorraine*, 29 September 1925, 'Les syndicats ouvriers du Bas-Rhin protestant contre les menées neutralistes des communistes en Alsace'; *Le Peuple*, 6 October 1925. 'Le manifeste de l'Union departementale des syndicats ouvriers du Bas-Rhin (CGT). Aux travailleurs des villes et des campagnes.'

in the aftermath of the split described the Alsatian working class as 'never more divided than at this moment', and their divisions persisted throughout the 1920s and hampered the effectiveness of the organized labour movement.[130] The three rival unions maintained patchworks of support across the region that reflected the strength of their associate parties; the CGTU measured greater strength in the Bas-Rhin, and the CGT and UGB both counted more supporters in the Haut-Rhin than in the Bas-Rhin. They also had strongholds in particular industries; for example, the CGTU boasted large numbers of members in the railway industry and potash mines, and amongst municipal workers of Strasbourg and Colmar.[131] Nevertheless, no union managed to sustain the levels of support achieved in the months after the armistice; the prefect of the Haut-Rhin noted that union membership in Mulhouse dropped from a peak of between 85 and 90 per cent of the working population in 1918 to 64 per cent in 1921.[132] The report of the central committee of the powerful *Union des Syndicats des Cheminots d'Alsace et de Lorraine* told a similar story, with the number of members falling from 22,195 on 1 April 1920 to 14,625 by 31 December of that year, and the number of groups falling from 52 to 48 over the same period.[133] Part of the reason for the decline in levels of union membership was a widespread perception that the unions had failed to achieve the workers' demands in the strikes of 1920–1.

When the SFIO and PCF edged towards joint anti-fascist activity within the Popular Front from 1934, the Alsatian CGT and CGTU also took the first tentative steps towards cooperation. However, the two unions' divergence over the question of Alsace-Lorraine proved difficult to overcome. For Eugene Imbs, leader of the Bas-Rhin CGT, it was a fundamental condition of unification that the CGTU refute their demand for the free disposition of Alsace and Lorraine.[134] But the CGTU's leaders pointed out that while this was a Communist Party demand, it had never been part of the union's official programme, meaning that they were unable to drop it. With the CGTU's position firm, Imbs was unable to secure the support of the federations of the Haut-Rhin or the Moselle in his demand, and he was forced to abandon it, much to his frustration. In this case, the close links between party and union meant that labour relations mirrored political tensions, as well as party concerns. In April 1936 the CGT and CGTU unified in Alsace and the Moselle, three months after the national reunification of the two unions. The mood of optimism and reconciliation created by the formation of the Popular Front prompted a flow of workers from the UGB to the reunified CGT, and the new union's meetings invited UGB members to attend under the banner of unity.[135]

[130] ADBR 121AL 882 Commissaire Spécial de Mulhouse, Mulhouse, 13 August 1922.

[131] The CGT and CGTU were reunified nationally in January 1936, and in Alsace in April 1936.

[132] ADBR 121AL 880 Préfet du Haut-Rhin to Commissaire Général, Colmar, 24 March 1921.

[133] ADBR 121AL 878 Union des Syndicats des Cheminots d'Alsace et de Lorraine, Rapport du Comité du 1 janvier au 31 décembre 1920. Confédération Générale du Travail.

[134] ADBR 98AL 1280 Commissaire Divisionnaire de Police Spéciale to Préfet du Bas-Rhin, Strasbourg, 28 October 1935.

[135] ADBR 98AL 684/1 Commssaire Divisionnaire to Préfet du Bas-Rhin, Strasbourg, 19 March 1937.

The Alsatian unions shared many of the concerns that worried workers across France, including wage levels, the working day, and international political events such as the occupation of the Ruhr or the Rif War in Morocco.[136] But unions in Alsace also supported the work of the SFIO, PCF, and UPR through organizing political meetings and conferences, publishing circulars, and contributing to the party press.[137] They devoted attention to the problems of reintegrating the recovered departments, the ownership of the railways and potash mines, and the status of Alsatian and Mosellan workers and *fonctionnaires*.[138]

The Alsatian socialist unions maintained their links with the Free Trade Unions in the Weimar Republic, which sent speakers and subsidies to help the movement in Alsace. In 1921 the *Textilarbeiterverband* of Berlin granted the *Syndicat du Textile de Mulhouse* a subsidy of 1,678,305 francs. In the atmosphere of post-war Franco–German tension, Charles Valette, prefect of the Haut Rhin, interpreted the donation as a gift aimed at spreading German propaganda in France.[139] Many union leaders adopted the position that Alsace could be a bridge between France and Germany supported by the international labour movement. But the socialist unions also attempted to claim the heritage of the French revolutionary tradition, and to identify themselves with it through familial metaphors or direct references to the role played in the revolution by their own ancestors.[140] Brandt, leader of the Brewers' Union, distinguished his anti-capitalist opposition to the French government from his previous rejection of the German government, which he said reflected his rejection 'of the entire German nation'.[141] This was associated with professions of the loyalty that the labour movement had maintained to

[136] See, for example, ADBR 121AL 882 Direction des Services de Police. Rapport, Guebwiller, 1 November 1922; 121AL 882 Commissaire Spécial, St Louis 11 November 1922; AN F7 13014 Commissaire Central of Belfort to Directeur de la Surete General, 25 April 1924; AN F7 13381 Commissaire Spécial de la Gare de Strasbourg to Préfet du Bas-Rhin, Strasbourg, 25 September 1925.

[137] In an outline of its activity in 1920, the Union des Syndicats des Cheminots d'Alsace et de Lorraine described the activity of its new Haut-Rhin section, which, since its foundation in April that year, had organized fourteen meetings and given thirty-one propaganda conferences. In 1920 the union issued sixty-seven circulars. Its organ, *La Tribune des Cheminots*, appeared 25 times over the year, published 27 articles in the socialist press on the railways and their administration, and intervened 146 times with the director and 44 times with the different *chefs de service*. ADBR 121AL 878. Union des Syndicats des Cheminots d'Alsace et de Lorraine, Rapport du Comité du 1 janvier au 31 décembre 1920. Confédération Générale du Travail.

[138] For example, at a 1921 meeting of different professional groups, Kessler, the secretary of the PTT, outlined the advantages of the position of German *fonctionnaires*, and criticized the slow manner in which the government was attempting to regulate the situation of Alsatian-Lorrain *fonctionnaires*, while Simon of the teachers' union criticized the government for treating Alsatian-Lorrainer teachers badly. ADBR 121AL 880. Direction de Police, Rapport, Strasbourg, 23 October 1921. Also, the Rapport du Comité of the Union des Syndicats des Cheminots d'Alsace et de Lorraine, du 1 janvier au 31 décembre 1920, stated that the union has participated vigorously in the propaganda in favour of nationalization of the railways of Alsace and Lorraine; thus, during the general strike of May it held more than seventeen propaganda meetings in Alsace and Moselle on one Sunday. ADBR 121AL 878.

[139] ADBR 121AL 881 Préfet du Haut-Rhin to the Commissaire Général, Colmar, 25 July 1921.

[140] ADBR 121AL 878 Commissaire Spécial de Police, Saverne, 10 May 1920. Report on meeting in Saverne of employees affiliated to the CGT.

[141] ADBR 121AL 877 Direction de Police, Report on meeting of delegates of the *Union des brasseurs*, 11 October 1919.

France during the years of annexation.[142] In this way, notions of the borderland's double culture were mobilized for party-political purposes.

The unions' political priorities changed over time: after the depression hit in 1931, unions organized strikes to try to protect working conditions and wage levels. Upon Hitler's seizure of power in 1933, labour leaders used their links with German unionists to present themselves as authorities on the perilous situation in which many German union leaders now found themselves. After the Popular Front's victory in France in 1936, unions preoccupied themselves with ensuring that the new laws on holidays and the 40-hour week were being applied by Alsatian bosses.[143] With unemployment and the cost of living rising in the eastern departments throughout the 1930s, union leaders called for government intervention to provide work and wage increases.[144] Their political priorities also shifted to fighting fascism and opposing the policy of non-intervention in the Spanish Civil War.[145] The unions' practical activities similarly evolved and, after the Popular Front's introduction of paid holidays, the Alsatian CGT organized subsidized trips to destinations in the mountains or at the sea, as well as visits to the 1937 International Exhibition in Paris.[146] Throughout, labour relations reflected the region's cross-border links, as the unions demonstrated their German heritage and maintained cross-border connections. As was the case across the regional economy, such transnational associations were deeply embedded in the local context, as they responded to the ebbs and flows of reintegration in terms of the unions' activities and outlook. But while Alsatian unions maintained these cross-border links, once again their contact with unionists in Germany represented a constant reminder of the distinct challenges that the two national movements faced. In this sense, it served to reinforce a sense of difference and emphasize the meaning of the border.

CONCLUSION

The return to France triggered a transformation in Alsatian economic structures. Alsace returned to French rule in the throes of an economic slump brought on by the First World War, with land and crops destroyed by the fighting and stagnation across regional industry. Upon its return, a new currency, new customs regime, the

[142] ADBR 98AL 1280 Commissaire Spécial to Préfet du Haut-Rhin, Rapport, 9 July 1934. Report on congress of *ouvriers du sous-sol*, held Mulhouse 4–8 July.
[143] ADBR 98AL 684 Commissaire Divisionnaire to Préfet du Bas-Rhin, Strasbourg, 22 April 1937. Report on meeting in Bischheim of the Syndicat Unifié des Cheminots des Ateliers de Bischheim, attended by 600; Commissaire Spécial to Préfet du Haut-Rhin, Saint-Louis, 18 January 1937, report on meeting of syndicat unifié, held 17 January in Saint-Louis.
[144] ADBR 98AL 1280 Commissaire Divisionnaire to Préfet du Bas-Rhin, Strasbourg, 18 April 1937; 98AL 1280 Préfet du Haut-Rhin to Ministre de l'Intérieur, Colmar, 27 May 1937.
[145] ADBR 98AL 1280 Préfet du Haut-Rhin to Ministre de l'Intérieur, Colmar, 23 March 1937; 98AL 1280 Commissaire Divisionnaire to Préfet du Bas-Rhin, Strasbourg, 20 March 1937.
[146] ADBR 98AL 1280 Commissaire Spécial to Préfet du Haut-Rhin, Saint-Louis, 23 April 1937, report on meeting of Union locale held on 22 April in Hégenheim; 98AL 1280 Commissaire Spécial to Préfet du Haut-Rhin, Saint-Louis, 22 April 1937, report on meeting of Union locale of Saint-Louis-Huningue in Hésingue, 21 April.

upheaval caused by sequestration, and the need to realign Alsatian products to French markets all meant that the region's economy faltered throughout the 1920s. During the 1930s, the impact of the global economic crisis and the threat of war combined to create further problems, as the economy stuttered in the face of a lack of investment and the requisition of land for military use. In spite of some early successes, and in spite of the best efforts of local producers, Chambers of Commerce, and politicians, the regional economy could not escape the impact of national policy decisions and global change. When war broke out in 1939, the Alsatian economy remained in the grip of crisis.

The problems of economic reintegration prompted discussions about how best to realign the region's systems and institutions towards France. A primary goal for the French government was the removal of German influence; after all, as we have seen, what was 'German' could not be 'French'. This triggered the sequestration of certain German companies, leading the Alsatian public to call for the nationalization of these sequestered firms. However, the desire to bring the region into line with the rest of France, along with the potential profit to be made in privatization, ensured that these appeals went unheeded. As the economy veered from one crisis to another, the population demonstrated an evolving sense of difference. First, between Alsatians and the French from the interior, as Alsatians clashed with Paris over sequestration and reintegration, and as the Alsatian labour movement expressed a distinct set of concerns in strikes that left them out of step with workers west of the Vosges. Second, a sense of difference emerged between Alsace and Germany. In spite of the connections that the Alsatian labour movement maintained with unions in Germany, there was a widespread awareness that Alsatians faced a separate set of problems to their neighbours across the Rhine, whether as a result of the requirements of reintegration in the 1920s or because of the distinction between the Alsatian economy and the boom and political change in the Third Reich in the 1930s. Competition with German products and the presence of German shoppers in the region's towns only served to increase this sense of otherness. This helped to build the border between France and Germany, but it did not result in a feeling of greater connection to France, as the region's economic problems contributed to a sharp sense of Alsatian distinctiveness.

Economic reintegration thus increased the dissatisfaction experienced and expressed across politics, laws, and administration. As Renaud Jean established in his survey of the border departments, a malaise had gripped the Alsatian population that was connected to the problems of reintegration and the preparations for war. The uncertainty caused by the threat of conflict compounded the impact of the crises triggered by the problems of reintegration in the 1920s, and by the effects of the global financial crisis in the 1930s. This led to a crystallization of identities, and of how Alsatians expressed their sense of their situation. It is to these questions of identity that we turn in the next chapter.

5

Reimagining Alsatian Identities

This chapter considers attempts to reimagine what it meant to be Alsatian after the region's return to France. It focuses on two areas of daily life: language and festivities. Through their debates over the use of French, German, and Alsatian dialect, and discussions over how the region's past and present should be presented, voices from across Alsace, France, and Germany offered views of Alsatianness that drew upon the region's social and cultural practices, as well as its local context, position in France, and cross-border links. These discussions were characterized by a sense that the Alsatian population could shape the region's return through their attitudes and activity, and had implications for identities, revealing them to be multiple, contested, and dependent upon context and purpose. Indeed, the Alsatian population had a number of languages that they could, and did, draw upon, strategically invoking notions of Alsace's double culture or ties to France or Germany to explain themselves and their situation. And the choices that they made in doing so are illuminating of the ways in which ideas about locality, nation, and international connection interacted, suggesting that the return of Alsace to France was never understood as a purely 'local' problem.

The regional population was characterized by diversity, as previous chapters have argued. Yet shared experience of annexation, war, and return led to a deep-rooted attachment to frameworks below the nation, including the region, the village, or the locality, as well as to those above it, such as the Catholic Church. One result of this was certain commonalities in how Alsatians described their situation, most notably in the widespread notion that Alsace represented a 'bridge' between France and Germany and that this was reflected in its double culture. According to its proponents, this dualism explained the region's wider connections and offered a justification for Alsatian distinctiveness within the borders of France. Nevertheless, the idea that Alsace's double culture allowed it to mediate between the two nations clashed with French concern about German influence. The region's border position represented a potential threat to security and, in any case, connections with Germany distinguished Alsatianness from other regional identities within France, as it offered the Alsatians an 'alternative nation'. This was an alternative nation that became particularly problematic at moments of Franco–German tension, but even in moments of peace it had the potential to destabilize Franco–Alsatian relations by provoking question marks over Alsatian loyalty and attachment to the French state. As a result, ongoing concern about Alsatian ambivalence to France led to closer attempts to redefine the borders of the national community.

Parisian concerns about German influence in Alsace interacted with Alsatian efforts to describe the regional situation. After all, as Richard Jenkins has suggested, how an individual understands their own identity is inseparable from how others view them.[1] The government in Paris read expressions of identity and ideas about society and culture through the prism of national attachment, and civil servants, police officers, and politicians worried about German influence. Concern about apparent Alsatian ambivalence to the nation fed into descriptions of the population, such as the caricatures of Alsatians as the indecisive Hans im Schnokeloch of folk tales, and could have potentially serious ramifications. To take one example, when the mayor of Niederroedern faced trial for Germanophily in 1919, the verdict noted that he had 'excellent French sentiments, just as he had good German sentiments' before 1918.[2] Alsatians also adopted such assumptions and criticized each other for their apparent fickleness: Philippe Husser mocked those Alsatians who turned out to receive the French troops on 17 November 1918 'sporting a tricolour rosette, when just a few hours earlier they had been wearing a German military cross', and regionalist artist Charles Spindler described the 'hyperbolic demonstrations' of French patriotism on the part of those who had been 'perfectly integrated into the German regime' before the war.[3] Neither the language employed nor the behaviour demonstrated by the Alsatian population was consistent, and the same people could make arguments for both the region's double culture and integral place within the French nation. Thus debates about what it meant to be Alsatian suggest that nationalization could not be understood in simple, binary terms of for or against France, and would be better considered as a spectrum that allowed for the expression of multiple loyalties and attachments.

LANGUAGE, CULTURE, AND IDENTITY

Language proved one of the most contentious issues triggered by the return of Alsace to France; as General Commissioner Henri Cacaud wrote, 'No subject has been the subject of more careful study, or has proved more polemical.'[4] The 'linguistic problem' was rooted in the fact that the majority of the region's population did not speak French and instead spoke a Germanic dialect, while standard German (*Hochdeutsch*) was frequently used in the press, primary schools, and much of everyday life, such as the theatre and cinema.[5] Indeed, in 1919 just 6.1 per cent of the Haut-Rhin population and only 3.8 per cent of Bas-Rhinois spoke French

---

[1] Richard Jenkins, *Social Identity* (Oxford, 2004), p. 5.

[2] Alfred Wahl and Jean-Claude Richez, *La Vie Quotidienne en Alsace entre France et Allemagne 1850–1950* (Paris, 1993), pp. 238–9.

[3] Philippe Husser, *Un Instituteur Alsacien. Entre France et Allemagne. Le Journal de Philippe Husser, 1914–1951* (Paris, 1989), p. 125; Charles Spindler, *L'âge d'or d'un artiste en Alsace. Mémoires inédits 1889–1914* (Colmar and Nancy, 2009), p. 251.

[4] AN Cacaud papers, 485AP8, Report 'La Question de la Langue', nd.

[5] The use of *Hochdeutsch* in these forums was a result of regional variations in Alsatian dialect.

as their first language.[6] This was the result of long-standing connections between Alsace and the communities across the Rhine, and had been compounded by almost half a century of German rule after 1871, although many French administrators who arrived in the region after 1918 assumed that the situation had been created purely by an aggressive programme of Germanization, and could be reversed by a similar process.

The French assessment of the situation was underpinned by an understanding that it was essential that the Alsatians speak French if they were to become fully fledged French citizens. To quote lawyer Marcel-Henri Nast, the Third Republic viewed language as the vehicle of 'national ideas, thought and mentality'.[7] Concern spread that the failure to introduce French effectively would not only close the door to French ideas and prevent the population from becoming French, but that it could also leave the region open to German influence.[8] And, given the apparent connection between language use and national sentiment, many administrators and politicians worried about the security implications of the presence of a German-speaking population on the nation's border.[9] As a result, language and questions of loyalty were closely connected to those of security and national cohesion; as Paul Bastier, sub-prefect of Sélestat, wrote in October 1925, 'The main German claim on Alsace results from the Alsatians speaking German dialect. Therefore, in Alsace, the political problem is actually a linguistic problem.'[10] This sentiment was echoed four years later by Strasbourg's Special Commissioner: 'No-one contests the usefulness of bilingualism in a border region. But, German irredentist leagues...and autonomist agitators have given this question a special character by connecting it with separatism.'[11]

For many Alsatians, meanwhile, it was important to distinguish between language and nationality as, in their eyes, language had nothing to do with patriotism.[12] The population demonstrated considerable attachment to local dialect, which Monsieur Spittler, director of the Alsatian-dialect theatre, said had been 'a shield...against the *Boches*' that allowed Alsatians to play tricks on the Germans.[13] As a result,

---

[6] Fischer, *Alsace to the Alsatians?* p. 135. On the other hand, 93 per cent of the Haut-Rhin and 95.8 per cent of the Bas-Rhin population were able to speak dialect in 1910. The number of Bas-Rhinois who spoke only French increased from 26,365 to 60,465 (or 3.9 to 9.9 per cent), and in the Haut-Rhin the total increased from 31,760 to 53,351 (or 6.3 to 11.6 per cent) by 1931; and the number who spoke French as their habitual language increased in the Bas-Rhin from 4.1 per cent to 20.2 per cent and in the Haut-Rhin from 6.5 to 22.5 per cent. According to the 1910 census, 93 per cent of the Haut-Rhin and 95.8 per cent of the Bas-Rhin population spoke dialect as their first language. Marcel Koch, 'Les Mouvements de la Population', in Comité alsacien d'études et d'informations, *L'Alsace depuis son retour à la France*, 3 vols, vol. 1 (Strasbourg, 1932), pp. 345–6.

[7] Marcel Nast, 'Inévitable Choc', *Le Journal d'Alsace et de Lorraine*, 28 April 1920.

[8] ADBR 286D 44 André Helmer to Raymond Poincaré, 3 March 1927.

[9] ADBR 286D 46 Inspecteur de l'Académie to Préfet du Bas-Rhin, Strasbourg, 6 November 1925.

[10] ADBR 286D 46 Sous-préfet de Sélestat to Préfet du Bas-Rhin, 29 October 1925.

[11] ADBR 286D 44 Commissaire Spécial to Préfet du Bas-Rhin, Strasbourg, 19 December 1929.

[12] *Le Journal d'Alsace et de Lorraine*, 26 November 1924.

[13] Paul Smith, 'From the Reich to the Republic: Alsace 1918–1925', in Michael Kelly and Rosemary Bock (eds), *France: Nations and Regions* (Southampton, 1993), pp. 182–9, p. 184.

voices from across the region argued that return to France should not trigger the suppression of German or dialect in favour of French; rather, it created the opportunity to spread bilingualism, which would offer economic, cultural, and political benefits in a borderland.[14] Once again, Alsatian connections with Germany and French concern over German influence complicated return. The resulting clash between such divergent understandings of language meant that controversy over language proved both highly divisive and durable. Whenever dialect or German appeared to be threatened, the Alsatian population reacted with letters of protest and demands for linguistic equality. What is more, competing views in Paris and Alsace prevented the smooth dissemination of the new national language, and meant that the question of language became a major battleground for contested visions of what it meant to be Alsatian in French Alsace.

Two broad issues dominated debate: first, the introduction of French; and second, the question of bilingualism. In Paris, while there was general agreement that French should be introduced into the recovered departments, questions remained over the appropriate method of introduction and whether there was any place for bilingualism. In Alsace, opinion was even more divided. Initial agreement amongst local politicians over the introduction of French broke down in the face of frustrations with government policy in the recovered departments. Debates about bilingualism and how French should be introduced persisted throughout the interwar years, while the nationalist press in Germany criticized France's suppression of Alsatian dialect.

One of the first measures taken by the French government was to introduce French on street signs, in education, the judiciary, and the press, as disseminating the language was viewed as 'the best way to assure the future of French Alsace'.[15] But this rapid introduction meant that many lawyers, administrators, teachers, and civil servants found their jobs threatened and opportunities for promotion thwarted. Private-sector employees often fared little better, and workers or agricultural labourers who had no need for French in their working lives found themselves unable to understand official communications, signs, or judicial process. In courts, the accused, witnesses, and jurors complained about the requirement to speak and understand French.[16]

As the government became increasingly concerned about the problems of reintegrating Alsace, the prefect of the Bas-Rhin requested an in-depth investigation into language use in the department in 1925. The resulting reports reveal not only the ongoing complaints about linguistic discrimination, but also the complexities of the situation that the French government faced. French use varied widely between different districts, while class, gender, religion, and geography compounded this fragmentation. Nevertheless, local administrators were able to identify some common themes. French use was more frequent amongst the young (particularly

[14] *Die Freie Presse*, 23 July 1939.

[15] Marcel Nast, 'Inévitable Choc', *Le Journal d'Alsace et de Lorraine*, 28 April 1920.

[16] ADBR 286D 44 Préfet du Bas-Rhin to Président du Conseil, 27 March 1928; Préfet du Bas-Rhin to Président du Conseil, 12 February 1927; *Die Freie Presse*, 2 September 1925.

children), who had been exposed to French in primary schools, and amongst women, who were frequently identified as having better knowledge of French by teachers and officials.[17] It was also more widespread in the liberal professions, and amongst small businessmen and industrialists, for whom French offered an economic advantage, than it was amongst peasants or workers.[18] This contributed to greater French use in towns than in the countryside.[19]

While such facts offer a useful insight into who was speaking French and where it was spoken, all figures on language must be treated with caution; answers about linguistic habits may have been coloured by the desire to please the census taker, or exaggerated by the administrators collecting results in order to satisfy their superiors. And these reports, written by sub-prefects across the Bas-Rhin department, are similarly shaped by the ideological assumptions of their authors. What is more, the picture would have been affected by the influx of Germans before 1918 and French from the interior afterwards. Nevertheless, they offer an important insight into the situation in Alsace, and notably into the widespread use of German and the way that this was interpreted by the French government.

The reports also highlight the interaction of language and religion. In the early Third Republic, republican reformers had attempted to introduce French to limit the control that the clergy were able to wield over regional populations. Similarly, in Alsace the German authorities had worried about the potential for national propaganda exercised by the French-speaking clergy. After 1918, some members of the Alsatian Catholic Church lived up to this Francophile reputation. The sub-prefect of Saverne highlighted the good work that nuns were doing in improving their students' French.[20] But in Sélestat and Erstein the clergy was delivering fewer sermons in French than they had before 1918, and in some cases they had stopped using French altogether.[21] Moreover, in Saverne the curate went so far as to promote German, while concerns abounded about how far Lutheranism bound the Protestant clergy to the German nation.[22]

The reports suggested some progress; seven years of French rule had seen an increase in the number of mayors and communes using French in communication,

---

[17] ADBR 286D 46 Sous-préfet d'Erstein (Hoerter) to Préfet du Bas-Rhin, 27 October 1925; Sous-préfet de Saverne (Peyromaure-Debord) to Préfet du Bas-Rhin, 30 October 1925; Sous-préfet de Molsheim (Amade) to Préfet du Bas-Rhin, 30 October 1925; Sous-préfet de Wissembourg (Chathonet) to Préfet du Bas-Rhin, 23 October 1925.

[18] ADBR 286D 46. Sous-préfet d'Erstein (Hoerter) to Préfet du Bas-Rhin, 27 October 1925; Sous-préfet de Haguenau (Le Hoc) to Préfet du Bas-Rhin, 29 October 1925; Sous-préfet de Molsheim (Amade) to Préfet du Bas-Rhin, 30 October 1925.

[19] Again, these figures vary. In the north Alsatian district of Wissembourg one-third of the urban population understood French compared to around 10 per cent in the surrounding countryside, while in the western district of Saverne the equivalent figures were 15 and 10 per cent. ADBR 286D 46 Sous-préfet de Saverne (Peyromaure-Debord) to Préfet du Bas-Rhin; Sous-préfet de Wissembourg (Chathonet) to Préfet du Bas-Rhin, 23 October 1925.

[20] ADBR 286D 46 Sous-préfet de Saverne (Peyromaure-Debord) to Préfet du Bas-Rhin, 30 October 1925.

[21] ADBR 286D 46 Sous-préfet d'Erstein (Hoerter) to Préfet du Bas-Rhin, 27 October 1925; Sous-préfet de Sélestat (Bastier) to Préfet du Bas-Rhin, 29 October 1925.

[22] ADBR 286D 46 Sous-préfet de Saverne (Peyromaure-Debord) to Préfet du Bas-Rhin, 30 October 1925.

improvements in basic knowledge of French amongst the majority of pupils leaving primary school, and wider sectors of the population able to use French for the 'necessities of life'.[23] Nevertheless, attendance at adult-education classes had declined, many men who used French in their professional life continued to speak dialect amongst their families, and the vast majority of the population remained unable to communicate in French at all.[24] The dissemination of French continued in this gradual, halting fashion. In 1931, while just over half of Alsace's population spoke some French and 5.6 per cent spoke only French, 43.9 per cent still spoke only dialect or German.[25] The Francophile association *Renaissance Alsacienne* had estimated that 90 per cent of Alsatians read a German language newspaper in 1922, and this figure had barely dropped over a decade later when the *Courier cinématographique* pointed out that 80 per cent of the population still read the German press.[26] In 1938 the Bas-Rhin Socialist women's section was still translating articles into German, 'as the majority of Alsatian women [didn't] read French well enough to read *La Tribune* in its original version'.[27] Behind these figures there is considerable regional variation. In 1930 a British diplomat recorded his surprise that in Mulhouse 'everyone, even French officials, seemed to be speaking German', but that, in Strasbourg, if he asked a question in German he received his reply in French, albeit 'sometimes very poor French'.[28]

While almost all in Alsace were in favour of the introduction of French, many also argued that bilingualism should be given official status. This was a position shared by all major political parties, as it reflected, in the words of the *Journal d'Alsace et de Lorraine*, the region's history and geography; after all, nature had placed Alsace 'on the edge of two linguistic domains, two civilizations and two great political nations', and its people had adapted to this borderland position.[29] Politicians from left and right described Alsace as a 'bridge' between France and Germany, and treated bilingualism as the best means to achieve this.[30] In this way, bilingualism in Alsace became a means to ensure Franco–German reconciliation, and a strength of Alsatian culture that reflected the quote from Goethe that was

[23] ADBR 286D 46 Sous-préfet de Sélestat (Bastier) to Préfet du Bas-Rhin, 29 October 1925; Sous-préfet de Saverne (Peyromaure-Debord) to Préfet du Bas-Rhin, 30 October 1925; Sous-préfet de Wissembourg (Chathonet) to Préfet du Bas-Rhin, 23 October 1925; Sous-préfet de Haguenau (Le Hoc) to Préfet du Bas-Rhin, 29 October 1925; Sous-préfet d'Erstein (Hoerter) to Préfet du Bas-Rhin, 27 October 1925.

[24] ADBR 286D 46 Sous-préfet de Wissembourg (Chathonet) to Préfet du Bas-Rhin, 23 October 1925; Sous-préfet de Molsheim (Amade) to Préfet du Bas-Rhin, 30 October 1925; Sous-préfet de Haguenau (Le Hoc) to Préfet du Bas-Rhin, 29 October 1925.

[25] See J. Rossé, M. Stürmel, A. Bleicher, F. Deiber, and J. Keppi, *Das Elsass von 1870–1932*, 4 vols (Colmar, 1936–8), vol. 4, p. 199.

[26] ADBR 98AL 624 Courrier cinématographique de Colmar et Ribeauvillé, 15 April 1933.

[27] OURS SFIO Fonds 41, Liste 1, Dossier 21. Liselotte Wernher to Suzanne Buisson, Strasbourg, 20 November 1938.

[28] TNA FO371/14901 (W13614). Foreign Office Commander Maxs, 18 December 1930.

[29] 'Les Grandes Problèmes d'Alsace et de Lorraine. Bilinguisme et Religion', *Le Journal d'Alsace et de Lorraine*, 9 April 1920.

[30] ADBR 121AL 1059 Rapport sur la question de langue en Alsace-Lorraine (unsigned, nd); 121AL 1059 Debate in Chambre des députés sur la langue de l'enseignement primaire, 16 December 1925.

often repeated in interwar regional newspapers: 'Speaking one language makes one a man. Speaking two makes one a cultivated man.'[31] Proponents of bilingualism referred to successful examples elsewhere, in Belgium or Switzerland, and argued that linguistic unity had not always guaranteed loyalty to the nation, as the case of Ireland demonstrated.[32]

Supporters of bilingualism also mobilized arguments of practicality. First, it offered real economic benefits to the region by facilitating contact and exchange with the neighbouring German states on the right bank of the Rhine. Second, it would avoid the sacrifice of a generation who had built their careers in German and were unable to adapt to a strict imposition of the French language.[33] Third, it could ease the reintegration process by ensuring that the populations of the recovered departments were able to read and understand French laws and literature in the language with which they were most familiar.[34] The degree of common ground over this issue was reflected in 1927 when the Radical politician Georges Wolff proposed a joint political front on the issue of language. However, this common ground was unable to overcome the political divisions between the region's parties, and the front failed to get off the ground after the SFIO refused to work with the Catholic clergy.

The French authorities were unprepared for the extent of local support for bilingualism. The government initially met demands for bilingualism with concern, fearful that tolerance of German in the region might either 'foster the creation of a centre of German thought' or encourage other regional populations to demand bilingualism and, as a result, fundamentally undermine the unity of the Republic.[35] But, over the course of the 1920s, administrators in Alsace warned that refusal to allow German would simply provide fodder for the growing regional discontent.[36] In response, successive governments introduced a series of compromises, including the provision of translators in courts, the translation of important documents, allowing correspondence in German, and printing bilingual election materials.[37] In 1927, at the height of the tensions provoked by the emergence of the autonomist movement, Premier Raymond Poincaré insisted that all communication with Alsatian mayors include German translations, and advised sub-prefects to use

---

[31] 'Les Grandes Problèmes d'Alsace et de Lorraine. Bilinguisme et Religion', *Le Journal d'Alsace et de Lorraine*, 9 April 1920.

[32] ADBR 286D 44 Commissaire Spécial to Préfet du Bas-Rhin, Strasbourg 19 December 1929; 'Les trois Enfants', *La République*, 20 September 1921.

[33] See, for example, Camille Dahlet, 'Les Trois Enfants', *La République*, 30 September 1921; *Elsässer Kurier*, 11 December 1922; 'Les Grandes Problèmes d'Alsace et de Lorraine. Bilingualism et Religion', *Le Journal d'Alsace et de Lorraine*, 9 April 1920; ADBR 286D 44 Préfet du Bas-Rhin to Président du Conseil, 26 January 1929.

[34] AMC Délibérations du Conseil Municipal de la Ville de Colmar, 17 séance du Conseil Municipal, 20 July 1920, p. 340.

[35] ADBR 121AL 1059 Rapport sur la question de langue en Alsace-Lorraine (unsigned, nd); 121AL 1059 Debate in Chambre des députés sur la langue de l'enseignement primaire, 16 December 1925.

[36] ADBR 286D 46 Préfet du Bas-Rhin to Président du Conseil, 12 February 1927.

[37] ADBR 286D 44 Président de la Cour d'Appel de Colmar to Préfet du Bas-Rhin, 30 October 1927.

German or dialect in their dealings with the population if this would improve communication.[38] After Hitler seized power in 1933, French administrators again raised concern about the use of German in Alsace, but a popular campaign against the proposed ban on German at Radio Strasbourg demonstrated continued local support for bilingualism.[39] Recognition that French use was not as widespread as the government had hoped is reflected in official communications; in 1928 important communications were 'rarely' sent out only in French, and almost ten years later the government still included German translations alongside its French-language communiqués about the International Exhibition of 1937.[40] When discussion moved to evacuation of the frontier departments in 1939, the parliamentary committee charged with planning advised that all documents on mobilization and evacuation should be available in both French and German.[41]

The most contentious discussions over language focused upon education, and, as a result, primary schooling became emblematic of many of the problems of reintegrating Alsace and the Moselle.[42] This was partly because the French education system had been an area of rapid change and fundamental republican reform since 1871. The focus of the reformers had been secularity; Premier Jules Ferry's laws had famously made primary education free, secular, and compulsory, and Emile Combes's ministry had banned religious orders from teaching in 1904, and abrogated the Napoleonic Concordat and instituted the separation of church and state the following year. But primary schools had also become an important means of spreading the French language in areas where local languages and dialects dominated. *Instituteurs* thus played a crucial role in shaping the development of their pupils' sense of Frenchness and in encouraging the coexistence of French and local language in the early Third Republic.[43]

Many politicians and education reformers assumed that a similar process would occur in Alsace, but they soon found the situation to be different as the region returned to a nation where French was the language of the majority, which, as Eugen Weber famously pointed out, had been far from the case in 1871.[44] As a result, many Alsatian and Mosellan teachers were concerned about how their calls for the use of dialect in primary schools would be interpreted by the government. Their worries were increased by the connection between Alsatian dialect and the

---

[38] 286D 44 Poincaré to Préfet du Bas-Rhin, 16 July 1927.

[39] *Der Republikaner*, 17 March 1933.

[40] ADBR 391D 33 Circulaire relative au congé exceptionnel à accorder au personnel communal pour lui permettre de visiter l'Exposition international à Paris, 10 June 1937. Signé Léon Blum.

[41] AMVES 106Z 1 Rapport fait au nom de la délégation chargée par la Commission de l'Agriculture d'effectuer une enquête sur la situation des populations rurales des régions de l'Est et du Nord Est, par M. Renaud Jean, député (February 1939).

[42] Alison Carrol, 'Regional Republicans: The Alsatian Socialists and the Politics of Primary Schooling in Alsace, 1918–1939', *French Historical Studies*, 32:2 (2011), pp. 299–325.

[43] Jean-François Chanet, *L'Ecole Républicaine et les petites patries, 1879–1940* (Paris, 1990); Deborah Reed-Danahay, *Education and Identity in Rural France: The Politics of Schooling* (Cambridge, 1996); Anne-Marie Thiesse, *Ils apprenaient la France* (Paris, 1997), and Thiesse, *La création des identités nationales* (Paris, 1999).

[44] Eugen Weber, *Peasants into Frenchmen. The Modernization of Rural France 1870–1914* (Stanford, 1976).

German language, as German was the language of France's main perceived threat and a potential 'alternative nation' for the Alsatian population. This meant that the introduction of French was treated with an urgency that distinguished it from earlier linguistic projects, and created a context where Alsatians worried that calls for the use of dialect could be read as unpatriotic. The intersection of language and religion polarized the politics of primary schooling further, and pastors and priests reported problems with religious education as children taught in French could not understand sermons and so were unable to fully engage with the teachings of the Church.[45] As a result, the clergy and its political representatives became closely associated with the defence of regional language in Alsace, although of course defence of regional language was by no means a policy restricted to the Church.

Immediately after the armistice, the French government introduced the 'direct method', which consisted of immersing Alsatian children in French from their first day at school. The method had been used successfully in the areas of Alsace occupied by the French army during the war, and was presented by many as the best way of giving schoolchildren a good level of French as quickly as possible.[46] Evidence suggests that many schools embraced the new system; Philippe Husser records a meeting on 21 November 1918, when the teachers in his school were informed that all instruction was now to be given in French and that anyone unable to do so should report to the office. The experiment did not meet with success in Husser's school, however. He described his students' difficulties with the method, and noted that, left to 'sink or swim', most children found themselves sinking.[47]

Husser's students were not alone in experiencing difficulties with the direct method. While French administrators wrote that most parents were happy with their children's progress and that all complaints were an 'autonomist tactic', politicians and teachers from across the political spectrum argued that the government was creating a generation which could not understand French or German.[48] In 1927 this formed the basis of a proposal to the Chamber of Deputies that a commission be established to revise educational methods in the recovered departments.[49] Across the region, discussion focused upon the 'sacrificed generation', and all parties agreed that this problem could be corrected by the introduction of bilingualism. This view was supported by local councils, the Conseils Généraux, by certain subprefects, and by the clergy.[50] Nevertheless, some administrators suggested that

[45] ADBR 286D 44 Letter from Pasteur Victor Nessman, Westhoffen to Président du Conseil, 24 March 1927; Motion of the Consistoire Supérieure de la Confession d'Augsbourg, 13 July 1925.
[46] Albert Scheurer 'L'enseignement de l'allemand dans les territoires d'Alsace-Lorraine reconquis depuis 1914', *Journal d'Alsace et de Lorraine*, 4 March 1920.
[47] Husser, *Un Instituteur Alsacien*, pp. 127–8.
[48] AN F7 12751 Commissaire Spécial de Sélestat, Rapport mensuel, Sélestat 4 November 1926.
[49] AMVES 125Z 37 'Proposition de résolution invitant le Gouvernement à constituer, à Strasbourg, une Commission scolaire, chargée d'amener une prompte résolution du problème des langues de l'enseignement primaire des trois départements d'Alsace et de Lorraine'. Présentée par Seltz, Walter, Brom, Meyer, Burger, Oberkirch, Bilger, Pfleger, Silbermann. Chambre des députés, 14 January 1927.
[50] In 1925, the Conseil Général passed a resolution demanding greater recognition of the necessity of knowledge of both languages, especially in education, and that German be used by judicial authorities and administration; also that its use be facilitated by the employment of *fonctionnaires* and judges

bilingualism was more of a priority amongst Alsatian politicians and clergy than the population. The Bas-Rhin academic inspector noted in 1925 that few families demanded bilingualism, and that, when given the choice of a primary school where German was taught or an elementary class for the *lycée* where German was only introduced in the sixth year, most families chose the *lycée*.[51]

Alongside the apparently punitive direct method, local councils and associations rewarded students who achieved particular success in the language.[52] The *Association des Professeurs de Langues Vivantes* sent high-achieving language students on holiday to the French interior to improve their French and create links between the recovered departments and the rest of the nation.[53] Such measures were not only directed at the young: teachers were also given the option of taking a short placement in the interior to help them improve their linguistic skills, although for some teachers this was a requirement rather than a choice. Husser recorded the case of his friend Augst, who killed himself following a bout of depression that resulted from just such an enforced placement.[54]

Concerns over the direct method contributed to discussion of alternative means of teaching Alsatian children to speak French, some of which placed French alongside German or dialect to allow children to get used to the language, while being able to keep up with their lessons. In November 1918 the academic inspector at Colmar reported that all capable teachers would teach two hours of French daily, and that half of all other subjects should be in French.[55] Reports throughout the 1920s stress the importance of ensuring that any teachers sent to Alsace from the interior were able to speak German.[56] In 1927 Poincaré's government fixed the education of German from the beginning of school, and introduced a German test into the programme of studies. In addition, German would be used for the four hours of religious education that Alsatian schoolchildren still received, although anti-clerical critics of this policy pointed out that it worked against students who wished to opt out of religious education, as in doing so they would miss out on four hours of

who spoke both languages, and that arrangements be made for those who only spoke German or dialect. For correspondence on this issue, see ADBR 286D 46 Préfet du Bas-Rhin to Sous-préfet de Strasbourg Campagne, 20 October 1925; Sous-préfet de Saverne to Préfet du Bas-Rhin, 30 October 1925; Sous-préfet de Wissembourg (Chathonet) to Préfet du Bas-Rhin, 23 October 1925. See also Motion of the Consistoire Superieur de la Confession d'Augsberg, 13 July.

[51] ADBR 286D 46 Inspecteur de l'Académie du Bas-Rhin (Hourticq) to Préfet du Bas-Rhin, Strasbourg, 6 November 1925.

[52] AMVES 4MW 14 Jacques Peirotes to E. Tonnelat, Professeur à l'université de Strasbourg, Strasbourg, 20 July 1923; 4MW 14 Note, Office municipal de Jeunesse, 30 July 1924.

[53] AMVES 4MW 14 G. Guibillon to Jacques Peirotes, Strasbourg 1 February 1928. The association sent twenty-two students in 1926, twenty-three in 1924, and twenty-seven in 1927.

[54] AMVES 4MW 14 Mayor of Strasbourg to M. Schont, Professeur at Lycée Fustel de Coulanges, Strasbourg, 20 May 1922; Husser, *Un Instituteur Alsacien*, p. 241.

[55] Harp, *Learning to be Loyal*, p. 196. The government also instructed teachers that German should not be introduced until children could read, write, and speak French in a 'semi-fluent fashion'. See AN, AJ30 204, Le Recteur d'Académie, Directeur Général de l'Instruction publique et des Beaux Arts to Monsieur l'Inspecteur d'Académie, Strasbourg, 19 October 1920.

[56] ADBR 286D 46 Inspecteur de l'Académie du Bas-Rhin to Préfet du Bas-Rhin, Strasbourg, 6 November 1925.

German instruction per week. Throughout the period, Socialists and Radicals continued their attempts to disassociate regional language from religion.

The success of these attempts to introduce French into Alsatian primary schools is difficult to judge. Prefectural reports classed children as a group with the best knowledge of French in the region. This assessment was made as levels of French use increased, so that by 1931 the census indicated that the number of the population able to speak French (either as a sole language or as well as dialect or German) had increased to 50.2 per cent in the Bas-Rhin, and 54.6 per cent in the Haut-Rhin.[57] But, as we have seen, this view was countered by many regional politicians who argued that the system had produced a generation unable to express themselves in either French or German. Moreover, Stephen Harp has shown that not only did Alsatian students' knowledge of French remain considerably weaker than elsewhere in France up to the Second World War, but also interwar literacy rates signalled a drop from the pre-war level in the region.[58]

While primary schools attempted to introduce the French language to young Alsatians, a number of societies and associations emerged after 1918 to spread the French language (and nurture French values) amongst adults through conferences, adult language classes, plays, and libraries. Organized across the region, these associations attempted, in the words of the Haut-Rhin association *La Cigogne*, to 'alter a mentality formed through forty-eight years of German domination'.[59] Associations rapidly emerged to cover all sections of the population, and the *Société des cours populaires de français* even offered German classes to *Français de l'Intérieur* to promote bilingualism in the region.[60] Within two and a half years of the armistice, the network of classes covered around 70 per cent of communes across the two Alsatian departments.[61] Table 5.1 shows their distribution. In total, these language associations organized 905 classes and counted 14,672 students in the Bas-Rhin, and 701 classes for 11,698 students in the Haut-Rhin.[62] This represented around 2.5 per cent of the region's population.

The associations were creative in their use of new media, embracing film alongside poetry readings, songs, and children's shows; and *Renaissance Alsacienne* also came up with the idea of publishing a weekly French-literature supplement for

[57] Marcel Koch, 'Les Mouvements de la Population', in Comité alsacien d'études et d'informations, *L'Alsace depuis son retour à la France*, 3 vols, vol. 1 (Strasbourg, 1932), p. 346.

[58] Harp, *Learning to be Loyal*, p. 195.

[59] ADBR 121AL 158 Comité de propagande 'La Cigogne' Colmar, 24 September 1919.

[60] 121AL 518 Cours Populaires de Langue Française en Alsace, 18 December 1920. Rapport.

[61] 69 per cent of Bas-Rhin and 68 per cent of Haut-Rhin communes offered a language course.

[62] Rapport sur le fonctionnement des oeuvres post-scolaires d'Alsace et Lorraine, 1920–1921, Strasbourg, 1 April 1921. In 1921 *Renaissance Alsacienne*, which focused on workers with top-up classes for children who wanted to improve the French that they learned in primary school offered 75 classes in the Haut-Rhin as well as 121 basic and 51 advanced classes in the Bas-Rhin. *La conference au village* offered 51 classes in the Bas-Rhin and 346 in the Haut-Rhin, *La Cigogne* (which operated only in the Haut-Rhin) provided 234 classes to students in Colmar, Guebwiller, and Ribeauvillé, and the *Société des cours populaires de français* offered 99 classes and taught 1,826 students in Strasbourg, its suburbs, and the surrounding countryside. In addition, a number of communes in the Haut-Rhin offered their own classes, amounting to 46 classes with 738 students.

Table 5.1. Language Associations in Alsace in 1920–1.

NAME OF ASSOCIATION	CLASSES OFFERED IN THE HAUT-RHIN	CLASSES OFFERED IN THE BAS-RHIN
Renaissance Alsacienne	75	121 BASIC 51 ADVANCED
La conférence au village	346	51
La Cigogne	234	–
La société des cours populaires de français		99
Communal classes	46	–
Other	–	579

Source: ADBR 121AL 158 'La Renaissance Alsacienne'; 'Comité de Propagande de la Cigogne, Colmar, 10 April 1920'; Rapport sur le fonctionnement des oeuvres post-scolaires d'Alsace et Lorraine, 1920–1921, Strasbourg, 1 April 1921.

distribution with the bestselling regional newspapers, the *Dernières Nouvelles de Strasbourg*, the *Journal de Mulhouse*, and the *Metzer Freies Journal*. The *Société de livre français en Alsace et Lorraine* collected books for distribution in the departments. By 1921 it had distributed 32,568 books to libraries, 11,554 books to schools, and 41,356 propaganda texts across the departments. It also created 388 libraries in the Bas-Rhin, 354 in the Haut-Rhin, and 212 in the Moselle, as well as mobile libraries that covered the Alsatian Jura and Vosges valleys, and organized conferences and readings across the departments.[63] The *Institut d'études françaises modernes* organized summer courses that covered the French language alongside history, literature, and contemporary issues, as well as excursions and visits across Alsace. But, in 1920, the Alsatians taking the course were outnumbered by foreign students; the majority came from England, and American, Chinese, and Czech students made up the numbers.[64] Five years later, the number of Alsatians registered had dropped further, and they represented just two of twenty-five students in the winter and two of thirty-two in the summer.[65] This reflected the general decrease in Alsatians taking courses in the French language, as initial enthusiasm for return ebbed away and increased frustration with French rule set in.

These associations described their work as 'patriotic tasks'.[66] This patriotic duty meant that many associations branched out beyond language to cover the history, geography, and culture of France and its colonies, and they received state and communal subsidies to cover the cost of heating the classrooms, paying teachers, and organizing courses. *La Conférence au Village* also called upon local industrialists

[63] ADBR 121AL 158 Rapport sur le fonctionnement des oeuvres post-scolaires d'Alsace et Lorraine, 1920–1921, Strasbourg, 1 April 1921; 81Z 39 Le Livre Français en Alsace et Lorraine. Appel.

[64] AMVES 4MW 14 Rapport sur l'Institut d'Etudes Françaises. Exercise d'été 1920. The group included ten English students, seven Alsatians, four Americans, two Czechs, and one Chinese student.

[65] AMVES 4MW 14 Direction de l'Institute d'Etudes Françaises Modernes to Jacques Peirotes, 19 January 1925.

[66] ADBR 121AL 158 Cours Populaire de Langue Française en Alsace. Appel.

and businessmen to support their activity.[67] The *Livre Français* associated their work with the protest against annexation made by the Alsatian deputies at Bordeaux in 1871, while other associations made use of the familial metaphors that had become a mainstay of the cult of the lost provinces after 1871 by describing the recovered departments as 'lost children'.[68] Such language was common amongst these associations; the *Cigogne* stated that it was through the French language that Alsatians could return to their place within the French 'family', and the *Cours Populaire* stated that the Alsatian population would gratefully learn French to merit their place within the nation that had rescued Alsace so heroically.[69]

This 'patriotic duty' raised questions over student participation. At first students paid subscriptions to attend class but, as sections of the region began to face economic difficulties in 1921, Jean Gentzbourger, head of *Renaissance Alsacienne*, argued that unemployed workers should not be required to pay to learn French.[70] His view was countered by Monsieur Kuntz, head of *La Cigogne*, who argued against making the courses free to students, as paying for language classes repre-sented another dimension of the Alsatians' 'daily plebiscite' and was an important signal of their French patriotism. Kuntz stressed that, with every development in the region closely monitored in Germany, it was important to be able to claim that the Alsatians not only followed French courses but paid to do so.[71] The 'patriotic duty' also meant that the government was careful to check the backgrounds of the organizers of these private associations; Gentzbourger's wartime conscription into the German army was deemed to be worthy of note, while Kuntz raised no cause for concern as he had been 'left destitute by the boche'.[72]

In 1919 it became clear that some German nationals were attending French language courses, and the General Commissioner was placed in a difficult position over how best to intervene. He was concerned that their presence could prove disruptive, but regretted that he was unable to give direct instructions to the associations as they were private bodies and outside government control.[73] In any case, their presence allowed the aim of using Alsace as a site to spread the French language and culture outside France's national borders, and this was one area where French administrators did treat Alsace as the heart of a broader, Rhineland community. From 1920, members of Alsatian administrative bodies worked to support French administrators in the Rhineland who established a new course in Mainz for French and German students, which allowed them to study French law and commerce together with the aim of preparing them for peaceful relations

[67] ADBR 121AL 158 La Conférence au Village. Comité du Bas-Rhin.

[68] ADBR 121AL 158 Le Livre Français en Alsace et Lorraine. Appel.

[69] ADBR 121AL 158 Le Livre Français en Alsace et Lorraine. Appel; 81Z 39 Exposé sur l'organisation des cours d'adultes en Alsace.

[70] ADBR 121AL 158 M. Gentzbourger to M. Charléty, Directeur de l'Instruction Publique, Strasbourg, 25 April 1921.

[71] ADBR 121AL 158 Report on activity of la Cigogne, signed Kuntz.

[72] ADBR 121AL 158 Chef du service de la propagande pour M. le Commissaire Général, Strasbourg, 29 (month obscured) 1920; Exposé sur l'organisation des cours d'adultes en Alsace.

[73] ADBR 121 AL 1059 Recteur d'academie to Haut Commissaire de la République, Strasbourg, 18 January 1919.

in the future.[74] This reflected some degree of acceptance of the Alsatian argument that the region's 'double culture' would allow it to act as a bridge between France and Germany.

A further battleground for ideas about language and its role in making Alsatian identities was the theatre. Under German rule municipal theatres across the region had disseminated German cultural products through the staging of the major works of German literature, while the regional *théâtre alsacien* did an equally important job of maintaining a sense of Alsatian distinctiveness through its dialect plays and depiction of Alsatian culture.[75] After 1918, attention focused upon these institutions and their role in shaping identities. For many in both the French administration and amongst Alsace's cultural and political elites, the theatre was the means by which the Alsatians would become 'definitively French', by exposing themselves to the new national language and values, to quote Mayor of Strasbourg Jacques Peirotes.[76] Thus French troupes toured the recovered departments after 1918, staging plays in French in the region's theatres and schools.[77] Treating these tours as an act of patriotism, the *Théâtre d'art français* (TAF), established in May 1919 by Francophile Alsatians, had staged more than 220 shows in 17 different towns in the recovered departments by April 1921.[78] The problem was that they found the Alsatian public unwilling to pay for shows that they were unable to understand, and reductions in their state subsidies forced the TAF to reduce the number of shows on offer by the middle of the 1920s, and their tours gradually petered out towards the end of the decade.[79]

Similar problems faced the *théâtre alsacien*. After the war, Hansi argued for the closure of this regional theatre. He acknowledged that it had been established as an anti-German cultural product, but stated that it had since been brought under the control of the imperial authorities in order to prevent the diffusion of French. It was, as a result, a potentially dangerous element of counter-propaganda that offered a forum for 'Germanophile elements' of the Alsatian population to rally together and should be banned.[80] The theatre was saved by the Commissioner in Colmar, who argued that the widespread demand for plays in Alsatian gave the theatre an important role, but suggested that as a compromise each show should

[74] 'Le Droit Français sur le Rhin', *L'Echo du Rhin du samedi*, 17 May 1920.
[75] Dominique Huck, 'Le "Théâtre Alsacien de Strasbourg" et la production dramatique de ses fondateurs (1898–1914)', in Jeanne Benay and Jean-March Leveratto, *Culture et Histoire des spectacles en Alsace et en Lorraine: de l'annexion à la decentralisation (1871–1946)* (Berne, 2005), pp. 197–222.
[76] AMVES 125Z 15 Discours pronouncé par Jacques Peirotes au Théâtre municipal de Strasbourg, Centenaire de l'inauguration du théâtre municipal le 21 mai 1921; 1MW 262, 42 séance du Conseil Municipal de la Ville de Strasbourg, 31 December 1926, p. 719; AMM 13 séance, 30 December 1929, p. 693.
[77] ADBR 121AL 186 M. et Melle Soudart, Direction du Théâtre la fontaine to Préfet du Bas-Rhin, Paris, 17 April 1922.
[78] ADBR 121AL 186 Rapport, Théâtre d'art français, April 1921.
[79] ADBR 121AL 186 Ministre de la Justice to Commissaire Général de la République, Paris, 23 February 1924. In 1923 the TAF received a subsidy of 300,000 francs. This dropped to 150,000 francs in 1924, and the Minister of Justice saw no means of increasing the subsidy in 1925.
[80] ADBR 121AL 186 Hansi to Président du Conseil, Paris, 20 January 1919.

open with a French song to allow the people to keep their theatre while 'gradually developing a taste for French literature'.[81]

In the region's municipal theatres, the French government's concerns about German influence led to a ban on the staging of German or Alsatian plays in the first years after the armistice. Instead, prefects urged the region's municipal theatres to focus on French plays.[82] As the theatres relied on state subsidies alongside local taxation and ticket receipts to fund their productions, they had little choice other than to follow the new rules.[83] But the city councils argued that the population would be reluctant to see plays that they could not understand, and therefore the theatres should be allowed to stage German plays alongside French ones. The local press came out in support of this position; the Conservative daily *Le Journal de l'Est* stressed its benefits for tourism as well as the population, while the Socialist *Republikaner* argued that German plays in Alsatian theatres would signal a new era of Franco–German reconciliation.[84] Eventually, a more open attitude developed; Premier Edouard Herriot personally granted permission for the Strasbourg municipal theatre to stage Schiller's *Don Carlos* in German in 1924, and the first part of Goethe's *Faust* played in Strasbourg in 1925, in spite of General Commissioner Alapetite's reservation that it was still 'too soon' to have German plays in Alsace's flagship theatre.[85]

The retention of the Alsatian theatre and the permission to stage German plays signalled a more relaxed attitude on the part of the French government, but in 1930 the autonomist Camille Dahlet nonetheless complained that France had adopted a less tolerant attitude than the German authorities had done prior to 1918.[86] Not only had the French government failed to create a German-language troupe, Dahlet argued, but it had also banned the staging of any German plays at all for some time after the region's return to France. Three years later, Colmar's Socialist Mayor Edouard Richard was still attempting to convince the government to allow German plays, stressing that the topic under discussion was not 'German plays' but plays in the German language, and arguing that it would help the

[81] ADBR 121 AL 186 Commissaire de la République, Colmar to Haut Commissaire in Strasbourg, 6 February 1919.
[82] 'L'Alsace et Lorraine. Un conflit de langues', *L'Express*, 15 December 1920. This continued, in 1924, when *Die Freie Presse* reported on the fact that the director of the Eden Theatre had been called to the prefecture, as his troupe left songs in German after translating its plays into dialect. *Die Freie Presse*, 11 April 1924.
[83] In February 1919, the French writer Louis Payen took over the Mulhouse municipal theatre. Payen staged classic works, modern pieces, and more popular plays at reduced rates, but he relied on a subsidy of 250 francs per classic matinée staged at a reduced price in Colmar or Mulhouse. ADBR 121AL 186 Louis Payen to Pierre Rameil, Paris, 8 February 1919; Commissaire de la République to Président du Conseil, Colmar, 20 March 1919; Under Secretary of State at Président du Conseil to the Commissaire de la République, Colmar (nd); Commissaire Général, Decision 6 May 1922 (on state subsidies for theatre); Colmar sample programme.
[84] *Le Journal de l'Est*, 27 November 1924; *Der Republikaner*, 23 October 1924.
[85] ADBR 121AL 856 Commissaire Général to Préfet du Bas-Rhin, 9 March 1925. On the response to the decision, see *Le Courrier de Strasbourg*, 28 November 1924; *Le Journal de l'Est*, 27 November 1924.
[86] AMVES Comptes rendus des séances du Conseil Municipale de la Ville de Strasbourg, 18 séance 3 February 1930.

population to learn French if they were able to watch works of French literature such as those by Molière, Victor Hugo, and Racine in the language most familiar to them.[87]

As Richard indicated, part of the problem was the need to separate plays in German from the German nation. The Alsatian population was well aware of the distinctions between Germany and Alsace; as we have seen, greater contact had bred a clearly defined sense of difference. But this clashed with how the French government viewed the region. Thus successive governments' reluctance to allow German plays was reflective of the broader aim of expunging German influence in the recovered departments, whether through removing suspect German nationals, abrogating German laws, or sequestering German companies. And assumptions about the close connection between language and identity led to a widespread reluctance to allow this inroad into German culture.

The task of sealing the region against German influence became more pressing after Hitler seized power in 1933. In the spring of that year a performance by the Freiburg troupe at Strasbourg's municipal theatre was interrupted by youths with stink bombs.[88] In the aftermath of the protest, autonomist politician Klein worried that the protest suggested anti-German sentiments, which he argued bore no connection to the feelings of the majority in Alsace, but the Conservative councillor Streisguth argued that the protest had been an anti-Hitler demonstration rather than an attack on German culture, and so did reflect popular opinion: 'We would very willingly have a Goethe-inspired theatre here in our town, but we will not tolerate in any way a Hitlerist theatre.'[89] The notion of two Germanies was a way of attempting to make Alsace's ongoing connections to German culture permissible in spite of the changing domestic context in Germany. Nevertheless, shifting Franco–German relations affected what was possible in Alsace, and made much more problematic any expression of loyalties that could be labelled as 'German'.

Separating 'German' from 'Germany' was not only a problem faced by Alsace's theatres, as concerns over German influence also affected what was shown in the region's cinemas. While French cinema hit what has been labelled its 'golden age' following the birth of sound in 1927, many in Alsace expressed their concern that the cinema offered a further means of exposing the population to German cultural exports.[90] As a result, discussion focused upon limiting the number of German films

---

[87] AMC CM 30 Ville de Colmar. Délibérations du Conseil municipal, 1919, pp. 142–4; CM 30 Ville de Colmar, Délibérations du Conseil municipal, 17e séance du Conseil Municipal, 20 July 1920, p. 340. This was not the view taken by all, however. In Strasbourg, the Progressist councillor Klein argued that the Alsatians had distinct tastes. He recognized the important contribution that works of French literature had made to the theatre, but argued that these tended to be Parisian tales of adultery. The Alsatians, on the other hand, had more serious tastes and wanted plays by Goethe, Shakespeare, and Bernard Shaw, and he added that these plays were not offered by French troupes. AMVES Comptes rendus des séances du Conseil Municipale de la Ville de Strasbourg, 91 séance, 10 April 1933, p. 246.

[88] AMVES Comptes rendus des séances du Conseil Municipale de la Ville de Strasbourg, 91 séance, 10 April 1933, p. 227.

[89] AMVES Comptes rendus des séances du Conseil Municipale de la Ville de Strasbourg, 91 séance, 10 April 1933, pp. 227–46.

[90] On interwar French cinema, see Rémi Fournier Lanzoni, *French Cinema: From its Beginnings to the Present* (New York, 2002), especially chapter 5, 'The Golden Age of French Cinema'. On the

shown, and numerous films were censored to avoid anti-French messages reaching the Alsatian audience. Nevertheless, administrators noted subtle ways in which German film could influence cinemagoers in Alsace. One report described the 1930 film *Der Sohn der weißen Berge* (*The Son of the White Mountain*), which featured a scene in which the French character was challenged by the German hero, and his response was to hide behind his skis and whistle the Marseillaise. The apparently anti-French message of the character's emasculation was not lost upon the prefect's office, which encouraged closer censorship to ensure that such films could no longer be shown in the recovered departments, and suggested a quota of 50 per cent for French-language films shown in Alsace to make such embarrassments less likely.[91] In his report on the situation, commentator Gérard Stroobants recognized that this measure was likely to be unpopular with cinema owners, who found that both their audiences and takings went down whenever too many French films were shown. But, Stroobants reasoned, the demands of owners and distributors needed to be balanced with the 'political imperative to introduce French to the region'.[92] Introducing French was, of course, an important means of making Alsace French.

By the interwar years, an assumption had taken root across the Third Republic that French nationality went hand in hand with speaking French. The return of Alsace represented a challenge to ideas about the connection between language and nationality, and ideas about bilingualism represented a practical expression of the 'double culture'. But just as problems of reintegration and shifting Franco–German relations made expressions of the border as a meeting point increasingly difficult, so this was the case for arguments about Alsatian connection to Germany through language. As a result, discussions over language came to emphasize the importance of speaking French. All the same, language was not the only marker of national identity and national belonging, and attempts to create a sense of Alsatianness also questioned how to create a shared culture. Such discussions increasingly came to focus upon festivities and exhibitions as means to develop common cultural under-standings as a way of reimagining the region's place within France.

FESTIVALS AND EXHIBITIONS

Questions of culture and of history arose as Alsatian elites discussed holidays and festivities in the recovered region. The initial, practical questions over what should be a holiday (given that in 1918 Alsace celebrated Good Friday and Saint-Étienne, which were not holidays in the rest of France) eventually gave way to discussion over the presentation of the region's past and present through such festivities, and

situation in Alsace, see ADBR 98AL 624 *Courrier cinématographique de Colmar et Ribeauvillé*, 15 April 1933.

[91] ADBR 98AL 624 Rapport sur la question du langue et du film en Alsace-Lorrain (nd); 98AL 624 Gérard Stroobants, 'La Question du langue et du film en Alsace-Lorraine', Strasbourg, 13 February 1933.

[92] ADBR 98AL 624 Gérard Stroobants, 'La Question du langue et du film en Alsace-Lorraine', Strasbourg, 13 February 1933.

what popular engagement revealed about the population's national sentiments.[93] At first Alsace came together for national festivals such as 14 July, Bastille Day, which had been introduced in France in 1880. Prior to 1918, Francophile Alsatians had used the day as a means to demonstrate their French patriotism by heading for the border to demonstrate, and Robert Redslob's memoirs describe the evenings when older generations would tell the children crouched around them about 'before 1870', which always ended with the advice, 'You should go to Nancy to celebrate 14 July'.[94] On the first Bastille Day after the region's return, 14 July 1919, Strasbourg's interim city council produced detailed instructions that called upon residents to decorate or illuminate their houses with banners or ribbons 'so that the appearance of the city will correspond with the sentiments that animate its citizens on this memorable day', while the Colmar council issued the same instructions, reminding its population that 14 July was their opportunity to show their gratitude to the '*mère patrie*' for its wartime sacrifices to secure the region's 'liberation'.[95]

Subsequent Bastille Days saw similar combinations of detailed directives and grass-roots enthusiasm. In 1920 large numbers turned out to celebrate the fiftieth anniversary of the establishment of the Third Republic in towns across Alsace in September, and the second anniversary of the entry of French troops into Strasbourg on 22 November.[96] After the heady atmosphere following 1918 had passed, anniversaries remained a way to signal popular attitudes. So, in 1935 when the Socialist city council in Colmar used the 300th anniversary of Colmar's attachment to France to stir up patriotism, they did so with an eye on both autonomist groups in the region and the increasingly belligerent Third Reich. Hansi's poster for the event depicted a tricolour-coloured rainbow shining over the town, while Mayor Edouard Richard concluded his speech with the cry, 'Colmar has been a French town for the last three hundred years, and she will remain so forever!'[97] A similar sentiment motivated attempts to recapture the atmosphere of November 1919 in Strasbourg's celebrations of the twentieth anniversary of the city's liberation by the French army on 22 November 1938. Processions marched along the streets, while the surviving members of the reception committee reunited, wearing their original armbands from 1918.[98] In 1939, when the region commemorated the 150th anniversary of the French Revolution of 1789, the press encouraged the population to celebrate with as much fervour as possible, given that Germany would keep a close eye on events in the city.[99]

[93] See the correspondence held under ADBR 121AL 579.

[94] AMM Fonds Martin 40TT 8 *Der Republikaner*, 9 December 1918; Robert Redslob, *Entre la France et l'Allemagne. Souvenirs d'un Alsacien* (Paris, 1933), p. 40.

[95] AMVES 1AFF Affiche, 14 July 1919; AMC 08 40 3 Avis, Colmar 12 July 1920.

[96] AMC 08 40 2 'La fête du Cinquantenaire de la République sera célébrée dans toute la France avec la plus grande solennité'.

[97] *L'Ère Nouvelle*, 16 September 1935.

[98] *Journal d'Alsace et de Lorraine*, 20 November 1938; AMVES 81Z 39 Fonds Haug, Survivants du Comité Central de Réception de 1918 (Altorffer, Braun, Hahn, Stephen, and Wagner) to Hugo Haug, Strasbourg, 16 November 1938.

[99] *Journal d'Alsace et de Lorraine*, 15 July 1939.

As with language, such events were inseparable from how the Alsatians were viewed from outside the region, and, for the government, participation in such festivities represented a means of checking loyalties and attitudes in the recovered departments. So, as the first reports of Alsatian discontent arrived at the Interior Ministry in 1921, police officers reassured the government that Strasbourg's population had celebrated 14 July enthusiastically, 'in spite of the developing malaise'.[100] By the mid-1920s, as autonomism gained in momentum and found its first official expression in the *Heimatbund* manifesto of 1926, the Socialist daily *Die Freie Presse* described Strasbourg's 'spontaneous' celebration of 14 July as a 'categorical response' to the autonomist movement and affirmation of the city's patriotism.[101] In 1929, after the victory of the Volksfront coalition of autonomists, Communists, and Catholics in municipal elections in Strasbourg and Colmar, editor of *La France Moderne* Paul Yves Sebillot reported that the tricolour flags at Strasbourg's 1929 celebrations for Joan of Arc were 'as numerous as those on the Île de France on 14 July'. What is more, some were so old that they were embossed with the imperial eagle, a 'testament', Sebillot noted, 'to a half century of loyalty to France'.[102] Further reassurance came when the tricolour flew from Strasbourg's town hall and the city was illuminated as usual on 14 July 1929.[103]

But concerns rose after the Strasbourg Volksfront voted against staging a firework display or illuminating Strasbourg's buildings on Bastille Day in 1931.[104] The council put this decision down to its poor relations with Paris, while the prefect of the Bas-Rhin dismissed the Volksfront's refusal to celebrate as the result of the Alsatians' 'natural tendency towards opposition and criticism'.[105] However, Socialist councillor Marcel-Edmund Naegelen interpreted the protest as Germanophily, informing a rally that Mayor Hueber had gone to Germany on 14 July 1930, in a reversal of the pre-war Alsatian habit of heading to France to celebrate the national festival.[106] This reflected a broader concern that the Volksfront was 'anti-French', '*boches*', or '*amis de boches*'.[107] In this sense, many Alsatians adopted national language in their descriptions of themselves and each other, and the distinction between what was German and what was Alsatian became more important than ever.

New or existing festivals also raised questions over Alsace's future and brought into conversation other aspects of Alsatian identities. So, when the Conservative government introduced a holiday commemorating Joan of Arc in the aftermath of her 1920 canonization, it provoked lively debate in Alsace. On the first Joan of Arc

---

[100] ADBR 121AL 855 Rapport sur l'activité des services de police d'Alsace et de Lorraine pendant le mois de Juillet 1921. Strasbourg, 10 August 1921.

[101] *Die Freie Presse*, 15 July 1926.

[102] ADBR 98AL 634 Minister of Interior to Président du Conseil, Paris, 8 June 1929.

[103] 'La municipalité pavoisé aux couleurs nationales', *Le Journal d'Alsace et de Lorraine*, 14 July 1929.

[104] *Dernières Nouvelles de Strasbourg*, 11 July 1930; 'La mairie et la fête nationale', *Dernières Nouvelles de Strasbourg*, 12 July 1930; Compte-rendu du conseil municipal, 52 séance, 6 July 1931, p. 427.

[105] ADBR 286D 348 Préfet du Bas-Rhin to Président du Conseil, 16 August 1929. For the council's discussion, see AMVES Compte-rendu du conseil municipal, 52 séance, 6 July 1931, Discours de Mohn, pp. 424–6.

[106] *Dernières Nouvelles de Strasbourg*, 1 October 1930.

[107] AMVES Compte-rendu du Conseil Municipal de la Ville de Strasbourg, 18 séance, 3 February 1930, Discours de Staehling, p. 203.

Day Strasbourg's council failed to illuminate all of the town's buildings, as it did on Bastille Day and other important commemorations. This triggered harsh criticism of the Socialist council from the Catholic councillor Schies. Mayor Peirotes denied Schies' charge of unpatriotic behaviour, and pointed out that as he had received no instructions from the government on how the festival should be celebrated, the town decorated several important buildings but avoided wasting money on 'unnecessary illuminations'.[108]

Peirotes' motivations were not as wholly practical as he implied, of course. Since the end of the nineteenth century, the French left had wrestled to prevent the Catholic right's annexation of Joan of Arc and attempted to present Joan as a republican figure.[109] In many ways, Peirotes' response represented a continuation of this struggle. But it was also a reaction to local circumstances, as the region's Socialists experienced mounting frustration that their demands for the introduction of the separation of church and state in Alsace went unheeded in Paris, and, as a result, the mayor was keen not to celebrate a Catholic heroine with too much enthusiasm. Indeed, refusal to celebrate sent a potent signal about attitudes towards the religious question in the city, and Peirotes pointed out that the city's population had not indicated any desire to celebrate the festival.[110]

Mulhouse's Socialist city council made a similar point in July 1931, when it used celebrations for the fiftieth anniversary of secular education in France to protest against the failure to introduce secular education in Alsace. With both the Concordat and confessional schooling still in place, the council organized festivities and the city's primary-school children received cakes topped with a card that read 'secularity means the utmost respect of the law and rights of the individual'.[111] Frustrated by successive governments' failure to introduce secular education, the council used this festival to offer their view of Alsace's place within the French republic.

Other occasions were similarly politicized; for example, the festival of 1 May was given a particularly Alsatian flavour and spoke to questions of the place of the Alsatian labour movement in Europe. At events throughout Alsace families were welcomed, and marches were usually accompanied by musicians and often followed by a trip to the forest or a get-together in the evening, while party leaders called for internationalism, peace, and unity in the labour movement or focused upon specific threats to peace, such as the French occupation of the Ruhr.[112]

[108] AMVES Compte-rendu du conseil municipal, 50 séance, 11 May 1921, pp. 495–8. Discours de Schies et discours de Jacques Peirotes.
[109] Michel Winock, 'Jeanne d'Arc', in Pierre Nora (ed.), *Les lieux de mémoire, III: Les Frances* (Paris, 1992), pp. 675–732.
[110] AMVES Compte-rendu du conseil municipal, 50 séance, 11 May 1921, pp. 495–8. Discours de Schies et discours de Jacques Peirotes.
[111] ADBR 98AL 326 Recteur de l'Académie publique to the Préfet du Haut-Rhin, Strasbourg, 10 July 1931.
[112] May 1st was treated as a Socialist festival in Alsace, as the CFTC in Alsace did not celebrate the day in the region. See Bénédicte Zimmermann, 'Les Premiers Mai de la CFTC/CFDT: logique identaire et pratique syndicale', *Le Mouvement Social*, 157 (1991), pp. 87–102. On the celebration, see ADBR 121AL 103 Chef d'Escadron Richard, Commandant de la Cie de la Gendarmerie du Haut-Rhin to the Commissaire Général, Colmar, 2 May 1922; *Die Freie Presse*, 29 April 1924; ADBR 121AL 103 Chef d'Escadron Richard, Commandant de la Cie de la Gendarmerie du Haut-Rhin to

The appeals for internationalism were, as had been the case before 1918, frequently focused on Franco–German reconciliation and stressed Alsace's favourable position to comment on events and developments in Germany and to mediate between Germany and France. In the Socialist daily *Die Freie Presse*'s 1 May edition in 1924, Léon Blum appealed to the German Socialists, stating that peace would suffer should the nationalists win in the German elections.[113] The decision to print this appeal in the Alsatian newspaper underscored the idea of Alsace as a bridge between two cultures.

This idea also lay at the heart of the Alsatian celebrations of the centenary of Goethe's death. At an event organized by Strasbourg's *Union locale des syndicats*, Hermann Wendel of Frankfurt described Goethe as 'a friend of France and admirer of Napoleon 1er', and called on Strasbourg to be proud of its association with both Rouget de l'Isle, who had first sung the Marseillaise, and Goethe, 'the precursor of Franco–German entente'.[114] Later that year, in July 1932, Strasbourg councillors Camille Dahlet and Jean-Pierre Mourer proposed that Strasbourg host the international congress against war, stressing that should war break out the city would be at the heart of the battlefield.[115] Moreover, having been a 'seed of discontent' in the past, it was likely to find itself in a similar position in the future and should take the lead in setting the pacifist agenda.[116] In proposing the congress, Dahlet and Mourer attempted (unsuccessfully) to stress that the city's role as a bridge could be useful in geopolitical terms as well as in culture.

Local politicians and economic and cultural elites also attempted to disseminate their vision of identities through museums and exhibitions. In the summer of 1919 Strasbourg's city council established a Historic Museum, and through the early years of French rule a number of new museums were discussed, including the Museum to the Marseillaise on Place Broglie in Strasbourg, on the site of Mayor Dietrich's house where the anthem had reportedly been composed and performed for the first time.[117] Exhibitions on France and Louis Pasteur in Strasbourg equally served the purpose of presenting the links between France and Alsace during these early years. At the colonial exhibition held in Strasbourg in 1924, organizers attempted to stir up a sense of Alsace's connection to Greater France through exhibits, displays, and brochures that described daily life in the colonies, and the

Commissaire Général, Colmar, 2 May 1922; ADBR 121AL 103 Commissaire Spécial de Police to Préfet du Haut-Rhin, Colmar, 2 May 1922; ADBR 121 AL 103 Commissaire Spécial, Rapport, Strasbourg, 1 May 1923; ADBR 121AL 103 Commissaire de Police, Rapport, Sainte Marie-aux-Mines, 2 May 1923; ADBR 121AL 103 Telegramme Officielle, 1 May 1923. Alapetite (Commissariat Général) to Ministère de la Justice; ADBR 121AL 103 Inspecteur, Rapport, Strasbourg 1 May 1923; ADBR 121AL 103 Commissaire Spécial. Rapport, Guebwiller 2 May 1923; ADBR 121AL 103 Préfet du Haut-Rhin to Garde des Sceaux, 4 May 1923.

[113] *Die Freie Presse*, 29 April 1924.
[114] ADBR 286D 47 Commissaire Spécial to Préfet du Bas-Rhin, 3 April 1932.
[115] AMVES Compte-rendu du conseil municipal, 75 séance, 18 July 1932, p. 560.
[116] AMVES Compte-rendu du conseil municipal, 75 séance, 18 July 1932, pp. 555–6.
[117] ADBR 121AL 1091 Le Maire de Strasbourg to M. le Commissaire Général de Strasbourg, 21 January 1921; Extrait de la Séance du 21 Fevrier 1921 de la Commisssion de l'Architecture et des Beaux-Arts. Conservation des Immeubles situés en façade sur le Broglie.

reciprocal advantages of the relationship between France and its empire.[118] Exhibition brochures featured maps detailing the goods produced by individual colonies, while pointing out France's good works in installing hospitals and schools where there had previously been 'prisons' and 'penal colonies', and describing the loyalty that it could command from its colonial subjects.[119] Reproduced ceremonies, such as the baptism of babies born during the passage, marriages, and the coronation of King Bouppé I, aimed to offer visitors an insight into daily life.[120]

As well as stressing France's grandeur and global influence, these colonial exhibits were placed alongside information on Alsatian industry and agriculture, while concerts by the Strasbourg orchestra and athletic displays took place beside the colonial-themed ceremonies in an attempt to stress the links between Alsace and Greater France.[121] Organizer Louis Proust stressed Alsace's continuous interest in French colonial life, while Minister of Colonies Edouard Daladier paid tribute to those famous 'fils d'Alsace' who had sacrificed their lives for the colonial idea; and his colleague on the organizing committee, Professor Auguste Sartory, pointed to the Alsatians who had led France's colonial adventures.[122] For Mayor Peirotes, meanwhile,

> Alsace…has a colonial past. In spite of being separated from the motherland for almost half a century, it was always interested in France's colonial expansion. The Alsatian didn't restrict himself to the soil of his birth…he looked further, paying attention to the peaceful conquests of our armies on the burning soil of Africa or in far-away Asia. Many of Alsace's sons died heroically on these new lands, where our flag flies today. And numerous great colonialists have Alsatian origins.[123]

Presenting Alsace as an integral part of France with long-standing commitments to the empire was of course a concerted economic strategy and a political response to the burgeoning autonomist movement. Linking region and nation in this way stressed the indivisibility of France and represented an emphatic statement to those sections of the autonomist movement that argued for Alsatian neutrality.[124]

---

[118] It recorded a 40,000-franc profit, which compared favourably with the loss of 150,000 francs recorded at the national exhibition and the 1,437,000 francs loss of the Pasteur exhibition, AMVES 234MW 343. Liste d'expositions et foires expositions à Strasbourg, 1919–1928; AMVES 234MW 295 Jacques Peirotes to M. le Ministre des Finances, Strasbourg, 26 July 1924.

[119] AMVES, 234MW 296 Brochure de l'Exposition Coloniale, Industrielle et Agricole de 1924, 4 October 1924; AMVES 234MW 295. Brochure de l'Exposition Coloniale, Industrielle et Agricole de 1924.

[120] AMVES 234 MW 295 Brochure de l'Exposition Coloniale, Industrielle et Agricole de 1924.

[121] 'L'Exposition Coloniale de Strasbourg. Participation Etrangère, *Dernières Nouvelles de Strasbourg*, 8 February 1924; AMVES 234MW 297. Correspondance du secrétaire général du Comité des Fêtes de l'Exposition Coloniale Agricole et Industrielle, June 1924; Brochure de l'Exposition Coloniale, Industrielle et Agricole de 1924, 9 August 1924, 16 August 1924; AMVES 234MW 295. Exposition Coloniale, Agricole et Industrielle. Guide spéciale éditée par les *Dernières Nouvelles de Strasbourg*, 1924; Louis Proust, 'L'Exposition Coloniale de Strasbourg', *Dernières Nouvelles de Strasbourg*, 22 February 1924.

[122] *Die Freie Presse*, 7 July 1924.

[123] AMVES 234MW 295 Brochure de l'Exposition Coloniale, Industrielle et Agricole de 1924, 4 October 1924.

[124] AMVES 234MW 296 Brochure de l'Exposition Coloniale, Industrielle et Agricole de 1924, 'Exposition coloniale de Strasbourg', 5 July 1924; AMVES 234MW 295 Exposition Coloniale, Agricole et Industrielle. Guide spéciale éditée par les *Dernières Nouvelles de Strasbourg*, 1924.

In this sense, festivities and exhibitions offered forums for elite groups to set out their visions for Alsace and Alsatian cultural life, and many of the debates over the region's reintegration were reproduced in these discussions over festivals and exhibitions. But what made them distinctive was the outlet they offered for the expression of attitudes, and the sense that the population could 'make' culture affected the nature of these debates. As always, the idea that Germany would be monitoring cultural developments in Alsace raised their stakes.

CONCLUSION

Ideas about Alsatian identities were expressed through discussions of different areas of life. This chapter has traced these debates in areas that became battlegrounds for understandings of what was distinctly *Alsatian*: language, festivals, and exhibitions. Across each area, attempts to carve out a space for Alsatianness within the borders of France grappled with how to reconcile the interaction between the local context, the return to the French nation, and Alsace's broader connections. Many Alsatians from different walks of life articulated this interaction through the notion of the region's 'double culture', which connected it to France and Germany. This idea allowed the reconciliation of the specificities and uniqueness of Alsatian culture with its cross-border connections, and served to relabel aspects of the region's culture, such as the use of the German language or attachment to German literature as *Alsatian* rather than *German*. As in the case of legislative and administrative structures, this relabelling was important as it allowed Alsatians to argue in favour of the retention of regional cultural particularities, and in so doing it was able to unify diverse sections of the regional population.

Problems arose, however, as many of these arguments from Alsace clashed with assumptions west of the Vosges, where the dominant understanding of Alsace was as the limits of France and of Frenchness. The problem for those Alsatians who tried to explain regional culture to Paris was that any connections with Germany were awkward in interwar France. Long before Hitler seized power in 1933, French administrators were concerned with sealing their border against German influence, and in this light even a staging of Goethe's *Faust* in Strasbourg in 1925 presented a potential security risk. As a result, the notion that Alsace's double culture would allow it to act as a bridge between the two great European cultures of France and Germany never supplanted the idea that Alsatian culture had to be a barrier against German influence. At the heart of this understanding was a view of the national boundary as the limits of the nation.

Behind this clash were divergent ways of seeing borders, but also nationalization. As Alsatians attempted to reconcile use of the German language, interest in German culture, and connections to French history, they revealed an understanding of these different aspects of identity as compatible. Such connections to both France and Germany explained the region's cultural distinctiveness, and were presented as a natural and historic state of affairs in a borderland. Nationalization, therefore, was never viewed in binary terms, and Strasbourg's municipal council could consequently demand to stage Goethe's work in German in the municipal theatre, all the while putting extraordinary effort into celebrating Bastille Day. After all, as we have seen, cross-border contact had created a clear understanding of difference between Germany and Alsace, and many Alsatians saw no contradiction in the council's behaviour. In Paris, however, things appeared in more straightforward terms as 'for' or 'against' France. Concern over use of the German language, and the presentation of France in exhibitions and festivities all reflected uncertainty over the Alsatian population's loyalty towards France. And, in the face of such national ambiguity, French policy focused on more closely defining the borders of what was permitted for members of the national community.

BORDER CREATES A CLEAR
UNDERSTANDING OF
    DIFFERENCE
      BETWEEN GERMANY
AND ALSACE
(in Alsace at least)

6

The Border Landscape

All the same, we still had one great and valuable asset...It was the land.
We clung to it with every fibre of our being. This land was ours, and no-one
would take it from us.

Robert Redslob (1933)[1]

This chapter considers the remaking of the Alsatian landscape after 1918. While
the national boundary between France and Germany shifted in 1871 and 1918,
there was only one change in the borders of Alsace, when Belfort withstood the
siege of 1870–1 and remained within France, as the rest of Alsace was annexed into
the German Empire. Such constancy in regional boundaries contributed to a sense
of place that was connected to the Alsatian territory. And, just as fluid national
boundaries led to a reinforcement of existing social structures, so consistency in
place led to a deeply rooted attachment to the physical Alsatian *Heimat* (homeland). This was an attachment that was expressed through discussions of the
regional landscape and historic ideas of the region and the border. Throughout, the
Alsatian landscape was remarkable in the certainty it offered, in spite of the instability of national boundaries.

There is a wide-ranging historiography on the relationship between landscape
and human society. The *annalistes* stressed the formative and even deterministic
influence that landscape and the environment exerted upon society, shaping
human action and agency, and driving historical change.[2] Alternatively, the landscape has been treated as a cultural construction, and research has demonstrated its
symbolic power through consideration of the myths and memories invested in it.[3]

---

[1] Robert Redslob, *Entre la France et l'Allemagne. Souvenirs d'un Alsacien* (Paris, 1933), p. 234.
[2] Peter Burke, *The French Historical Revolution: The Annales School, 1929–1989* (Stanford, 1990).
See in particular Braudel's *Mediterranean*, which traced the slow, almost imperceptible transformations initiated by the environment, as its repetition and its cycles shaped the lives of those who lived
from the sea and upon the areas that bordered it. Fernand Braudel, *La Méditerranée et le monde méditerranéen à l'époque de Philippe II* (Paris, 1949). In a similar vein, Marc Cioc's eco-biography of the
Rhine treats the river as 'the means whereby Germany rose to industrial greatness in the nineteenth
and twentieth centuries': it supplied the water necessary for the factories lining its banks, while carrying
the ships that brought supplies to the factories and sent their products to market. Marc Cioc, *The Rhine:
An Eco-Biography, 1815–2000* (Seattle, 2002).
[3] Dennis E. Cosgrove, *Social Formation and Symbolic Landscape* (Madison, WI, 1984); Simon Schama,
Landscape and Memory (New York, 1995). As Alexandra Walsham has put it, in this analysis the landscape is 'conceptualised not merely as a by-product of the economic and social activities and processes
which unfolded upon it, but also as a dense and complex system of signs and symbols that can be

Such understandings and experiences did not remain static and changed over time, meaning that each generation inscribed its own values and preoccupations onto the landscape, all the while finding it impossible to entirely erase those of the preceding one.[4] In this sense, the landscape represented a site, or 'realm of memory', to quote Pierre Nora.[5] What is more, work on the built environment and the commemorative landscape has recognized its role in shaping experiences, and in building national cultures.[6]

Building on this focus on the landscape (both natural and built) as a site of memory, recent literature on European identities has stressed the importance of a connection to landscape. Work on modern Germany has shown the role of an idealized landscape of home as a focus for emotional solace at moments of trauma and change.[7] And recent research on France has shown the multiple practical and symbolic ways in which populations have rooted themselves in a sense of place, and stressed the importance of local sensibilities in forging understandings of the French nation.[8] Similarly, in interwar Alsace the sense of Alsatianness discussed in previous chapters was not connected solely to language, culture, or other markers of identity; it was also rooted in the Alsatian landscape—the Vosges mountains, the Rhine river and its plain, the dense forests, the half-timbered houses depicted by Hansi, the ruins of castles and abbeys that spoke to the region's history, and the distinct *quartiers* and districts of its towns and cities.

In this sense, it was impossible to separate the Alsatian landscape from the myths and symbolism invested in it. As we have seen, French thinkers and politicians since the time of Louis XIV had described the Rhine as the nation's natural frontier, with Strasbourg as the great citadel in the east. After 1871 the 'blue line of the

decoded and deciphered'. See Alexandra Walsham, *The Reformation of the Landscape: Religion, Identity and Memory in Early Modern Britain and Ireland* (Oxford, 2011), p. 6.

  [4] Alain Corbin, *L'homme dans le paysage* (Paris, 2001). See also Caroline Ford, 'Nature's Fortunes: New Directions in the Writing of European Environmental History', *Journal of Modern History*, 79 (2007), pp. 112–33.

  [5] Pierre Nora, *Les Lieux de mémoire*, 3 vols (Paris, 1984–92). See also W. G. Hoskins, who described the landscape as the 'richest historical record we possess'; W. G. Hoskins, *The Making of the English Landscape* (London, 1955), p. 14.

  [6] See Andrew Lees and Lynn Hollen Lees, *Cities and the Making of Modern Europe, 1750–1914* (Cambridge, 2007); Martin Simpson, 'Republicanizing the City: Radical Republicans in Toulouse, 1880–90', *European History Quarterly*, 34: 2 (2004), pp. 157–90; Janice Best, *Les Monuments de Paris sous la Troisième République: Contestation et commémoration du passé* (Paris, 2010). Notably, Maurice Agulhon's pioneering work on 'statuomania' has pointed to the use of statues and monuments in the construction of a national symbolism in Third Republican France. See Maurice Agulhon, 'La «statuomanie» et l'histoire', *Ethnologie Française*, 8: 2/3(1978), pp. 145–72; Maurice Agulhon, 'La statuomanie et l'histoire', *Histoire vagabonde*, 3 vols (Paris, 1988–96); Maurice Agulhon, *Marianne into Battle: Republican Imagery and Symbolism in France, 1789–1880* (Cambridge, 1981); Antoine Prost, *Les anciens combattants et la société française*, 3 vols (Paris, 1977).

  [7] Thomas Lekan, *Imagining the Nation in Nature: Landscape Preservation and German Identity, 1885–1945* (Cambridge, MA, 2004), p. 254; Celia Applegate, *A Nation of Provincials: The German Idea of Heimat* (Oxford, 1990), pp. 228–36; David Blackbourn, '"The Garden of our Hearts": Landscape, Nature and Local Identity in the German East', in David Blackbourn and James Retallack (eds), *Localism, landscape and the ambiguities of place: German-speaking central Europe, 1860–1930* (Toronto, Buffalo, and London, 2007).

  [8] Philip Whalen and Patrick Young (eds), *Place and Locality in Modern France* (London, 2014).

Vosges' (in reference to the blue colour that the mountain range adopts when viewed from a distance) became a symbol of revanchism, and of France's dismemberment following the loss of Alsace-Lorraine.[9] For Germany, meanwhile, the Rhine had long served as a potent symbol of German nationalism flowing through the body of the fatherland. This metaphor clashed with French ideas of the Rhine, as it was based upon both banks belonging within the German nation.[10] Yet it was through such descriptions, and through their role in shaping relations between France and Germany, that the border became a symbol of national unity. Of course, this meant that the post-1918 border seemed natural to some and artificial to others, a reminder that both supposedly 'natural' and 'artificial' borders lie in the eye of the beholder.

While the border became a symbol of national unity, the interwar borderland was the site of boundary markers that signalled the division between French and German territory, and also of former border points that indicated the sites of older borders that were no longer in force. Disused border stations became tourist sites highlighted by the Michelin guide, while a series of auberges, war monuments, commemorative plaques, and other symbols marked the former boundary, and inns were renamed as '*à l'ancienne frontière*' as a reminder of where the border had once stood.[11] The region also achieved new symbolic status because of both the importance of return as a central French war aim after 1914, and its renewed status as France's frontier against Germany and symbol of military might. Tourists and observers poured in; for example, the *Touring Club de France* chose it as the site for their first group tour, and Stephen Harp has described their flight to the city where they ate pâté de Strasbourg, choucroute, and tarte aux quetsches d'Alsace, all washed down with Strasbourgeois beer and wines from Ribeauvillé, and served by women dressed in traditional Alsatian costume.[12] In this way, the symbolism of border sites became intertwined with other symbols of Alsatian identity, such as regional cuisine or dress.

This chapter considers the ways in which the border landscape was shaped, invented, and reinvented after 1918, while recognizing that it also represented an actor in the change that the region experienced in these years. In Alsace, the landscape moulded the regional economy by dictating what was grown, grazed, and mined, and it fashioned lives by connecting or isolating populations. But it was also shaped by the humans who lived on it, described it, or built on it, and the interwar Alsatian landscape reflected both the particular experience of annexation, and how Alsatians saw themselves in relation to the rest of France, to Germany, and to Europe. It was not unchanging: different aspects were willed into and out of existence by city planners, politicians, commemorative societies, engineers, hiking clubs, and others. And Alsatians were not alone in reflecting upon the Alsatian

[9] Aude Dontenwille-Gerbaud, 'La ligne bleue des Vosges', *Mots. Languages du Politique,* 105 (2014), pp. 13–26.
[10] Schama, *Landscape and Memory*, p. 363.
[11] *Pneu Michelin Guide Régional Alsace de Strasbourg à Mulhouse Hautes Vosges* (Paris, 1935–6), p. 30.
[12] Stephen L. Harp, *Marketing Michelin: Advertising and Cultural Identity in Twentieth Century France* (Baltimore, 2001).

landscape after 1918; Germans visiting the region reflected upon their loss, while one of the first steps taken by the returning French was to construct a new commemorative landscape.[13]

In common with earlier chapters, this chapter suggests that it is impossible to consider the interwar landscape in isolation; both continuity and change are closely linked to the preceding period. Yet it is also important to recognize the scale of the transition triggered by return in 1918. The chapter's focus is upon how insiders and outsiders viewed and described the landscape, and how their 'imaginings' connected to transformations of the landscape by larger processes of social, economic, or political change. It also suggests the impossibility of separating the natural from the man-made and points to the long interaction between the two, whether through alterations to the path of the Rhine by engineers and planners in an attempt to rationalize its natural vagaries, through the deforestation of woodland for hunting or firewood, or through the construction of houses adapted to local circumstances and 'traditional' regional style, such as Louis Sezille's noted 1909 example of a typical Alsatian house built from local materials to withstand the regional weather.[14] Meanwhile, groups and individuals from inside and outside the region built monuments, reconstructed ruins, and worked on fortifications with a wide range of aims, whether it was to remove traces of German identity, to inscribe a sense of Frenchness, to offer a picture of a traditional Alsatian past, or to secure the region. Throughout, ideas about Alsace as a frontier of France and of Frenchness interacted with, and were challenged by, the notion of the region as the heart of a cross-border community. The tension between the two understandings lies at the heart of Alsace's return to France.

IMAGINING AND REIMAGINING THE ALSATIAN LANDSCAPE

The distinct features of the Alsatian landscape represented a common theme in descriptions of Alsace in memoirs, literature, and tourist guides. But, of course, attitudes towards the landscape were never fixed: on the one hand, they changed over time; on the other, they could vary in different national contexts.[15] The latter point is of particular pertinence for border regions, which were sites where such

---

[13] ADBR 286D 326 *Der Republikaner*, 10 August 1939. On Strasbourg's commemorative landscape, see Alison Carrol, 'In the Border's Shadow: Reimagining Urban Spaces in Strasbourg, 1918–39', *Journal of Contemporary History*, 48 (2013), pp. 666–87.

[14] Eric Storm, *The culture of regionalism: Art, architecture and international exhibitions in France, Germany and Spain, 1890–1939* (Manchester, 2010), pp. 126–7.

[15] On changing views over time, see, for example, the work of Alain Corbin, which has charted the changing views of the sea and seaside. Corbin describes their transformation from objects of fear into sites of admiration and desire between the eighteenth and twentieth centuries. Alain Corbin, *Le territoire du vide. L'Occident et le désir du rivage, 1750–1840* (Paris, 1988). On distinct national contexts, Simon Schama has pointed to the different national 'landscape myths' which shaped perceptions of the landscape, such as the German association between the forest and patriotism that could be traced back to Tacitus. See Schama, *Landscape and Memory*, p. 83.

different national views of the landscape interacted. Thus nineteenth-century French and German travellers visiting the Rhine viewed it with very different ideas of how it fitted into their own national histories; while France laid claim to the river as the nation's natural and historic frontier, for German nationalists it was, in the words of Bonn professor Ernst Moritz Arndt, 'Germany's river, but not Germany's border'.[16] Indeed, the symbolism invested in the river meant that after 1871 the entire Rhine valley became a privileged site for new memorials built to solidify attachment to the Kaiserreich, notably the Germania monument overlooking the village of Rüdesheim and the Kaiser Wilhelm statue in Koblenz.

These national ideas of the landscape became entangled with ideas of which natural features of the landscape constituted a border. Written in the aftermath of the loss of Alsace, Ernest Renan's celebrated 'What is a Nation?' had rejected the suggestion that 'a nation's frontiers are inscribed on the map, and that this nation has the right to take for itself what is necessary in order to round out certain contours' as arbitrary and fatal. Of course, Renan was writing with 1871 in mind and arguing against German claims on Alsace as ethnically German and bound to Germany by the River Rhine: 'Soil no more makes the nation than does race.'[17] Yet, as we have seen, ideas about the Rhine's role as a natural and a historic frontier had a long history in France.

Such understandings of the Rhine as a border were picked up in Alsace, and for Alsatian regionalist Anselme Laugel the Rhine had long been 'the border between two distinct civilizations', or 'between civilization and barbarity'. In his view, for 'many centuries the Rhine represented the limits of the known world. While on the left bank, the vast network of Roman Roads extended to the Atlantic Ocean, its right bank was covered with the immense German forests, and inhabited only by savage people, amongst whom no traveller would dare to tread.'[18] This understanding was depicted by a Hansi cartoon showing the ancient Germans gazing longingly at Alsace from across the Rhine as they think about invasion (Figure 6.1). In common with other Hansi cartoons, the Germans are caricatured in their spectacles and their physiques, which Hansi depicted as extremely thin or very stocky.

As Laugel's comments suggest, during the nineteenth century French and German ideas of the Rhine as a border developed in interaction with each other, and national hostilities and rivalry crystallized on the river. Thus the understanding of the Rhine as a symbol of Germany's cultural and political unity was based on Germany's continued struggle against the French. Over the course of the 1840s German poets and songwriters penned some 400 patriotic Rhine tunes in the span of that single decade, most notably Nikolaus Becker's *Rheinlied,* which included the line 'They shall not have it / The free German Rhine', and Max Schneckenburger's *Die Wacht am Rhein,* which proclaimed 'Dear Fatherland, have no fear / The watch

---

[16] Lekan, *Imagining the Nation in Nature,* p. 27; Cioc, *The Rhine: An Eco-Biography,* p. 9.

[17] Ernest Renan, *Qu'est-ce que c'est une nation? Conférence faite en Sorbonne le 11 mars 1882,* 2nd edn (Paris, 1892), p. 57.

[18] Anselme Laugel, *Costumes et coutumes d'Alsace* (Colmar and Nancy, 2008; 1st edn 1902), p. 318.

Les Germains aperçoivent l'Alsace de l'autre côté du Rhin.

Figure 6.1. Hansi, 'Les Germains aperçoivent l'Alsace de l'autre côté du Rhin'.

on the Rhine stands fast and true'. The latter was resurrected as a military anthem during the Franco–Prussian War.[19] After war broke out in 1914 French claims to the river became increasingly vocal, and publications such as Camille Jullian's *Le Rhin Gaulois* stressed that the Rhine's history was indelibly bound up with that of the rest of France and painted a picture of the population's resistance to the

[19] Cioc, *The Rhine: An Eco-Biography*, p. 9.

German 'invasions' and described the invading forces as 'barbarians'.[20] Of course, as Peter Schöttler has pointed out, the term 'barbarian invasion' was one with a double historical and political meaning when Jullian's work was published in 1915.[21] These competing ideas of the Rhine shaped interwar understandings of the river, and history became an important instrument to advance such claims. In the period after Versailles, German nationalist historians turned to history to fight the clauses of the Treaty and above all the territorial losses and new frontiers it included. This so-called '*Grenz- und Volkstumskampf*' ('struggle over borders and nationhood') was not restricted to the Rhine, as it offered Weimar Germany the possibility to continue by other means the political struggle over territories lost at Versailles. But it took on a particular force in the study of the Rhineland as a result of the river's symbolic importance. Following the establishment of the *Institut für geschichtliche Landeskunde der Rheinlande* (Institute for Historical Geography of the Rhineland) at the University of Bonn in 1920, a flurry of works stressing the Rhineland's Teutonic, or German, history and character appeared.[22] For the French, on the other hand, Versailles represented the restoration of the Rhine as France's natural, historical, and rightful frontier. Yet some thinkers took seriously the notion that the Rhine was a 'frontier' rather than a 'limit'. At Versailles Clemenceau had demanded the separation of the right bank of the Rhine from Germany in order to create an independent and neutral state, and during the war and in its immediate aftermath French historians published works which stressed that the Rhinelanders' biological roots were Gallic and Roman rather than Teutonic, and argued that the French Revolution and Napoleonic rule had reunited Rhinelanders with their kin in France.[23]

Paul Tirard, chairman of the Inter-Allied Rhineland High Commission, even exempted Rhinelanders from German war guilt by claiming that they had suffered more than a hundred years of Prussian oppression and called upon them to join the French to allow themselves to once again participate fully in Western modernity.[24] When the French occupied the Ruhr valley in 1923 in response to Weimar's failure to continue its payments for wartime reparations, this gave greater urgency to the sense of French threat to the Rhine as a German river. Thus, in 1925 German authorities celebrated the millennium of the Rhineland as a German territory, and the following year organized the illumination of the Germania monument. Meanwhile, a 1929 poem printed in the *Neuwieder Zeitung* in December 1929 recalled the original 'Watch on the Rhine' with the words, 'The enemy still keeps watch, but the river must remain German like the force of Nature.'

Ideas of the Rhine as France's natural boundary coexisted with the notion that the river represented a point of connection. Indeed, in the aftermath of Alsace's annexation into Germany, diplomat and historian Albert Sorel stressed the 'linking'

---

[20] Camille Jullian, *Le Rhin Gaulois: le Rhin français* (Paris, 1915), pp. 22 and 52.
[21] Peter Schöttler, 'The Rhine as an Object of Historical Controversy in the Inter-war Years. Towards a History of Frontier Mentalities', *History Workshop Journal*, 39 (1995), pp. 1–22, p. 5.
[22] Schöttler, 'The Rhine as an Object of Historical Controversy', pp. 7–8.
[23] *Le Rhin dans l'histoire*, 2 vols (Paris, 1917); Jullian, *Le Rhin Gaulois*.
[24] Lekan, *Imagining the Nation in Nature*, p. 90.

function that rivers had historically played, and argued that transforming a river into a frontier thus violated nature 'by separating arbitrarily that which history has united'.[25] In the interwar years, this idea of the connecting role played by rivers was developed in Lucien Febvre and Albert Demangeon's 1935 survey *Le Rhin: Problèmes d'Histoire et d'Economie*.[26] The survey was commissioned by the *Société Générale Alsacienne de Banque* to celebrate its fiftieth anniversary in 1931, and it commissioned Demangeon, a Sorbonne-based geographer, to write the geographical and economic sections and Febvre, a historian best known for his role in the *Annales* journal, to write the historical section.

Febvre's section on the Rhine's history outlined certain problems in the hope of 'dispelling catastrophe-laden stormclouds, to substitute for a particularistic history of wars and hatreds a peaceful history of exchanges and unions'.[27] Febvre's analysis stressed that there are no 'natural frontiers'. Rather, they are constructed by humans and, as a result, the Rhine was a product of human history that had been transformed by human action. What is more, the Rhine's role as a frontier was relatively recent, and only dated back to the sixteenth century. Similarly, it is important to recognize the 'otherness' of ancient and medieval societies, rendering it impossible to draw any retrospective identification between Germans and Teutons, or between the modern Rhineland and that of Roman and Frankish times.[28] Febvre characterized the Rhine as a European river, linking and binding together the various economies, cultures, and languages, and he treated the Rhinelands (plural) as a historical landscape between East and West. While this rejected the French notion of the Rhine as a 'natural' and 'historic' frontier, it also challenged the idea of the Rhine as the 'sacred river' of Germany. This did not go unnoticed; Friedrich Metz, a geographer and regional specialist at the University of Freiburg, criticized Febvre for turning the Rhine from a German river into a European one, and in doing so offering a 'new scholarly justification of the Versailles diktat'.[29]

When describing the Rhine as a European river, Lucien Febvre built upon a deeper-rooted idea, which could be traced back beyond the revolutionary wars when French troops poured across the Rhine and swept away existing political and economic structures. The new cross-national institutions and organizations that they created formed the basis of the free trade zone and Rhine Commission created at the Congress of Vienna, and in the following years the advent of steamship travel and the inauguration of Baden engineer Johann G. Tulla's project to 'tame' the meandering Rhine in 1817 transformed the river: the multiple river tolls disappeared, as did any natural impediments such as the fabled Lorelei rock, while the introduction of mechanized transport and straightening of the Rhine's bed enabled freighters to move upstream with ease. The French accepted and maintained these

[25] A. Sorel and T. Funck-Brentano, *Précis du Droit des gens* (Paris, 1887), pp. 18–19; this critique was taken up by the historian Gaston Zeller in 'Histoire d'une idée fausse', *Revue de Synthèse*, 56:2 (1936), pp. 115–32.

[26] Albert Demangeon et Lucien Febvre, *Le Rhin. Problemes d'Histoire et d'Economie* (Paris, 1935).

[27] Demangeon et Febvre, *Le Rhin*, pp. xi–xii.

[28] Demangeon et Febvre, *Le Rhin*, pp. x and 22–59.

[29] Schöttler, 'The Rhine as an Object of Historical Controversy', p. 16.

structures and changes after reclaiming Alsace and Lorraine in 1918, and they also moved the Rhine Commission's headquarters to Strasbourg and included Belgium, Italy, and Britain on the Commission.[30] This was no acceptance of the Rhine as a 'European' river, however. Rather, it represented a concerted effort to dilute German influence. These measures, and France's plans for a Rhine–Rhône canal to tie the river more closely to the French sphere of influence caused concern in Germany and led the Duisburg newspaper, *Die Rhein- und Ruhrzeitung*, to call for the 'genuine internationalization' of the Rhine, along with all the great European rivers (the Escaut, Meuse, Rhône, and Danube), as the only way to ensure that economic concerns would be able to take precedence over political ones.[31]

In a similar vein, ideas about regional history coloured many interwar accounts of the Alsatian landscape. Robert Redslob's memoirs talked of the 'solace' that the Alsatian forests had offered during the years of German rule, and connected his experiences of retreating to the forest to escape the German rulers with those of the 'Celts of Alsace' who had hidden in the very same forests to avoid German invasions.[32] Tourist guides similarly helped to shape ideas about the landscape for tourists and non-tourists alike. The *Michelin Guide*, for example, pointed out notably 'Alsatian' towns, like Obernai, and brushed over the period of German rule by referring to the 'much criticized restoration of [the twelfth century castle] Haut-Koenigsbourg' without going into the specifics of who had restored it or why.[33] This castle had famously been restored by Kaiser Wilhelm II after he was gifted it by the town of Sélestat, and had become a focal point for opposition to German rule during the later years of annexation, not least after Wilhelm proclaimed, 'May Hohköningsburg here in the West as Marienburg in the East stand as a symbol of German culture and power for all time'.[34] For the population, rather than a symbol of shared German culture across a bounded territory, the castle instead became a symbol of the empire's unpopular attempts to assimilate the region into the German nation.

Michelin also described Strasbourg as possessing two sides: first, the old medieval town and, second, the modern town, 'created over the last sixty years around the old town, which offers large avenues bordered by characterless buildings and vast squares containing massive monuments'.[35] These recent changes were instantly recognizable as the *quartier allemand*, built during the years after 1871 but described by *Michelin* in a way vague enough to avoid any specific mention of German rule. German publications similarly made omissions, but these proved a source of more immediate concern on the left bank of the Rhine. In 1939 a German railway

[30] Articles 354–62 of the Treaty of Versailles.
[31] ADBR 286D 160 Le Commissaire Spécial to M.le Directeur des Services Généraux de Police d'Alsace et de Lorraine à Strasbourg, Kehl, 4 December 1929. Report on article in the *Rhein- und Ruhrzeitung* on 29 November 1929. 'La Lutte pour l'Embouchure du Rhin. Les Plans Français Rhin-Rhone. Les divergences de vue belgico-hollandaise'. Speech by Dr Osswald von Potsdam.
[32] Robert Redslob, *Entre la France et l'Allemagne. Souvenirs d'un Alsacien* (Paris, 1933), p. 247.
[33] *Pneu Michelin Guide Régional Alsace de Strasbourg à Mulhouse Hautes Vosges* (Paris, 1935–6), p. 35.
[34] Fischer, *Alsace to the Alsatians?*, pp. 53–60.
[35] *Pneu Michelin Guide Régional Alsace de Strasbourg à Mulhouse Hautes Vosges* (Paris, 1935–6), p. 115.

company's holiday brochure for a south German tour of 'the Black Forest, the Rhine, the Battlefields and Alsace' was greeted with alarm by the Haut-Rhin Socialist daily *Der Republikaner* because of its failure to mention the border.[36]

The rhetoric surrounding the border landscape changed over time, and the notion that the border represented a limit rather than a meeting point tended to triumph in moments of international tension or domestic crisis. What is more, as we have seen in previous chapters, Alsatians were no more united in their ideas about the landscape than were French from the interior or Germans from east of the Rhine, and just as this was the case for ideas about the landscape, so it affected the attempts to make Alsatian territory French after the return to France.

TRANSFORMATION AND CHANGE

The first change in the Alsatian landscape was the redrawing of the border between France and Germany. Article 51 of the Treaty of Versailles had specified that the territories ceded to Germany in 1871 would be reintegrated into French sovereignty, provided that the provisions of the pre-1871 delimitation treaties were put into force.[37] Thus it restored France's eastern border to the boundary line that had existed on 18 July 1870. This line had, in turn, been fixed by treaties dating back to 1829 and 1830 between France and Prussia's Rhineland territories, back to 1825 and 1828 for the boundary between France and the Bavarian Palatinate, and by the 1840 convention between France and the Grand Duchy of Baden. The Versailles Treaty left the question of whether to modify this line open to the respective governments, but it soon became clear that the straightforward restoration of the old border would be unfeasible as a result of changes in the border landscape in the years since 1871: new railway lines had been built, villages had expanded, and sections of the Rhine had been rerouted. As a result, in places the former border now cut through railway stations, villages, and, in a few cases, individual houses. Elsewhere, communes found themselves cut off from their communal forests by the boundary line, or needing to cross the border in order to access territories to which they held hunting or fishing rights.[38]

Unsurprisingly, therefore, when Colonel de Lavalette du Coetlosquet of the army's Geographic Service was called to Strasbourg to study the question of border delimitation, he argued for the creation of a commission of border delimitation.[39] This joined the commission created by Article 48 of the Treaty of Versailles to delineate the border between France and the newly neutral Saarland, and the commission formed to regulate the Franco–Swiss boundary line, as Alsace's return

---

[36] ADBR 286D 326 *Der Republikaner*, 10 August 1939.

[37] ADBR 121AL 524 Régime des Propriétés Communales situées sur le rive droite du Rhin et en général de toutes les propriétés françaises, situées en Allemagne à moins de 5 kilomètres de la frontière.

[38] ADBR 121AL 521 Délimitation des Frontières de l'Alsace et de Lorraine. Rapport du Lieutenant-Colonel de Lavalette du Coetlosquet du Service Géographique de l'Armée. 27 November 1919.

[39] ADBR 121AL 521 Délimitation des Frontières de l'Alsace et de Lorraine. Rapport du Lieutenant-Colonel de Lavalette du Coetlosquet du Service Géographique de l'Armée. 27 November 1919.

created a new border between France and Switzerland.[40] This meant that the new border was the result of negotiation between France and the Weimar Republic in the east, with the Saar in the north-east, and with Switzerland in the south. The nineteenth-century idea that good borders make good neighbours persisted in these discussions, in spite of changing notions of boundaries and border rhetoric. Indeed, Premier Aristide Briand made specific reference to the 'rapports de bon voisinage' when negotiating the access of border inhabitants to their territories on the other side of the Rhine in 1922.[41]

The commissions formed to fix the new boundary included representatives of the army and Minister of War, local administrators, and nominated delegates.[42] Crucially, the public were consulted, and the president of the Delimitation Committee sent a copy of the nineteenth-century conventions agreed between France, Bavaria, and Prussia to each town hall in the recovered departments, and called local administrators to send their comments (and particularly on any change of use) to the Commission.[43] Local communities also sent petitions to the premier demanding the finalization of border protocols and arrangements to guarantee 'facilités fron-talières'.[44] The correspondence of the commissions reveals that while they were officially granted free passage across the border in order to complete their work, on numerous occasions border-commission delegates were stopped at the frontier despite the markings on their cars and their paperwork, and many experienced repeated difficulties in crossing.[45] Following one such incident, the Ministry of Foreign Affairs contacted the General Commissioner to bring to a stop 'with a matter of urgency' such problems for the commissions when crossing 'our frontier'.[46]

As the commissions began work on the new borders, their decisions reveal the interconnection of different guiding concerns, as security, economics, practicality,

[40] ADBR 121AL 520 Protocole relative à l'entretien de la frontière du territoire du bassin de la sarre (partie franco-saaroise).

[41] ADBR 121AL 524 M. Briand (Président du Conseil, Ministre des Affaires Etrangères) to M. le Dr Mayer, Ambassadeur d'Allemagne à Paris, Paris, 12 January 1922.

[42] For example, the Franco-Swiss commission was headed by the Lieutenant Colonel de Lavalette du Coetlosquet of the army's Geographic Service, while delegates from the Swiss side were appointed by the new chief of the *Département politique fédéral*. See ADBR 121AL 519 Ministre de l'Intérieur to M. le Garde des Sceaux, Ministre de la Justice, Paris, 30 November 1923; 121AL 519 Président du Conseil to Ministres de l'Intérieur et de la Guerre, Paris, 12 February 1924; 121AL 519 Ministre de l'Intérieur to M. Garde des Sceaux, Ministre de la Justice, Paris, 30 November 1923; 121AL 520 Président du Conseil de la délimitation du bassin de la Saar to M. le Haut Commissaire de la République française à Strasbourg, 4 June 1920.

[43] ADBR 121AL 520 Président du Conseil de la délimitation du bassin de la Saar to M. le Haut Commissaire de la République française à Strasbourg, 4 June 1920.

[44] ADBR 121AL 520 Président du Conseil, Ministre des Affaires Etrangères to M. le Haut-Commissaire de la République à Strasbourg, Paris, 5 November 1921.

[45] ADBR 121AL 521 Président du Conseil de la délimitation du bassin de la Saar to M. le Haut Commissaire de l'Alsace-Lorraine, Sarrebruck, 28 April 1920; 121AL 518 Le Lieutenant Colonel de Lavalette du Coetlosquet, Président de la Commission de Délimitation to M. le Directeur de l'Intérieur, Strasbourg le 14 March 1922; 121AL 520 Télégramme chiffre. Affaires étrangères to Commissaire Général, Strasbourg. Off. Paris 71378 85 7 April, 21h10; 121AL 520 Président de la Commission de délimitation du bassin de la Sarre to M. le Haut Commissaire à Strasbourg, Sarrebruck, 22 February 1922 (marked urgent).

[46] ADBR 121AL 520 Télégramme chiffre. Affaires étrangères to Commissaire Générale, Strasbourg. Off. Paris 71378 85 7 April, 21h10.

and prestige all played a part in designating the new boundary line. The commission presented some decisions as based on sheer practicality, but it is possible to detect interconnecting motives; for example, in the north of the recovered departments the border cut through the middle of the station in the town of Guerstling. The French commissions proposed moving the border so that the entire station was on the French side, while the German delegate proposed leaving the border in place and agreeing to a convention to resolve any difficulties provoked by having the border divide the station.[47] Elsewhere, in the village of Schönecken two houses were cut in half by the border, while a third was separated from the village, meaning that its inhabitants would need to pass through a border control every time they needed to visit the village shops, bar, or post office. The French commission demanded that the line be moved to unite the three houses with the rest of the village, while the German commission proposed maintaining the status quo but introducing a slight deviation to allow the inhabitants of one of the houses to enter their building without crossing the border.[48] In both cases, the French made arguments of practicality, but were concerned not to lose face should the border divide French villages or stations.

Some concerns were connected to national security, such as the Waldwisse tunnel on the railway line towards Merzig in the Moselle. The tunnel itself lay under French territory but was cut by the boundary line so that both its entrances were located on the Saar side of the border, which the director of the Alsace-Lorraine railways pointed out could represent a security concern for France should the Saar vote to return to Germany in 1935.[49] In the discussions, the proposal to grant France one of the tunnel entrances was quashed following opposition from representatives of the commune of Waldwisse, who protested that this would mean that their access to the communal woodland would be cut off.[50] So, to remedy the situation, the Conference of Ambassadors decided to modify the border between France and the Saar.[51] Thus security and economic concerns interacted, but this case also reveals the range of individuals involved in making the border and the level of consultation of local populations in fixing the eventual line.

There was a similar intersection of economic concerns with security, practicality, and prestige in the negotiations and decisions taken over the problem of French communities holding communal land on the east bank of the Rhine, and vice versa. In many cases this was a long-standing state of affairs, resulting from the rerouting of the Rhine or from earlier territorial agreements. But the Treaty of

---

[47] ADBR 121AL 520 Conférence des Ambassadeurs, Paris 18 April 1921 to M. le Président. (Signed J. Cambon.)

[48] ADBR 121AL 520 Conférence des Ambassadeurs, Paris 18 April 1921 to M. le Président. (Signed J. Cambon); 121AL 520 Ambassade d'Allemagne en France (Dr Mayer) to M. le Président de la Conférence des Ambassadeurs, Paris 7 October 1921.

[49] ADBR 121AL 520 Directeur des chemins de Fer d'Alsace et de Lorraine to M. le Commissaire Général de la République (Direction de l'Intérieur), Strasbourg 23 September 1921; 121AL 520 Le Directeur des chemins de fer d'Alsace et de Lorraine to M. le Commissaire Général, Strasbourg, 16 May 1921.

[50] ADBR 121AL 520 Note pour la Sous Direction d'Europe, Paris 23 June 1921.

[51] ADBR 121AL 520 Note pour la Sous Direction d'Europe, Paris 23 June 1921.

Versailles fixed the border between France and Germany along the Rhine's mid-point, and Article 56 stated that any forests belonging to Baden, the Palatinate, or Saar communities should become the property of the French state. Correspondence from French officials reveals the consensus that it would no longer be possible to continue the usage rights enjoyed by German communities to French land prior to 1918, principally on the basis of national security.[52] In the case of individual or ecclesiastical property, the Treaty left the decision to the French government, and many cases were treated on a case-by-case basis, with the final decision delayed until the conclusion of the Franco-German delimitation commission's discussions.[53]

Further complications arose with regard to French property on the German side, which was protected by Article 60 of the Treaty, which restored all rights and interests to Alsatians in possession of goods on German territory.[54] But the German government questioned whether continued free access would help to foster peace between inhabitants of the two sides of the border, and after 1918 many Alsatian citizens reported difficulties in accessing their land. In some cases, border inhabitants reported that the German government had gone so far as to deny them access.[55] While French administrators pointed out that Baden had no right to limit the access of Alsatians to their communal land on the east bank of the Rhine, the Minister of Foreign Affairs took the lead in encouraging Alsatian communes to accept the German government's offer to buy their land to remove the need to cross.[56]

Problems emerged as many communes argued that financial compensation was inadequate recompense for the loss of forests which generated revenue through the production of wood, and they demanded compensation through equivalent forests close to their communes where they would have rights to hunt and fish.[57] The town of Rhinau became a cause célèbre after its case was taken to the premier by the town's UPR parliamentary deputy Thomas Seltz.[58] As a result of the regularization of the Rhine (completed in 1872), Rhinau possessed around 1,000 hectares on the east bank of the river.[59] For the town's inhabitants, this meant that when

---

[52] ADBR 121AL 522 le Directeur des Eaux et Fôrets to M. le directeur de l'intérieur, Strasbourg, 12 May 1921; 121AL 520 Directeur des Eaux et Fôrets to M. le Commissaire Général de la République, Strasbourg, 15 March 1921.

[53] ADBR 121AL 524 M. Briand (Président du Conseil, Ministre des Affaires Etrangères) to M. le Dr Mayer, Ambassadeur d'Allemagne à Paris, Paris, 12 January 1922.

[54] ADBR 121AL 524 Régime des Propriétés Communales situées sur le rive droite du Rhin et en général de toutes les propriétés françaises, situées en Allemagne à moins de 5 kilomètres de la frontière.

[55] ADBR 121AL 524 M. Briand (Président du Conseil, Ministre des Affaires Etrangères) to M. le Dr Mayer, Ambassadeur d'Allemagne à Paris, Paris, 12 January 1922; 121AL 524 Régime des Propriétés Communales situées sur le rive droite du Rhin et en général de toutes les propriétés françaises, situées en Allemagne à moins de 5 kilomètres de la frontière.

[56] ADBR 121AL 521 Directeur de l'Intérieur to Commissaire Général, 9 November 1919; 121AL 552 Rapport de la Seconde Commission sur les Biens Communaux alsaciens sur la rive droit du Rhin.

[57] ADBR 121AL 552 Sous-préfet de Wissembourg to Commissaire Général, Wissembourg, 18 February 1925; 121AL 552 Extrait du registre des délibérations du Conseil Municipal de la Commune de Beinheim, séance du 2 février 1925; 121AL 552 Note sur la Convention de 1829 et les avis du commissaire français; 121AL 523 Seltz (député) to Ministre, Paris, 30 January 1921; 121AL 552 Préfet du Haut-Rhin to Commissaire Général, Colmar, 23 February 1921.

[58] ADBR 121AL 523 Seltz (député) to Ministre, Paris, 30 January 1921.

[59] ADBR 121AL 523 Seltz (députe) to Ministre, Paris, 30 January 1921.

they crossed to tend their fields, they needed to pass through customs points as they left and returned into France.[60] Despite Seltz's efforts, the case remained unresolved throughout the 1920s, and the town retained its east-bank possessions. This became especially problematic as Franco–German relations deteriorated, and in 1932 Kern, the Conseilleur Général of the canton, once again raised the difficulties that the town's inhabitants had in accessing their land on the right bank.[61]

Others called for the maintenance of historic rights to neighbouring communes. In the case of the commune of Leidingen in the Saar, village inhabitants had assumed that an 1838 treaty had granted the Leidingers rights to the territory on the west bank of the Rhine, and these rights had been recognized by both sides in the following years. But when the treaty was checked with a view to its inclusion in discussions over the new border, no mention of Leidingen was found.[62] In other cases, local administrators called on the French government to consider the implications of sequestering German-owned property on French territory; the subprefect of Wissembourg suggested that the seizure of the forest belonging to the Dahn church might lead Bavaria to take revenge by creating difficulties in accessing the much larger forest that Wissembourg possessed in the Palatinate.[63] The mayor of Wissembourg had previously urged the General Commissioner not to sequester the buildings and vines owned on French territory by Palatinate communes, as he feared that those affected would sabotage vines belonging to Wissembourg on the east bank in retaliation. In any case, he added, the only ones to benefit from sequestering buildings and vineyards would be the 'speculators'.[64]

Such negotiations reveal changing ideas about what a border should be. Whereas the nineteenth-century boundaries had allowed for the ownership of land and resources in a neighbouring national territory, by the twentieth century it was widely accepted by all involved in the negotiations that the best solution was a 'neat border', that is, one single border for both territory and ownership. Nevertheless, there was continuity in ideas about the role of neighbourly relations, and the idea that good neighbours make good borders was a constant in these discussions.

The treaty delimiting the Franco–Saar border was signed on 21 December 1921, the Franco–Swiss delimitation treaty was signed on 30 July 1924, and the delimitation treaty for the Franco–German border was signed on 14 August 1924.[65] Once the new national boundaries had been fixed, the region's mayors were able to

[60] ADBR 121AL 552 *Le Temps*, 'Le cas de la ville de Rhinau', 20 May 1924.

[61] ADBR 286D 385 M. Haelling to Chief Engineer, 6 October 1932.

[62] ADBR 121AL 552 M. le Maire de Leidingen to Président de la Commission de délibération de la Sarre, 1 June 1921.

[63] ADBR 121AL 524 Sous-préfet de Wissembourg to Préfet du Bas-Rhin à Strasbourg, Wissembourg, 25 June 1924.

[64] ADBR 121AL 518 Maire de Wissembourg to M. le Commissaire Général de la Republique à Strasbourg, 9 May 1922.

[65] ADBR 121AL 520 Préfet de la Moselle to Commissaire Général, Metz, 3 August 1925; 121AL 520 Président du Conseil de la délimitation du bassin de la Saar to M. le Haut Commissaire de la République française à Strasbourg, 17 December 1920; 121AL 518 l'Officier d'Administration du 2e classe du génie colson, du service géographique de l'armée to M. le Directeur de l'Intérieur Commissaire Général d'Alsace-Lorraine à Strasbourg, 8 October 1925; 121AL 519 Président du Conseil, Ministre des Affaires Etrangères to M. le Commissaire Général de la République to Strasbourg, 30 August 1924.

unload the border posts that they had received in 1920 and install them in position, and the French also stepped up the work of removing the symbols of the old border.[66] In 1922 there were still around 3,000 border posts marked with 'D' on one side and 'F' on the other along the line of the old boundary, and administrators noted that the population living along the border found them to be a painful reminder of 'German domination' and 'forcefully demanded their removal'.[67] The French focused upon removing those that lined major roads, but for others the relevant authorities simply removed the 'D's and 'F's in order to 'make any indication of the limits of the state disappear'; the posts were left in place, but they now signified the limits of communes rather than nation states.[68] This was completed in the Bas-Rhin and the Moselle by June 1922, leaving just the Haut-Rhin border, which had been complicated by the ongoing boundary negotiations with Switzerland.[69]

The border commission also had an eye on aesthetics. When considering the placement of tricolour-coloured signposts to signal that the border was close, it discussed the contrast between the simplicity of plaques indicating a French customs posts and the more heavily decorated German signposts, noting that it was desirable to ensure that the signs of French sovereignty 'can sustain comparison with those of Germany'.[70] As a point where symbols of the two states could be viewed next to each other, the border represented an important space for national statement. Consequently, the prefect of the Moselle insisted that regular checks be conducted by the local authorities or specially constituted commissions every two or three years to check the state of the borderline.[71] Nevertheless, reports continued of vandalism to border posts, including one case in 1932 when the posts were reversed, so the 'F' pointed towards Germany and the 'D' towards France.[72] While such cases of vandalism were generally pranks, each was thoroughly investigated to ensure that it was not intended as a political statement about the position of the new border.

After fixing the borders, all three commissions were dissolved and Colonel de Lavalette was sent to Morocco.

[66] ADBR 121AL 520 Président du Conseil de la délimitation du bassin de la Saar to M. le Haut Commissaire de la République française à Strasbourg, 4 June 1920.

[67] ADBR 121AL 518 Directeur des voies ferrés et des routes to M. le Directeur de l'Intérieur, Strasbourg, 7 June 1922; Directeur des Eaux et Forêts to M. le Directeur des Services de l'Intérieur, 27 February 1923; 121AL 519 Le Commissaire Général de la République (Direction de l'Intérieur) to M. le Ministre de l'Intérieur, Strasbourg, 9 October 1922.

[68] ADBR 121AL 518 Directeur des voies ferrés et des routes to M. le Directeur de l'Intérieur, Strasbourg, 7 June 1922; Le Lieutenant Colonel de Lavalette du Coetlosquet (Président de la Commission de Délimitation) to M. le Directeur de l'Intérieur, Strasbourg, 24 June 1922.

[69] ADBR 121AL 519 Le Commissaire Général de la République (Direction de l'Intérieur) to M. le Préfet du Haut-Rhin, 4 March 1923; Le Commissaire Général de la République (Direction de l'Intérieur) to M. le Préfet de la Moselle, 8 June 1922; Le Commissaire Général de la République (Direction de l'Intérieur) to Préfet du Bas-Rhin, 8 June 1922.

[70] ADBR 121AL 518 Le Lieutenant Colonel de Lavalette du Coetlosquet (Président de la Commission de Délimitation) to M. le Directeur de l'Intérieur, Strasbourg, 24 June 1922.

[71] ADBR 121AL 520 Préfet de la Moselle to Commissaire Général de la République, Metz, 17 March 1921.

[72] ADBR 121AL 520 Ministre de l'Intérieur to Président du Conseil, Paris, 10 February 1921; 286D 385.

As well as introducing symbols to mark the new border, the territory of Alsace also needed to be connected to that of the rest of France. With this in mind, politicians and representatives of the region's Chambers of Commerce planned new transport links; one early proposal suggested the building of railways through the Vosges to connect the Alsatian network with French lines, to improve the canals between the Rhine and the Rhône, Marne and Ill, and to enlarge the port of Strasbourg.[73] Many of these measures had been planned before the region's return to France, with an eye not only on their economic and military utility, but also on the fact that they would mark the landscape with France's presence.[74] The plans met with support in Alsace; petitions signed by inhabitants of towns across the region demanded the construction of new railways, while mayors, trade unions, and the *Conseil supérieur d'Alsace et de Lorraine* all voiced their backing for the project, and local councils offered financial support. In order to construct the proposed line between Sainte-Marie-aux-Mines and Sélestat, the councils of the two towns voted 150,000 and 500,000 francs respectively, while Colmar voted 3 million francs and La Bresse voted 2.5 million francs for the La Bresse–Metzeral line.[75]

The face of Alsatian towns and cities also changed after 1918. In response to the challenges of wartime destruction, the newly constituted *Ministère des Régions Libérées* oversaw the reconstruction of devastated buildings, including forty-eight churches.[76] And in those Haut-Rhin villages that had been transformed into battlefields, villagers themselves set to work on rebuilding their houses, churches, and public buildings.[77] Meanwhile, the ravages of war and increased population led councils in towns and cities across Alsace to construct pavements, create new roads, repave public areas, tarmac and extend existing streets, install street lamps, improve the public transport network, modernize the water and sewage systems, expand electricity and gas provision, create new cemeteries and crematorium facilities, and open allotments.[78] New green spaces were created as parks were built, military

[73] ADBR 121AL 44 'L'Accroissement des Voies de Communications en Alsace-Lorraine' Programme et conséquences économiques' Fernand Jacq. (nd); *Journal d'Alsace et de Lorraine*, no. 206, 2 August 1920. 'Le Rapport de M. le General Bourgeois'; Association nationale d'expansion économique Commission de l'outillage national. Rapport sur les chemins de fer à travers les Vosges par M. Gerardin, Directeur de la compagnie des chemins de fer de l'est, Paris, 1919.

[74] ADBR 121AL 44 Association nationale d'expansion économique Commission de l'outillage national. Rapport sur les chemins de fer à travers les Vosges par M. Gerardin, directeur de la compagnie des chemins de fer de l'est. Paris, 1919.

[75] ADBR 121AL 44 Conseil supérieur d'Alsace et Lorraine, Session octobre 1919. Rapport de la section permanente. 'Rapport de M. Laugel sur la question de la percée des Vosges', Association nationale d'expansion économique, Commission de l'outillage national. Rapport sur les chemins de fer à travers les Vosges par M. Gerardin, Directeur de la Compagnie des chemins de fer de l'est. Paris, 1919.

[76] Jean de Leusse, 'La Renaissance des Eglises Devastees', in Comité alsacien d'études et d'informations, *L'Alsace depuis son retour à la France. Premier supplement: Vie politique administrative et sociale; Vie intellectuelle; artisistique et spirituelle; Vie economique* (Strasbourg, 1937), p. 157.

[77] Abbe Vital Bourgeois 'L'œuvre de Reconstruction des Eglises Catholiques', in Comité alsacien d'études et d'informations, *L'Alsace depuis son retour à la France. Premier supplement: Vie politique administrative et sociale; Vie intellectuelle; artisistique et spirituelle; Vie economique* (Strasbourg, 1937), p. 159.

[78] AMVES US 240 *Compte rendu de l'administration de la ville de Strasbourg 1919–1935*; US 240 *Activité du Conseil Municipal et de l'Administration de la Ville de Strasbourg, 1925–1929*, Bureau Municipal de Statistique, Strasbourg, 1929; *Dix Années d'activité municipale, 1925–1935*, Ville de Mulhouse, Haut-Rhin, imprimerie Union Mulhouse, 1935; AMC, 50 10/1. Commissaire Central

land was declassified, and *jardins ouvriers* (workers' allotments) opened.[79] Flagship developments such as the Wacken exhibition centre in Strasbourg and the riverside sports stadium in Mulhouse asserted their modernity, while reminding all of the political identity of the Socialist-dominated councils of the two cities.[80] Town and city councils also constructed housing, particularly low-rent housing built under the auspices of newly created municipal offices for *habitation à bon marché*.[81] These offices oversaw the construction of *cités ouvrières* in the towns, the larger of which had public baths, libraries, primary and nursery schools, and social centres.[82] Four major *cités ouvrières* opened in each of the three major cities, Strasbourg, Colmar, and Mulhouse, while in Strasbourg the '*Grande Percée*' saw the replacement of a number of small, medieval streets and buildings with a modern complex of shops with social housing on their first and second floors.

An immediate priority in response to the change of national regime was the translation of German street names into French, and villages, towns, and cities worked to replace those names that honoured the Hohenzollern royal family or German military victories, as well as to restore the region's towns and cities' former French names and to replace the signs for both. In the cities, the translation of street names proved an enormous undertaking, and in Strasbourg the number of replacements necessary meant that it was over two years before the majority of signs were replaced.[83] Given the political importance of language, the delay created concern amongst Strasbourg councillors and residents that their tardiness might be misinterpreted as a signal of the city's lack of French patriotism.[84] A decade later, in the midst of the tensions that followed the election of the Volksfront in Strasbourg, autonomist councillor Karl Roos complained that the placement of French street names in the city had been at the expense of German translations and argued that the city's bilingual population warranted the display of names in both languages.[85] That street names were still a source of controversy in 1929 is suggestive of both the division amongst the Alsatian population and the lengthy process of transforming the Alsatian landscape.

to Sous-préfet de Colmar, Colmar 10 November 1926; *Société pour le développement des jardins ouvriers*, p. 19; *Société pour le développement des jardins ouvriers, Congrès Fédéral et exposition*, Colmar, 9 September 1928, Salle des Catherinettes, p. 17.

[79] These *jardins* built on a longer Alsatian tradition of workers maintaining some land to grow their own food. See AMVES US 240 *Activité du Conseil Municipal et de l'Administration de la Ville de Strasbourg, 1925–1929*, p. 244; *Société pour le développement des jardins ouvriers, Congrès Fédéral et exposition*, Colmar, 9 September 1928, Salle des Catherinettes, p. 17. As the economic crisis hit Mulhouse, more than 40 per cent of workers cultivated their own food in their *jardins*. US 240 *Activité du Conseil Municipal et de l'Administration de la Ville de Strasbourg, 1925–1929*, p. 315.

[80] AMVES 1MW 258 Compte rendu du Conseil municipal, 81 séance, 26 April 1922, p. 402; AMM D1 a1 1936, 1 séance, 24 January 1930, p. 32.

[81] Stéphane Jonas, 'La Politique Urbain et du Logement de Jacques Peirotes, Député-Maire Socialiste de Strasbourg', *Revue des Sciences Sociales de la France de l'Est*, 15 (1986–7), pp. 143–9.

[82] *Une génération d'activité municipale*, Mulhouse, pp. 42–3; Albert Fix, *100 Ans de Politique de l'Habitat. L'Office du Logement de la Ville de Strasbourg* (Obernai, 1978); *Collection Le Patrimoine des Communes de France: Haut-Rhin*, p. 263.

[83] AMVES *Compte rendu du Conseil municipal*, 20 séance, 15 September 1920, pp. 1409–10.

[84] AMVES *Compte rendu du Conseil municipal*, 4 séance, 17 December 1919, pp. 1025–6.

[85] AMVES *Compte rendu du Conseil municipal*. 7 séance, 16 September 1929, p. 624.

This transformation was also a process that reflected connections to France and Germany. In 1929 the Mulhouse council sent a commission to Germany to try to draw lessons for the city's housing policy, while Strasbourg's *cité* Jules Siegfried, which opened in February 1928, was inspired by similar projects in Vienna, and the city's Mayor Jacques Peirotes looked to Henri Sellier's flagship Socialist housing projects in the Parisian suburbs as a model for housing policy.[86] In light of such influences, Stéphane Jonas' work on housing has presented Alsatian towns a site of scientific, artistic, and social transfer and exchange between France and Germany.[87] The Alsatian councils themselves looked to capitalize upon their international networks to set a new agenda, and in 1923 Peirotes organized an international town planning conference in Strasbourg that brought together leading politicians, including Edouard Herriot and Léon Bourgeois, with architects such as Le Corbusier.[88]

Town planning also became a vehicle for commenting on the process of reintegration. Socialist-dominated councils in Colmar and Mulhouse consistently refused to grant funds for the repair to, or construction of, ecclesiastical buildings, leading the prefect of the Haut-Rhin to request that the charges be inscribed into the budget. The resulting toing and froing (which always culminated in the prefect insisting on their insertion) was, according to Mulhousian Socialist adjunct Jean Wagner, 'the only occasion to remind the government that we still demand the introduction of the French secular legislation'.[89] But these contests over funding for religious buildings also reflected regional political rivalries, and in 1928 Wagner's appeal to the council to refuse funding for ecclesiastical buildings and personnel betrayed his frustration that Alsatian 'taxpayers have contributed enough to individuals who are, in sum, the secretary and propagandists of a Party rather than church ministers'.[90]

In these early years, the population of Alsace witnessed the tearing down of fortifications as former military constructions, barracks, and fortifications were declassified for use as housing or infrastructure, such as Strasbourg's port.[91] The decision to demolish the old defences reflected recognition of the changing nature of conflict.

[86] AMM D1 a1 1929 séance, 22 March 1929, pp. 140–2; *Collection Le Patrimoine des Communes de France: Bas-Rhin*, p. 1405.

[87] Stéphane Jonas, 'Les Jardins d'Ungemach à Strasbourg: une Cité-Jardin d'origine nataliste, 1923–1950', in Paulette Girard and Bruno Lussac Fayolle, *Cités, Cités-Jardins: Une Histoire Européenne* (Talence, 1996), p. 66.

[88] Jean-Claude Richez, Léon Strauss, François Igersheim, and Stéphane Jonas, *Jacques Peirotes, 1869–1935 et le socialisme en Alsace* (Strasbourg, 1989), p. 161.

[89] AMM, D1a1 Comptes rendus des séances du Conseil Municipale de la Ville de Mulhouse, 1926, 2 séance, 26 February 1926, p. 47.

[90] AMM, D1 a1, Comptes rendus des séances du Conseil Municipale de la Ville de Mulhouse, 6 séance, 28 June 1928. p. 245. This was also demonstrated in 1930, when the council in Mulhouse refused to grant credits for the personnel of staff at the newly created parish of Sainte-Jeanne-d'Arc. The council's argument was that as the parish was created after 1918, the council was not obliged to grant credits to pay for its clerical personnel or the upkeep of the church. However, a resolution advanced by the Radicals and supported by the Socialists in the council admitted that a major objection to the new parish was that it would benefit the Catholic Party. This had been tacitly admitted by Wagner in an earlier meeting, when he compared churches relying on the town to fund them with the Socialist Party finding the funds from its own members whenever it wished to establish a new office in a section of town. AMM D1a1 1930, 7 séance, 25 July 1930, p. 513.

[91] ADBR 121AL 395 Colonel Winkler, Directeur de Genie à Strasbourg to M. le Commissaire Général de la République, Strasbourg, 13 February 1925; Président du Conseil, Minister of War to

Aware of the lessons of the Great War, and principally of the impact of modern artillery on any area where fighting took place, the army's General Staff turned its attention to the question of border fortifications in 1919 and decided that the old battlements in the centre of cities would no longer be a useful defence.[92] Nevertheless, the pulling down of existing fortifications represented an important visual symbol that fed Alsatian hopes that the region would no longer be a site of battle.

While cities built housing where once there had been defences, the army continued to consider the question of the best way to fortify the eastern border. The problem was tricky; as General Armau de Pouydraguin, the former military governor of Strasbourg, stated in 1937, the new border may have restored France's historic frontier, but it also left it with an open one.[93] In 1920 the *Conseil Superieur de Guerre* took over consideration of the border fortifications, and from 1922 two special commissions were created to tackle the issue. The first was headed initially by Marshall Joffre and subsequently by General Guillaumat. Guillaumat maintained leadership of the second commission, which produced the eventual report of 1926 on border fortifications that proposed the creation of fortified regions. The first attempt to act on the report ran out of finances, but after André Maginot became Minister of War in 1929, he embraced the project and won the Chamber's support and the sum of 2.9 million francs for his proposed works.[94] The construction of fortifications posed practical problems as it involved the expropriation of land and damage to roads, but it also had a significant psychological impact and the increasingly visible construction of fortifications offered a stirring visual reminder of the region's identity as a defensive frontier.[95]

The construction of fortifications was coupled with the presence of troops after Hitler sent the German army into the Rhineland in March 1936.[96] Proximity to the border meant that rumours swirled about what was happening in the Third Reich, and in the aftermath of the arrival of Wehrmacht troops in the Rhineland, the news spread through Alsace that border villages in Baden had started laying tubing across the roads, reportedly in order to make the roads unusable in the case of invasion.[97] In this way, transformations reshaped the border landscape as the boundary was redrawn and its markers designated the new limits between France and Germany. The transformation of the Alsatian landscape is suggestive of the ways in which making and maintaining the border was a collective process,

---

M. le Commissaire Général de la République Française, Mission Militaire et Administrative de la Basse Alsace, Paris, 5 June 1919.

[92] General Armau de Pouydraguin 'Les Fortifications du Nord-Est', in Comité alsacien d'études et d'informations, *L'Alsace depuis son retour à la France. Premier supplement: Vie politique administrative et sociale; Vie intellectuelle; artisistique et spirituelle; Vie economique* (Strasbourg, 1937), p. 31.

[93] General Armau de Pouydraguin, 'Les Fortifications du Nord-Est', in *L'Alsace depuis son retour à la France*, p. 30.

[94] General Armau de Pouydraguin, 'Les Fortifications du Nord-Est', in *L'Alsace depuis son retour à la France*, p. 35.

[95] ADBR 286D 100 *Die Freie Presse*, 'Ne construisez pas de mur autour de nous' 6 December 1928.

[96] General Armau de Pouydraguin 'Les Fortifications du Nord-Est', *L'Alsace depuis son retour à la France* (Paris, 1937), p. 36.

[97] ADBR 286D 161 Rapport, P. Elbling, Inspecteur de Police Special, Schoenau, 5 November 1936.

involving diplomats and commissions, but also the population who lived alongside the boundary. What is more, this was a process that took time and reflected the evolving political situation. As a result, there was little clear agreement about either the priorities or what exactly was necessary to remake the Alsatian landscape within the boundaries of France. Such divisions were even more marked with regard to the next step in terms of transformation: the fixing of the border's commemorative landscape.

THE COMMEMORATIVE LANDSCAPE

The interwar Alsatian commemorative landscape built upon the region's existing monuments and sites of commemoration. During the years of German rule, new architecture—such as Strasbourg's railway station, which was decorated with friezes of Friedrich Barbarossa in Alsace, or the Kaiserplatz with its statue of Wilhelm I—attempted to introduce the symbols of the German monarchy and empire, and to tie Alsace to the medieval German past. These commemorative sites from the years of German rule had underlined the historic links between Alsace and Germany, but they shared space with monuments that acted as reminders of the region's French past, such as the Mont Sainte-Odile, a medieval monastery built by the Duke of Alsace for his daughter, Odile, who became its abbess, and which became a symbol of Alsatian resistance to German rule.[98] Odile's story of recovery from blindness and patronage of the blind had led to a cult of Saint Odile in Charlemagne's empire, and her unofficial status as patron saint of Alsace was formalized when she was canonized by Pope Pius VII in 1807. During the early nineteenth century the mountain became a popular site for day trippers, and after 1871 the mountain and monastery were treated as a point of connection with an eternal Alsace that the Germans had not touched. This incarnation of Alsace was not simply for the region's Catholics; the Protestant academic Robert Redslob would later talk of climbing the sacred mountain. In Redslob's eyes, Mont Sainte-Odile served as a reminder that a 'few years' of German occupation could not undo centuries of connection to France.[99]

Both French and German monuments also served as a reminder of the region's recent past as the site of battle between France and Germany, and across Alsace the battlefields of 1870–1 and of the Napoleonic Wars attracted tourists.[100] Of course, this presentation of history was rooted in a sense of place. The Geisberg monument built to commemorate all French soldiers killed during battles on the site since the eighteenth century represented a reminder of the many battles fought in and for Alsace, while the monument to the revolutionary General Desaix offered a reminder of a military front forged at the foundation of the French First Republic, and as a

---

[98] Redslob, *Entre la France et l'Allemagne*, p. 248.
[99] Redslob, *Entre la France et l'Allemagne*, p. 248.
[100] On battlefield tourism, seea Karine Varley, *Under the Shadow of Defeat. The French of 1870–71 in French Memory* (Basingstoke, 2008), pp. 112–20.

result, of a historic French frontier that coincided with the idea of the Rhine as France's natural frontier.

After 1918 a number of monuments dating from the years of German rule were destroyed. In Saint-Privat in the Moselle, the town's population announced that *rupture* they would melt down the bronze eagles that topped the memorial to the war of 1870–1 and use them to replace the church bells removed by the Germans before their departure.[101] And in Strasbourg, images of the decapitated statues of Kaiser Wilhelm II, along with his father and grandfather, on the Strasbourg post office were captured in postcards that circulated after the armistice (see Figures 6.2 and 6.3).[102] The destruction or neglect of German monuments gave the region's prefects cause for concern over the potential effects upon the still uncertain *in renown* peace.[103] And in 1923 the Premier ensured that the Ministry of War and Pensions allocated a sum of 25,000 francs to allow the repair of German commemorative monuments in the region.[104]

But in many cases the prefects were alone in their concerns; the sub-prefect of Wissembourg informed the prefect of the Bas-Rhin that the Wissembourg monument was not 'abandoned', as a recent newspaper article had alleged. Rather, it

Figure 6.2. Postcard showing the decapitated statues of Wilhelm I, Friedrich III, and Wilhelm II at the Strasbourg post office, decapitated during the night of 20–1 November 1918.

Source: AMVES, 81Z 39, Fonds Hugo Haug, Carte postale.

[101] ADBR 121AL 1091 Le Président du Conseil to M. Charles Laurent, Ambassadeur de la République Française à Berlin, Paris, 14 October 1921.
[102] AMVES 81Z 39 Fonds Hugo Haug. Cartes postales.
[103] AN 313AP 225 Préfet du Bas-Rhin to Commisssaire Général de la République, 20 November 1923.
[104] ADBR 121AL 1091 Le Commissaire Général de la République to M. le Président du Conseil, Strasbourg, July 1923.

Figure 6.3. Postcard showing the head of the statue of Wilhelm I.
Source: AMVES, 81Z 39, Fonds Hugo Haug, Carte postale.

was in an adequate state of repair and the vandalism described had been done by retreating German soldiers at the end of the war.[105] The *Union Nationale des Combattants* (UNC) and *Souvenir Français* also argued that any damage to German monuments at the armistice reflected a population in a moment of enthusiasm following years of struggle against Germany, and thus it was not possible to compare the monuments constructed on the Rhine by the French state to commemorate combats conducted 'for the liberation of the world' with those erected by Germany 'following a war of conquest in an annexed territory'.[106] Indeed, they suggested, most German monuments had less a commemorative character and were, rather, provocative and aggressive, and therefore measures to repair them should be postponed, any provocative elements should be removed, and the monuments themselves should be relocated to military cemeteries. This would allow the liberation of public spaces and also place the commemorative monuments alongside those that they sought to remember.[107]

---

[105] AN 313AP 225 Sous-Préfet de Wissembourg to Préfet du Bas-Rhin, 6 November 1923.
[106] AN 313AP 225 President of the sections of the Union Nationale des Combattants et du Souvenir Français to Haut-Commissaire, Strasbourg.
[107] AN 313AP 225 President of the sections of the Union Nationale des Combattants and of Souvenir Français to Haut-Commissaire, Strasbourg.

In the Moselle, demands to destroy or remove German monuments adopted particular force; the local population protested against the repairs to German monuments undertaken in the early 1920s, and between 1923 and 1925 the municipal council of Sainte-Marie-aux-Chênes campaigned for the replacement of the German war memorial on Place de la Victoire with a monument to those who had died for France during the war of 1914–18.[108] The municipal council argued that the German monument could then be moved to one of the town's military cemeteries, which would avoid having it in a public place.[109] Their campaigns met with support from Premier Poincaré, who wrote to the General Commissioner in 1923 to offer his approval of the project, and to suggest that it would be best if their demands were supported as quickly as possible.[110] Poincaré's intervention also reflected official sanction of the destruction or removal of monuments. In 1919 the *Directeur Général des Finances d'Alsace-Lorraine* announced that following an investigation he had established that the bronze statue to the kaisers in the city of Metz 'did not belong to anyone', and that, as the city had been the primary subscriber, it was free to melt down the monuments and use the metal for other projects.

As these cases indicate, for many in Alsace, the Moselle, and beyond the removal of the markers of the region's German past was not enough. On the contrary, signalling the new French identity of the recovered departments also required the introduction of the symbols of French history and culture to the region, through erecting statues and monuments and renaming streets or public areas to honour the national past. Consequently, the early years after 1918 saw a flurry of such cultural and commemorative projects, and committees, societies, newspapers, and individuals from across the globe offered gifts of statues, sculptures, and busts to the city.[111] This went some way to filling the empty spaces left by the destruction of German monuments, but it also represented a concerted attempt to encourage identification with the French nation.

As streets and squares were renamed, many recalled the recent experience of war through the date of the particular town's 'liberation', or paid tribute to heroes of those efforts. Many municipal councils also attempted to signal the new political culture of their towns by naming streets after notable French republicans, including Emile Zola, Voltaire, Pascal, and Jules Ferry, while others recognized notable Alsatians, such as Marguerite Spoerling or Emile Noltig.[112] That streets were renamed in such overtly political circumstances meant that they retained their political importance.

---

[108] ADBR 121AL 1091 Le Commissaire Général de la République to M. le Président du Conseil, Strasbourg, July 1923.

[109] AN 313AP 225 Extrait du registre des deliberations du Conseil municipal, séance du 5 mai 1925. The Conseil municipal de la commune de Sainte-Marie-aux-Chenes ; 121AL 1091 Le Préfet de la Moselle to M. le Commissaire General de la République, 25 July 1923.

[110] AN 313AP 225 Préfet de la Moselle to Commissaire Générale, Metz, 2 July 1923.

[111] AMCVUS Fonds Haug 81 Z 37 Jacques Peirotes to members of the Conseil Municipal, 18 November 1920. A delegation of citizens of Milwaukee agreed to give the town of Strasbourg a bronze of the Marseillaise; 81Z 39 Peirotes to Hugo Haug, 8 November 1919.

[112] ADBR 121AL 770 Records of the Commissariat Général, March 1923; AMC 35 séance, 20 December 1921, p. 1053; 35 séance, 20 December 1921, p. 1053; AMM 11 séance, 22 October 1925, pp. 527–8; 98AL 1036 Extrait du registre des délibérations du Conseil municipal de Colmar, séance du 27 October 1936.

In 1926 news broke out that the newly elected council in the Bas-Rhin town of Sélestat had decided to restore the old names to streets renamed after the armistice.[113] As the 1918 names included a mixture of republican heroes and names reminiscent of the Great War, including rues Turenne, Thiers, Gambetta, Deroulede, Jacques Preiss, Poincaré, Joffre, Castelnau, Foch, Gouraud, de Verdun, and du 17 novembre, controversy broke out across the region and the town's patriotic societies were moved to protest.[114] The president of the local veterans' association, the UNC, wrote to the prefect to complain that in the context of the ongoing autonomist crisis it was politically unthinkable that the council should change these names.[115] In particular, the idea of changing the names 'de Verdun' and 'Poincaré', who was an honorary citizen of the town, provoked widespread indignation.[116]

When questioned, the Socialist Mayor Dr Bronner explained that the council had not wanted the 1918 name changed in the first place. They saw street names as 'sacred', akin to family names, and, regardless, the population continued to use the 1918 names. While they rejected the Heimatbund, he explained, they also wanted nothing of the 'exaggerated and unhealthy chauvinism' which would insist upon a further change in the names.[117] Bronner's appeal to French patriotism did not sway Prefect Henri Borromé, who insisted that the council change the names back, although he did warn Premier Raymond Poincaré not to view the incident from the perspective of 'the interior'.[118] In the eyes of the prefect, the decision was an attack on the former municipality, rather than upon France, and neither the mayor nor the majority of the council had recognized the implications of their motion.[119]

In a later case, the Mulhouse council decided in 1937 to rename a street in honour of Alfred Dreyfus, the Jewish army captain falsely accused of espionage in 1894. Dreyfus had been born in the town and died two years earlier, in 1935. The city's *Baumeister* objected to the instruction that 'rue du Barrage' become 'rue du Capitaine Alfred Dreyfus', stating that as Dreyfus had died a colonel rather than a captain, the street should be 'rue du Colonel Alfred Dreyfus'. Socialist councillor Falck responded, 'We are not interested in the man as a colonel. We want to commemorate the time when he was a captain.'[120] The council got their way. The battle was important for the town's Socialist council, as the new name did not simply pay tribute to a famous former son, but also signalled Mulhouse's political culture by making reference to the struggle for the future of

[113] ADBR 286D 44 Sous-préfet Sélestat to Préfet du Bas-Rhin, 27 July 1926; Extrait du Registre des délibérations du Conseil Municipal, 17 July 1926; AN F7 12751 Commissaire Spécial de Sélestat, Sélestat, 31 August 1926. Rapport Mensuel.

[114] ADBR 286D 44 Sous-préfet de Sélestat to Préfet du Bas-Rhin, 26 July 1926.

[115] ADBR 286D 44 Président de la Section de Sélestat de l'Union Nationale des Combattants (G. Trouillot) to Préfet du Bas-Rhin, 26 July 1926.

[116] ADBR 286D 44 Sous-préfet de Sélestat to Préfet du Bas-Rhin, 26 July 1926.

[117] ADBR 286D 44 Dr Bronner, Mayor of Sélestat to Préfet du Bas-Rhin, Sélestat, 28 July 1926.

[118] ADBR 286D 44 Préfet du Bas-Rhin to Président du Conseil, Direction Générale des Affairs d'Alsace et Lorraine, Strasbourg, 28 July 1926.

[119] ADBR 286D 44 Préfet du Bas-Rhin to Président du Conseil, Direction Générale des Affairs d'Alsace et Lorraine, Strasbourg, 28 July 1926.

[120] AMM D1 a1 1937 séance, 29 April 1937, p. 155.

the Republic triggered by the Dreyfus case, and aligned Alsace with France's republican past. With proto-fascist parties and groups linked to Nazi Germany increasing their appeal in the region, Mulhouse's council was keen to make a statement about which side they were on.

The new commemorative landscape was not restricted to street names alone, and debates about monument construction in Alsace, and particularly in the high-profile city of Strasbourg, formed another site of the battle over the remaking of the border's commemorative landscape. Notably, they reveal the coexistence and competition of ideas of Alsace as an integral part of France, as a regional centre, and as the heart of a cross-border community. Thus, plans for statues focused first upon national history. This was the case for Alsace's first major interwar monument, a statue honouring the Marseillaise in Strasbourg. For this statue the initiative was taken outside the city when President Raymond Poincaré and Albert de Dietrich, a descendant of Strasbourg's eighteenth-century mayor Friedrich de Dietrich, formed a monument committee to commemorate the national anthem's composition in the city in 1792.[121] The committee was formed during the war and planned the monument to celebrate Alsace's return to France in the event of a French victory.[122] After the armistice, the committee rapidly decided upon a sculptor, commissioned the form of the statue (which depicted three soldiers brandishing the tricolour), and proposed that the monument should be placed in the Place de la République, the former Kaiserplatz and the heart of the German new town, as a highly symbolic replacement for the statue of Wilhelm I, which had been torn down in November 1918.[123]

In May 1919 Strasbourg's council subscribed to the committee as a founding member and pledged 100,000 francs to the statue.[124] The council then chose the construction materials and the statue's eventual site, in Place Broglie close to de Dietrich's former house.[125] The change of location is suggestive of the different attitudes towards the statue held by the council and by the monument committee. The council rejected the straightforward replacement of the Kaiser by the Marseillaise and instead opted to place the statue in the old town, close to the house in which it was composed. This location underlined the region's role in national history; for the council there was no need to replace one set of national symbols with another, as the city had its own, existing symbolism and history. Similarly, there was no need to impose a French identity on the recovered region,

[121] AMVES 154MW 61 Albert de Dietrich to Jacque Peirotes, Paris, 3 May 1919; ADBR 121AL 1091. The Committee was made up of Pierre Bucher, Paul Helmer, F. Kieffer, Anselme Laugel, Daniel Mieg, Jules Siegfried, and C. Staehling.

[122] AMVES 154MW 62 Committee de la Marseillaise to Mayor of Strasbourg, Paris, 7 February 1922.

[123] AMVES 154MW 61 Albert de Dietrich to Jacques Peirotes, Paris, 2 May 1919.

[124] AMVES 154MW 61 Président du Conseil Municipal to M. Baron Albert de Dietrich Strasbourg (nd); 154MW 61 Président du Conseil Municipal to Président du comité national de la Marseillaise, Strasbourg, 17 July 1919; Compte rendu du Conseil Municipal de la Ville de Strasbourg, 20 séance, 20 June 1919, p. 458.

[125] Compte rendu du Conseil Municipal de la Ville de Strasbourg, 12 séance, 31 March 1920, pp. 480–1.

as Alsatians would be actively involved in the reimagining of their region's place within France.

The filtering of national symbols through local understandings was reinforced at the placement of the first stone in June 1922, when Radical councillor François Oesinger paid tribute to Alsace, which was 'at the forefront of all the great republican and revolutionary movements which made France one and indivisible, and which created the magnificent, democratic France of 1918'.[126] In speeches and pamphlets the city council presented the monument as the fusion of national and local history, stressing the Strasbourgeois origins of the anthem and the role of Alsatians in the Revolution of 1789. At the monument's unveiling on 14 July 1922, Socialist Mayor Jacques Peirotes took pains to show that, while the statue may have been a 'top-down' initiative thought up by a Parisian committee, Strasbourg had embraced it as its own:

> Since our election [in 1919], the Municipality has understood that, in effect, it needed to perpetuate in Strasbourg the memory of this happy event through a monument which would express simultaneously our joy at being returned to the mother country, our recognition of the sacrifices … and our attachment which has stayed so firm to all of the republican institutions. And we believed that these sentiments could only be expressed by a concrete glorification of the Marseillaise.[127]

Peirotes added that, in spite of forty-seven years of annexation into Germany, in its attachment 'to the ideas of liberty and equality that inspired the Marseillaise' the city shared celebrations of Bastille Day with the rest of France.[128] Nevertheless, local political controversies ensured that Peirotes also made reference to the population's continued attachment to all 'republican institutions'.[129] By this, of course, he meant the laws of religious separation, and by making them part of his speech he transformed the monument into an intervention into the debate about the reintegration of Alsace into France.

Similar political imperatives guided Strasbourg council's rejection of the Joan of Arc monument in 1925, offered by a Parisian committee after Joan's 1921 canonization by the Vatican and the announcement of a national Joan of Arc Day by the Conservative Bloc national government. The Socialist- and Radical-dominated council, which had come under criticism for its failure to celebrate the festival in 1921, also refused the statue, rejecting it as an unsuitable aspect of the French past to commemorate in a region they presented as affirmably republican. The statue was eventually situated in the garden of the Palais du Rhin.[130]

---

[126] AMVES 154MW 62 'Discours de Oesinger'; *Journal d'Alsace et de Lorraine*, 17 June 1922.

[127] AMVES Fonds Jacques Peirotes 125Z 33. Discours prononcé lors de l'inauguration de la statue représentant La Marseillaise, Place Broglie, 14 July 1922.

[128] *Dernières Nouvelles de Strasbourg*, 15 July 1922 ; 'L'Inauguration du Monument de la Marseillaise', *Journal d'Alsace et de Lorraine*, 15 July 1922.

[129] AMVES 154MW 62 Discours de Oesinger; *Journal d'Alsace et de Lorraine*, 17 June 1922; *Dernières Nouvelles de Strasbourg*, 15 June 1922 ; 'L'Inauguration du Monument de la Marseillaise', *Journal d'Alsace et de Lorraine*, 15 July 1922; Fonds Jacques Peirotes 125Z 33. Discours prononcé lors de l'inauguration de la statue représentant La Marseillaise, Place Broglie, 14 July 1922.

[130] *Le Journal de l'Est*, 21 February 1925.

If the Marseillaise and Joan of Arc revealed divergent attitudes towards Alsace's place within France, monuments could also reveal a variety of attitudes towards its position upon the border. And, of course, these two aspects of its position were inseparable. In December 1928 Fritz Beblo, chief architect of the Bavarian city of Munich and former *Stadtbauinspektor* of Strasbourg, proposed that Strasbourg swap its statue of Father Rhine, which had been installed by the imperial government in 1903, for a monument of the Meiselocker, or 'Bird-catcher'.[131] The Meiselocker paid homage to an ancient nickname that the Strasbourgeois held in Alsace, and depicted a young boy with a flute, which, according to the legend, he used to attract birds that he then sold in the city's markets. Socialist Mayor Peirotes accepted the offer, and Father Rhine was unveiled in its new position in Munich in 1932. Although Father Rhine had never been a particularly popular monument in Strasbourg, its replacement did not meet with approval in the city; the Sculptors' Guild protested at the replacement of the well-known 'Vater Rhein' by the unknown Meiselocker, and inhabitants of the Place Saint-Etienne, in which the council planned to place the new monument, complained about its aesthetics.[132]

Controversy over the statue went beyond its appearance, however. At its unveiling the Volksfront, which had recently won the town hall, attempted to offer the Meiselocker as an alternative symbol for Alsace: one that reflected its position as a bridge between France and Germany. Autonomist councillor Heil made a speech which focused on the need for further cultural exchange across the Rhine.[133] This reflected the attitudes of the new council to Strasbourg's role as a border city; three months later Communist-Autonomist Mayor Hueber would stress that 'the Rhine separates countries, not men'.[134] But while this view reflected widely held and long-standing understandings of Strasbourg, Franco–German tension meant that its articulation in 1930 was problematic. The Socialists and Conservatives on the city's council boycotted the event, condemning its neglect of 'true' Alsatian traditions and criticizing its invitation to student societies that aped German customs.[135] Meanwhile, the Conservative Alsatian press labelled Heil's speech a 'provocation' to the majority of the Strasbourg population and a 'challenge' to France, concerns which were echoed both in other Alsatian political circles and in

[131] AMVES 154MW 67 Extrait des délibérations du Conseil municipal de la ville de Strasbourg, Séance 10 December 1928.

[132] AMVES 154MW 67 Corporation obligatoire des patrons sculpteurs sur pierre et entrepreneurs de monuments du Bas-Rhin to Jacques Peirotes, Strasbourg, 22 April 1929; Résidents de la Place Saint-Etienne to Charles Hueber, Strasbourg, 16 May 1929.

[133] 'L'inauguration du Meiselocker a été une manifestation autonomiste', *Journal d'Alsace et de Lorraine*, 18 November 1929.

[134] Compte-rendu du Conseil Municipal de la Ville de Strasbourg, 18 séance, 3 February 1930, Discours de Charles Hueber, 204. This was not simply Communist internationalism. By this point, Hueber had been expelled from the PCF and embarked upon the political trajectory that would lead to his reinstatement as mayor of Strasbourg by Gauleiter Robert Wagner, after the city's annexation into the Third Reich. Thus the label 'Communist-Autonomist' reflects his origins in the PCF and commitment to autonomism. See Samuel H. Goodfellow, 'From Communism to Nazism'.

[135] AMVES Compte rendu du Conseil Municipal de la Ville de Strasbourg, 12 séance, 25 November 1929, pp. 835–6 and 842.

the corridors of power in Paris.[136] In the eyes of the new council, however, the event's stress on Franco–German rapprochement reflected popular attitudes in Alsace. In this sense, Heil's speech represented one of the clearest challenges to the idea of Strasbourg as a boundary, while the response he received is revealing of the splintering of Alsatian opinion by the beginning of the 1930s.

These differences crystallized the following year, 1931, during discussions over the statue of Victor Hugo and Lamartine. This statue was the idea of a Strasbourg-based committee of Conservative, Francophile Alsatians including university Rector Christian Pfister and Professor Robert Redslob.[137] The committee envisaged the monument as a vibrant national symbol depicting Strasbourg's return to France, and requested Parisian help in financing the project by stressing Alsace's constant loyalty to France during the years of annexation.[138] The monument would thus be a great French patriotic gesture: a statement that Alsace 'was to be definitively French, and that the German era was forgotten'.[139] Moreover, like the councillors who had embraced the statue of the Marseillaise, the committee connected the monument with the history of Strasbourg: Hugo had written of the Cathedral, while Lamartine had paid homage to Gutenberg and the Marseillaise.[140]

But, like the Meiselocker, this monument also needed to reflect Strasbourg's position on the border. This gave the city a double duty, first to inform and warn France of any potential hostility as and when necessary, and second to bring the 'treasures of German culture to France'.[141] Redslob envisioned the Hugo-Lamartine statue alongside the existing statues of Schiller and Goethe as a signal of Alsace's position as a bridge, and a sign that Strasbourg merited its moniker 'city of roads'.[142] That Redslob would argue for both the erasure of memories of the German era and for Strasbourg as a bridge is suggestive of his view that it was possible to remove German influence without destroying Alsace's cultural heritage of links to both France and Germany. In this sense, the monument offered an expression of Alsatianness based upon the region's connections to France and Germany that was distinct from both.

The Conservative Francophile Redslob and the autonomist Heil both articulated a view of Alsace as a cultural meeting point, yet the two men used this idea in very different ways. For Redslob it was an integral part of the region's French patriotism, while for Heil it reflected Alsatian uniqueness and underscored his argument against the introduction of French laws, language, and institutions into

[136] 'L'inauguration du Meiselocker a été une manifestation autonomiste', *Journal d'Alsace et de Lorraine*, 18 November 1929; 'Une protestation de groupements d'étudiants', *Journal de l'Est*, 20 November 1929; *Journal d'Alsace et de Lorraine*, 20 November 1929.

[137] AMVES 154MW 53 'Pour le monument Lamartine-Victor Hugo'.

[138] AMVES 154MW 55 668 Christian Pfister Recteur de l'Université to M. le Baron Henri de Rothschild, Strasbourg, 23 December 1927; 154MW 53 'Pour le monument Lamartine-Victor Hugo'. Discours de Gaston Kern.

[139] AMVES 154MW 53 Robert Redslob to Jacques Peirotes, Strasbourg, 17 December 1927; 154MW 54, Appel en faveur d'un monument Lamartine-Victor Hugo à ériger à l'orangerie de Strasbourg.

[140] AMVES Compte-rendu du Conseil Municipal de la Ville de Strasbourg, 98 séance, 15 April 1929, p. 194.

[141] AMVES 154MW 53 'Pour le monument Lamartine-Victor Hugo'. Discours de Christian Pfister.

[142] AMVES 154MW 53 'Pour le monument Lamartine-Victor Hugo'. Discours de Robert Redslob.

the region. But, in spite of the similarities between the attitude of the monument committee and the Volksfront council, the local administration boycotted the unveiling ceremony in protest against the failure of the committee to inform the council where the monument would be placed.[143] When the council discussed the events, autonomist councillor Camille Dahlet criticized the committee's handling of the affair, treating it as reflective of a broader problem in relations between Paris and Alsace. For Dahlet, the imposition of the monument represented an attempt to enforce a 'Parisian' national identity onto the Alsatian population, and a rejection of the sense of identity which Alsatians had forged for themselves. Dahlet warned that the French were not only failing in their attempt to demonstrate the Alsatians' French patriotism to German observers, but were also repeating the mistakes that the Germans had made during the years of the region's annexation into the German Empire. As a result, national governments would be advised instead to give the Alsatians 'standardized monuments' with 'detachable heads'. This would remove the need to destroy entire monuments at moments of change of national regime and, had this been the case earlier, Strasbourg could have simply replaced the heads of the three Hohenzollern emperors that adorned the facade of the city's post office with the heads of their liberators, Marshals Foch, Joffre, and Pétain.[144]

The common ground between the monument committee and the Volksfront council was overshadowed by their very different understandings of the relationship between France and Alsace. The Volksfront deemed French policy in the recovered provinces to have been heavy-handed and insensitive. For the monument committee, on the other hand, mistakes made by the French in their treatment of Alsace did not merit rejection of the French nation. When the monument's placement was decided upon, the council learned from the press that it would be placed in the Rhine Palace, just as the Joan of Arc monument had been in 1925.[145] For Dahlet, it was fitting that the Palace, itself constructed with no account of local views, should be home to a growing collection of unwanted monuments. Yet it was also, in his view, an example of the French failure to take account of Alsatian attitudes, and another work of national propaganda, of the type inflicted upon the region since the years of German rule, along with Vater Rhein, Wilhelm I, Goethe, the Marseillaise, Joan of Arc, Pasteur, and now Hugo-Lamartine.[146] The monument thus became emblematic of the problems of reconciling regional and national identity with Alsace's position on the border through the commemorative landscape.

An acutely politically sensitive question in the region's new commemorative landscape was how Alsace should memorialize its Great War dead. As monuments sprung up in towns across the region after 1918, concerned civil servants contacted

[143] AMVES Compte rendu du Conseil Municipal de la Ville de Strasbourg, Séance 22 June 1931, p. 399.

[144] AMVES Compte rendu du Conseil Municipal de la Ville de Strasbourg, Séance 22 June 1931, p. 397.

[145] AMVES Compte rendu du Conseil Municipal de la Ville de Strasbourg, Séance 22 June 1931, p. 392.

[146] AMVES Compte rendu du Conseil Municipal de la Ville de Strasbourg, Séance 22 June 1931, p. 398.

the Interior Minister about the 'tasteless' character of many war memorials.[147] But more than aesthetics, the Alsatians faced a problem with the form, language, and message of their *monuments aux morts*. As the region's war dead had fought for Germany but since become citizens of France, the question of how to commemorate them (and of if and how to distinguish between those who had indeed fought for Germany and those who had fought for France) was a particularly sensitive one. The result was what William Shane Story has identified as a general reluctance to embark upon commemorative projects to avoid the airing of discord or uncertainty about the past.[148]

Such divisions over commemoration were frequently contentious; in Sélestat in 1924 the council received criticism after it voted 35,000 francs for a war monument that would recognize the dead of all three confessions, and then placed it in the Catholic cemetery.[149] The intervention of commemorative associations often complicated situations further, and in Mulhouse problems emerged over the town's memorial when the *Souvenir Français* protested against commemorating enemy soldiers, which, of course, included the vast majority of Alsatians who had fought in the German army. The project artist managed to resolve the crisis by designing a statue with two soldiers, which he argued honoured all dead while celebrating French liberty.[150] In Strasbourg, meanwhile, the war memorial was unveiled in October 1936 and filled the space at the centre of the Place de la République, which had been much coveted as a symbolic commemorative space.[151] The monument featured a mother as an allegory for Alsace holding her two dead sons in her arms; one son represented the Alsatians who had fought for France and the other those who had fought for Germany. Elizabeth Vlossak has pointed out that the Strasbourg memorial is unusual amongst Alsatian monuments to the Great War, as most of the region's towns opted to depict either solitary women or female allegories. In these monuments, mothers were not simply a universal figure of collective sorrow. They also allowed the avoidance of the awkward question of whether to depict Alsatian soldiers in French or German uniform.[152]

Strasbourg's monument instead attempted to capture the pacifist mood of the mid-1930s through its depiction of two dead soldiers who linked hands in death, with neither wearing his uniform. Its inscription read '*A Nos Morts*' without specifying the nation for which the men had died. But it did not go so far as a bilingual inscription, as the committee feared that this might prove too controversial. The speech delivered by President Albert Lebrun at the unveiling reflected the pacifist tone of the monument; after stressing the historic links between Alsace and France,

[147] ADBR 121AL 583 M. Le Directeur d'Architecture et des Beaux Arts to M. le Directeur de l'Interieur, 9 December 1920.

[148] William Shane Story, 'Constructing French Alsace: A state, region, and nation in Europe, 1918–1925' (PhD Dissertation, Rice University, 2001), p. 226.

[149] *Die Freie Presse*, 24 September 1924.

[150] Shane Story, 'Constructing French Alsace', pp. 229–30.

[151] AMVES Compte-rendu du Conseil Municipal de la Ville de Strasbourg, 19 séance, 6 April 1936, p. 175. On the construction of memorials, see Daniel J. Sherman, *The Construction of Memory in Interwar France* (London, 1999).

[152] Vlossak, *Marianne or Germania*, p. 166.

he recalled the tragedy of 1918, when brothers were called upon to fight against each other, and he appealed, 'Let our hands, like theirs, seek and find each other. That they would also reach across borders in a generous gesture, a movement of rapprochement, entente and peace.'[153] Through the monument, ideas of Alsatian victimhood interacted with understandings of the region's history and with local and international politics. In an atmosphere of Franco–German tension, the monument reflected broader European sentiments and an appeal for peace and unity that marked it apart from the monuments of the 1920s.

The major war memorial in interwar Alsace was the enormous monument and ossuary at Hartmannswillerkopf. During the war, the rocky 'mountain of death' became the scene of fierce fighting and totalled a rate of casualties equivalent to that at Verdun or Artois, with more than four soldiers killed per metre of front.[154] After the war, the increasing numbers of battlefield tourists visiting the site led General Commissioner Alapetite and head of the military in Strasbourg General Boisseau to express concerns about the behaviour of tourists and the commercialization of the battlefield.[155] Thus the *Association des Dames Françaises* proposed the erection of a monument on the mountain.[156] Their proposal was taken up by the *Souvenir Français*, and in 1922 the former battlefield was classified as a historic monument.[157] Under the auspices of the Commission of Architecture and Fine Arts, discussion began in Paris over the monument's form, and the planners agreed that, while honouring the dead, the monument should also reflect the 'glory' of the victory and the 'gratitude' of the Alsatians who owed their liberation to the French troops. Thus the eventual monument encompassed a crypt containing the unidentified remains of fallen soldiers, three separate chapels to represent the Catholic, Protestant, and Jewish dead, twelve tablets engraved with the details of the troops, and an enormous bronze cross at the summit, which had two figures to represent Alsace and Lorraine at its feet.[158]

The monument's landscape and location influenced planners' considerations. The mountain's thick covering of forest had been destroyed during the war, and the commission agreed that the battlefield should be maintained in its 'state of devastation'.[159] As the monument was 'opposite the French Rhine', it was important that it pay fitting tribute to the extent of France's efforts to recover its lost provinces.[160] Senator Jules Scheurer based his appeal for financial support on the mountain's traditional role as a defensive frontier against German tribes, while

---

[153] 'Strasbourg en Fête a donné un sens national à la visite de M. Lebrun', *Le Figaro*, 19 October 1936; 'Le Discours du President de la République à l'inauguration du monument aux morts de Strasbourg', *Le Temps*, 19 October 1936.

[154] ADBR 121 AL 1092 Monument de l'Hartmann. Résumé historique; ADBR 98AL 626 'Appel' Signé Pouydraguin Strasbourg (nd).

[155] ADBR 121 AL 1091 Monuments.

[156] ADBR 121 AL 1092 Monument de l'Hartmann. Résumé historique.

[157] ADBR 121 AL 1092 Rapport addressé à M. le Commissaire Général de la République sur les travaux projetées au champ de bataille de l'Hartmannswillerkopf.

[158] ADBR 121 AL 1092 Rapport addressé à M. le Commissaire Général de la République sur les travaux projetées au champ de bataille de l'Hartmannswillerkopf.

[159] ADBR 121 AL 1092 Monument de l'Hartmann. Resumé historique.

[160] ADBR 98AL 626 'Appel' Signé Pouydraguin Strasbourg (nd).

Philippe Pétain's description of the monument focused on the views from its peak, which displayed France's former frontier, 'the blue line of the Vosges', as well as its restored, 'rightful' border on the Rhine.[161] Ideas about borders thus contributed to the region's commemorative landscape. Work on the monument was suspended in 1928 when public subscriptions dried up, but a new appeal in Strasbourg raised a further 185,000 francs. This brought the committee close to the total necessary for the monument's construction and left it with just another 800,000 francs to raise.[162] The Hartmannswillerkopf *monument aux morts* was eventually inaugurated by President Lebrun in October 1932.

Debates and disputes over Alsace's commemorative landscape after 1918 were dominated by questions of how to memorialize the region's past through street names, statues, and monuments. And, as had been the case with administrative and legal reintegration, politics, economics, society, and culture, discussions over the landscape brought to the fore the divisions amongst Alsatians over how to best remake the border landscape. Throughout these discussions, the idea of the region as France's boundary coexisted alongside the idea that it represented the heart of a cross-border community, reflected in its double culture. These ideas coexisted, but at moments of crisis (and particularly moments of tension in Franco–German relations), the rhetoric of the border came to focus upon its role as France's boundary, leaving no space for understandings of it as a point of connection. But these two ideas of the border were not simply rhetorical constructions; they also reflected lived experience in Alsace, where the population lived with the points of contact and limitations that were part of life on France's eastern frontier.

CONCLUSION

The Alsatian landscape determined the shape of much of the region's economic and social life. This was the case for the long, sunny autumns so suited to the production of Riesling wine, to the potash below the earth that triggered new industrialization in the late nineteenth century, and to the Rhine, which connected populations on both banks but which also represented a clear visual marker between French and German national territory after 1918. Of course, all three examples remind us that the influence of the landscape was never straightforward. Interwar commentators wrote that the production of wine linked the region to French cultures of consumption, especially as Alsatian *vignerons* tried to alter their wines to cater for French tastes, while potash was a symbol of the economic success of German rule and of the problems associated with economic reintegration into French system. And, with regard to the Rhine, not only do rivers flood and burst their banks, leading to changes in national boundaries, but they are also reimagined for a range of different purposes, as we saw in the rival ideas of the Rhine as

---

[161] ADBR 98AL 626 Brochure. Le Monument National de l'Hartmannswillerkopf, préface de M. le Maréchal Pétain (Paris, 1927).
[162] ADBR 98AL 626 G. E. Pouydraguin, Strasbourg. 2 July 1928.

France's national and historic frontier, Germany's national river, and a great European river. In this sense, the landscape was both a driver of change and a cultural construction. This had implications for identities, which were shaped by the landscape's impact upon social and economic structures, but which were also articulated with reference to the landscape.

The remaking of the Alsatian landscape after 1918 involved establishing the new border, redesigning the region's towns, and fixing its commemorative landscape. This was completed through both practical measures and discussions about how the landscape should be transformed and what it represented. Each of these steps involved voices from across Alsace, France, and further afield. While the Treaty of Versailles restored the border to its 1871 position, the exact line that it took followed consultation with the public, and the border commissions took account of popular attitudes when making their final decisions about its position. After the boundary was established, changes to the Alsatian landscape were designed to make a statement, and it was through these changes that the aesthetics of the border were fixed and it began to appear as a meaningful division between the two national communities on the left and right banks of the Rhine. This border, therefore, was a collective construction drawn against the backdrop of shifting relations between Alsace and France, and between France and Germany.

The remaking of the landscape saw some of the most overt and explicit articulations of the two ideas of the borderland that shaped debates about the return of Alsace to France; that on the one hand Alsace represented France's limits, and on the other that Alsace was the heart of a cross-border, transnational community. From the discussions over the form that the customs posts should take to the stress upon the Hartmannswillerkopf monument's position upon France's natural and historic frontier, efforts to remake the border landscape were informed by the sense that Alsace represented a boundary not just of France, but also of Frenchness. This understanding coexisted with the idea of Alsace that stressed the region's deep-rooted and continued connections to France and Germany. The two notions coexisted, and both were mobilized to argue for Alsatian distinctiveness. Both were also underpinned by the daily experience of the border as the nation's limits, and as a site of cross-border contact. And, as had been the case with all areas of return, Alsatians were far from united in how they viewed the landscape.

The impact of the return of Alsace to France upon the region's landscape is revealing of the dynamics of return in a number of ways, from the role of popular participation in the construction of borders, to the competing and intermingling notions of Alsace as France's limits and as the heart of a cross-border community, and to the remaking of the landscape which involved the removal of evidence of the German past (or what was perceived to be German) to replace it with symbols and statements of the region's place within France. These tasks engaged individuals in Alsace, in the French interior, and in Germany. Within debates about reintegration, there was diversity in the opinions advanced from all sides. Yet there was unity in the ultimate aim of reimagining Alsace's position within France and reconciling Alsace's connections to Germany. This task remained incomplete when war broke out in 1939 and the region found itself once again upon the front line of Franco–German antagonism. In 1940 German troops marched into Alsace, and the region was attached to Baden as part of the Gau Baden-Elsass. Annexation brought new challenges for the population left on the home front, for those Alsatians who were sent elsewhere in the Third Reich to work, and for the young men who were conscripted into or volunteered for the Wehrmacht.[163] The fractured memories that resulted posed fresh problems of reintegration when Alsace once again returned to France at the end of the Second World War.

[163] See Thomas Williams, 'Remaking the Franco–German Borderlands: Historical Claims and Commemorative Practices in the Upper Rhine, 1940–49' (unpublished DPhil, University of Oxford, 2010).

I like this

USE IN MY DISSO

Conclusion

Studying the history of a border raises new questions about the locality, the nation, and the international, and demands new conceptual tools for its analysis. This book has considered how the Franco–German border shaped the return of Alsace to France after 1918, and rather than consider the border as the geographical location of the study, it has treated the border as a driver of change. Adopting this approach encourages greater attention to the interaction between the different scales of analysis of the local, national, and international, and avoids a binary view of Alsace as either French or German, or as falling between two nations. Instead, Alsace emerges as a dynamic force, and our lens is focused upon the multiple languages that its population adopted to describe return. These languages were neither consistent nor fixed in time, as voices from across Alsace attempted to shape their place within the French nation and to reconcile this with local particularities and cross-border connections. Their attempts to do so covered all the areas charted in this book and have implications that extend far beyond the region of Alsace: the perceived ambiguity that France encountered in Alsace led to new efforts to redefine the boundaries of the French nation (and notably to a greater focus upon race and ethnicity). As this ambiguity resulted from Alsace's cross-border connections with Germany, Alsace's return to France is inseparable from Europe's interwar history, and reminds us that nations are not formed in isolation. The border was the site of contact, interaction, and tension, and was formed from the interaction between top-down initiatives and grass-roots experience, as the Alsatian population adapted to the new boundary after their return to France.

THE RETURN OF ALSACE TO FRANCE

In 1918 the end of the First World War triggered the return of Alsace to France. The following years saw debate across society, administrative and legislative institutions, politics, economics, culture, and the landscape, as voices from Alsace, the French interior, and Europe offered their views on reintegration. In this multicentred struggle, a central aim guiding the majority of French initiatives was the complete and total removal of German influence. But this raised a series of related (and interconnected) questions: What was German? What was French? What was Alsatian? Navigating these questions proved problematic. Years of interactions across the Rhine and the Vosges, as well as transfers between French and German rule, meant that Alsace had been shaped by its ties to both France and Germany, and the removal of German influence was not as clear-cut as first assumed. What is more, as a result of these connections the task of renegotiating Alsace's place within France was inseparable from Franco–German relations, which evolved across the interwar years. As the thaw around the Locarno Agreement gave way to concerns and hostility after Hitler seized power in 1933, escalating tensions were given concrete form in Alsace through the construction of border fortifications. These shifting relations affected Alsace's relationship with both France and Germany, yet, throughout, the region was a site of contact between the French and German nations.

This contact took a variety of forms: citizens of Baden and the Palatinate shopped in Alsace's towns, Alsatians crossed the Rhine to visit family in Germany, German ideas about housing informed the development of *Habitation à Bon Marché* in Strasbourg and Mulhouse, and Alsatian wines competed with Rhineland vintages. Of course, not all of this contact was positive. Many cross-border encounters produced grumbles, complaints, or outright conflict. This suggests that borders do not create a sense of difference by isolating populations, but instead by creating a space for contact and by generating frictions. Indeed, cross-border encounters played a significant part in the sense of otherness that developed between the population of Alsace and those living across the border in Germany. This arose in spite of commonalities in language, culture, and family ties, and the fact that they had recently been members of the same nation state.

This sense of difference from populations across the Rhine did not lead to feelings of greater connection to France amongst the Alsatian population, however. Alsace shared with France the history of the key moments of revolution in 1789 and 1848, of restored monarchy, and the Second French Empire. Yet after 1918 contact with *Français de l'Intérieur* informed a sense of Alsatian distinctiveness within the French nation, especially as the feeling took root that France was failing to understand Alsace. This failure found its most obvious expression in the reports that Alsatians were being called '*boches*' when they encountered French citizens from other regions, but it informed all of the discussions over integration between Alsatians and French from the interior. Indeed, the very notion of '*France de l'Intérieur*' or '*Français de l'Intérieur*' speaks to a sense of Alsatian difference within France. Crucially, however, it also suggests that Alsatians did not separate themselves from France and instead understood that there was more than one France; there was the *France de l'Intérieur* and the France that they hoped to belong to. This was a France with multiple and varied customs and mores, but it nevertheless represented a national whole.

Of course, Alsatians were not alone in identifying varied customs and mores across the corners of the French hexagon; Ernest Renan's *What is a Nation?* had recognized the diverse groups that made up France: 'A Frenchman', he stressed, 'is neither a Gaul, nor a Frank, nor a Burgundian. Rather he is what has emerged out of the cauldron in which, presided over by the King of France, the most diverse elements have together been simmering.'[1] Renan's notion of a 'cauldron' (*chaudière*)

---

[1] Renan, *Qu'est-ce qu'une nation?* (Paris, 1882), p. 17.

has found parallels in many subsequent historical accounts of the integration of regional or immigrant populations into the French nation, which demonstrate that it was not necessary to shed a regional identity to become French, and which stress the role of grass-roots agency in refashioning Frenchness.[2] Nevertheless, the underlying premise behind such an understanding of integration is that becoming French was a process, and one that was both progressive and beneficial. From this perspective, Frenchification may have adopted a more complex and twisting path than once thought, but it remains a path to the nation, which is the natural unit.

This view (which was equally displayed by successive governments and administrators in their dealings with interwar Alsace) was one that came into conflict with Alsatian notions of national heterogeneity. On France's eastern border, Alsatians who had accepted or even celebrated the return to French rule became increasingly frustrated at the lack of space for regional particularities within the hegemonic notions of Frenchness that they encountered after 1918. As the late Third Republic struggled to negotiate local distinctiveness, and successive governments proved unable or unwilling to pay heed to Alsatian attempts to differentiate themselves from Germany, they revealed their own increasing cultural and political insecurities. The result was an uneasy compromise, where regional legal and administrative structures were left in place, but Alsatian suggestions that the region could represent a model for national reform died out during the 1930s. The focus upon the region that emerged as a key feature of Alsatian public life in the interwar years was a response to the trauma of change of national regime, but its persistence is testament to the uneasy position that Alsace occupied within the Third Republic.

BUILDING THE BORDER

Through their encounters across the Rhine and the Vosges, Alsatians shaped and developed their understanding of the world. Many in Alsace were aware of the roots and importance of their region's cross-border connections to France and Germany. Thus, they made reference to their double culture, called upon their international networks, and made use of German words when the French word failed to capture the historical and cultural sense that they sought to convey—such as *Kulturkampf* or *Heimat*. In this way, these links informed Alsatian understandings of their own situation, and such contact also created a clear sense of what was distinctly Alsatian. This was not the view from the French interior, however, as the authorities' concerns about German influence on their eastern border led them to read such connections with suspicion.

This contact was, nevertheless, one of the ways in which the Alsatian population helped to 'make' the border between France and Germany after 1918. After all, the

[2] Caroline Ford, *Creating the Nation in Provincial France: Religion and Political Identity in Brittany* (Princeton, 1993); Patrick Young, *Enacting Brittany: Tourism and Culture in Provincial France, 1871–1939* (Farnham, 2012); Gérard Noiriel, *Le Creuset Français. Histoire de l'immigration (XIXe–XXe siècle)* (Paris, 1988).

new Franco–German boundary was a collective construction. As we have seen, the discussions at Versailles restored the boundary line to its 1871 position, then the exact path that it took followed consultation with the public, and the border commissions considered popular attitudes when making their final decisions about its precise course. The discussions over where the border should go reveal the interconnection of different concerns, as security, economics, practicality, and prestige all played a part in designating the new boundary line. They are also suggestive of changing ideas about borders, as the nineteenth-century boundaries had allowed for the ownership of land and resources on a neighbouring national territory, but by the twentieth century it was widely accepted by all involved in the negotiations that the best solution was a 'neat border', that is, one single border for both territory and ownership. This was connected to changing ideas about nations. The collapse of the multinational empires of central and eastern Europe during the war fed into the guiding principle at Versailles that national boundaries should, as far as possible, contain national populations and national territory. Nevertheless, one constant was the underlying principle that good borders make good neighbours.

After the establishment of the boundary line, the Franco–German border was then transformed into a meaningful division by the introduction of new laws, new administrative institutions, the French franc, new customs posts, a new commemorative landscape, and the French language. Each of these elements of the French nation separated the population in Alsace from neighbouring populations in the Weimar Republic. Then, cross-border interactions and transgressions created the sense that the border was a meaningful boundary, whether through encounters with German or Swiss shoppers, who visited the region's shops and reportedly pushed local prices up, or through the act of smuggling tobacco or sugar, which showed the border to be a division that mattered.

Furthermore, this border was solidified by how it was imagined and described. After the annexation of the 'lost provinces' into the German Empire in 1871, Alsace-Lorraine acquired a symbolism that formed an important part of the cultures of nationalism of the French Third Republic; the notion of the blue line of the Vosges, the maps that showed the lost provinces shrouded in black or purple as the colours of mourning, and the references to the loss as an 'amputation' that had destabilized the French hexagon, all helped to rally France's citizens to the new regime. This was not simply a top-down phenomenon: the population engaged with this symbolism at the grass roots, and the '*ancienne frontière*' became a site of popular tourism in the late nineteenth century. This symbolism persisted and evolved after 1918, as Alsatians and *Français de l'Intérieur* attempted to imprint the region with the symbols of France, from the statue of the Marseillaise in Strasbourg right down to the border posts, which faced the equivalent German signposts and therefore needed to be able to 'sustain comparison with those of Germany'.[3]

This symbolism helped to make the border, with the result that attempts to reimagine Alsace within France took place within the confines of two ideas that competed and interacted throughout the interwar years. The first was that Alsace

---

[3] ADBR 121AL 518 Le Lieutenant Colonel de Lavalette du Coetlosquet (President de la Commission de Delimitation) to M. le Directeur de l'Interieur, Strasbourg, 24 June 1922.

represented France's limits, and a frontier of Frenchness. The second was that it represented a point of cross-border contact, or a bridge across the Rhine. These ideas were important rhetorical tools, but they also reflected lived experience, as Alsatians lived alongside the boundary posts and border guards that offered a reminder that the Rhine marked the limits of French territory, while maintaining cultural and linguistic links across the border. Crucially, both ideas were based upon the premise that it was impossible to renegotiate Alsace's place within France without taking account of its relationship to Germany.

The notion of Alsace as a bridge fed into the idea that the region had a 'double culture' that drew upon French and German influences. This was articulated throughout the interwar years as a means of protecting Alsatian distinctiveness within the French nation, and of retaining economic, cultural, and social ties to Germany. Yet an understanding and acceptance of German influence in Alsace did not lead to endorsement of all that was German amongst the majority of the regional population. On the contrary, laws dating from the years of German rule were relabelled as 'local' or 'Alsatian' rather than 'German', the German language was treated as a local particularity, and the term '*boche*' became an insult that Alsatians turned upon each other. Crucially, the fact that the region remained a site of contact throughout reveals that the binary opposition that is frequently drawn between borders as 'limits' on the one hand and 'sites of contact' on the other is a false dichotomy. The sense of difference that resulted from cross-border contact did not preclude interaction. Quite the reverse, it informed it.

Nonetheless, not everyone viewed cross-border traffic in quite the same way, and we find fluid interpretations across time. Not only was it the case that at moments of tension Alsatians increasingly adopted the language of the boundary as a 'limit' (rather than a bridge), but border guards interpreted traffic in different ways at discrete moments. To take one example, whereas border crossings to go shopping or visit family were treated as a sign of peace at moments of détente in Franco-German relations, this changed when relations became more difficult. Then, they were viewed as potentially hostile and destabilizing. Thus in the tense atmosphere immediately following the end of the First World War those Germans who crossed into the region were treated as troublemakers, and after Hitler's seizure of power the *Contrôleur Général chargé des Affaires d'Alsace et de Lorraine* interpreted the increased number of crossings as a result of 'more spies, more political refugees and more smugglers'.[4] Through these means, the physical and imagined boundaries between the French and German nations arose together after 1918.

BORDERS, IDENTITIES, AND PROCESSES

All of this goes to show that people make borders. But it is also the case that borders shape identities. Living alongside the border (and its associated symbols) offered daily reminders of the French nation, while the context of return meant that the

---

[4] ADBR 286D 385 M. Le Contrôleur Général to M. le Préfet du Département du Bas-Rhin, Strasbourg, 26 August 1933.

nation acquired acute importance in daily life in Alsace. From political and economic debates to cultural life or the commemorative landscape, the actions and words of Alsatians were frequently read through the prism of national attachment. Equally, the experience of regime change also led to the reinforcement of existing social structures and frameworks smaller than the nation (most notably the region), and larger than the nation, such as the Catholic Church. As a result, the use of national language did not necessarily reflect attachment to France. Rather, it was the dominant and accepted language of power, and Alsatians juggled national attachment with a series of conversant, and occasionally competing, loyalties.

Crucially, Alsatians did not have the same definition of Frenchness as those administrators who arrived in the region with the aim of removing German influence. For Alsace, years of contact with Germany had led to a clear understanding of difference, and Alsatians attempted to distinguish between what was German and what was Alsatian. Part of the problem lay in the fact that local expressions of belonging were not consistent, and the range of attitudes displayed by the population and their political, economic, and religious representatives is suggestive of the competing sensibilities that interacted in negotiations over the region's place within the nation. Yet in spite of such differences, and in spite of the political, class-based, confessional, geographical, gendered, or linguistic fractures in the population, they were united in expressing a sense of Alsatian identity. In many ways this was a result of the experience of transfer of national regime and the crisis that this triggered. Indeed, this book has suggested that one impact of crisis is that it squeezed identities and their articulation, with the result that existing social structures were reinforced and Alsatians took refuge in their Alsatianness.

In addition to shaping identities, the border also shaped processes, and crucially the reintegration of Alsace into France cannot be understood without consideration of how it was affected by the border. The fact that Alsace had been recovered from (and now formed the border with) France's major continental rival guided the central French aim of removing German influence from the region. Continued Franco–German tension after 1918 overlaid the devastating impact of the First World War, whereby the centrality of the return of Alsace-Lorraine in France's war aims led to a perception of French sacrifice to secure the 'liberation' of the lost provinces. This increased the stakes in terms of reintegration, as a clash of expectations and misunderstandings developed rapidly. These problems were unexpected, and many of the arriving *Français de l'Intérieur* had trouble reconciling a region that had been presented as the epitome of Frenchness in the years since 1871 with the reality of the German-speaking region with strong attachments to regional particularities. The result was a clash that affected all areas of daily life, as Alsatians endeavoured to reimagine the region's future amidst concerns that their attempts to do so appeared to threaten the very unity of the French nation.[5]

There was unity in the ultimate aim of reimagining Alsace's position within France, and reconciling Alsace's connections to Germany. Yet this was expressed in different

---

[5] Marcel Nast, *Le Malaise Alsacien-Lorrain* (Paris, 1920).

ways, from the notions of the double culture to references to Napoleon's reported quote that it mattered little if the Alsatians spoke German, as long as they 'fought in French'.[6] Of course, how those in Alsace and the French interior attempted to reimagine the region's place within the boundaries of the nation evolved over time. Early efforts to present Alsace as a model for widespread national reform gradually gave way to efforts to retain regional particularities, and this reflects a general drift towards the prioritization of regional issues above all else across Alsatian life. This suggested increasing frustration with the narrow and rigid definition of Frenchness that Alsace encountered after 1918, and the French tendency to label any ideas or activities that did not fit existing ideas about centralization as 'anti-national' or 'pro-German'. This binary view reflected failings in accommodating regional particularity and a growing stress upon race in the late Third Republic, and clashed with Alsatian expressions of loyalty and attachment which were not consistent, and might be best understood as positions on a spectrum.

What is more, interventions into the debates about Alsace's future did not come only from Alsace and the French interior; they also came from Germany as the press, nationalist politicians, research institutes, and historians all commented on French treatment of the region or made a case for its historic connections to the German lands. These debates took place in the context of ideas about national self-determination and minorities that proliferated after Versailles, and took shape within this international context. National integration in this case, therefore, was not a two-way interaction between centre and periphery, as neither Paris nor Alsace were united in their ideas about the region's future, and as the debate was not restricted to within France's borders. Instead, Alsace's return to France was shaped through cross-border interactions, and the periphery emerges as a motive force in the creation of the French nation, which must be understood as a fluid process. Borderland populations helped to forge the nation through their grass-roots encounters, just as diplomats, political actors, and cultural intermediaries negotiated the limits of state power, competed with each other, and imitated and reflected developments in rival nations.

ENTANGLED HISTORIES AND THE PARADOX OF ALSACE

Just as recent work on transnational history has stressed the importance of taking account of the multiple scales of past existence (the transnational, the national, the local), this story is impossible to tell without taking account of the various 'scales' that shaped Alsatian life. Cross-border flows of visitors, shoppers, migrants, goods, and ideas coexisted in a region with an acute and well-developed sense of local identity where everyone adopted national rhetoric. Yet such impulses were not contradictory. On the contrary, they were entangled and motivated each other. Thus, to return to the example of autonomism, the movement emerged in order to

---

[6] *Pneu Michelin Guide Régional Alsace de Strasbourg à Mulhouse Hautes Vosges* (Paris, 1935–6).

protect local rights and sensibilities, but was fuelled by both German money and the French authorities' concerns that it was a German import. In turn, these dual impulses affected how the autonomists described themselves, and how other Alsatians responded to their ideas about integration. In this way the local, national, and transnational became enmeshed and affected the development of each other. And as we have seen, not all transnational contact was positive; it could equally take the form of conflict, while misunderstandings and misinterpretations could arise from actors coming from distinct national contexts. Such interaction between these distinct scales was not unique to Alsace. But while it reflected broader realities, they were particularly exposed in the Alsatian case as a result of the region's borderland position.

Given these multiple and contradictory impulses, this book argues that neither national attachment nor nations can be viewed as having been formed in isolation. In this way, this book builds upon literature that has stressed the importance of national rivalries and the emergence of a sense of self-differentiation in the creation of understandings of nationhood and national identity.[7] It also builds upon the studies of modern Europe that have stressed the crucial role played by regional populations in filtering, interpreting, and building a sense of nationhood in peripheral regions, and upon literature that has suggested that borders represent sites of contact more than they represent limits.[8] Yet its aim has not been to simply join up the dots of histories of national integration in Europe. In seeking to understand the forms that contact took and the dynamics of these processes, it has underlined the implications of cross-border contact. This contact, this book argues, bred both transnational understandings and a clear sense of difference, with the result that the border was built through cross-border contact, whether encounters, transgressions, or border rhetoric. Of course, this sense of difference did not only lead to conflict; it also contributed to better understandings and cohabitation.

Through cross-border contact, the interwar Franco–German border became a meaningful division between two communities who shared a language, culture, and recent history. And in doing so, the border contributed to Alsatian identities within France. Yet just as the border shaped people, it also shaped processes. Indeed, its influence upon the return of Alsace to France meant that cross-border encounters helped to build the French nation, contributing to France's heterogeneity and to the subjectivity of its citizens. Meanwhile, the French government's problems in coming to terms with Alsatian particularities reveal just how difficult its operating assumptions could be for its regional populations, as well as the

---

[7] Peter Sahlins, *Boundaries: The Making of France and Spain in the Pyrenees* (Berkeley, 1989); Linda Colley, *Britons: Forging the Nation, 1707–1837* (New Haven, 1992).

[8] Caroline Ford, *Creating the Nation in Provincial France: Religion and Political Identity in Brittany* (Princeton, 1993); Timothy Baycroft, *Culture, Identity and Nationalism: French Flanders in the Nineteenth and Twentieth Centuries* (Woodbridge, 2004); Abigail Green, *Fatherlands: State-Building and Nationhood in Nineteenth Century Germany* (Cambridge, 2001); Alon Confino, *The Nation as a Local Metaphor: Württemberg, Imperial Germany and National Memory, 1871–1918* (London, 1997); Celia Applegate, *A Nation of Provincials: The German Idea of Heimat* (Oxford, 1990); Patrick Young, *Enacting Brittany: Tourism and Culture in Provincial France, 1871–1939* (Farnham, 2012).

insecurities of the regime itself. In spite of the government's concerns, Alsatian attempts to renegotiate the region's place within France were informed by their connections to Germany, and by a clearly defined sense of difference between Alsace and its neighbours across the Rhine. The resulting negotiation between the transnationality that defined daily life and the region's status as symbol of the nation's territorial limits was the paradox of the Alsatian borderland.

Bibliography

ARCHIVAL SOURCES

Archives Départementales du Bas-Rhin (ADBR)
98AL 326–340: Education
98AL 614–624: Language
98AL 626: Cultural Affairs
98AL 634–6, 661, 673/2, 683, 684/1: Politics
98AL 1064–1076/2: Elections
98AL 1083 2: Press
98AL 1280: Unions
121AL 1, 20, 33: General Commission
121AL 44: Cartography in Alsace-Lorraine
121AL 93: Finance
121AL 94–5: Churches
121AL 99–100: Presidential and Ministerial Visits
121AL 102–3: Political parties and public opinion
121AL 156: The Economy
121AL 158: Religion and Language
121AL 162: Press
121AL 186: French-language theatre
121AL 198–9: Commissioners of the Republic
121AL 204: Administration of Alsace-Lorraine
121AL 205: Senate Commission for Alsace-Lorraine
121AL 206–7: Legislative Reintegration
121AL 394–5: Border Fortifications
121AL 518–525: Border Regime
121AL 547–562: Elections
121AL 579: Festivals
121AL 583–4: Monuments
121AL 740: Municipal Law of 1884
121AL 770: Denomination des rues
121AL 855–7: Rapports de Police
121AL 878–882: Trade Unions
121 899–908: Commissions de triage
121AL 1059: Language and Education
121AL 1091–2: Monuments
121AL 1105: Railways
121AL 1256: Potash
121AL 1260–1: Wine
286D 100–102: Maginot Line
286D 160–1: Border Circulation
286D 174: Livrets de Famille
286D 325–341: The Press
286D 343–349: Elections

286D 353–4: Socialist Party
286D 385: Border Incidents
286D 44: Relations with mayors
286D 46–47: Bilingualism

Archives Municipales de la Ville et de l'Eurométropole de Strasbourg (AMVES)
1AFF: Posters
81Z 29, 37, 39: Archives Hugo Haug
113Z 29–30, 43, 48: Archives Eugène Muller
125Z 15–64: Archives Jacques Peirotes
1MW: Minutes of the Municipal Council of the Town of Strasbourg, 1919–39
151MW 68–69: Unemployment
154MW 32, 34–37, 53–55, 58, 60, 61–63, 67: Monuments
155MW: Street names
204MW 15–18: Municipal Law/Local Law
204MW 25: Association of Mayors of France
204MW 34–35: Conference of Mayors of Alsace-Lorraine
204MW 71–79: Minutes of the Commissions of the Municipal Council
204MW 193: Winter works
234MW 131–136: Festivals
234MW 168: Meiselocker Monument
234MW 295–298: Colonial Exhibition
234MW 341–345: Diverse Exhibitions

Archives Nationales de France (AN)
313 AP 225: Archives Paul Painlevé
470 AP 44: Archives Alexandre Millerand
485 AP: Archives Henri Cacaud
AJ30 170: Reports of the Haut Commissaire de la République
AJ30 171–4: Conseil Consultative
AJ30 204–8: Education
AJ30 223: Pasteur Exhibition
AJ30 232–234: Elections
C14640, C14849, C14877, C14952, C14982, C15209: Commission of Alsace-Lorraine
F7 12567–12571, 12726, 12933: (Police Général) Border situation
F7 12751–12755: (Police Général) The economic and social situation in the Bas-Rhin and the Haut-Rhin
F7 13014: (Police Général) The political situation in the Bas-Rhin and the Haut-Rhin
F7 13028, F7 13040: (Police Général) Reports of the Prefect of the Bas-Rhin
F7 13261, 13404: (Police Général) Elections
F7 13377–13394: (Police Général) Political Situation Alsace-Lorraine
F7 13527, 13528, 13540, 13550, 13556, 13561: (Police Général) Unemployment
F7 14614: (Police Général) The separation of Church and state
F7 14841: (Police Général) Drug Trafficking
F7 15990: Fonds Panthéon (Jacques Peirotes)
F715961–F715963: Fonds Panthéon (Salomon Grumbach)

The National Archives, Kew (TNA)
FO371: Foreign Office General Correspondence

Archives Départementales du Haut-Rhin (ADHR)
8AL 200578-200580-200590: Electoral Materials, 1919–36

Office Universitaire de Recherche Socialiste (OURS)
Fonds SFIO 41, Liste 1, Dossier 21–23: Correspondence with SFIO Women's Sections of the Bas-Rhin and the Haut-Rhin

Archives Municipales de Mulhouse (AMM)
Aa10: Elections of the Mayors of the Town of Mulhouse, 1901–35
D1a1- 1925–39: Minutes of the Municipal Council
D1 a2: Resolutions of the Municipal Council
D111 Cb1-3: Municipal commissions, 1924–34
1Q 149–149b, 164: Unemployment
40TT 1–11: Fonds Jean Martin
4Q 17: Office for *Habitation à Bon Marché*

Archives Municipales de Colmar (AMC)
Minutes of the Meetings of the Municipal Council of the Town of Colmar, 1919–39
CM 30-31-33-35-38-42-46-63-66 Town of Colmar. Discussions of the Municipal Council
00 43 1 *Office Public de l'Habitation à Bon Marché*
00 144 1 Motions and Resolutions of the Municipal Council
08 40 2–3, 08 41 5–6 Festivals (14 July, 11 November, Joan of Arc)
50 10-11/1-11/2 Hygiene Office
66 5/762- Street names

NEWSPAPERS

Das Mulhäuser Volksblatt
Der Elsässer
Der Elsässer Bote
Der Republikaner
Die Freie Presse.
Die Lothringer Volkszeitung
Elsässer Kurier
L'Ami du peuple
L'Echo du Rhin du samedi
L'Ère Nouvelle
L'Evénement
L'Excelsior
L'Express
L'Express de Mulhouse
L'Humanité
La France de l'Est
La République
Le Courrier de Strasbourg
Le Figaro
Le Journal d'Alsace et de Lorraine
Le Journal de l'Est
Le Journal de Mulhouse

Le Nouveau Rhin Français
Le Petit Parisien
Le Quotidien
Le Temps
Les Dernières Nouvelles de Strasbourg
The Daily News
The New York Times

PRINTED PRIMARY SOURCES

Activité du Conseil Municipal et de l'Administration de la Ville de Strasbourg, 1925–1929, Bureau Municipal de Statistique (Strasbourg, 1929).

Bazin, René, *Les Oberlé* (Paris, 1901).

Boissiere, Emile, *Vingt ans à Mulhouse, 1855–1875* (Macon, 1876).

Bruno, G., *Le Tour de la France par deux enfants* (Paris, 1877).

Chambre des Députes, *Journal Officiel*, 1925.

Comité alsacien d'études et d'informations, *L'Alsace depuis son retour à la France*. 3 vols (Strasbourg, 1932).

Comité alsacien d'études et d'informations, *L'Alsace depuis son retour à la France. Premier supplement: Vie politique administrative et sociale; Vie intellectuelle; artisistique et spirituelle; Vie economique* (Strasbourg, 1937).

Compte rendu de l'administration de la ville de Strasbourg 1919–1935 (Strasbourg, 1935).

Daudet, Alphonse, *La dernière classe. Récit d'un petit Alsacien* (Paris, 1873).

Demangeon, Albert and Febvre, Lucien, *Le Rhin. Problemes d'Histoire et d'Economie* (Paris, 1935).

Dix Années d'activité municipale, 1925–1935, Ville de Mulhouse, Haut-Rhin (imprimerie Union Mulhouse, 1935).

Grimm, Johann Friedrich Carl, *Bemerkungen eines Reisenden durch Deutschland, Frankreich, England und Holland in Briefen an seine Freunde*, 3 vols (Altenburg, 1775).

Hugo, Victor, *Le Rhin. Lettres à un ami.* 2 vols, vol. 1 (Paris, 1912).

Husser, Philippe, *Un Instituteur Alsacien. Entre France et Allemagne. Le Journal de Philippe Husser, 1914–1951* (Paris, 1989).

Jullian, Camille, *Le Rhin Gaulois: le Rhin français* (Paris, 1915).

L'œuvre sociale de la Ville de Mulhous (Mulhouse, 1931).

Lambert, Charles, *La France et ses étrangers* (Paris, 1928).

Laugel, Anselme, *Costumes et coutumes d'Alsace*, (Colmar and Nancy, 2008; 1st edn 1902).

Le Rhin dans l'histoire, 2 vols (Paris, 1917).

Libmann, Jean, *Mes Mémoires, Chronique d'une famille en marge de l'histoire* (Strasbourg, 1989).

Manifeste du Heimatbund (Strasbourg, 1926).

Mauco, Georges, *Les Etrangers en France. Leur rôle dans l'activité économique* (Paris, 1932).

Meinecke, Friedrich, *Straßburg, Freiburg, Berlin. Erinnerungen 1901–1919* (Berlin, 1949).

Millerand, Alexandre, *Le retour de l'Alsace-Lorraine à la France* (Strasbourg, 1923).

Moeder, Marcel, *Notes sur l'industrie de Mulhouse et de ses environs* (Mulhouse, 1923).

Nast, Marcel, *Le Malaise Alsacien-Lorrain* (Paris, 1920).

Paira, René, *Affaires d'Alsace, Souvenirs d'un préfet* (Strasbourg, 1990).

Parti Socialiste: Section Française de l'International Ouvrière. XXVe Congrès National, tenu à Toulouse, les 26, 27, 28 et 29 mai 1928. Compte Rendu Sténographique (Limoges, 1928).

Pluyette, Jean, *La Doctrine des races et la sélection de l'immigration en France* (Paris, 1930).

Pneu Michelin Guide Régional Alsace de Strasbourg à Mulhouse Hautes Vosges (Paris, 1935–6).

Redslob, Robert, *Entre la France et l'Allemagne. Souvenirs d'un Alsacien* (Paris, 1933).

Renan, Ernest, *Qu'est-ce que c'est une nation? Conférence faite en Sorbonne le 11 mars 1882*, 2nd edn (Paris, 1892).

Roche, Sophie von La, *Journal einer Reise durch Frankreich* (Altenburg, 1787).

Rossé, J., Stürmel, M., Bleicher, A., Deiber, F., and Keppi, J. *Das Elsass von 1870–1932*, 4 vols (Colmar, 1936–38), vol. 4.

Rousseau, Jean-Jacques, 'Extrait du projet du paix perpétuelle de l'Abbé de Saint Pierre [1756]', in C. E. Vaughn (ed.) *The Political Writings of Jean-Jacques Rousseau* (Cambridge, 1915).

Société pour le développement des jardins ouvriers, Congrès Fédéral et exposition, Colmar, 9 September 1928, Salle des Catherinettes.

Sorel, A. and Funck-Brentano, T., *Précis du Droit des gens* (Paris, 1887).

Spindler, Charles, *L'âge d'or d'un artiste en Alsace. Mémoires inédits 1889–1914* (Colmar and Nancy, 2009).

Une génération d'activité municipal (Mulhouse, 1947).

Young, Arthur, *Arthur Young's travels in France during the years 1787, 1788, 1789* (New York, 1906).

Zeller, Gaston, 'Histoire d'une idée fausse', *Revue de Synthèse*, 56, 2 (1936), pp. 115–32.

SECONDARY SOURCES

Agulhon, Maurice, 'La «statuomanie» et l'histoire', *Ethnologie Française*, 8: 2/3 (1978), pp. 145–72.

Agulhon, Maurice, *Marianne into Battle: Republican Imagery and Symbolism in France, 1789–1880* (Cambridge, 1981).

Agulhon, Maurice, 'La statuomanie et l'histoire', *Histoire vagabonde*, 3 vols (Paris, 1988–96).

Altink, Henrice and Gemie, Sharif (eds), *At The Border: Margins And Peripheries In Modern France* (Cardiff, 2008).

Anderson, Benedict, *Imagined Communities: Reflections on the Origin and Spread of Nationalism* (London, 1983).

Anderson, Malcolm, 'Regional Identity and Political Change: the Case of Alsace from the Third to the Fifth Republic', *Political Studies*, 20 (1972), pp. 17–30.

Applegate, Celia, *A Nation of Provincials: The German Idea of Heimat* (Oxford, 1990).

Audoin-Rouzeau, Stéphane and Becker, Annette, *14–18: Understanding the Great War* (London, 2002).

Baas, Genevieve, *Le malaise alsacien, 1919–1924* (Strasbourg, 1972).

Baechler, Christian, *Le Parti Catholique Alsacien 1890–1939: Du Reichsland à la République Jacobine* (Strasbourg, 1982).

Baechler, Christian, 'Le Clergé Catholique alsacien et la politique, 1871–1939', *Revue d'Alsace*, 111 (1985), pp. 125–48.

Baechler, Christian, 'Espoirs et désillusions: l'entre-deux-guerres et l'occupation nazie (1918–1944)', in Georges Livet and François Rapp (eds), *Histoire de Strasbourg* (Toulouse, 1987).

Baechler, Christian (ed.), *Alfred Oberkirch 1876–1947. Un médecin alsacien dans la tourmente politique* (Strasbourg, 1990).

Baechler, Christian, 'L'autonomisme alsacien entre les deux guerres', *Historiens et Géographes*, 347 (1995), pp. 249–55.

Baechler, Christian, *Clergé Catholique et Politique en Alsace, 1871–1940* (Strasbourg, 2013).

Bankwitz, Philip Charles Fairwell, *Alsatian Autonomist Leaders. 1919–1947* (Kansas, 1978).

Baud, Michel and van Schendel, Willem, 'Toward a Comparative History of Borderlands', *Journal of World History*, 8 (1997), pp. 211–42.

Baycroft, Timothy, *Nationalism in Europe, 1789–1945* (Cambridge, 1998).

Baycroft, Timothy, 'Changing Identities in the Franco-Belgian Borderland in the Nineteenth and Twentieth Centuries', *French History*, 13:4 (1999), pp. 417–38.

Baycroft, Timothy, *Culture, Identity and Nationalism. French Flanders in the Nineteenth and Twentieth Centuries* (Woodbridge, 2004).

Baycroft, Timothy, *France. Inventing the Nation* (London, 2008).

Baycroft, Timothy and Hewitson, Mark, *What is a Nation? Europe 1789–1914* (Oxford, 2006).

Bayly, C.A. et al., 'AHR Conversation: on transnational history', *American Historical Review*, 111: 5 (2006), pp. 1441–64.

Becker, Jean-Jacques and Berstein, Serge, *Victoire et frustrations 1914–1929* (Paris, 1990).

Bell, David A., 'Nation Building and Cultural Particularism in Eighteenth Century France: The Case of Alsace', *Eighteenth Century Studies*, 21:4 (1988), pp. 472–90.

Bell, David A., 'Lingua Populi, Lingua Dei: Language, Religion, and the Origins of French Revolutionary Nationalism', *American Historical Review*, 100 (1995), pp. 1403–37.

Bell, David A., *The Cult of the Nation in France. Inventing Nationalism, 1680–1800* (Cambridge, MA, 2001).

Berdahl, Daphne, *Where the World Ended. Reunification and Identity in the German Borderland* (Berkeley, 1999).

Berstein, Serge, 'Le Parti radical et le problème du centralisme (1870–1939)', in Christian Gras and Georges Livet (eds), *Régions et régionalisme en France du XVIIIe siècle à nos jours*, (Vendôme, 1977), pp. 225–40.

Best, Janice, *Les Monuments de Paris sous la Troisième République: Contestation et commémoration du passé* (Paris, 2010).

Bischoff, Georges, 'L'invention de l'Alsace', *Saisons d'Alsace*, 119 (1993), pp. 35–70.

Bjork, James E., *Neither German nor Pole. Catholicism and National Indifference in a Central European Borderland* (Michigan, 2008).

Blackbourn, David and Retallack, James (eds), *Localism, landscape and the ambiguities of place: German-speaking central Europe, 1860–1930* (Toronto, Buffalo, and London, 2007).

Bloch, Marc, 'Pour une histoire comparée des sociétés européenes', in Bloch, *Mélanges historiques*, 2 vols, (Paris, 1963).

Boswell, Laird, 'Franco-Alsatian Conflict and the Crisis of National Sentiment during the Phoney War', *Journal of Modern History*, 71 (1999), pp. 552–84.

Boswell, Laird, 'From Liberation to Purge Trials in the "Mythic Provinces": Recasting French Identities in Alsace and Lorraine, 1918–1920', *French Historical Studies*, 23:1 (2000), pp. 129–62.

Boswell, Laird, 'Rethinking the Nation at the Periphery', *French Politics, Culture & Society*, 27 (2009), pp. 111–26.

Bouhet, Agnès, 'L'Affaire Saverne: Novembre 1913-Janvier 1914 (Un exemple de conditionnement international indirect)', *Guerres mondiales et conflits contemporains*, 173 (1994), pp. 5–17.

Boyce, Robert, *The Great Interwar Crisis and the Collapse of Globalisation* (Basingstoke, 2009).

Bracke, Maud Anne and Mark (eds), 'Between Decolonization and the Cold War: Transnational Activism and its Limits in Europe, 1950s–90s', *Special Issue of the Journal of Contemporary History,* 50:3 (2015).

Braudel, Fernand, *La Méditerranée et le monde méditerranéen à l'époque de Philippe II* (Paris, 1949).

Breuilly, John, *Nationalism and the State,* (Manchester, 1982).

Broch, Ludivine and Carrol, Alison (eds), *France in an Era of Global War 1914–1945: Occupation, Politics, Empire and Entanglements* (Basingstoke, 2015).

Brubaker, Rogers, *Citizenship and Nationhood in France and Germany,* (Cambridge, MA, 1992).

Burgess, Greg, 'The Foreign Presence in the early-industrial Haut-Rhin, 1820-22: a short history from the pre-history of immigration to France', *French History,* 28 (2014), pp. 366–84.

Burke, Peter, *The French Historical Revolution: The Annales School, 1929–1989* (Stanford, 1990).

Cabo, Miguel and Molina, Fernando, 'The Long and Winding Road of Nationalization: Eugen Weber's Peasants into Frenchmen in Modern European History', *European History Quarterly,* 39 (2009), pp. 264–86.

Camiscoli, Elisa, *Reproducing the French Race: Immigration, Intimacy and Embodiment in the Early Twentieth Century* (Durham and London, 2009).

Caplan, Jane (ed.), *Nazi Germany* (Oxford, 2008).

Caron, Vicki, *Between France and Germany. The Jews of Alsace-Lorraine, 1871–1918* (Stanford, 1988).

Caron, Vicki, 'The anti-Semitic revival in France in the 1930s: the Socio-Economic Dimension reconsidered', *Journal of Modern History,* 70 (1998), pp. 24–73.

Carr, E. H. *Twenty Years Crisis. An Introduction to the Study of International Relations* (Basingstoke, 2001).

Carrol, Alison, 'Regional Republicans: The Alsatian Socialists and the Politics of Primary Schooling in Alsace, 1918–1939', *French Historical Studies,* 32:2 (2011), pp. 299–325.

Carrol, Alison, 'Les anglophones et l'Alsace: une fascination durable', *Revue d'Alsace,* 138 (2012), pp. 265–83.

Carrol, Alison, 'The Socialist Party and the Return of Alsace to France', in Brian Sudlow (ed.), *National Identities in France* (Rutgers, 2012), pp. 47–64.

Carrol, Alison, 'In the Border's Shadow: Reimagining Urban Spaces in Strasbourg, 1918–39', *Journal of Contemporary History,* 48 (2013), pp. 666–87.

Carrol, Alison and Zanoun, Louisa, 'The View from the Border. A Comparative Study of Autonomism in Alsace and the Moselle, 1918–1929' *European Review of History,* 18:4 (2011), pp. 465–86.

Chanet, Jean-François, *L'Ecole Républicaine et les petites patries, 1879–1940* (Paris, 1990).

Chapman, Herrick and Frader, Laura L. (eds), *Race in France: Interdisciplinary Perspectives on the Politics of Difference* (New York, 2004).

Chrastil, Rachel, *The Siege of Strasbourg* (Cambridge, MA, 2014).

Cioc, Marc, *The Rhine: An Eco-Biography, 1815–2000* (Seattle, 2002).

Cointet, Jean-Paul, *Pierre Laval* (Paris, 1993).

Colley, Linda, *Britons: Forging the Nation, 1707–1837* (New Haven, 1992).

Confino, Alon, *The Nation as a Local Metaphor: Württemberg, Imperial Germany and National Memory, 1871–1918* (London, 1997).

Conklin, Alice, *A Mission to Civilize: The Republican Idea of Empire in France and West Africa, 1895–1930* (Stanford, 1997).

Conway, Martin, *Catholic Parties in Europe, 1918–1945* (London, 1997).

Corbin, Alain, *Archaïsme et modernité en Limousin au XIX siècle*, 2 vols (Paris, 1975).

Corbin, Alain, *Le territoire du vide. L'Occident et le désir du rivage, 1750–1840* (Paris, 1988).

Corbin, Alain, *L'homme dans le paysage* (Paris, 2001).

Cosgrove, Dennis E., *Social Formation and Symbolic Landscape* (Madison, WI, 1998).

Craig, John E., *Scholarship and Nation Building. The Universities of Strasbourg and Alsatian Society, 1870–1939* (Chicago, 1984).

Curthoys, Ann and Lake, Marilyn (eds), *Connected worlds: History in transnational perspective* (Canberra, 2005).

Demangeon, Albert and Febvre, Lucien, *Le Rhin. Problèmes d'Histoire et d'Economie* (Paris, 1935).

Donnan, Hastings and Wilson, Thomas, *Border Identities. Nation and State at International Frontiers* (Cambridge, 1998).

Dontenwille-Gerbaud, Aude, 'La ligne bleue des Vosges', *Mots. Languages du Politique*, 105 (2014), pp. 13–26.

Dreyfus, François G., 'Les socialismes en Alsace de 1912 à 1962', *Bulletin de la Faculté des Lettres de Strasbourg*, 44:1 (1965): pp. 511–34.

Dreyfus, François G., *La vie politique en Alsace, 1919–1936* (Paris, 1969).

Dreyfus, François G., *Histoire de l'Alsace* (Paris, 1979).

Dunlop, Catherine Tatiana, *Cartophilia. Maps and the Search for Identity in the French-German Borderland* (Chicago, 2015).

Dutton, Paul V., 'French versus German approaches to Family Welfare in Lorraine, 1918–1940', *French History*, 13 (1999), pp. 439–63.

Dutton, Paul V., *Origins of the French Welfare State. The Struggle for Social Reform in France, 1914–1947* (Cambridge, 2002)

Edelstein, Melvin, 'Aux Urnes Citoyens! The Transformation of French Electoral Participation 1789–1870', in Gail M. Schwab and John R. Jeanneney (eds), *The French Revolution of 1789 and its Impact* (Westport, 1995).

Espagne, Michel, 'Sur les limites du comparatisme en histoire culturelle', *Genèse*, 17 (1994), pp. 112–21.

Evans, Richard J., *The Coming of the Third Reich* (London, 2003).

Fahrmeir, Andreas, *Citizens and Aliens: Foreigners and the Law in Britain and the German States, 1789–1870* (New York, 2000).

Fischer, Christopher J., *Alsace to the Alsatians? Visions and Divisions of Alsatian Regionalism, 1870–1939* (New York and Oxford, 2010).

Fischer, Conan, 'The Failed European Union: Franco-German Relations during the Great Depression of 1929–32', *International History Review*, 34:4 (2012), pp. 705–24.

Fischer, Fabienne, *Alsaciens et Lorrains en Algérie. Histoire d'une migration, 1830–1914* (Nice, 1998).

Fix, Albert, *100 Ans de Politique de l'Habitat. L'Office du Logement de la Ville de Strasbourg* (Obernai, 1978).

Flohic, Jean-Luc (ed.), *Collection Le Patrimoine des Communes de France: Bas-Rhin* (Paris, 1999).

Flohic, Jean-Luc (ed.), *Collection Le Patrimoine des Communes de France: Haut-Rhin* (Paris, 1999).

Ford, Caroline, *Creating the Nation in Provincial France: Religion and Political Identity in Brittany* (Princeton, 1993).

Ford, Caroline, 'Nature's Fortunes: New Directions in the Writing of European Environmental History', *Journal of Modern History*, 79 (2007), pp. 112–33.

Gellner, Ernest, *Nations and Nationalism* (Oxford, 1983).

Gemie, Sharif, *Brittany 1750–1950: The Invisible Nation* (Cardiff, 2007).

Gibbs, N. H., *Grand Strategy* (London, 1976), p. 43.

Gildea, Robert and Tompkins, Andrew, 'The Transnational in the Local: The Larzac as a site of Transnational Activism since 1970', *Journal of Contemporary History,* 50:3 (2015), pp. 581–605.

Goodfellow, Samuel Huston, *Between the Swastika and the Cross of Lorraine, Fascisms in Interwar Alsace* (DeKalb, 1999).

Graham, Helen, *The Spanish Civil War. A Very Short Introduction* (Oxford, 2005).

Gras, Solange, 'La presse francaise et l'autonomisme alsacien en 1926', in Christian Gras and Georges Livet (eds), *Régions et régionalisme en France du XVIIIe siècle à nos jours,* (Presses Universitaires de France: Vendôme, 1977), pp. 337–61.

Green, Abigail, *Fatherlands: State- Building and Nationhood in Nineteenth Century Germany* (Cambridge, 2001).

Green, Nancy, 'French History and the Transnational Turn', *French Historical Studies,* 37: 4 (2014), pp. 551–64.

Grohmann, Carolyn, 'From Lothringen to Lorraine: Expulsion and Voluntary Repatriation', *Diplomacy and Statecraft,* 16 (2005), pp. 571–87.

Grünewald, Irmgard, *Die Elsass-Lothringer im Reich, 1918–1933* (Frankfurt, 1984).

Harp, Stephen L., *Learning to be Loyal. Primary Schooling as Nation Building in Alsace and Lorraine, 1850–1940* (Illinois, 1998).

Harp, Stephen L., *Marketing Michelin: Advertising and Cultural Identity in Twentieth Century France* (Baltimore, 2001).

Harvey, David Allen, 'Lost Children or Enemy Aliens? Classifying the Population of Alsace after the First World War', *Journal of Contemporary History,* 71:3, (1999), pp. 552–84.

Harvey, David Allen, *Constructing Class and Nationality in Alsace, 1830–1945* (DeKalb, 2001).

Hastings, Adrian, *The Construction of Nationhood: Ethnicity, Religion and Nationalism* (Cambridge, 1997).

Hau, Michel and Stoskopf, Nicolas, *Les dynasties alsaciennes du XVIème siècle à nos jours* (Paris, 2005).

Hobsbawm, Eric, *Nations and nationalism since 1780. Programme, myth, reality* (Cambridge, 1990).

Hobsbawm, Eric and Ranger, Terence (eds), *The Invention of Tradition* (Cambridge, 1983).

Höpel, Thomas, 'The French-German Borderlands: Borderlands and Nation-Building in the 19th and 20th Centuries', *European History Online* (August 2012).

Horne, John, 'Demobilizing the Mind: France and the Legacy of the Great War, 1919–1939', *French history and civilization: papers from the George Rudé Seminar* (2009), pp. 101–19.

Hoskins, W. G., *The Making of the English Landscape,* (London, 1955).

Howard, Sarah, *Les images de l'alcool en France entre 1915 et 1945* (Paris, 2006).

Huck, Dominique, 'Le "Théâtre Alsacien de Strasbourg" et la production dramatique de ses fondateurs (1898–1914)', in Jeanne Benay and Jean-March Leveratto, *Culture et Histoire des spectacles en Alsace et en Lorraine: de l'annexion à la decentralisation (1871–1946)* (Berne, 2005), pp. 197–222.

Hyman, Paula E., 'Citizenship. Regionalism and Identity. The Case of Alsatian Jewry, 1871–1914', in Judith Frishman, David J. Wertheim, Ido de Haan, and Joël Cahen (eds), *Borders and Boundaries in and Around Dutch History* (Amsterdam, 2011).

Igersheim, François, *Politique et Administration dans le Bas-Rhin, 1848–1870* (Strasbourg, 1993).

Jackson, Julian, *The Popular Front in France: Defending Democracy 1934–1938* (Cambridge, 1998).

Jackson, Peter, *Beyond the Balance of Power. France and the Politics of National Security in the Era of the First World War* (Cambridge, 2013).

Jeanneney, Jean-Noël, *Leçon d'histoire pour une gauche au pouvoir. La faillite du Cartel 1924–1926* (Paris, 1977).

Jenkins, Brian and Millington, Chris, *France and Fascism. February 1934 and the Dynamics of Political Crisis* (Oxford, 2015).

Jenkins, Richard, *Social Identity* (Oxford, 2004).

Jonas, Stéphane, 'La Politique Urbain et du Logement de Jacques Peirotes, Député-Maire Socialiste de Strasbourg', *Revue des Sciences Sociales de la France de l'Est*, 15 (1986–7), pp. 143–9.

Jonas, Stéphane, 'Les Jardins d'Ungemach à Strasbourg: une Cité-Jardin d'origine nataliste, 1923–1950', in Paulette Girard and Bruno Lussac Fayolle, *Cités, Cités-Jardins: Une Histoire Européenne* (Talence, 1996).

Judson, Pieter M., *Guardians of the Nation. Activists on the Language Frontier of Imperial Austria* (Harvard, MA, 2006).

Judt, Tony, *Socialism in Provence, 1871–1914. A Study in the Origins of the Modern French Left* (Cambridge, 1979).

Kaiser, Wolfram, *Christian Democracy and the Origins of European Union*, (Cambridge, 2007).

Kalman, Samuel, *The Extreme Right in Interwar France: The Faisceau and the Croix de Feu* (Aldershot, 2008).

Kedward, Rod, *La Vie en Bleu. France and the French since 1900* (London, 2005).

Keiflin, Claude, *L'été 36 en Alsace* (Strasbourg, 1996).

Keiger, J. F. V. *Raymond Poincaré* (Cambridge, 1997).

Keiger, J. F. V., *France and the World since 1870* (London, 2001).

Keller, Richard, 'À l'atelier, à l'usine, au bureau', in Bernard Vogler (ed.), *Chroniques d'Alsace 1918–1939* (Barcelona, 2004).

Keller, Richard, 'L'Alsace Rurale: Un monde inchangé', in Bernard Vogler (ed.), *Chroniques d'Alsace 1918–1939* (Barcelona, 2004).

Kennedy, Sean, *Reconciling France Against Democracy: The Croix de Feu and the Parti Social Français, 1929–1935* (Montreal, 2007).

King, Jeremy, *Budweisers into Czechs and Germans: A Local History of Bohemian Politics, 1848–1948* (Princeton, NJ, 2005).

Kintz, Jean-Pierre, 'Vers une autre économie et une autre société', in Philippe Dollinger (ed.), *L'histoire de l'Alsace de 1900 à nos jours* (Toulouse, 1979).

Klein, Detmar, 'The Virgin with the Sword. Marian Apparitions, Religion and National Identity in Alsace in the 1870s', *French History*, 21: 4 (2007), pp. 411–30.

Klein, Detmar, 'Folklore as a Weapon: National Identity in German Annexed Alsace, 1890–1914', in Timothy Baycroft and David Hopkin (eds), *Folklore and Nationalism in Europe during the Long Nineteenth Century* (Brill, 2012), pp. 161–91.

Kovar, Jean-François, 'Religion et Éducation: De la concorde à la discorde', in Bernard Vogler (ed.), *Chroniques d'Alsace 1918–1939* (Barcelona, 2004).

Kramer, Alan, 'Wackes at War: Alsace-Lorraine and the Failure of German national mobilization, 1914–1918', in John Horne (ed.), *State, Society and Mobilisation in Europe During the First World War* (Cambridge, 1997), pp. 105–21.

Kurlander, Eric, *The Price of Exclusion. Ethnicity, National Identity and the Decline of German Liberalism, 1918–1933* (New York and Oxford, 2006).

'La direction générale du travail, de la législation ouvrière et des assurances sociales au commissariat général d'Alsace-Lorraine: laboratoire du droit social (1919–1925)', *Les Cahiers du Comité d'Histoire*, Colloque organisé sous la responsabilité scientifique de Jeanne-Marie Tuffery-Andrieu le 11 décembre 2009.

Lanzoni, Rémi Fournier, *French Cinema: From its Beginnings to the Present* (New York, 2002).

Laven, David and Baycroft, Timothy, 'Border Regions and Identity', *European Review of History–Revue Européenne d'histoire*, 15 (2008), pp. 255–75.

Lees, Andrew and Lees, Lynn Hollen, *Cities and the Making of Modern Europe, 1750–1914* (Cambridge, 2007).

Lekan, Thomas, *Imagining the Nation in Nature: Landscape Preservation and German Identity, 1885–1945* (Cambridge, MA, 2004).

Lewis, Mary Dewhurst, *The Boundaries of the Republic: Migrant Rights and the Limits of Universalism in France, 1918–1940* (Stanford, CA., 2007).

L'Huillier, Fernand, 'Remarques sur les grèves de 1920 et de 1936 en Alsace', *Bulletin de la Societe d'Histoire Moderne*, 3 (1972), pp. 9–17.

Lidtke, Vernon, *The Outlawed Party: Social Democracy in Germany, 1878–1890* (Princeton, NJ, 1966).

Livet, Georges, *Histoire de Mulhouse. Des origines à nos jours* (Strasbourg, 1977).

Macartney, C. A., *National States and National Minorities* (London, 1934), p. 482.

McMillan, James, *Modern France, 1880–2002* (Oxford, 2003).

MacMillan, Margaret, *Peacemakers. Six Months that Changed the World* (London, 2001).

Mayeur, Jean-Marie, 'Une memoire frontière: L'Alsace', in Pierre Nora (ed.), *Les lieux de memoire, vol. II: La Nation* (Paris, 1966), pp. 14–20.

Mayeur, Jean-Marie, *Autonomie et Politique en Alsace: La constitution de 1911* (Paris, 1970).

Milbank Farrar, Marjorie, *Principled Pragmatist. The Political Career of Alexandre Millerand* (Oxford, 1991).

Morgan, Philip, *Italian Fascism, 1919–1945* (Basingstoke, 2001).

Mouré, Kenneth, *Gold Standard Illusions: France, the Bank of France and the International gold standard* (Oxford, 2002).

Mushaben, Joyce, *The Changing Face of Citizenship: Integration and Mobilization among Ethnic Minorities in Germany* (New York, 2008).

Nathans, Eli, *The Politics of Citizenship in Germany: Ethnicity, Utility and Nationalism* (New York, 2004)

Noiriel, Gerard, *Le Creuset français: Histoire de l'immigration XIXe–XXe siècle* (Paris, 2006).

Nolan, Michael E., *The Inverted Mirror. Mythologizing the Enemy in France and Germany, 1898–1914* (Oxford, 2005).

Nora, Pierre, *Les Lieux de mémoire*, 3 vols (Paris, 1984–92).

Nordman, Daniel, 'Des limites de l'Etat aux frontières naturelles', in Pierre Nora (ed.), *Les Lieux de mémoire*, vol. 1 (Paris, 1997), pp. 1125–46.

Overy, Richard, *The Interwar Crisis* (Harlow, 2007)

Ozouf, Jacques and Ozouf, Mona, 'Le tour de la France par deux enfants: Le petit livre rouge de la République', in Pierre Nora (ed.), *Lieux de Mémoire* (Paris, 1984).

Ozouf, Mona, 'L'Alsace-Lorraine, mode d'emploi. La question d'Alsace-Lorraine dans le Manuel général, 1871–1914', in *L'école de la France: essais sur la Révolution, l'utopie, et l'enseignement* (Paris, 1984), pp. 214–30.

Passmore, Kevin, 'La droite et l'extrême droite Française et la Grande Bretagne, 1870–1940: préjugés antiméridionaux, préjugés anticeltiques', in Philippe Vervaecke (ed.) *À droite de la droite. Les droites radicales en France et en Grande Bretagne au XXe siècle* (Villeneuve d'Ascq, 2012).

Passmore, Kevin, *The Right in France. From the Third Republic to Vichy* (Oxford, 2012).

Peer, Shanny, *France on Display: Peasants, Provincials and Folklore in the 1937's World Fair* (Albany, NY, 1998).

Perry, Matt, *Prisoners of Want. The Experience and Protest of the Unemployed in France, 1921–1945* (Aldershot, 2007).

Persil, Raoul, *Alexandre Millerand 1859–1943* (Paris, 1949).Prost, Antoine, *Les anciens combattants et la société française*, 3 vols (Paris, 1977).

Reed-Danahay, Deborah, *Education and Identity in Rural France: The Politics of Schooling* (Cambridge, 1996).

Reiss, Matthias and Perry, Matt, *Unemployment and Protest. Two Centuries of Contention* (Oxford, 2011).

Reynolds, Sian, *France between the Wars. Gender and Politics* (London, 1996).

Richez, Jean-Claude, 'Novembre 1918 en Alsace: Conseils Ouvriers et Conseils de Soldats', *Cahiers de l'Alsace Rouge*, 1 (1977), pp. 1–22.

Richez, Jean-Claude, 'La Révolution de Novembre 1918 en Alsace dans les petites villes et les campagnes', *Revue d'Alsace*, 107 (1981), pp. 153–68.

Richez, Jean-Claude, 'Ordre et Désordre dans la fête- Les fêtes de réception des troupes françaises en Alsace en Novembre 1918', *Revue des sciences sociales de la France de l'Est*, 12 (1983), pp. 157–77.

Richez, Jean-Claude, 'Malaises et crises après le retour a la France', *Langue et culture régionales*, 15 (1990), pp. 65–92.

Richez, Jean-Claude, 'L'Alsace revue et inventée. La Revue Alsacienne Illustrée 1895–1914', *Saisons d'Alsace*, 119 (1993), pp. 83–94.

Richez, Jean-Claude, with François Igersheim and Peter Armand, *Il y a cinquante ans, le Front Populaire... Sorglos sunnen? Travail et Temps libre en Alsace*, Exposition présenté par La CFDT et l'Atelier Alsacien le 23 au 28 juin 1986 en la Salle de la Mairie de Schiltigheim.

Richez, Jean-Claude and Strauss, Léon, 'Tradition et renouvellement des pratiques de loisirs en milieu ouvrier dans l'Alsace des années trente', *Revue d'Alsace*, 113 (1987), pp. 217–37.

Richez, Jean-Claude, Strauss, Léon, Igersheim, François, and Jonas, Stéphane, *Jacques Peirotes, 1869–1935 et le socialisme en Alsace* (Strasbourg, 1989).

Robertson, Roland 'Globalisation or glocalisation?', *Journal of International Communication*, 1: 1 (1994), pp. 33–52.

Rosenberg, Clifford D., *Policing Paris: The Origins of Modern Immigration Control between the Wars* (Ithaca and London, 2006).

Roth, François, 'La frontière franco-allemande 1871–1918', in Wolfgang Haubrichs and Reinhard Schneider (eds), *Grenzen und Grenzregionen* (Saarbrücken, 1994), pp. 131–45.

Roudmetof, Victor, 'Transnationalism, Cosmopolitanism and Glocalisation', *Current Sociology*, 53, 1 (2005), pp. 113–35.

Rowe, Michael, 'Between Empire and Home Town: Napoleonic Rule on the Rhine, 1700–1814', *Historical Journal*, 42:3 (1999), pp. 643–74.

Rowe, Michael, *From Reich to State: the Rhineland in the Revolutionary Age, 1780–1830* (Cambridge, 2003).

Rüger, Jan, 'OXO: Or, the Challenges of Transnational History', *European History Quarterly* 40: 4 (2010): pp. 656–68.

Sahlins, Peter, *Boundaries: The Making of France and Spain in the Pyrenees*, (Berkeley, 1989).

Sahlins, Peter, 'Natural Frontiers Revisited: France's Boundaries since the Seventeenth Century', *American Historical Review*, 95 (1990), pp. 1423–51.

Sahlins, Peter, *Unnaturally French: Foreign Citizens in the Old Regime and After* (Ithaca, NY, 2004).

Schama, Simon, *Landscape and Memory* (New York, 1995).

Schlögel, Karl, 'Europe and the Culture of Borders: Rethinking Borders after 1989', in Manfred Hildermeier (ed.), *Historical Concepts Between Eastern and Western Europe* (New York and Oxford, 2007).

Schöttler, Peter, 'The Rhine as an Object of Historical Controversy in the Inter-war Years. Towards a History of Frontier Mentalities', *History Workshop Journal*, 39 (1995), pp. 1–22.

Scott, Joan Wallach, 'Gender as a Useful Category of Analysis', *American Historical Review*, 91: 5, (1986), pp. 1053–75.

Seigel, Micol, 'Beyond Compare: Comparative Method after the Transnational Turn', *Radical History Review*, 91 (2005), pp. 62–90.

Sheffer, Edith, *Burned Bridge: How East and West Germans Made the Iron Curtain* (Oxford, 2011).

Sherman, Daniel J., *The Construction of Memory in Interwar France* (London, 1999).

Siegel, Mona L., *The Moral Disarmament of France: Education, Pacifism, and Patriotism, 1914–1940* (Cambridge, 2004).

Silverman, Dan P., *Reluctant Union: Alsace-Lorraine and Imperial Germany, 1871–1918* (Pennsylvania, 1972).

Simpson, Martin, 'Republicanizing the City: Radical Republicans in Toulouse, 1880–90', *European History Quarterly*, 34: 2 (2004), pp. 157–90.

Smith, Anthony D., *The Ethnic Origins of Nations* (Oxford, 1986).

Smith, Paul, 'From the Reich to the Republic: Alsace 1918–1925', in Michael Kelly and Rosemary Bock (eds), *France: Nations and Regions* (Southampton, 1993), pp. 182–9.

Smith, Paul, 'A la recherche d'une identité alsacienne', *Vingtième Siècle*, 50 (1996), pp. 23–35.

Smith, Timothy B., *Creating the Welfare State in France, 1880–1940* (Quebec, 2003).

Soucy, Robert, *French Fascism: The Second Wave* (New Haven, 1995).

Sowerwine, Charles, *France Since 1870: Culture, Politics and Society* (Basingstoke, 2001).

Steiner, Zara, *The Lights that Failed. European International History, 1919–1933* (Oxford, 2005).

Steiner, Zara, *The Triumph of the Dark. European International History, 1933–1939* (Oxford, 2011).

Steinhoff, Anthony, *The Gods of the City. Protestantism and Religious Culture in Strasbourg 1870–1914* (Boston, 2008).

Stevenson, David, 'French War Aims and the American Challenge, 1914–1918', *Historical Journal*, 22 (1979), pp. 877–94.

Storm, Eric, *The culture of regionalism: Art, architecture and international exhibitions in France, Germany and Spain, 1890–1939* (Manchester, 2010).

Strachan, John, 'Romance, Religion and the Republic: Bruno's Le Tour de France par deux Enfants', *French History*, 18 (2004), pp. 96–118.

Strauss, Léon, 'Les militants alsaciens et lorrains et les rapports entre les mouvements ouvriers français et allemands entre 1900 et 1923', *Revue d'Allemagne*, 4 (1972), pp. 3–23.

Strauss, Léon, 'La Crise de Munich en Alsace (Septembre 1938)', *Revue d'Alsace*, 105 (1979), pp. 173–88.

Strauss, Léon, 'Monde ouvrier et mouvement ouvrier du XVIIIe siècle à la Seconde Guerre Mondiale', in P. Klein, *L'Alsace* (Paris, 1981), pp. 261–4.

Strauss, Léon, 'Les organisations sportives ouvrières en Alsace et en Lorraine, 1899–1935', in Wahl, Alfred (ed.), *Des jeux et des sports* (Metz, 1986).

Strauss, Léon, 'Le malaise alsacien et le développement de l'autonomisme. La vie politique en Alsace dans l'entre-deux guerres', *Historiens et Géographes*, 345 (1995), pp. 227–36.

Strauss, Léon, 'L'Alsace de 1918 à 1945 - d'une libération à l'autre', *La Presse en Alsace au XXe siècle* (Strasbourg, 2002).

Strauss, Léon, 'L'anti-sémitisme en Alsace dans les années trente', *XVIIIe Conférence de la Société d'Histoire des Israelites d'Alsace et de Lorraine, Strasbourg 10–11 Février 1996* (Strasbourg, 1996), pp. 77–89.

Struck, Bernhard, 'Conquered Territories and Entangled Histories: The Perception of Franco-German and German-Polish Borderlands in German Travelogues, 1792–1820', in Karen Hagemann, Allan Forrest, and Etienne François (eds.), *War Memories: The Revolutionary and Napoleonic Wars in 19th and 20th Century Europe*, (Basingstoke, 2012), pp. 95–113, pp. 103–4.

Struck, Bernhard, 'Crossroads: Border Regions', *European History Online* (January 2013).

Struck, Bernhard, Ferris, Kate, and Revel, Jacques, 'Introduction: Space and Scale in Transnational History', *International History Review*, 33:4 (2011): pp. 573–84.

Swenson, Astrid, *The Rise of Heritage. Preserving the Past in France, Germany and England, 1789–1914* (Cambridge, 2013).

Thaler, Peter, 'Fluid Identities in Central European Borderlands', *European History Quarterly*, 31 (2001), pp. 519–48.

Thaler, Peter, *Of Mind and Matter: The Duality of National Identity in the German-Danish Borderlands* (Purdue University Press, 2009).

Thiesse, Anne-Marie, *Ils apprenaient la France* (Paris, 1997).

Thiesse, Anne-Marie, *La création des identités nationales* (Paris, 1999).

Thomas, Martin, *The French Empire between the Wars* (Manchester, 2005).

Tombs, Robert (ed.), *Nationhood and Nationalism in France from Boulangism to the Great War, 1889–1919* (London, 1991).

Tooze, Adam, *The Deluge. The Great War and the Remaking of the Global Order, 1916–1931* (London, 2014).

Torpey, John, *The Invention of the Passport. Surveillance, Citizenship and the State* (Cambridge, 2000).

Turetti, Laurence, *Quand la France pleurait l'Alsace-Lorraine. Les 'provinces perdues' aux sources du patriotisme républicain, 1870–1914* (Strasbourg, 2008).

Turner, Frederick Jackson, *The Significance of the Frontier in American History* (New York, 1920).

Uberfill, François, *Mariages entre Alsaciens et Allemands à Strasbourg de 1871 à 1914. Etude de processus du formation des unions mixtes* (Strasbourg, 1993).

Uberfill, François, *La Société strasbourgeoise entre France et Allemagne (1871–1924)* (Strasbourg, 2001).

Varley, Karine, *Under the Shadow of Defeat. The War of 1870–71 in French Memory* (Basingstoke, 2008).

Vlossak, Elizabeth, *Marianne or Germania? Nationalizing Women in Alsace, 1870–1946* (Oxford, 2010).

Vogler, Bernard, *Histoire Politique de l'Alsace* (Strasbourg, 1995).

Vogler, Bernard (ed.), *Chroniques d'Alsace 1918–1939* (Barcelona, 2004).

Wahl, Alfred, *L'Option et L'Emigration des Alsaciens-Lorrains (1871–1872)* (Paris, 1974).

Wahl, Alfred, 'L'immigration allemande en Alsace-Lorraine (1871–1918)', *Recherches germaniques*, 3 (1973), pp. 202–17.

Wahl, Alfred and Richez, Jean-Claude, *La Vie Quotidienne en Alsace entre France et Allemagne, 1850–1950* (Paris, 1993).

Wahrman, Dror, *The Making of the Modern Self. Identity and Culture in Eighteenth Century England* (New Haven and London, 2006).

Walsham, Alexandra, *The Reformation of the Landscape: Religion, Identity and Memory in Early Modern Britain and Ireland* (Oxford, 2011).

Wardhaugh, Jessica, *In Pursuit of the People. Political Culture in France, 1934–1939* (Basingstoke, 2009).

Watson, Alexander, 'Fighting for Another Fatherland: the Polish Minority in the German Army, 1914–1918', *English Historical Review,* 126 (2011), pp. 1137–66.

Weber, Eugen, *Peasants into Frenchmen. The Modernization of Rural France 1870–1914* (Stanford, 1976).

Weil, Patrick, *La France et ses étrangers: L'aventure d'une politique d'immigration, 1938–1991* (Paris, 1991).

Weil, Patrick, *How to be French: Nationality in the Making since 1789,* (Durham, NC, 2008).

Whalen, Philip and Young, Patrick (eds), *Place and Locality in Modern France* (London, 2014).

Winock, Michel, *Nationalisme, antisémitisme et fascisme en France,* (Paris, 1990).

Winock, Michel, 'Jeanne d'Arc', in Pierre Nora (ed.), *Les lieux de mémoire, III: Les Frances* (Paris, 1992), pp. 675–732.

Young, Patrick, *Enacting Brittany: Tourism and Culture in Provincial France, 1871–1939* (Farnham, 2012).

Zahra, Tara, 'Looking East: East Central European "Borderlands" in German History and Historiography', *History Compass,* 3: 1 (2005), pp. 1–23.

Zahra, Tara, *Kidnapped Souls: National Indifference and the Battle for Children in the Bohemian Lands, 1900–1948* (Ithaca, NY, 2008).

Zahra, Tara, 'The Minority Problem: National Classification in the French and Czechoslovak Borderlands', *Contemporary European History,* 17 (2008), pp. 137–65.

Zahra, Tara, 'Imagined Noncommunities: National Indifference as a Category of Analysis', *Slavic Review,* 69 (2010), pp. 93–119.

Zimmer, Oliver, *Nationalism in Europe 1890–1940* (Basingstoke, 2003).

Zimmermann, Bénédicte, 'Les Premiers Mai de la CFTC/CFDT: logique identaire et pratique syndicale', *Le Mouvement Social,* 157 (1991), pp. 87–102.

UNPUBLISHED PHD THESES

Baechler, Christian, 'L'Alsace entre la Guerre et la Paix: Recherches sur l'opinion publique, 1917–1918' (Thèse pour le Doctorat de Troisième Cycle, Université de Strasbourg, 1969).

Grohmann, Carolyn, 'Problems of Reintegrating Annexed Lorraine into France, 1918–1925' (PhD dissertation, University of Stirling, 2000).

Klein, Detmar, 'Battleground of Cultures: "Politics of Identities" and the National Question in Alsace under German Imperial Rule (1870–1914)' (PhD dissertation, Royal Holloway, University of London, 2004).

Shane Story, William, 'Constructing French Alsace: A state, region, and nation in Europe, 1918–1925' (PhD dissertation, Rice University, 2001).

Williams, Thomas, 'Remaking the Franco-German Borderlands: Historical Claims and Commemorative Practices in the Upper Rhine, 1940–49' (DPhil dissertation, University of Oxford, 2010).

Index